# RECONFIGURING IDENTITIES AND BUILDING TERRITORIES IN INDIA AND SOUTH AFRICA

*Centre de Sciences Humaines* (Centre for Social Sciences and Humanities): Created in New Delhi in 1989, the CSH is part of the network of research centres of the French Ministry of Foreign Affairs. The Centre's research work is primarily oriented towards the study of issues concerning the contemporary dynamics of development in India and South Asia. The activities of the Centre are focused on four main areas, namely: Economic transition and sustainable development, Political dynamics, institutional set-up and social transformations, Regional dynamics in South Asia and international relations and Urban dynamics.

Centre de Sciences Humaines, 2, Aurangzeb Road, New Delhi 110011, India,
Tel: (91) 11 3041 00 74, Fax: (91) 11 3041 00 79
E-mail: public@csh-delhi.com Website: http://www.csh-delhi.com

*Institut Français de Pondichéry* (French Institute of Pondicherry): Created in 1955, the IFP is a multidisciplinary research and advanced educational institute. Major research works are focusing on Sanskrit and Tamil Languages and literatures—in close collaboration with the Ecole Française d'Extrême-Orient—ecosystems, biodiversity and sustainability, dynamics of population and socio-economic development.

Institut Français de Pondichéry, 11 Saint Louis Street, PB 33,
Pondicherry 605001, Tel: (91) 413 2334 168
Fax: (91) 413 2339 534
E-mail: ifpdir@ifpindia.org Website: http://www.ifpindia.org

The *French Institute of South Africa*, founded in 1995 in Johannesburg, promotes French cultural presence in South Africa. The Institute, under the French Ministry of Foreign Affairs, is also a centre of research in Social Sciences and Humanities aiming to promote and support French academic and scientific research on South and Southern Africa.

French Institute of Africa, 66, Wolhuter Street, PO. Box 542,
Newton 2113, Johannesburg, Afrique du Sud
Tel.: 21 11 836 05 61 Fax: 27 11 836 58 50
E-mail: secretariatrecherche@ifas.org.za Website: www.ifas.org.za

*GECKO* (*ex-Géotropiques*) is a research centre of comparative geography at the University of Paris X. Researchers analyse the process occuring between globalization and local dynamics in Southern and Northern countries, and the interactions between social, economical, political and cultural factors in these processes. Issues of identities and territories are a key part of this work.

Département de Géographie, Université de Paris X, 92001 Nanterre cedex,
France. Website: http://geotropoiques.net

# Reconfiguring Identities and Building Territories in India and South Africa

*Edited by*

PHILIPPE GERVAIS-LAMBONY
FRÉDÉRIC LANDY
SOPHIE OLDFIELD

MANOHAR

CENTRE DE SCIENCES HUMAINES
2005

First published 2005



ISBN 81-7304-666-2

*Published by*
Ajay Kumar Jain *for*
Manohar Publishers & Distributors
4753/23 Ansari Road, Daryaganj
New Delhi 110 002

*Printed at*
Lordson Publishers Pvt Ltd
Delhi 110 007

*Distributed in South Asia by*
FOUNDATION BOOKS
4381/4, Ansari Road
Daryaganj, New Delhi 110 002
and its branches at Mumbai, Hyderabad,
Bangalore, Chennai, Kolkata

# Contents

# Acknowledgements

The project from which this book has been developed was organized by the Laboratory Géotropiques (now GECKO) at the University of Paris X, Nanterre and the Institut Francais d'Afrique du Sud (Johannesburg), in collaboration with the Department of Environmental and Geographical Science at the University of Cape Town, the Centre de Sciences Humaines (New Delhi) and the Human Sciences Research Council (Pretoria). We thank each of these institutions, as well as the participating project authors, for their support and participation in the project. This book is the outcome of an international conference held in Nanterre in November 2001. With the exception of Chapter 4, it was originally published in French *Espaces arc-en-ciel: identités et territories en Afrique du Sud et en Inde*, by Karthala, Paris in 2003.

# Introduction

PHILIPPE GERVAIS-LAMBONY, FRÉDÉRIC LANDY
and SOPHIE OLDFIELD

*Samathuvapuram* (village of equality) is the name of a housing scheme launched in the South Indian State of Tamil Nadu in the 1990s. This scheme seeks to break with tradition by constructing permanent housing for 'Untouchables'. More often authorities launch housing development schemes on the outskirts of villages reserved exclusively for these categories, thus perpetuating and exacerbating the ostracism that victimizes most 'Untouchables' in rural India. In this programme, however, the beneficiaries were selected on the basis of poverty, not according to caste affiliations. The title deeds were signed over to women in order to promote their empowerment. A school, a dairy, as well as a playground were provided. Each family was required and agreed to pledge 'not to install statues of religious or community leaders, not to sell or pledge houses for 15 years, to accept using a common burial ground, not to create separate places of worship, not to consume liquor, not to let the houses [and to] maintain hygiene' (Jothi Sivagnanam and Sivaraj, 2002, p. 3992).

Another tradition which has been challenged is immediately west of Johannesburg's town centre in the Newtown area, on South African national railways property and on a site previously occupied by a slum. The South African government has provided social housing for the poorest sections of society. Built on large, inexpensive tracts of land, the provincial and national authorities normally undertake low-income housing construction in peripheral zones far from the city centre. Seeking to reduce construction costs, they end up reproducing the infamous *township* model. The Newtown project aims at just the opposite: to construct affordable housing for the poor and middle classes, in terms of small apartment complexes rather than individual houses, and near the city centre rather than on the urban periphery.

Both projects attempt to create social change through spatial intervention, in particular the transformation of inherited spaces and territories that are problematic because of their propensity to segregate. Although the contrast of projects in Tamil Nadu and Johannesburg draws together the rural and urban in two vastly different places, it highlights the complex constitution of identities and space and the nature of state intervention in both cases. Questions of territory, space and identity are critical in the contemporary international, global context, as well as central issues for research in the social sciences. Processes connected with globalization have reconfigured identities and territories at multiple scales, connecting and disconnecting places in complex ways and reinforcing old while producing new forms of segregation and polarization.

Global discourse and process overlays however complex and specific South African and Indian geographies of inequality, expressed at the national, regional and local scales in cities and rural areas. In the South African case, a political imperative to transform the legacies of racial inequality from colonial and apartheid rule underscores the centrality of racial identities. But racial discourse and differentiation embody and at times mask a complex mix of place-based (urban/rural), gender, class and cultural identities, expressed in a multi-scalar politics of territory. More than fifty years into independent rule, Indian identity politics continues to build to a large extent on caste and the intricate ways in which caste affiliation merges with religious, socio-economic, political and place-based identities. In both contexts, the politics of identity and territory unify and divide at the national, regional and local scales.

The scales at which these processes operate and the spaces, territories and identities produced lie at the heart of the project for which the papers in this volume have been written. Collectively, the contributions represent the culmination of research[1] that has attempted to draw together comparative analysis of the relationship and reconfiguration of Indian and South African identities and territories through a dialogue between geographers, and other social scientists, from France, India and South Africa.

## THE DIALECTICAL RELATIONSHIP BETWEEN IDENTITY, TERRITORY AND SPACE

Geographers and other social scientists are interested in the ways in which space and territory relate dialectically at a variety of scales to reinforce and justify affiliation to a particular identity or, on the contrary, to minimize it (Keith and Pile, 1993). This literature poses space, territory and identity as complex and contingent expressions of regional and local identities that emerge in everyday practice embedded in social, economic and political relationships. While social, economic and political networks are central to the construction of space and territory, spatial and territorial processes also reinforce and support networks. At the same time the relationship between top-down (such as state-driven) and bottom-up (for example, communally built) constructions of territory and identity are made specific in particular contexts.[2] Both are central to identity formation and its politics. As a result, identity is not just projected on to space and territory, but it is also produced by space and scale that, in turn, generates a politics of territory (Marston, 2000). An analysis of the dynamic relationship between space and identity, and the production of territory, therefore requires research that is both systematic and historical, and situated in time and place.[3]

Space and territory, respectively, and their relationships with identity formation have become increasingly important in social science debates in anglophone and French academic literature. The usage of 'territory' in French literature is ubiquitous and there is growing interest in space in disciplines other than geography in English language research. Arguments in both contexts can be categorized (Jolivet and Léna, 2000). The first treats territory and space from a geopolitical perspective, addressing the issue of its restructuring through processes of globalization. In this context, territory and space are integral to discussions on borders, international relations, and decentralization. The second body of work relates more closely to economics, raising issues of local development and the organization of civil society in space. In this literature, theories of territory underpin arguments about industrial districts, social capital, participatory democracy and decentralization. The third set of debates views territory from a social and anthropological perspective on identity, conceptualizing the relationship between identity and territory as representational and as socially constructed in everyday practice. These three literatures do not operate in isolation from each other because identity itself is eminently political, as well as social and economic.

In this volume, while identities in India are understood as built primarily on ethnic, caste and religious foundations, in South Africa race and class predominate in analyses. Yet, the authors agree that identities are always contextual as well as variable, an interwoven mix of structurally imposed and locally generated elements. Thus, contributions with a historical theme demonstrate that the contingencies arising in the long-term play a decisive role in the structuring of identities. Surajan Das recounts in chapter 8 how the Nagas from the eastern Himalayas remained extremely segmented at the level of the clan or the village until intervention by British colonial administrators and later the post-colonial Indian state generated a politics demanding 'a' Naga regional identity. François-Xavier Fauvelle-Aymar's paper on (Chapter 9) *Bastards* in the Northern Cape in South Africa illustrates a parallel process of shifting territories and identities where the historical complexities of race, ethnicity and locational identity were subsumed under the naming of a Bastard ethnicity and then a broader classification of 'coloured' or 'white' in the more recent apartheid period.

Whether ethnic or racial, identities and their relationship to territory and space are clearly expressions of power (or the lack thereof), essentialist analyses of identity (ethnic, racial or otherwise) are inadequate. Contact with the 'Other' is critical for the formation of identity along necessarily contextual 'frontiers' (Barth, 1969) as demonstrated by Das' argument, that '(e)thnicity is the result of contact, not of isolation' (Das, 2001, p. 12). Although in India caste classifications and identities are deeply rooted historically in Hinduism and presently in the consciousness of individuals and groups, the watertight compartments in which they exist and operate also reflect colonial powers and ethnography (Amselle and M'Bokolo, 1985), particularly the intervention of oriental classificatory thinking, for instance in the implementation of the Census (see Christopher's contribution in Chapter 5 in this volume). Likewise, in South Africa racial classification of the apartheid period persists, although mediated by a range of post-apartheid cleavages and social and politcial processes. Identities, therefore, are not solely ethnic or racial, but characterized by a multitude of familial, religious, professional and social linkages. These pieces do not fit together like a jigsaw puzzle, but coalesce and diverge in particular moments, processes and places (Oldfield, 2004). Identities (and the territories and spaces that they generate and are produced in) are, therefore, always heterogeneous and 'multi-layered' (Mainet-Valleix, 2002), constructed and drawn on by individuals, groups and societies in strategic and specific ways. Far from being absolute, identity, space and territory conceptually and materially reinforce each other in social- and political-economic contexts (Godelier, 1984).

## COMPARING SOCIETY AND TERRITORY IN SOUTH AFRICA AND INDIA

The following discussion outlines the specificity of the South African and Indian contexts as well as highlights the points from which the volume's comparative analysis proceeds.

### THE SOUTH AFRICAN CASE

The colonial and apartheid project imposed racial identities on South African society, categories that were then used to design and implement segregation at a national level (where various categories of 'African' 'homelands' were designated) and within cities, town and rural areas where neighbourhoods were designated by race. Coupled with an intricate legal, political and economic infrastructure, this system of social and spatial engineering produced massive inequalities that persist in territorial and identity-based politics in the post-apartheid period (Turole, 2001). Although racial identities are important, they reveal and mask other identities grounded in places and experiences in urban and rural contexts.

Spatial and identity constructs inherited from the old regime persist in racially based socio-economic inequality and the ways in which towns, cities and rural areas are spatially and territorially divided (Zegeye, 2001). The new government has redefined the internal territorial limits as a political and social tool to facilitate redistribution and to reconstruct South African democracy as a 'non-racial' project (Cameron, 1999). The reconstruction of identities and the reorganization of space are critical in the post-apartheid period (see Map 1). These processes are especially complex as systematic racial segregation has over the years obscured other social and spatial divisions in South African society, based on socio-economic, linguistic, cultural, religious and political inequalities (Christopher, 2004). Therefore, South African territorial and spatial identities must be analysed in all their complexity, particularly because in the post-apartheid context communities tend to redefine themselves in terms of new territories and use identity in support of claims that are often spatial in nature. The challenges of constructing democracy and addressing stark inequalities—of making a 'rainbow nation' to use Desmond Tutu's famous expression—in a highly segregated country are not unique however to South Africa.

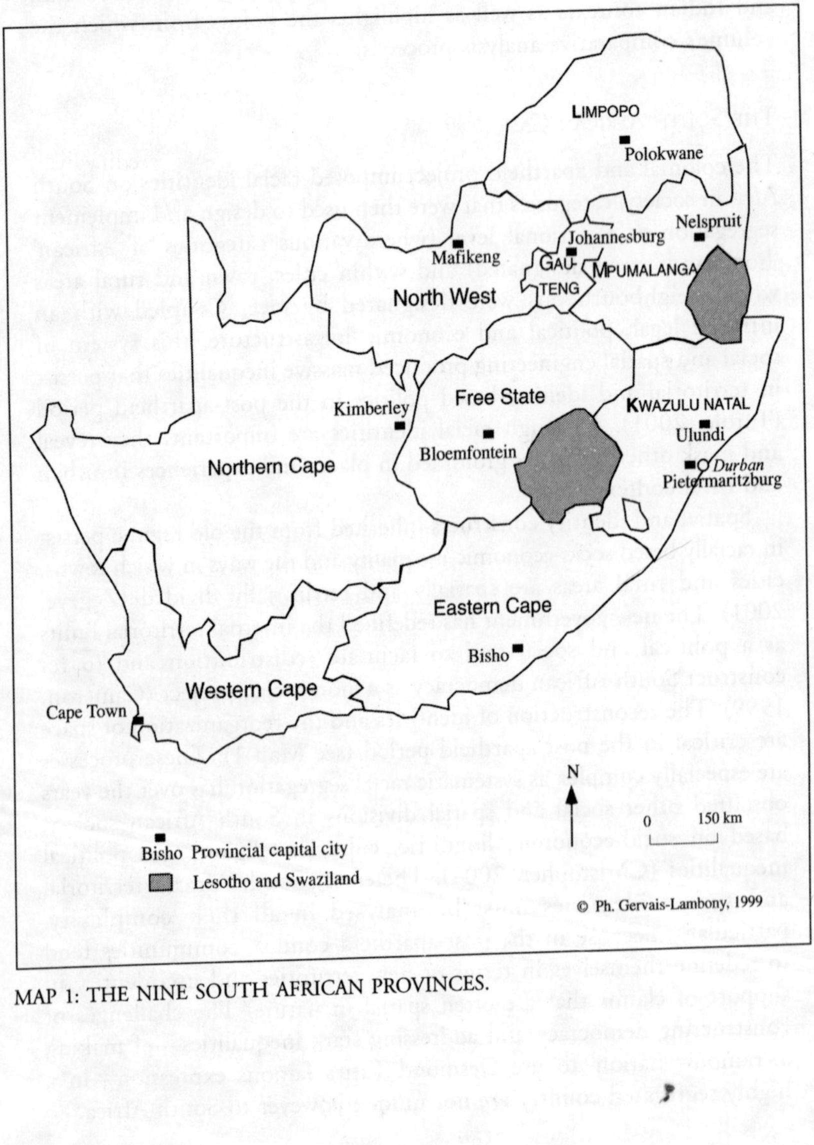


MAP 1: THE NINE SOUTH AFRICAN PROVINCES.

## The Indian Case

India is also characterized by segregated, often hierarchical social structures that constitute one of the obstacles to development and the generation of national identities. Social and political divisions are drawn along different lines, of course. Apart from the conventional socio-economic factors, there are three aspects of segmentation in India. Religion, particularly the existence of a substantial Muslim minority in a country with 81 per cent Hindus; the caste system, which hereditarily defines groups according to a hierarchy based on so-called purity; and regional origin, primarily sustained by linguistic differences, which determined territorial division into twenty-eight states (see Map 2), and has produced xenophoia in some instances, setting the 'sons of the soil' against migrants from other regions of India. The relatively substantial legislative powers conferred by the Constitution to the states of the Union enhances the importance of the regional question. These three systems of segmentation and the socio-economic hierarchy overlay each other, making Indian society highly complex and dynamic.

Can segregation in the two countries be compared? In South Africa, segregation based on race was introduced through legislation. In India, segregation based on caste or 'community' was founded on religion. Thus, it is possible to distinguish sources of South African and Indian spatial and territorial division. Under apartheid, a racial hierarchy of the population and systematic territorialization of the different groups was imposed in South Africa. In India, territorialization has always been more flexible and less deliberate. This is especially true of the caste system. On the one hand, for thousands of castes there is no pan-Indian hierarchy (caste is merely regional), while on the other, the definition of castes is never strictly spatial as, for it to work, the social system traditionally necessitated the coexistence of complementary castes in the same space. The caste system implies spatial segregation only at the local and even micro local levels (Dupont, 2004). Last, it should be recalled that caste can sometimes transcend state boundaries (for instance, Jat networks in north India).

These factors have major geographical repercussions. In India, poverty is visible practically everywhere, even on the pavements of upmarket urban areas. In South Africa, it is better concealed, because functional, social and racial segregation operates at a macro rather than micro level—by neighbourhood and area rather than household and street. As Mainet-Valleix (2002) argues, sections of the ethnic Indian

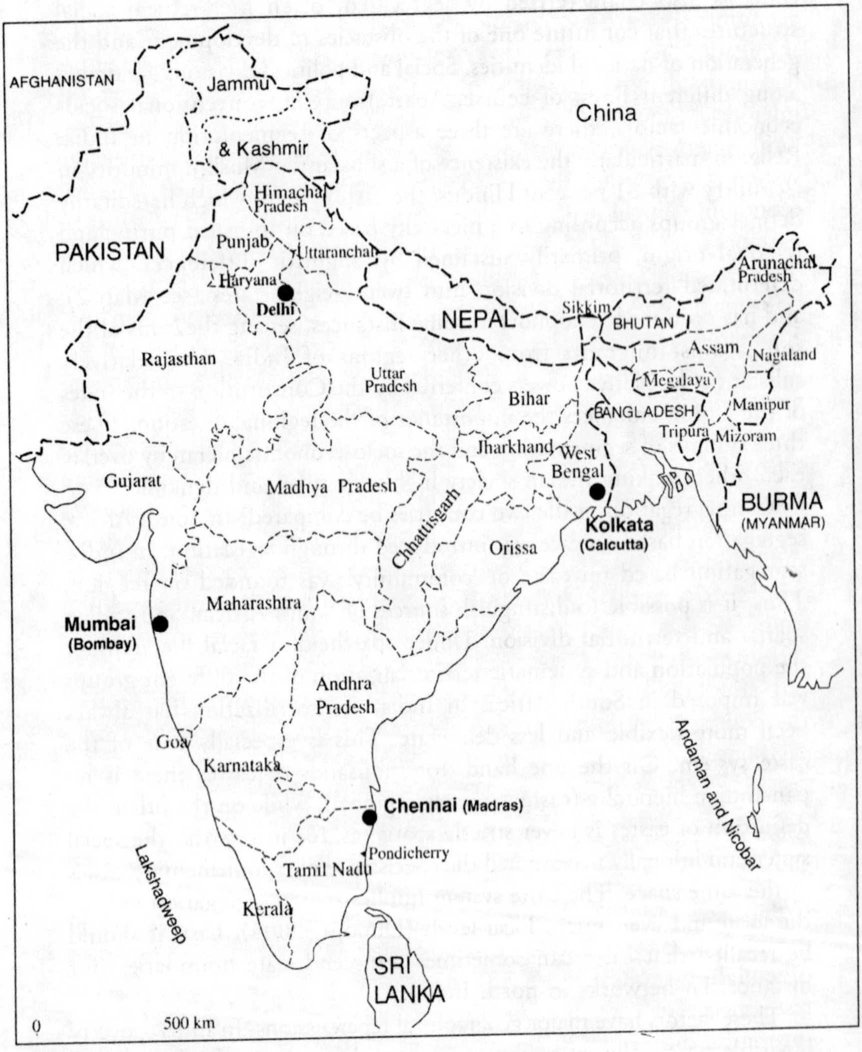


MAP 2: THE STATES OF INDIA.

community in South Africa would have accepted residential segregation even before apartheid, if it had not been accompanied by penalizing economic segregation. In India, the country of its ancestors, residential segregation had always existed; thus the community's imported culture had probably prepared it for this. But it was practised more at the microlevel, given that economic segregation in India did not prevent local systems based on complementarity from operating (the *jajmani* system prevailing in some villages, for example). In South Africa, this economic complementarity was encountered more at the regional or national levels (in townships and 'Bantustans', for example).

Both countries are officially engaged in the process of expunging traditional divisions through policies of 'national integration', such as: affirmative action (measures in favour of blacks in South Africa, ex-untouchables, tribals and low castes in India) and economic development policies for poorer regions. Moreover, in South Africa different racial groups are brought together within internal political-administrative boundaries, regionally and within cities, local authorities and ward (voting) blocks. In India, the linguistic division of states has not extinguished the hope of a 'secular' India triumphing over a 'communal' India. But, in both countries, the results are often disappointing: in South Africa, the policy of *black empowerment* has been compared to a cappuccino as whites continue to remain at the top. In reality, these measures often create new schisms (between regions or within regions, but also between and within communities) that are symptoms of the complex interplay between identities and spatial and territorial divisions.

## CROSSING NATIONAL, DISCIPLINARY AND LINGUISTIC TRADITIONS: THE CHALLENGE OF COMPARATIVE STUDIES

Comparing India and South Africa raised a host of difficulties that the project grappled with. These were merged with the challenges of collaboration between English-speaking and French-speaking researchers. The collaboration raised methodological, terminological and theoretical differences in the context of subjects as complex and often ill defined as those of identity, space and territory. The following discussions, therefore, outlines the comparative and theoretical assumptions underpinning the project and highlights the inherent difficulties, weaknesses and strengths of comparison across national, disciplinary and linguistic boundaries.

The terms 'race' and 'ethnicity' are defined and politicized in different ways in France, India and South Africa. Discussions between researchers at the symposium revealed that 'community' was another ambiguous term. Many English-speaking planners use community in the sense of 'locality', in a purely spatial sense that is more or less synonymous with *neighbourhood*. But in the political language of India, community is also a euphemism for 'caste' or 'religion': in this way the print media systematically refers to Muslims as the 'minority community'. Similarly, in South Africa, 'community' most often designates 'racial groups'. While the French interpretation is probably closer to the Indian meaning, it is also ambiguous.

Moreover conceptualizations of 'space' and 'territory' do not have the same significance for social scientists from the English- and the French-speaking world. Many English-speaking geographers in particular never use the word 'territory', prefering to use 'place' to distinguish from 'space' (Tuan, 1977) and concepts of socio-spatial dialectics to consider how power and geography coalesce in complex and contingent ways (Benko and Strohmayer, 1997). In contrast, most of French geographers use 'space' as an apolitical, neutral concept and 'territory' to analyse power and politics. The fact that languages assign different meanings to the same words is in itself a sign of the diversity of modes of thinking and a reflection of cultural dynamism (see chapter 1 by Gervais-Lambony for an elaboration on these issues).

Apart from questions of terminology and concepts between academics, methodological differences were highlighted during the symposium; issues perhaps even more difficult to resolve. The questions raised by various researchers in relation to the comparative method were often different in nature as is evident in the various chapters. All these issues raise the limits of comparative processes, concepts and methods, the importance of transparency of method and the need for delineating and substantiating conceptual frameworks drawn on in the various research projects. These issues are particularly important in a comparison of two complex and quite different countries such as India and South Africa.

## ORGANIZATION OF THE BOOK

This book is structured according to the complexity of the concepts studied, the importance of a multidisciplinary approach, the differences between Anglo- and French scientific practices, and the diversity of the two nations studied. Although it is the study of the scales of territory and identity which must ultimately weave sections two through four together, it was necessary to devote the first part of the book to the theoretical issues that underpin the collection of papers and work on identity and territory in South Africa, India and France.

Gervais-Lambony lays the ground for a comparative Indian–South African project in his discussion on comparative practices, their constraints, limitations and advantages in Chapter 1. He argues that comparative research is critical and that social scientists with area-based specializations are ideally positioned to conduct comparative research across and between different cities, regions and countries. A comparison of processes across places and societies illustrates both the universal and the particular, facilitating critical reflection not only on each place and society but also on the processes themselves. In Chapter 2, Dupont and Landy define 'segregation' and 'territory' on the basis of the South African and Indian experiences. In the next chapter Kalam examines the question from the Indian perspective by drawing a parallel between tribal and Hindu territories within a nation-state in perpetual construction. Each time territory proves to be a space supporting the formation of identity. Hence, it is often an instrument of segregation—defined as the spatial form of discrimination—which is illustrated by caste discrimination in India and racial discrimination engendered by apartheid in South Africa. In each instance, the consequent superimposition of territories, the lack of correlation between spatial distance and social distance, as well as the forms of geographical mobility render the various relationships between segregation and territory extremely complex. Battersby (Chapter 4) examines South African discourses on race, nationalism and belonging, illustrating the re-inscription of race and ethnicity as central to discourses on socio-economic rights and cultural diversity in the post-apartheid period. These papers bring together the contexts in which comparative work on identity and territory are debated in India, South Africa and France.

The second part of the book focuses on the study of the national and regional scale in India and South Africa. Regions and their power and political economies feature as central questions in India and South Africa. In both instances, regions may be understood as political tools for transcending and uniting territories and communities. But, regional identities may also constitute separatist tendencies as expressed in movements and regional politics. In practice, territorial boundaries overlap and are contested drawing on historical experiences and narratives and through the creation of new territories that consolidate regional identities. The dialectic between territory, space and identity, therefore, expresses itself at multiple scales and through overlapping and, sometimes, conflicting processes.

Christopher draws striking parallels between the Indian and South African colonial heritage in Chapter 5. The spatial policy of the British Empire had, in fact, already defined not only the major part of their borders, instituted the federal pattern, but also built new urban structures and landscapes and introduced a population census. In consequence, many uniform grids and practices in the Empire's territories were superimposed on (rather than substituted for) the existing structures in each country. It is in this colonial setting that most migrants of Indian origin arrived in East Africa living in an uneasy situation between whites and blacks, who made them 'scapegoats' after the countries attained independence. In the following chapter Maharaj explains this process and how 'ethnic frontiers' functioned in a rigid manner, creating contexts in which, for instance, 'Indians' could be expelled from Uganda en masse. Another case is examined by Das, who narrates the difficult birth of Nagaland in the north-eastern India. His analysis demonstrates that until 1975, the Nagas, an ethnic group, were refused statehood, not because the identity-based unity of the Nagas was a recent one, but because the federal government was wary of shattering the fragile unity of the Indian Union. The question of regional identities is also highly relevant in post-apartheid South Africa. The provinces, delineated on the basis of boundaries drawn after 1994, have well and truly become the new referents of territorial identity, especially in KwaZulu Natal and the Western Cape, areas where the African National Congress governs in coalition with opposition parties. The construction of identities in the latter province is analysed by Bekker, Leildé and Puttergill. Their discussion highlights the ways in which culture, class and urban/rural divisions further fragment South African racial identities.

The third part of the book dissects the difficult relations between 'minorities', territory and space at a local scale. 'Minority' status is contested in South Africa and India, often masking more complicated demographics and issues of identity politics. We approach these issues by analysing the complex processes underlying the formation of identities and territories, minority or otherwise. An initial approach at the regional level gauges the dynamics of the cohesion or, conversely, the fragmentation of minorities, taking into account historical disruptions that may have occurred. In other words, we assess the manner in which a 'sense of community' reacts, by disintegrating or by reinforcing itself when confronted with spatial rigidity, pressures from other groups and a range of political developments. These explorations highlight that identity is always contextual and contingent.

Kidwai's paper examines Muslims from two neighbouring regions of north India—Awadh and Rohilkhand. Her investigation analyses regional identities and history prior to consolidation under British colonialism and socio-religious identities formed in part because of minority status in a majority Hindu country, but also in relation to positionality as a dominant elite during the Nawab era. Teppo and Guillaume focus on 'poor whites' in Johannesburg, historically advantaged as 'whites' but now a minority adjusting to the post-apartheid period. Three chapters are devoted to South Africans of Indian origin. In Chapter 11 Landy contextualizes this group in the Indian 'diaspora' by examining the Indian South African community's relations with India as a country of origin. Because migration took place a long time ago and because of the interruption caused by apartheid, economic links are limited, and for many, India is a major cultural referent rather than a real material presence. Ebrahim-Vally's analysis focuses on the heterogeneity of the Indian South African community in its inclusion of Muslims and Hindus, 'north' Indians and 'south' Indians, and descendants of traders as well as agricultural labourers. She argues that the integration of 'Indians' into South African society is slow, but real, even though new referents do surface (such as links with the Muslim *umma*) that create new territorial identities. Mainet-Valleix describes Durban Indians' lived and perceptual spaces, such as the home as a matrix of familial identities and cultural difference and Indian townships and their transformation as Indian spaces. She argues that Indian urban spaces can be understood as 'territory as archipelago', interlinked internally but largely separated from other parts of the city.

The complex integration of these identities is seen more specifically at the local and urban levels in the fourth part of the book entitled 'Urban Territory and the Politics of Identity'. The world over cities present a fertile ground for the partial dilution of regional and local identities in a common melting-pot, which we call urban society, but also for an intensive territorialization of identity at the local, and indeed micro-local levels. The forms of and mechanisms that (re)produce segregation are common themes running through the contributions in this section that consider not only socio-economic segregation, but also ethnic, race, caste and religious spatial divisions in Indian and South African cities. In all these processes, scale becomes a critical analytical variable to understand the ways in which segregation and integration are produced and contested. A central question in this section is to what extent cities allow for the construction of new identities and a means to move beyond parochial and confining local identities.

A second theme running through the chapters pertains to the relationships between local authorities and processes of state intervention on urban identities. Both countries have powerful administrations and a political will at least to eliminate divisions. This has taken the form of redistribution of fiscal resources at the metropolitan level in South Africa or positive discrimination in favour of particular groups or spaces. The relationship between the metropolitan government and the agglomeration, taken as a system, largely explains the spatial limits ascribed to the metropolis, particularly in the examples studied in Johannesburg, Capetown, Durban and Delhi. Issues of the redistribution of resources and of urban growth as well as the reconfiguring of municipal boundaries highlight the interplay between identity, space, and territory as processes of planned integration, as well as a platform on which local 'community-based' representatives organize. The final theme draws a parallel between urban and rural identity. Urbanization in South Africa and India is characterized by links that the new arrivals maintain with their rural origin. Although the scale at which urbanization occurs is not comparable (approximately 30 per cent of the Indian population compared with 60 per cent in South Africa), the two countries possess dense urban networks and large cities. Over and above representations of the city in both contexts as a place of lost identities, broken social linkages and insecurity, we consider how caste, village and family relate with urbanization in concrete terms and the manner in which migrants are received in the city and settle down.

It is to these different issues that the contributions respond. Three build on the notion of urban fragmentation. In this respect the South African case is interesting as it questions the tension between political and administrative metropolization, on the one hand, and the continuation of the processes of socio-economic 'fragmentation', on the other. The contributions of Gervais-Lambony, and Bénit highlight that in reality there is no contradiction and, therefore, it is necessary to emphatically question the very notion of fragmentation as it is conceptualized theoretically. This is confirmed by a systematic comparative study of Cape Town and Delhi (by Dupont and Houssay-Holzschuch in chapter 16). All the approaches to urban space and territories highlight the importance of understanding the spatial and territorial construction of identity as embedded in the daily life of cities. The importance of urban conviviality and communal construction towards a specific goal is illustrated, for instance, by Oldfield's study in an area of Cape Town where a territorial and spatial identity is being forged, based not on race or ethnic group but in defence of the locality. In this case territorial and place-based strategies are grounded on the construction of identity, at the same time that they induce it. Once again, what is important is territorial construction in relation to the Other: it is constitutive of identity for it means distinguishing oneself as a community under threat and also identifying oneself as a group.

This comparative project has contributed not only to the development of this volume, but also to an interdisciplinary and cross-national collaboration in which we have analysed our fields of study and the national contexts in which we work. At the same time, the project has provided a unique opportunity to explore the links between India and South Africa and has facilitated exchanges between the three scientific communities. Foremost our research illustrates that the building of territories and places, whatever the terrain, is inevitably a matter of re-oconfiguring economic, political, cultural and social identities in rich and complex ways.

NOTES

1. This book includes papers presented at an international symposium held at the University of Paris X-Nanterre on 29 and 30 November 2001. It is also the outcome of a research programme launched in 1998 by the Laboratory Géotropiques (University of Paris X, Nanterre) and the Institut Français d'Afrique du Sud (Johannesburg), in collaboration with the Department of Environmental and Geographical Science at the University of Cape Town, the Centre des Sciences Humaines (New Delhi) and the Human Sciences Research Council (Pretoria). This programme, entitled 'Spaces, Territories and Identities in South Africa and India. A Comparative Perspective' brought together South African, Indian and French geographers, sociologists, historians, demographers, anthropologists and political scientists.
2. For instance, although the connection between the geopolitical territory of

India and South Africa retains minimal importance for South Africans of Indian origin (see Chapter 11 by Landy), Indian territories exist in Durban around temples, mosques and kinship, social and business networks.

3. We agree with Assayag and Bénéï and their argument that even discourse and research on identities must be grasped through the 'categorical imperative of locality' (2000, p. 22).

## REFERENCES

Amselle, J.-L., E. M'Bokolo, *Au cœur de l'ethnie*, Paris: La Découverte, 1985.

Assayag, J., V. Benei, 'A demeure en diaspora. Asie du Sud, Europe, Etats-Unis', *L'Homme*, Special Issue 'Intellectuels en diaspora et théories nomades', vol. 156, 2000, pp. 15-28.

Barth, F. (ed.), *Ethnic Groups and Boundaries: The Social Organization of Culture Difference*, Bergen-Oslo, Universitetsforlaget, 1969.

Benko, G., U. Strohmayer, *Space and Social Theory: Interpreting Modernity and Postmodernity*, Oxford: Blackwell Press, 1997.

Cameron, R., *Democratisation of South African Local Government: A Tale of Three Cities*, Pretoria: JL van Schaik, 1999.

Christopher, A.J., 'Linguistic Segregation in Urban South Africa, 1996', *Geoforum* 35, 2, pp. 145-56, 2004.

Das, S., *Kashmir and Sindh: Nation-Building, Ethnicity and Regional Politics in South Asia,* Kolkata, University of Calcutta, K.P. Bagchi, 2001.

Dupont, V., 'Socio-spatial Differentiation and Residential Segregation in Delhi: A Question of Scale?' *Geoforum* 35, 2, pp. 157-88, 2004.

Godelier, M., *L'idéel et le matériel*, Paris: Fayard, 1984.

Jolivet, M.-J., Ph. Lena, 'Des territoires aux identités', *Autrepart*, Special Issue 'Logiques Identitaires, Logiques Territoriales', 14, L'Aube-IRD, 2000, pp. 5-16.

Jothi Sivagnanam, K., M. Sivaraj, '*Samathuvapuram*: Towards Spatial Equality', *Economic and Political Weekly*, 37, 39, 28 September 2002, pp. 3990-2.

Keith, M., S. Pile, *Place and the Politics of Identity*, London: Routledge, 1993.

Mainet-Valleix, H., *Durban. Les Indiens, leurs territoires, leur identité,* Paris: IFAS-Karthala, 2002.

Martson, S., 'The Social Construction of Scale', *Progress in Human Geography*, 24, 2, pp. 219-42, 2000.

Oldfield, S., 'Urban Networks, Community Organising and Race: An Analysis of Racial Integration in a Desegrated South African Neighbourhood,' *Geoforum*, 35, 2, pp. 189-202, 2004.

Tuan Yi-Fu, *Space and Place: The Perspective of Experience*, Minneapolis: University of Minnesota Press, 1977.

Turole, I., 'Persistent Polarisation Post-aparthe id? Progress towards Urban Integration in Cape Town', *Urban Studies*, 38, 13, pp. 2349-77, 2001.

Zegeye, A. (ed), *Social Identities in the New South Africa*, Capetown: Kwela Books, 2001.

# PART ONE

# Comparing Identities and Territories in India and South Africa

CHAPTER 1

# The Challenge of Comparative Research in Geography and the Social Sciences

PHILIPPE GERVAIS-LAMBONY

When tourists visit a new place, they tend to recall the places they have visited earlier, their country of origin and their place of residence. Naturally, they compare. 'Scientists', researchers in the social sciences in particular, are warned, even forbidden, from conducting comparative research. Instead, academic practice promotes in-depth knowledge of a place or a society that generates awareness of its singularity. Comparisons are for the layman, the journalist or the 'humble' traveller. I argue instead that comparative research is critical and that social scientists with area-based specializations are ideally positioned to conduct comparative research across and between different cities, regions and countries.

Comparative research is difficult not only because it requires extensive knowledge, but also because it challenges the institutional organization of the academy. The concrete importance of this issue must be emphasized. For example, French research institutions are organized to support research on particular places. Funding supports collaboration between French researchers and researchers in the country of study, but knowledge is produced primarily in France, from and for French interests. This type of institutional architecture proves an obstacle for research projects that draw together multiple places—like the project on which this book is based. This project brought together scholars from three different countries, one from the 'North' and two from the 'South'. French research funding is not oriented towards creating academic triangles however. Indeed, in many senses, the challenge of comparative studies is institutional in the first place. France clearly is not exceptional in the way in which institutions of the academy are organized. Disciplinary compartmentalization also limits comparative work, often preventing a comparison of discipline specific approaches, not only because methodologies differ (in itself a major difficulty), but also because disciplines link with separate institutional bodies, funding agencies and literatures.

In the contemporary global context, however, comparative research has become increasingly common and critical. Globalization highlights the complex relationships between the local and the global, and the striking interdependence that characterizes relationships between cities, regions and countries. Comparative enquires have become increasingly legitimate as researchers become aware of the interdependent character of their economies, societies and knowledge. It is in this global context that I assert that comparative social science research is not only a researcher's prerogative, but also a duty. To establish this argument, I will define the comparative process and assess its benefits and limits. I will examine these issues in the context of my experience in organizing this project that drew together researchers from France, South Africa and India to compare territory, space and identity in India and South Africa.

## A COMPARISON OF DIFFERENCES

Comparative research on India and South Africa proves to be a challenge because the two countries are profoundly different. Let me briefly recall some geographical facts. On the one hand, India has a population of one billion, an area of more than three million square km; it is a South Asian giant, culturally marked by the Hindu religion but also by Islam and other 'smaller' religious groups. On the other, South Africa is situated at the southern tip of Africa, comprising a little over one million sq. km, with approximately 43 million inhabitants, its social and political fabric fragmented by apartheid legacies. This list of contrasts is just the beginning, as on one scale everything seems to differ: agriculture, cityscapes and cultural systems. Of course, with a little effort similarities can be seen between India and South Africa: both are former British colonies, southern-based democracies, national territories divided into provinces and states, and both encompass great social and spatial inequality as well as diverse peoples. Many links can be demonstrated between India and South Africa: from the migratory movement from India to South Africa at the end of the nineteenth century to current economic relations. But are these linkages and similarities sufficient to efface the fundamental differences that divide the Indian context from the South African?

This question is central to the project on territory and identity, the theme that draws together the papers in this book. Many researchers have argued or assumed that the South African example of racial segregation is so highly specific that it cannot be compared. For a long time the point of departure for any research on South Africa was based on the assumption that the policies of apartheid, because they were so very specific, had made the South African case unique, and therefore incomparable. Some years ago it would, therefore, have been inconceivable to draw a parallel between South Africa and other countries. Since then, however, the countless illusions about the singular character of the apartheid urban form have been deconstructed. More importantly, in the post-1994 period, it has been possible to trace the ways in which South African society and its cities and regions are moving away from apartheid racial segregation. In this context, the urban studies literature on fragmentation in North American cities, for instance, proves useful for understanding the transformation of space in South African cities. Clearly, South African cities can and should be compared. Apartheid can no longer be considered an isolated and exceptional episode. It should be seen in the context of its national history, not the result of a pre-established overall policy but an aggregation of a variety of policies and stages (Posel, 1991). One can also fruitfully draw on the South African case to better understand the ways in which territories and identities coalesce in other parts of the world. Parallel instances of the uniqueness and comparability of the Indian case can be illustrated as well.

The argument for or against comparison can always be validated and invalidated on the basis of a researcher's choice to draw upon similarities or differences between cases. The tension between uniqueness and generality builds on one fact that I believe is indisputable: at a certain level any and every geographical subject is absolutely different from another. Thus, at the same time, as it is impossible to find two countries absolutely identical, it is equally impossible to find two countries that are absolutely different. The basis of comparative work, therefore, cannot be simply determined on lines of difference and similarity. Different, more sophisticated, questions must be asked to alter the types of assumption on which comparative research has proceeded traditionally.

## COMPARISONS, EVERYBODY DOES IT

On one level, the question of the validity of comparisons can immediately be eliminated because comparison is, in fact, an integral part of the social sciences. In effect, scientific study assumes significance only in comparison with other studies. Whether a study seeks to demonstrate the absolute specificity of a people or of a place (for example, that South Africa is a unique case because apartheid was unique), or whether its purpose is to highlight that this population or this place reflects wider processes or experiences (for example, that South Africa shares common features with other African states, or other former British colonies), research will always refer to the rest of the world to validate differences or similarities in experiences or conceptualizations. Moreover, one's motivation for reading and drawing from area-specific work reflects a process of inbuilt comparison where one uses other researchers' analysis and theorization to draw contrasts and parallels with one's own research elsewhere.

For instance, French researchers working in contexts outside of France—in the south or the north—are by definition assuming a comparative posture. They look at spaces and societies that are not theirs and have always done this (it is still the case) from a Eurocentric perspective. In essence, the process of doing research elsewhere always draws on covert comparison, i.e. confronting the unfamiliar with one's own models of society from the basis of concepts embedded in one's own education and context. Even in instances where researchers focus on their 'own' societies, questions of 'insider' and 'outsider' remain important. On what basis could a researcher be considered an 'insider' and with what consequence? The class, race, gender and other identities of researchers make such categorizations difficult. To a degree then, research by definition is a process of comparative analysis. In the South African social sciences, for instance, one often finds 'white' researchers working on questions pertaining to 'black' society; in India, in comparison, issues of caste also fragment commonalities between researchers and 'subjects' of research. In the research process, a researcher could be considered a 'foreigner' or an 'outsider', if only because of his/her observer status and social position.

In all instances, the demonstration of uniqueness of a scientific case rests on its distinctiveness from other cases. The identity of a scientific object is at the same time related to its singularity and to its distinctness (just like the identity of an individual or a group). The process of affirming that South Africa, for example, is absolutely singular, is to affirm that it differs, an analysis that reflects comparison. Comparison is thus an integral part of any cognitive process. I see an apple; I know it is an apple because it resembles other apples. This identification is not in contradiction with the fact that this apple is unique, identical to none other. The difficulty with the comparative procedure lies in the permanent tension between the singularity and the universality of all objects. Comparison is an essential component of researchers' methodology and our training as scholars. Nonetheless, researchers working in the field of comparative studies must always justify themselves, and define (and defend) the basis on which comparative analysis has been made. In the process, they are compelled to explain what they mean by 'comparison'.

## TYPES OF COMPARISONS

Comparisons can be defined in various ways. In this section, I will group different types of comparative analyses on the basis of their conceptual objectives and discuss three broad groups.

The first group is the comparison of cases. In geography, for instance, this type of analysis compares different areas of land—cities, regions and countries. Area-based comparisons pose a simple and recurrent problem: are researchers comparing two similar cases or are they looking for similarities and differences between the two cases, whatever they be. Two radically different approaches can be adopted to answer this question.

First, a reductionist comparison involves a comparative approach, which is limited to similar cases: what is alike is comparable (similar). Comparing only similarities produces a restricted analysis and a restrictive definition of the comparative process (for a fuller discussion see Dufaux and Gervais-Lambony, 1993; Gervais-Lambony, 1994). I have described this as a tautological comparison for it merely corroborates a pre-established definition. Moreover, this approach is scientifically flawed: I know that each place is unique and that an identical place does not exist. If I pursue this approach seriously, in the end I cannot compare anything. This approach is thus an extremely limiting way to create knowledge. It reduces comparative work to contrasting two subjects in order to show that they are dissimilar in all aspects. Yet, is it possible for two geographical objects to be completely different if their components are of an identical nature (that is to say, when geographical entities are singular compositions of universal elements)? I would argue that such a proposition is not possible.

The second possibility attempts to find the general across many cases. The term 'general' is not really appropriate here however. Common elements or processes may exist between places, but one cannot ignore or demean the different contexts that enframe these similarities or that generate the unique elements of each case. Each place is different from the other and therefore unique, but each place also shares some common characteristics with others. Everything is singular, but everything is also universal at the same time, and neither of these dimensions should be reduced. From this perspective, a researcher may try to demonstrate what is different and what is similar, and explain why it is so. This is comparison *par excellence*; it enables one to assess the weight of the different components constituting a place, and the importance of external influences on the specific cases. This comparison helps to identify what is general and what is particular; and there can be no dispute about the advantages of this method. But at the same time, one cannot stop at this point, for comparison also can take many other forms.

The second group of comparisons contrasts cases to models. I can identify two, interrelated types of comparative analysis. The first is a classic scientific approach, which consists of comparing a particular case with a theoretical model: the model, qualitative or quantitative, has to be tested. Second, a closely related approach bases comparative analysis not on a model but on a broad, theoretically informed concept of a type of place or process. This method is used by Jacques Lévy in contemporary urban studies: he defines the relative urban-ness (co-habitation, density and diversity, for instance) while admitting that it is not found in equal measure in all cities, nor in all parts of a city. Without this approach, he has convincingly compared Amsterdam and Johannesburg and measured their degree of 'urbanité'.[1]

Last, the third grouping of comparisons differs from the first two categorizations: reality compared to representations, historical versus contemporary analyses, and comparisons between methodological approaches. A classical comparison in the social sciences is one that compares reality with representations such as the analysis of individual versus collective representations or the analysis of the various discourses on the subject studied. What is being compared are not two objects but one object and its representation. Often this type of research also aims at the comparison of two different representations, for instance, the Paris of the rich, the Paris of the poor, or the city viewed by urban authorities in contrast with the city viewed by its inhabitants. Comparison is equally relevant to historical work that compares the same society or the same place at different moments in time. The comparison of different investigative methodologies or of investigative research is another classical approach and forms the basis of inter-disciplinary work. Comparative discussions on methodologies underlie the type of teamwork envisioned in this project.

The tension between the undeniable singularity of a case studied and its universality is a common issue in the three comparative categories discussed here. Its negotiation is the central challenge to comparative research.

## THE SINGULAR AND THE UNIVERSAL

Do not all the different ways of using comparisons aim at resolving the difficulty underlying the transition from the particular to the general? It amounts to building a bridge between a local (or field) approach and a general approach. One cannot avoid either when trying to resolve the apparent contradiction between deductive analysis that seeks general laws through the construction of models and an inductive approach that starts with the uniqueness of places and societies and theorizes from this specificity. This problem is common to all the social sciences, although it is particularly marked in gography: 'One of the most constant tensions in geography is that which opposes a singularising methodology with a universalising methodology' (Robic, 1992, p. 56). In French geography, a traditional distinction is that between 'general' geography and 'regional' geography. 'General' geography has enjoyed full liberty to make comparisons; its very *raison d'être* has been to classify spaces wherever they are on the globe into types (based on regional or local studies). Conversely, the role of 'regional' geography has been to demonstrate the singularity of places through detailed description. Regional geographers usually do not draw comparisons at a general scale, their theorizing is based on the nuances of local cases. This division between area-focused regionalist and generalist geographers marks a strange contradiction within French geography.

For a French geographer, therefore, the question of the validity of comparisons is not a secondary question but a central one. It is possible to interpret the entire history of the discipline in this light. The objective has been a description of singular places or an explanation of universal spatial phenomena. In fact, there is no contradiction: places are singular, spatial phenomena are universal. In other words, the uniqueness of each place is not contradictory with the existence of 'laws of space'. For example, if one accepts that Paris is an absolutely singular place, the problems, of urban transport in Paris are not absolutely specific to it, but general to cities in many other areas. If one analyses a place individually, each place is unique for it represents a particular organization of space, distribution of resources, and set of representations. If one adopts an 'objective' point of view, each place is also unique for it is the result of a specific combination of processes. Take, for example, a zebra skin with its distinctive stripes or the uniqueness of each human being's fingerprints: both need to be under-stood as examples of general phenomena and unique expressions. Last, societies may represent a particular collective expression, but they also must be understood as the aggregate of individuals who have particular life experiences, and rules and symbols that come together in particular places and times. Each place is thus unique for it is a complex human construction. It is not only unique in space but also unique in time: for each place is immediate, it exists only in its immediacy.

Can comparisons help to resolve this tension between the unique and the universal? It cannot be resolved, but researchers must recognize and understand the ways in which the tension plays out in their research, their disciplines and in the social sciences in general. For instance, in the case of geography, geographers do not study spaces and places, or societies in their entirety. Moreover, they do not describe spaces; they describe human spatial constructions. Therefore, their methods need to be dynamic, to reflect the dynamism of the processes studied. The critical question often is not what are the differences between here and there, but what processes have led to a particular situation, and how the process shapes a society or place? The same process may shape two places or societies in a similar fashion at certain levels (for instance, the influence of British colonialism in India and South Africa). Similar processes may also lead to different situations (for instance 'affirmative action' or positively discriminating policies to address caste inequalities in India and racial inequalities in South Africa). A comparison of processes across places and societies illustrates both the universal and the particular, facilitating critical reflection not only on each place and society, but also on the processes themselves. The focus on process rather than a particular space or place is thus critical. Arguments that suggest comparative work as problematic because of the particular character of a place or society are misleading: one can compare processes occurring in different places.

Of course, research on unique cases is necessary, but only to the extent that such studies facilitate an understanding of process. This can well be the case with monographs on a place. Augustin Berque's work (1993) on the Japanese city aimed to determine what made the Japanese city unique in all its dimensions (physical, social and cultural). It demonstrated how the materiality of the city and urban society fused into an absolutely singular collective subject. Be that as it may, it is also necessary to describe the processes through which the particular character of a city is expressed in every case (or, at least, it is a condition for one to be able to talk about cities). In practice, the particular and the universal are studied jointly. The analysis of the particular case becomes a method and the conceptual foundation that is the route or instrument through which the comparison may then be constructed.

This volume's focus on the dialectic between territory[2] and identity is a thematic approach that lends itself to comparisons.[3] The various papers analyse the way in which people construct territories and the way in which territories and societies then evolve. Societal constructions are analysed as processes rather than static or unchanging objects. Comparison is necessary in order to understand the construction of territory and identity, and the processes that shape the relationship between the two. Moreover, it should be borne in mind that comparisons are necessary to avoid misconceptions that may occur when encountering concepts in different cultural spheres (Louiset, 1993). The contrast between town and countryside, a very European concept, is a good example. An analysis of Japanese cities, for instance, allows one to question the European assumption of division between urban and rural areas (Berque, 1993). South African cities also demonstrate a similar point: rural and urban universes are not in contradiction in the same way as they are in Europe or in North America. Through this comparative discussion, the idea of territoriality itself can thus be debated (Détienne, 2000). Comparative analyses and methodologies should focus, therefore, on concepts and categories rather than on places. From this perspective, the question of similarity and difference between places and societies becomes less important, and clearly does not invalidate a comparative research approach.

## THE LIMITS TO COMPARATIVE ANALYSIS

Although comparative research in the social sciences is important, theoretical and methodological limits do exist. First, the question of scale is important. Is it possible to compare processes that take place at different geographical scales, across towns, regions and countries? How is it possible to analyse urban segregation in India and South Africa when the scale of the two realities differs? If one focusses on multiple scales, what types of comparisons have been constructed? These issues are central to this volume with its focus on the urban and regional scale in India and South Africa

Second, comparisons raise the question of research subjectivity. Research is an individual act, which becomes useful only when it is shared with an audience. In various disciplines field research itself is nearly always done by the individual researcher. The role of the individual in shaping any interpretation immediately limits the potential for comparative analysis. A researcher cannot legitimately compare unless he/she has made an assessment of the subjectivity of his/her research. Transparency in methodology is critical for facilitating comparative research.

In an ideal comparative project, the same researcher should be in a position to conduct several field studies and thus systematically evolve a comparative approach. This, however, is extremely rare not only because of inadequate resources, but also because of the demands of understanding and accessing multiple contexts and literatures. Common research practice, therefore, leads to the comparison of one person's research area through reading on other places as well as discussion and exchange of ideas and information about particular places and processes with other scholars. Ideas flow through these types of collaborative conversations. In many senses, the research presented in this book represents the latter example. Although similar themes have been debated in the Indian and South African contexts and conceptual ideas have been discussed from French, Indian and South African academic traditions, only in a few, rare instances have cross-country, cross-region, cross-city, or cross-group studies been conducted.

Although truly comparative research would be ideal, a common vocabulary and conceptual apparatus may provide an excellent platform on which to build comparative research. A common vocabulary between researchers from different countries, across different languages, and between different academic traditions needs to also cross different social science disciplines. Although the issue of methodology remains a challenge, in itself it does not prohibit comparative research. If a common vocabulary and consensus on conceptual ideas has been achieved, I argue that a diversity of methods can provide the space for fertile comparative analysis that crosses traditional divisions between disciplines.

However, a critical material question should also be addressed: what does an Indian, South African, or French scholar gain from comparing different aspects of the situation in his or her country with that of another country? Comparisons should not be done for comparisons sake; there should be some sort of utility to ask questions and to conduct research across national and disciplinary boundaries.

Although there are challenges to comparative research and moments and places in which such projects are more useful than others, I would like to conclude on a positive note. Even if the 'scientific' character of comparative research can be debated, as Marcel Détienne (2001) pointed out: 'l'oeil comparatiste est primesautier'. Researchers should take pleasure in making comparisons; they are not noly a source of surprise, but also bring joy and lead to deeper insight.

## NOTES

1. Roughly translated as 'urban-ness' in English.
2. The concept of territory (*territoire*) is central in French geography, but cannot be directly translated into English. The French word 'territoire' is polysemic (see Chap. 2 by Dupont and Landy in this volume for a fuller discussion), referring simultaneously to a space on which a 'power' manifests its control (see Robert Sack's work for a similar conceptualization in English) and a space which has a symbolic sense for a community (this community identifies with that space and thus territory translates to identity). The word 'territoriality' describes the way in which human beings as individuals relate to space. This conceptualization is even more complex as each individual belongs to more than one territory and has multiple identities. The opposition between space and place in Anglophone geography is to some extent comparable to the distinction between space and territory in French geographical literature.
3. These concepts are 'comparables' to use Marcel Détienne's (2000) expression.

## REFERENCES

Augé, Marc, *Non-Lieux, Introduction à une anthropologie de la surmodernité*, Paris: Le Seuil, 1992.

Baby-Collin, Virginie, 'Marginaux et citadins. Construire une urbanité métisse en Amérique latine. Etude comparée des barrios de Caracas (Venezuela) et des villas d'El Alto de La Paz (Bolivie)', Ph.D. thesis, University Toulouse II-Le Mirail, 2000.

Berque, Agustin, *Le geste et la cité*, Paris: Gallimard, 1993.

Berque, Augustin and Nys Philippe (eds.), *Logique du lieu et œuvre humaine*, Bruxelles: Ousia, 1997.

Détienne, Marcel, *Comparer l'incomparable*, Paris: Le Seuil, 2000.

Donzelot, Jacques, 'La nouvelle question urbaine', *Esprit*, 258, 1999, pp. 87-114.

Dufaux, Frédéric and Philippe Gervais-Lambony (eds), *Afrique noire/Europe de l'Est, regards croisés*, Paris: Karthala-Géotropiques, 1993.

Gervais-Lambony, Philippe, *De Lomé à Harare: le Fait citadin*, Paris: Karthala, 1994.

Gourou, Pierre, *Pour une géographie humaine*, Paris: Flammarion, 1973.

Lévy, Jacques, *L'espace légitime. Sur la dimension géographique de la fonction politique*, Paris, Presses de la FNSP, 1994.

———, *Le tournant géographique. Penser l'espace pour lire le monde*, Paris: Belin, 1999.

Louiset, Odette, 'L'urbanité ailleurs', in *Logiques de l'espace, esprit des lieux*, ed. Jacques Lévy and Michel Lusault, Paris: Belin, 2000, pp. 157-64.

Posel, Deborah, *The Making of Apartheid*, Oxford: Clarendon Press, 1991.

Robic, Marie-Claire, 'Epistémologie de la géographie', in *Encyclopédie de Géographie*, ed. A. Bailly, R. Ferras and D. Pumain, Paris: Economica, 1992, pp. 55-73.

CHAPTER 2

# Segregation and Territory: What do We Mean? A Discussion in the Indian and South African Contexts

VÉRONIQUE DUPONT AND FRÉDÉRIC LANDY

Segregation intrinsically is linked to the relation between territory and identity and the connections between territoriality (the relationships with the territory) and identity markers. An analysis of these issues formed the core of the research programme discussed in this volume. Specifically, the project aimed to 'better understand how identities project onto space to create territories'. Debate on key concepts such as segregation, territory and identity is, however, a prerequisite for a productive, cross-disciplinary and international discussion of this topic. While there are numerous understandings of the terms 'territory' and 'segregation', we have chosen to draw from those that best express the relationship between identity and territory, and allow for a more productive comparison between the Indian and South African contexts.

## TERRITORY–SPACE DELINEATED BY IDENTITY

The term 'territory' is ambiguous. First, the definition based on identity, that we have adopted, is one out of many. Second, the concept can easily become overly rigid and used for purposes that are far from scientific.

### DEFINING TERRITORY

The term 'territory' is polysemous (Di Méo, 1998). Seen from a purely ethological perspective, territory may refer to the space demarcated by animal urine. But the concept may be used in multiple ways. For instance, it could be transposed to describe what occurs in Amazonia and Indonesia, where peripheral territories are demarcated by the presence of immigrants whose emigration from central areas is encouraged by government policies. Their presence is a way of expressing geopolitical appropriation of a zone, which requires a process of homogenization generated by the creation of networks (communications, transport, etc.) that enable persons and goods or information to circulate, the implementation of political decisions as well as the recognition of political power. In this frame of analysis, territory is understood as an 'integrated' space, closely tied to a geopolitical core and without excluded areas.

Territory can also be synonymous with 'mental/perceived space' (*espace perçu*) or 'lived-in space' (*espace vécu*). It is the space a person moves in during the course of a day or a year. Values and symbols have not necessarily been attributed to this space, however, which makes this type of definition too broad. 'Territory is more than "experienced"; it is learned and built by individuals through customs and beliefs that are social in nature. In the case of territory, psychological processes are subordinate to cultural models, which are either handed-down or constructed—appropriation, power, and representations come together' (Roncayolo, 1990, p. 189). Through this usage, the concept of 'territory' is, for the most part, based on feelings. Territory entails 'feelings of belongingness', 'this is where I'm from', and of appropriation, 'I am part of this place' (Brunet et al., 1992, p. 436).

Territory is therefore much more than just the space that is experienced or lived in. The definition adopted in this paper is one where territory is expressed as identity, which is then projected on to space. True, this is not a one-way relationship: conversely, identity can be partly produced by space (sometimes simply by proximity). In any case territory is the object of symbolic appropriation: the concept of 'territory' cannot exist without one of 'identity'. A clear example of this latter case could be Native American reservations in the United States where the term 'nation', which is laden with identity, has a spatial meaning that is almost synonymous with 'territory'. One can, for instance, even purchase maps of the 'Navajo nation'.

Reciprocally, is it possible to argue that there is no 'identity' without 'territory'? 'It is as if group thinking needed some visible form of space in order to exist, survive and become conscious' (Halbwachs, 1939, cited by Roncayolo, 1990, p. 183). It could be argued, however, that the new ties to space that have emerged because of globalization have now made it possible to have an identity without territory. A top executive working for a multinational corporation who stays two years in one country, three in another, and spends most of his time travelling on business could not be 'territorialized'. In France, for example, career military officers are forced to be mobile. Integration for these individuals and their families is limited. We believe, however, that even in such cases territories exist, although they are perhaps not deeply rooted and quickly forgotten. This is what Tarrius (1966, p. 191) described when referring to the 'international professional elite' who posses a 'circular territory that is extremely "technified" [*technicisé* in French, implying linkages generated through new technologies that reduce distance] and "exotified" [*exotisé* in French, arguing that previously unknown places are integrated into territories and identities].'

If space is understood as a medium for identity, in order for it to function as a territory, there has to be some mechanism by which it is appropriated. Appropriation may take place at the national level, i.e. the state: this allows for mutual recognition among inhabitants. Appropriation can take place at the local level through many types of mechanisms. The Roman law concept of ownership of property is only one of them. The French concept of *terroir* (village area) in Western Africa, 'a portion of appropriated territory that is prepared and used by the group residing there' (Sautter and Pélissier, 1964) is an example of space where *usus* (the right to use), *fructus* (the right to benefit from the fruits of the property) and *abusus* (the right to dispose of or alienate property) are separate. The 'holder' of the land (*maître de la terre*), the descendant of the first individuals who cleared the land, entrusts the land to the person who wishes to use it. In this case, the land is not legally owned. The person using the land is required to return the land to the 'holder' when he has ceased to use it. Except for a nominal gift, the land 'holder' does not receive any remuneration for lending the land.

It takes time to constitute a territory; people have to experience and use space. During the apartheid era, when Indians were expelled from inner Durban to the new neighbouring lands (townships) they had been allocated, these territories did not become 'theirs' immediately. They did not feel urban citizens in these new lands any more than they felt they were citizens of South Africa.[1] Initially, these zones were perceived as zones of forced concentration, hated rather than appropriated. In contrast, the government decided to leave Indian places of worship untouched, even though Hindu temples—such as the one in Cato Manor—were located in zones from where Indians had been expelled. The temples were still being used as places of worship; consequently, they remained part of Indian territory. The temples were like enclaves located in the space that the racist government had expropriated from the Indians and converted into a new *no-man's land*.[2]

## Rigid Territories

'Lived-in space' and 'territory' should be seen as distinct concepts. Lived-in spaces used by groups or individuals frequently overlap, without creating conflict. The overlapping of territories, however, usually leads to various types of tension. An example of conflict at a local level can be observed in India when members of a mosque or a temple have to cross a neighbourhood inhabited by the other religious community to reach their place of worship. At another scale, an unfortunate example of regional geopolitical conflict due to territory is north-east India,[3] where mountain tribes and tribes from the plains, Hindus, animists and Bangladeshi Muslim immigrants are, along with others, in competition for farming land, tea, or oil. There are as many ties to intertwined territories, as there are communities.

Because workplaces vary, the lived-in spaces of individuals belonging to the same group also vary enormously. Territoriality—the relationships with the territory—however, is similar for each individual within a group and usually corresponds to a clearly demarcated space. This can easily be observed in cities, where territories usually comprise a set of neighbourhoods that are contiguous in varying degrees with borders that become important in times of crisis. During the 1992-3 riots in Bombay, neighbourhood borders, which under normal conditions were fuzzy, were clearly delineated by the location of street barricades and police cars.[4] Political communal crises contribute to making the demarcation of territories more rigid. Spaces without identity or with multiple identities disappear under the pressure brought to bear by militants from all sides who want to mark their group of houses and do away with anything that is emblematic of any other identity but their own. Examples of this behaviour are people locked in their homes and burnt alive by the extremists of an opposing faction, and the 'purification' of the territory through the profanation or destruction of *dargahs*—graves of Sufi saints—symbols of identity.[5]

Movements such as the xenophobic Marathi Shiv Sena use their 210 local branches (*shakhas*), located in municipal constituencies, to demarcate Mumbai or at the least the centrally located Marathi-speaking neighbourhoods of Parel, Dadar, Lalbag, and Worli. The crenulated architecture of the *shakhas* is reminiscent of the forts built by Shivaji, a seventeenth-century Hindu hero. The banners, signs, and aggressive loudspeakers are usually located near mosques and mark the presence of the Shiv Sena (Heuzé, 1993). At the all-India scale, large processions (*yatras*) organized by the nationalist Hindu organizations like the RSS, the VHP and the BJP[6] have succeeded in delineating Hindu territory as the land from the southern end of the peninsula to the Himalayas, 'from Kanya Kumari to Mount Kailash'. The centre of this territory is both the geographical centre of India and the headquarters of the RSS: Nagpur (Assayag, 2001).

We will refrain, however, from believing that the territory of each Hindu is defined as clearly, aggressively and intransigently as the aforementioned examples, which, although striking, are exceptional. There are two reasons why less research has been done on moderate Hindu territories than on nationalist Hindu territories. In the former, the political stakes are less fearsome. Second, territories are more difficult to identify. They overlap and are so widespread that researchers have paid less attention to the ways in which territory reinforces identities, and vice versa, in these instances.

Until now we have only referred to religious territories. Ethnic or racial territories of the type found in South Africa may have other characteristics. To build a classification system for territories, we need to ask if the identity marker (ethnic group, religion, region, etc.) is an adequate classification criterion, or whether it is possible to include in the same class territories based on differing identity markers. For example, can we find some ethnic territories with the same characteristics as religious territories? The fact that certain identity markers are ambiguous makes the task of building such a typology more difficult. In India, for example, nationalist Hindu movements claim to speak on behalf of the nation rather than on behalf of their religious affiliation. The RSS uses the term 'Hindu' almost less often than it uses the terms *rashtriya* (national) or *bharatiya* (the adjective derived from the Sanskrit word *Bharat* meaning India) (Jaffrelot, 1993). The word 'Hindu' was originally used to designate anyone living on the land through which the Indus river flows: a religion therefore was named after a region and a river. Moreover, Hinduism is mostly practised in India, a fact that contributes to the ambiguity that Hindu nationalists skilfully use to transform the concept of Hinduism into a secular one. Nationalists claim that 'Hinduness' (*hindutva*) is only a 'way of life' and that it should be followed by all the nation's inhabitants, including those belonging to religious minorities.

### Flexible Territories

Identities are for the most part context-dependent. For instance, a South African of Indian ancestry, according to the context he finds himself in, may react on the basis of the place where he lives (a resident of Durban); his citizenship (a South African); his religion (a Hindu, Muslim, or Christian); his region of origin (descendant of Tamil or Hindi-speaking ancestors), among others.[7] If one person can have several identities, in various states of awareness, and each identity has a territory, does that person have at his disposal several territories, all of which are highly context-dependent? In Canada, outside Quebec, the French-speaking people have various territories: at the individual level, their territories are mixed seen from a linguistic perspective, since these people are living in an English-speaking milieu. At the collective level, however, one can find a purely French-speaking territory with specific associations, networks and places (Gilbert, 1999).

Territorial boundaries are often, therefore, flexible. In rural areas, territories are not as clearly defined as in cities because there are often fewer landmarks, and fewer streets and buildings that can be used to clearly delineate the boundaries. *Saltus* areas are poorly cleared, not cleared at all, or located at the periphery thus acting as a buffer zone between neighbouring territories.[8] The West African concept of village—*terroir*—is defined in terms of the centre and not the periphery. This meaning stands in contrast to modern European municipalities where territories (French *finages*) have 'outer', municipal 'limits' that are clearly demarcated. Indian villages, depending on the context, use concepts that lie somewhere between these African and European examples. When the village is located on land that has been completely cleared there are 'limits' like in a *finage*. When the village is located on partially wooded land where there is little farming activity, the boundaries are blurred as in the West African concept of *terroir*.

At one point India had this type of flexible system of territory at the national scale. The country was divided into political entities whose borders where defined by their centre rather than the peripheries, the opposite of the concept of *limes*, limits between states. That system continued till the reign of the Mughals (sixteenth to the eighteenth century), whose authority over certain local rulers was purely symbolic. A similar situation existed in France until the sixteenth century, when

French kings had to secure their authority by travelling throughout their kingdom, especially the fringes where the king had no local representatives to strengthen royal power.

Territory as defined by nomadic peoples is further proof of just how diverse the term is. The way nomads inscribe themselves into space may appear even more nebulous than that of farming communities, although the phenomenon is very real. This apparent lack of clear borders is one of the reasons why the Tuaregs inhabiting the Sahel, the cattle rearers of Thar in Rajasthan, or certain tribes living in central India encounter difficulties. National boundaries cut across the land used by nomadic people; forests are protected by the state or farmed by private firms without taking into account the practices of hunter-gatherers or shifting cultivation farmers. Hence, territoriality and permanent settlement should be considered as two separate phenomena. In defining 'circulatory territory', Tarrius (1996) clarified the complex relationships that developed between immigrants, their place of origin and their adopted homeland. There are thus many territories of mobility.

Generally speaking, rural areas in India have been inhabited for centuries; their inhabitants are thus deeply rooted in the land. Even the more recently settled frontiers (such as Punjab) are peopled by country-dwellers with a cultural heritage of intensive farming: every year land is improved and rarely do they leave their land fallow (Racine, 1997). The relatively low rate of Indian urbanization (28 per cent in 2001) reflects the importance of the relationship between rural people and rural areas. In the South African case the rural population is divided racially, supported historically by appropriation of land for 'white' farmers through forced eviction of black families and communities. 'White' farms tend to be located on productive farming land that was subsidized heavily by the apartheid state. In 1995, for instance, before land reforms, out of 55,000 commercial farmers only 1,500 were black (Gervais-Lambony, 1997). Rural population have connections to the land, but these connections have been shaped in the South African context by colonial and apartheid processes of displacement and the establishment of 'homelands'. In the apartheid and contemporary periods, homeland areas tend to be populated by the elderly and children, while working age people circulate between cities and the countryside to sustain their families' livelihoods. South Africa's long and turbulent history of massive displacement from the land produced complicated patterns of segregation that greatly contributed to the definition of complex territories.

## SEGREGATION AS A SPATIAL FORM OF DISCRIMINATION

### Finding a Definition

Etymologically, the word 'segregation' is derived from the Latin *segregatio*, from the verb *segregare*, i.e. 'to separate the herd'. The first meaning of 'segregation' is to separate, to set apart from the rest, to intentionally isolate. As J. Brun aptly put it: 'rather than denoting the end results, the word denotes the act' (1994, p. 23).

In the social sciences, however, the word 'segregation' denotes either a state—a descriptive form of the distribution of social groups in space, or a process—an act. The gamut of notions covered by the term segregation is very broad and encompasses a vast array of social-spatial configurations, with reference to a wide variety of processes. The question here is which definition facilitates a comparative approach?

A strict definition of segregation would denote the following: 'a form of institutionalised social distance which results in spatial separation' (*Dictionnaire de la sociologie*, 1989); 'policies of wilful separation of two different ethnic communities' (George, 1970, p. 421); 'forced, institutionalised, and regulated separation of population groups based on racial criteria' (Lapeyronnie and Rouleau, 1988, p. 611); or '. . . only cases where physical separation ensues from a principal of institutionalised social organization, [. . .] segregation [appears] as a spatial order for which the dominant group gives itself the means to impose on those it seeks to segregate' (Grafmeyer, 1994a, p. 87).

The two most frequently given examples of segregation are the segregation suffered by blacks in the southern United States, which was institutionalized by Jim Crow legislation in 1870 and continued till the 1964 Civil Rights Act, and apartheid in South Africa, literally 'separate development'. Apartheid segregation reflects a principle of separation of the 'white city' from the 'black city' (native city), which was the basis of British colonial urbanization in India as well.[9] Urban planning, as developed by the colonial authorities in cities under their control, was clearly wilful and organized separation. Spatial order was imposed on native populations, although it was not always backed by the type of radical and restrictive laws used for residential segregation in South Africa under apartheid.

The building of New Delhi in the 1910s and 1920s offers a good example of urban planning based on segregation (Dupont, 2001). The new imperial capital was deliberately built at a distance from the existing 'native' town, Old Delhi. A wide stretch of land was cleared and left undeveloped and used to mark the boundary between the two urban areas, not unlike the undeveloped buffer zones that separated 'black' and 'coloured' townships in South Africa from the 'white' city.[10] In New Delhi, the spatial organization of housing for civil servants directly reflected their position within the hierarchy. Moreover, housing for British employees was separate from that of Indian employees, with the latter housed as far away from the vice-regal palace as possible (Evenson, 1989).

If, however, we want to extend our analysis and go beyond the historical context (India ceased to be a colony in 1947 and the phasing out of apartheid in South Africa began in 1990), a definition of segregation limited to the concept of institutionalized separation would limit the analysis of current situations in post-apartheid South Africa and independent India.

On the other extreme, purely empirical and descriptive accounts would consider segregation as: 'spatial distinction among the residential zones of population groups living in the same agglomeration' (Brun, 1994, p. 22); 'lack of homogeneity of space in terms of population characteristics' (Castells, 1981, 219, a commentary on the work carried out by the Chicago School on American residential space); and 'differences in [residential] location of groups defined using criteria such as social position, ethnic origin, religion, etc., [that risk] having segregation likened to, ultimately, any type of social different-iation of space' (Grafmeyer, 1994a, p. 88; 1994b, p. 36).

These approaches may explain processes of aggregation or of 'spontaneous segregation' resulting from preferential residential clustering by individuals sharing similar characteristics and aspiring to live among one another. It is then possible, for example, to speak about 'rich ghettos'. In such cases, it needs to be proved that aggregation of the rich (active agents who chose to segregate themeslevs) is the same process as segregation of the poor (passive agents who are subjected to segregation). This conception would imply that in South Africa, whites are segregated to a greater extent than blacks, given the fact that they live, almost exclusively, in white zones, whereas some blacks lived in interstitial squatter settlements, or in servant quarters; moreover certain Blacks—members of the new bourgeoisie—live in predominantly white neighbourhoods. Also, if we adopt a very broad definition, the heuristic benefits of a comparative approach between India and South Africa would lose significance. In addition, we risk comparing and drawing irrelevant conclusions from phenomena and processes that are based on different rationales.[11]

We need to adopt a definition that is more rigorous and precise, which allows us 'to go beyond the ambiguities that are inherent in the indiscriminate use of the concept' (Brun, 1994, p. 48), but is not limited to the legal forms of separation imposed by governments. We believe that there are several principals that are essential to the concept of segregation: the original notion of separation and setting aside; discrimination (identified as essential by authors such as Brun, 1994; Grafmeyer, 1994a; 1994b; and Gervais-Lambony, 2001); the concept of 'hierarchical sorting' (Navez-Bouchainine, 2001); and inequality in relations among social groups (Brun, 1994).

According to Grafmeyer, 'segregation is always the creation of social distance coupled with physical separation' (Grafmeyer, 1994b, p. 39); consequently, we have adopted a definition of segregation as a process whereby social discrimination results in spatial separation.[12] We show how this definition of segregation permits study of the interrelations between segregation, territory and identity.

## Determining Relevant Scales and Spaces of Reference

Any discussion of the concept of segregation has to include reflection on the scale at which we are going to observe the phenomenon. If we are interested in studying the residential dimension of segregation, we must take note of Lévy's and Brun's (2000, p. 239) concern that: '. . . one is hesitant when it comes to using terms such as homogeneity or heterogeneity, since both concepts can change completely with a change in the scale at which one is observing the structure of the population'. On a city-wide scale, in a metropolis such as Delhi, a marked diversity in the socio-economic structure of the population and in housing at the level of large zones is coupled with highly salient segregation phenomena that can be observed at the scale of smaller spatial units. This is especially true in the case of the former untouchable castes—the scheduled castes.[13] On a neighbourhood scale, there is high residential concentration, but from a city-wide scale scheduled castes (as identified by the Census of India) reside in areas that are distributed throughout the capital (Dupont, 2004; Dupont and Mitra, 1995).[14] We must ask, therefore, a more general question: where do we draw the line between segregation and residential mixing?

Traditional quantitative analyses of residential segregation depend on how spatial units are demarcated within the entire space under study and on the size of the single units that have been selected for study.[15] The most frequently used segregation index[16] depends on the size and number of spatial units: the bigger the spatial unit, the lower the index and the larger the number of units, the higher the index. Researchers working on a comparative analysis of segregation in various regions or cities are faced with this type of problem. All the more reason why researchers conducting a comparative study, quantitative or otherwise, involving different countries must clearly define the spaces being studied and the scale of observation. In Europe and North America most of the research on segregation focuses on cities. In order to grasp the segregation phenomenon specific to South Africa and India we require a broader perspective, one that goes beyond the urban framework. At first glance, however, traditional segregation processes do not call into play the same spatial categories or the same scales.

In India, the Hindu[17] socio-religious hierarchy underpinning the traditional caste system implies a segmentation and hierarchy of space that can be observed (or were once observed) in the internal structure of every town or village. A village is generally characterized by heterogeneity of castes and it is at the microlocal scale—a hamlet, a neighbourhood, a street, or even a block of houses—that segmentation by caste becomes evident. The fact that members of each caste live in their own neighbourhood does not exclude certain observable types of caste mixing. Yet, the most flagrant and enduring example of residential segregation is the case of the former untouchable castes which are systematically relegated to hamlets outside the village (Deliège, 1999).

Sanskrit treatises on architecture recommended spatial separation (Begde, 1978). In cities, segregation was not always rigorously observed; this is especially true of cities in the south. Notwithstanding, the lines separating the castes at either end of the hierarchy have always been extremely clear: the Brahmins have invariably received special treatment (their neighbourhoods were usually located next to the temple) while at the other end of the social ladder, the Untouchables were segregated, relegated to the neighbourhoods located on the periphery. In pre-industrial cities in northern India, neighbourhoods located in the centre were segmented into blocks that housed the members of a specific community or sub-caste (for instance, *mohallas* in Delhi, *pols* in Ahmedabad).

Clearly, contemporary social dynamics are profoundly changing the segmentation in Indian society. The spatial growth of cities and villages tends to encapsulate and engulf segregated areas. As built-up areas become wider, groups that were initially relegated to the fringes find themselves inside the agglomeration. Notwithstanding these processes, many studies have shown that caste continues to be a key factor in socio-spatial organization in contemporary Indian cities (Gandhi, 1983; Noble and Dutt, 1977; Racine, 1990; Schenk, 1986; Trivedi, 1996; Vaguet, 1997). The Harijan[18] *bastis*, the neighbourhoods where the former untouchable castes live, are still an urban reality, although other residential neighbourhoods are the outcome of other complex economic and social dynamics. Therefore, the persistence of residential segregation according to caste should be studied at the intra-urban as well as the intra-village level.

In South Africa, the institutionalized system of separation for the population was applied to the entire country and not confined to urban areas. Even before the introduction of apartheid, which strictly speaking can be traced to the victory of the National Party in the 1948 elections, segregation laws were aimed at stemming the urbanization of blacks and controlling their stay in cities. The Land Act of 1913 established areas reserved for blacks—homelands or bantustans. Blacks could only acquire property on these reservations. The Native (Urban Areas) Act of 1923 instituted a system of passes, sojourner permits, for urban zones. The Group Areas Act of 1950, deemed to be the most powerful urban planning tool used for apartheid, established residential sections for each racial group: whites, black Africans, coloured and Indians. Racist legislation divided and created hierarchical divisions of space according to the four 'races'. Although in certain contexts these boundaries are blurring, they continue to broadly demarcate space. Race is thus closely linked to space, and belonging to a specific race strongly attaches one to a specific place (Christopher, 2001).

South African townships are frequently bigger than the caste-based neighbourhoods of India. They are also more diversified in socio-economic terms (a logical consequence of the effect of scale). For example, a Harijan *basti* in an Indian city is usually more homogeneous in socio-economic terms (there is an over-representation of the poor engaged in manual labour or demeaning services), whereas today in the formerly black townships, there are well-off black families who either do not have access, or do not wish to live in white neighbourhoods. Because of their high level of social and professional diversity, black townships in South Africa might rather resemble former Jewish ghettos in Europe.

## DOES RACIAL AND CASTE DISCRIMINATION CONSTITUTE A RELEVANT STARTING POINT FOR A COMPARATIVE APPROACH TO SEGREGATION IN SOUTH AFRICA AND INDIA?

What is the relationship between caste and race? Are they comparable? Studies comparing the caste system in India and social-racial stratification in the United States are fairly dated[19] and have been the subject of much criticism. Louis Dumont dedicated an entire chapter to this in his book *Homo Hierarchicus*, 'Caste, racism and "stratification"' (Dumont, 1966 and 1998). Dumont, unlike certain authors who are critical of this type of study (Deliège, 1999), does not, *a priori*, regard a comparative analysis of these two distant cultures as irrelevant. He does, however, state that certain conditions must be established:

> . . . comparative sociology requires concepts which take into account the values that different societies have chosen for themselves. [. . .] In so doing one will of course in no way impose upon a society the values of another, but only endeavour to set mutually 'in perspective' the various types of societies. (1998, p. 266)

While these debates go beyond the framework of this paper, we thought it important to point out their recent re-emergence[20] at the UN World Conference Against Racism, Racial Discrimination, Xenophobia and Related Intolerance held in Durban in September 2001—although the issues were clearly more political in nature. Indian NGOs speaking for the Dalits[21] requested that discrimination based on caste be put on the conference agenda against the official stance taken by the Indian government which argued that the issue was an internal affair. The action taken by the Dalit organizations was supported by the definition of racial discrimination proposed by the United Nations International Convention on the Elimination of All Forms of Racial Discrimination, 1965 (Article 1(i)):

> Any distinction, exclusion, restriction or preference based on race, colour, descent, or national or ethnic origin which has the purpose or effect of nullifying or impairing the recognition, enjoyment or exercise, on an equal footing, of human rights and fundamental freedoms in the political, economic, social, cultural or any other field of public life.

The debate focused on the definition of caste and race. A.S. Narang (2001, p. 2499) drew attention to the paradox in relation to this issue: 'Interestingly, the term "descent", which is not found in any other international document, was suggested by India during the elaboration of the Convention.' The term 'descent' can be used to refer to castes in India (or in Sub-Saharan Africa) as well as the Burakumins in Japan and the Roms in Europe. The term *jati* or caste has the same root as the Sanskrit word for 'birth'. Moreover, the literal meaning of the term for the four major caste groups, *varna*, is 'colour'. The *varnas* are described in the Vedas as different species: the highest *varna* (the Brahmins) is associated with white, while the lowest *varna* (the Shudras) is associated with black. The concept of race has pervaded, to some degree, caste ideology. At one point, a team of geneticists believed they had proven that the higher castes were genetically different from the lower castes, the former being closer to Europeans than to Asians.[22]

The controversy surrounding the nature of both social constructs—caste and race—and the stratification system they are part of are not as interesting, for our purposes, as the comparative analysis of racial discrimination and caste-based discrimination. Gail Omvedt's (2001) arguments about possible race and caste comparisons help us establish a basis for comparative Indian-South African research:

> Both [caste as a social system and 'racism'] (. . .) are systems of discrimination that attribute 'natural' or inherent qualities to people born in specific social groups. In other words, while caste has nothing to do with 'race', the justifications of caste discrimination have a lot to do with the social phenomenon of 'racism'.

To enhance our understanding of current segregation systems it is pertinent to draw parallels between the discrimination of blacks in South Africa and the practice of untouchability in India, and to examine how these systems are manifested in space and how that space is used. There are several underlying principles and mechanisms that merit our attention.[23]

In both countries discrimination systems are highly institutionalized although they rely on two different mechanisms: in South Africa, the political regime and the coercive legislation it created; and in India, social-religious ideology. In both cases, the justification of systems that deprived large parts of the population, blacks in South Africa and untouchables in India,[24] of their humanity, used sacred scriptures, even if it meant developing tendentious interpretations: the Bible, by the Dutch Reformed Church in South Africa, and the Vedas, by the Brahmins in India.

The period during which segregatory systems were established differ, of course. The science of architecture that advocated residential segmentation according to the four *varnas*, the *Vastu Vidya*, a legacy of the Vedic period (tenth to fifth century BC) is much older than the initial forms of South African segregation in the Cape Colony, which date back to the nineteetnth century (Houssay-Holzshuch, 1999). Articles 15 and 17, respectively, of the 1950 Indian Constitution prohibited caste-based discrimination and abolished untouchability. In South Africa apartheid was not completely eliminated until the new constitution was ratified in 1996 and came into effect in March 1997. Both systems of segregation, however, also present significant similarities: the determination to separate and create distance through certain principles and measures.

Both the caste system and apartheid, until its repeal in the early 1990s, disallow mixed marriages—marriage between members of different castes (or sub-castes), or different 'races'. According to the logic of both systems, endogamy is deemed necessary as it maintains the social hierarchy and prevents pollution from external groups.

In order to segregate populations, one needs to be able to discriminate. Discrimination criteria, which in both systems are determined by lineage, must remain clearly and easily identifiable; marriages and births must be regulated. The Prohibition of Mixed Marriage Act of 1949 in South Africa outlawed marriage between members of different races. The *Immorality Act*, strengthened in 1959, severely punished sexual relations outside of wedlock and between members of different races. In India, caste endogamy is still the dominant model; this is clearly illustrated in community and caste-wise classified marriage advertisements (where the mention of a preference for 'fair skin', a practice that would be considered illegal in South Africa, is nothing exceptional). Above all, for the higher castes, marriage with formerly untouchables is still unthinkable. As reported by Deliège (1999), death is often stated as the punishment required if a young woman runs away with a Harijan. Events corroborate these words.

In addition to the residential segregation, there is another equally restrictive dimension involved in the process of segregation: the banning of access to specific public spaces, or separating the use thereof. Under apartheid, there were a set of laws that severely regulated segregation in public places and within various institutions. The Reservation of Separate Amenities Act (1953) reinforced segregation in, among others, buses, toilets, post offices, beaches and benches. The State-Aided Institutions Act (1957) invested the power in authorities to institute segregation in libraries, stadiums, and theatres. The Extension of

University Education Act (1957) led to the setting up of separate universities for blacks, coloureds and Indians who only in exceptional circumstances had the right to register in white universities.

In India there were many restrictions on untouchables. These restrictions varied from one region to the next, according to local customs. Among the more widely observed restrictions were no admittance to temples, main wells, bathing *ghats*, certain roads, and restaurants. A survey carried out in 1982-3 by the Harijan Sevak Sangh[25] in a sample of villages located in twelve states showed that although the 1950 Constitution made all these restrictions illegal, thirty years later they were still common place.

While certain communities of untouchables in south India have converted to Christianity (a practice that dates back to the sixteenth century), even within churches, religious conversion has failed to put an end to segregation. Some eloquent examples can be quoted from Deliège (1999). In Tamil Nadu, there were churches with two naves to separate the untouchables, while in Vadakkankulam a 6-ft high brick wall had been built in the middle of the church to separate the Nadars (a lower caste) from the Vellalas (the higher caste). Until recently, in Trichy people fought to prevent converted untouchables from being buried in the same cemetery.

In India, as in South Africa, policies were designed to remedy the problems brought about by discriminatory practices aimed at former untouchables and blacks. Through affirmative action—a term that is rarely used in India—or 'black empowerment', South Africa provides blacks key posts in the public sector and black firms are given priority in calls for tender, for instance. In India, the policy of reservations keeps a certain quota of jobs for members of the scheduled castes or lower castes in the public sector (in the administration as well as in big firms); special education grants, loans, among others, are also available. Clearly, we could also compare the different types of civil society activism (by NGOs, and citizens groups, for instance) found in both countries.

## Processes of Segregation Today

Allowing for a broader concept than our own, Schelling (1978) described three processes of segregation. The first is a top-down process that is the result of collective determination or organized action, and can either be legal—such as apartheid, or illegal—unconstitutional restrictions imposed on untouchables in certain parts of India. A second process results from inequalities in resources, and is unintentional. The third process is due to the combining of individual discriminatory practices.[26] In real life these three processes intertwine. Untangling the mechanisms that serve to separate and exclude from aggregation phenomena based on affinity is not necessarily an easy task. Just as it is equally difficult to ascertain in certain preferential residential clusters which factors are due to spontaneous dynamics and which are due to imposed restrictions.

In the cases of India and South Africa the following questions must be addressed if we are to weed through current segregation processes:

Following the banning of untouchability and caste-based discrimination on the one hand and the abolition of apartheid on the other, what evidence remains of both of these institutionalized systems of segregation?

To what extent have these systems been taken over by individual discriminatory practices, reinforced by market forces, as well as social and economic inequality? And, to what extent do actions taken by institutional agents thwart or promote individual dynamics?

In India, there are strategies that combine exclusion (to the detriment of the lower castes) and clustering (practised by people of similar socio-economic strata, or belonging to castes of similar status). Among the various types of modern collective housing that have been developed in Indian cities, the co-operative housing societies provide a good illustration of combined practices leading to segregation. Such groups practise co-optation within the same communities, social group or professional circle to filter out potential buyers and tenants. This is in addition to the filtering mechanism based on the income required to access the various segments of the housing market (Dupont, 2004).

Although in South Africa the processes have shifted from being institutional to being spontaneous, they have remained very powerful. The 'nimby' (not in my backyard) attitudes taken by middle-class whites were clearly expressed in Johannesburg by '. . . a massive uprising of white residents against the building of housing for poorer families in the areas surrounding Bloubosrand [a middle-class neighbourhood]. The fear of being 'invaded' by corrugated metal shanties and thieves and 'murderers' made any discussion between the parties impossible' (Bénit, 2000, p. 275).[27]

In this context, social distance continues to be manifested by the desire for spatial distance: members of the upper social strata—whites—seeking distance from the lower-class, 'less white' who are still considered a threatening strata.

Lemon (1996, p. 64) eloquently described the inertia in the residential segregation model leftover from apartheid in South Africa and the current political obstacles to desegregation:

> Most urban Blacks who live in informal settlements, now the majority in most cities, cannot afford access to any formal housing, let alone former white areas. Even among township Blacks, only a relatively small minority can seriously contemplate such a move. Moves to some former Coloured and Indian areas may be more practicable economically, but the advantages may be small in relation to perceived social and cultural objections (which may deter many who could afford to move to former white areas).

Admittedly, there are some neighbourhoods inhabited by lower-class whites that are undergoing a process of rapid 'Africanization'. Yet, as pointed out by M. Houssay-Holzshuch (1999) when describing Cape Town, certain post-apartheid municipal public housing programmes '(. . .) reinforce the urban morphology created by segregation: the poorest segments of the population, which are also the less white, are housed in peripheral zones, far from employment centres', in these areas that were once buffer zones surrounding black and coloured townships. The private sector, which assumes an important role in housing production, has in any case limited interest in investing in the rental housing sector (Watson, 1999).

## SEGREGATION AND TERRITORY

### Is there Segregation without Territory?

'Segregation is inherently spatial as it involves creating distance between the segregating party and those who are set apart' (Gervais-Lambony, 2001, p. 33). Brun (1994, p. 37) also argued that the existence of 'spatial boundaries separating clearly defined groups' is essential to the concept of segregation. However, does the intrinsic link that exists between segregation and space imply that there is also an intrinsic link between segregation and territory? In other words, is there segregation without reference to a territory? Joye and Schuler (2001, p. 168), *a priori*, believed that this is not possible, 'Social segregation (. . .) by definition involves territory'. If by territory we mean the result of the projection of identity on to space, and if we also maintain that segregation is linked to discrimination—then the relation between segregation and territory is mediated through identity.

Without differentiation among social groups, based on race ethnicity, caste, religion, social standing, profession or geographical origin, in short without identity, it becomes impossible to discriminate and therefore to segregate. According to Gervais-Lambony (2001, p. 35):

> Segregation is linked to territory for two reasons. Firstly segregation is a territory-building process. Secondly, segregation leads populations into the process of building territorial community identity. (. . .) [These] identity building processes are what create similarities between segregation and territorialization. In both cases we are dealing with social constructs.

Before any of this can happen, populations first have to appropriate spaces. In the process of appropriation, such spaces become part of identities. This process takes time.

When blacks were displaced, because of apartheid, the new residential spaces they moved into were for the most part devoid of identity. Segregation was clearly in place, but at first there was no territory. We can assume that, if individuals and groups lay claim to spaces other than those they occupy, this is because they do not feel that the space they occupy is wholly their territory. Either the space is too small; or they have no ties to this space: they may have no cultural ties because they have been displaced to a space that is foreign to them, or they have no economic ties like in certain Indian resettlement colonies for evicted squatter settlement dwellers and, previously in South African townships, where inhabitants were not allowed to do business. Segregation creates territories just as territory can create segregation by fostering two opposite and complementary processes: clustering (voluntary) and exclusion (forced). 'A certain degree of territoriality can create social ties and solidarity while a high degree of territoriality annihilates them' (Brunet, 1992). Territory 'reduces distances within and creates infinite distance without' (Retaillé, cited by Di Méo, 1998, p. 39). The study of these dynamics is very complex because in addition to taking into account the dialectic between economic and political rationales (Castells, 1981), we also have to consider the strategies of individuals and households (Lévy and Brun, 2000).

## Social Distance and Spatial Distance: An Equivocal Relation

The fact that the relation between segregation and territory is highly significant does not mean that we should not consider other, non-spatial, facets of segregation. Social and cultural distance cannot always be correlated with spatial distance.

We have to keep in mind that segregation and isolation are two distinct things. Ethnic reservations are exceptional (to our knowledge, there are none in India; even in cases where tribal land can only be sold to tribe members and the tribe has a monopoly on all non-timber forest products). Segregated populations and spaces are, therefore, integral parts of society and of national space.

Untouchables in India and many blacks in South Africa are segments of the labour force that are indispensable to the economies of both countries. These segments usually perform tasks that other social groups refuse to perform. Untouchables and many blacks are discriminated against and oppressed, but they are not truly excluded. This is where the difference between 'segregation' and social 'fragmentation' comes into play. In extreme cases, the latter can be used to describe the type of isolation chosen by certain hermetic and almost autonomous groups (Navez-Bouchanine, 2001). As Gervais-Lambony (2001, p. 34), aptly put it, 'Segregation is separation without significant spatial distance. That is why the phenomenon is such a great paradox and why it is so effective: segregation creates social distance without creating too much spatial distance—the labour force has been distanced socially but must be economically exploitable.'[28]

In certain cases, Brun noted: '. . . cohabitation in a situation where distances are short and proximity is functional may go hand-in-hand with the existence of very rigid social barriers. The caste system and slavery are examples [of this type of cohabitation]. . .' (Brun, 1994, p. 26).

Spatial proximity does not determine modes of cohabitation nor does it preclude social distance.[29] In a Marxist analytical framework, according to Castells (1981, p. 233):

> . . . the degree of class struggle influences the forms and cadence of segregation: . . . an open struggle reinforces spatial fragmentation and may even lead to the creation of 'forbidden ghettos'. . . . However, in places where one class is completely subordinate and where domination by the other class is accepted at all levels, residential mixing is possible. This may happen in an atmosphere

of 'ecological paternalism' where dominating and dominated classes live in the same neighbourhood albeit in very different conditions.

The last remark is descriptive of situations in Indian cities, where the caste hierarchy and the socio-economic hierarchy are clearly reflected in housing conditions. In the same neighbourhood there may be a row of shabby huts next to affluent, luxury apartment buildings. It is also descriptive of a widespread phenomenon, servant quarters that are located in the apartments or houses of affluent families.

### Does the Existence of Spatial Mobility Call into Question the Relation between Segregation and Territory?

By highlighting the need to go beyond the purely residential aspects of segregation, spatial mobility and accessibility in general modify the relation between segregation and territory. According to Joye and Schuler (2001, p. 173), '. . . mobility has become crucial to the definition of segregation'.

In their words, the issue is

> . . . if everyone is equally mobile and functions in different spheres for work, recreation and residence, then how relevant is [a concept of] segregation based only on a residential dimension? On closer analysis we find that not everyone has access to the same degree of mobility. Mobility is determined by social standing and is an integral part of a system of inequalities.

In fact, 'unequal access to tangible and symbolic goods' (Grafmeyer, 1994a, p. 89) is another essential dimension of segregation. The most underprivileged segments of the population are affected by an accumulation of various forms of segregation,[30] whereas voluntary 'ghettoization', as practised by the rich living in gated communities, corresponds to a form of segregation made all the more relative by the fact that generally residents have the best access to urban facilities and services and are thus most mobile.

Circular mobility of individuals moving between different places of residence calls into question any concept of residential segregation based on an individual attached to a sole place (Brun, 1994, p. 47). In European countries weekend homes or secondary residences have become very significant; and in developing countries, such as India where the majority of the population is from a rural setting, people who have migrated to cities are still strongly attached to their native village.

Consequently, if we take spatial mobility into account, '. . . segregation, rather than being based exclusively on static place concepts, is based on the dynamic concepts of spatial and temporal accessibility. In other words, if we introduce the issue of accessibility, instead of dealing with space we are dealing with a network' (Kaufmann, Bassand and Joye, 2001, p. XV).

Social networks can easily extend beyond, overlap, and even disregard spatial limits, or in certain situations strengthen them (Offner and Pumain, 1996). According to Louiset (2000, p. 163), this is the case in India, where:

> . . . the boundary that counts is the one that serves to identify the group and not to demarcate space; the latter does not manifest itself in a continuous manner. A definition of urban identity based on territory is as problematic at a neighbourhood scale as it is at city scale.

To better understand the new forms of social and urban segregation Kaufmann (2001) proposed the introduction of the notions of 'motility' (defined here as 'an individual's or group's capacity to be mobile, spatially or virtually'[31]) and 'connectedness' (*connexité,* physical or virtual proximity via technology, namely the telephone, fax, e-mail, and the web). Kaufmann argued that with the emergence of virtual connection services, to the detriment of (physical) proximity services, '. . . the phenomenon [of connectedness] is creating a new form of social segregation and even exclusion; social integration has [the] tendency to become a function of an agent's potential for connected mobility' (2001, p. 101).

Motility, when taken into account, frees us from the constraints of geographical distance and underscores the inequalities in access to new technologies. But does it weaken the link between segregation and space? Probably not: the density of terminals with access to the Internet is far from being the same in all spaces. The 'digital fracture' is to a certain extent comparable to the types of fractures that appear in more common understandings of segregation.

## CONCLUSION

In addition to 'conventional' socio-economic inequalities, India and South Africa are both characterized by legacies of hierarchical systems based on alleged religious purity and racial superiority. The resulting 'segregation', comprising of a process of social discrimination and the projection on to space of the ensuing social distance, largely persists despite efforts to diminish it. Furthermore, cultural diversity in both countries has generated or maintained a multiplicity of identities all with their own 'territory' (defined here as the result of the projection of identity on to space).

The combination of both territory and segregation leads to complex situations: segregation can create territories, just as territories can reinforce segregation. Yet, we have argued here that we should try to avoid using an approach that exclusively addresses fractures and antagonisms. Many territories have fuzzy boundaries or overlap without leading to conflict. Many different identities co-exist within the same space or the same individual, creating particularly complex versions of territoriality. Moreover, if we factor in different forms of spatial mobility we construst a very different picture. We would be giving extremist factions of all sorts a free hand if we were to only reason in terms of opposites and exclusion. Even in highly segregated societies, there is no such thing as absolute territory or absolute segregation.

## NOTES

1. French and English use different concepts to express the relationships between individuals and a city and those between individuals and the nation. In French, the cognates *citadin* (city-dweller) and *citoyen* (citizen) express a feeling of belonging to a city and a feeling of belonging to a nation, respectively. If we use those terms, we can say that during apartheid South African townships were sometimes peopled with veritable *citadins*, who were not necessarily *citoyens*. In contrast, in India, as elsewhere, many rural immigrants living in cities are not integrated into the latter and are not veritable *citadins*, although they are fully-fledged *citoyens*. In English, a single term, 'citizen', is used for both concepts—*citadin* and *citoyen*—thus creating ambiguity.

   In English, however, 'city dweller' is a neutral term that can be applied to country folk living in, but not integrated into, cities, in other words, citizens who are not *citadins*. In French, the term *urbain* means 'urban'. But it generally denotes a very strong concept, *urbanité*, which describes a sense of 'used to the city', a concept which insinuates that an individual has appropriated the city in some way. Finally, the term *urbain* is not as neutral as 'urban-dweller'.
2. Cf. H. Mainet-Valleix's contribution in this volume.
3. Cf. S. Das' contribution in this volume.
4. The many ins and outs of community territories in Mumbai are described in G. Heuzé's (2000) autobiographical novel.

5. About the Gujarat riots, read for example *Frontline*, 7 June 2002.
6. Respectively, the Rashtriya Swayamsevak Sangh, the Vishva Hindu Parishad, and the Bharatiya Janata Party.
7. Cf. the contributions by R. Ebr.-Vally, F. Landy and H. Mainet-Valleix in this volume.
8. 'Saltus' refers in Latin to the space between fields around the central village ('ager') and the uncleared area ('silva' meaning forest) at the periphery of the territory. In India, this area is often called 'wasteland' by the government although it is commonly used as grazing land and as a source for firewood.
9. See A.J. Christopher's contribution in this volume.
10. One of the significant challenges of post-apartheid desegregation policies is the urbanization of these zones.
11. 'When the word "segregation" is used to describe complex or ambiguous situations, what is unfortunately implied, before it is proven, is that the situations are the result of the same rationale' (Brun, 1994, p. 32).
12. By discrimination we mean separating a social group from other social groups through unfair treatment. Thus, in South Africa blacks were barred from skilled jobs. In India, the hereditary transmission of professional specialization and crafts is an essential component of the caste system, and many castes carry the names of crafts and professions. The occupations deemed to be especially 'polluting' (because they involve waste disposal, i.e. scavengers, waste collectors, sweepers, the quartering of animal carcasses) explain specifically the origin of untouchability of communities which traditionally practised these occupations. Even today, many economic sectors remain segmented along caste or religious lines (Deliège, 1999; Gandhi, 1983).
13. Since this contribution focuses on issues related to segregation, we use preferentially the socio-anthropological term 'untouchables' (for references to the past, until Independence) or 'former untouchable castes' (for references to the period after the Indian Constitution abolished 'untouchability') that refers to discrimination by the higher castes, rather than the administrative term 'scheduled castes' that refers to the list of former untouchable castes that have been indexed by the government in order so that they benefit from a series of positive discriminatory measures, in accordance with the provisions of the Indian Constitution.
14. See also the contribution by V. Dupont and M. Houssay-Holzschuch in this volume.
15. For issues related to measuring segregation issues see C. Rhein (1994) and H. Le Bras (1994).
16. The segregation index is the sum, for the various areas within a spatial unit, of the differences in absolute terms of, on the one hand, the distribution of a given group in area 'i' relative to its overall numbers,

and on the other hand, that of other groups in area 'i' to their overall numbers. For South Africa, see A.J. Christopher (2001).

17. The Hindus accounted for 81 per cent of the population of India in 2001.
18. The term 'Harijan' (literally the people or children of Vishnu) was coined by Gandhi to refer to untouchables.
19. Namely the work of American sociologists carried out in the 1930s and 1940s, which refers to the *caste school of racial relations.* Among those reviewed by L. Dumont, were: L. Warner (1936), G. Myrdal (1944), J. Dollard (1937), and K. David (1941). More recently, another American sociologist, G. Berreman (1972, 1979, cited by Deliège, 1999), compared former Untouchables in India to Black Americans. He points out the similarity in the type of discrimination suffered by both groups and postulates that discrimination criteria—caste and race—are both tied to lineage and are the basis of social status.
20. The Indian newspaper *The Hindu* has been the sounding board for the controversy. See articles by Béteille (2001) and Omvedt (2001).
21. The use of the term 'Dalits' (the oppressed) was initially linked to a political movement, the Dalit Panthers, that was founded in Bombay in 1972. The movement used as a model the Black Panthers in America (Deliège, 1999). The various terms used to designate the same set of castes reflect the different facets of discrimination: 'untouchable' is descriptive of discrimination by the higher castes, 'scheduled castes' refers to affirmative action on the part of the state; Harijan is a term filled with compassion; and Dalit evokes revolt.
22. R. Ramachandran, 'The Genetics of Caste', *Frontline*, 22 June 2001, pp. 84-5, referring to the conclusions made by an international team co-ordinated by M.J. Bamshad of the University of Utah. The conclusions are highly questionable mainly because they are based on a sample of 265 subjects, all from the same district in Andhra Pradesh.
23. The Indian press published viewpoints during the international Conference Against Racism that were far from euphemistic, i.e. in his article entitled 'India's Apartheid', Rajeev Dhavan concluded, 'Casteism is not a social preference, but India's apartheid' (*The Hindu*, 24 August 2001). Dalits' campaign slogans during the conference in Durban did not hesitate to draw such analogies as, 'Annihilate the Apartheid of Caste in India'.
24. Black Africans in South Africa form the vast majority of the population (79 per cent in 2001), while the scheduled castes account for 16 per cent of the population in India; in absolute terms, however, the latter group is impressive in size: 167 million people in 2001.
25. According to this survey, reported by Herrenschmidt (1996, p. 412), in the villages that were visited, at that time, 'restaurants, temples, and wells [designated for other castes] were still barred to untouchables in Karnataka, Kerala, Orissa, and in the Madurai district of Tamil Nadu'.

26. For a critique see cf. Y. Grafmeyer (1994a).
27. Similar if not identical avoidance strategies aimed at the lowest classes can be observed in many other countries, including France.
28. See also M. Houssay-Holzchusch (2000) for the case of South Africa, and R. Deliège (1999) for the case of untouchables in India.
29. For further information on cohabitation in France see the now famous article by Jean-Claude Chamborédon and Madeleine Lemaire (1970) 'Proximité spatiale et distance sociale. Les grands ensembles et leur peuplement' (Spatial Proximity and Social Distance: Large Housing Complexes and Their Residents).
30. Y. Grafmeyer (1994a, p. 89) talked about 'triple segregation faced by blue collar workers' in big cities in France during the 1970s which was manifest in 'the location and quality of housing, utilities and public services, and the distances between the home and the workplace'.
31. According to V. Kaufmann (2001, pp. 94-6), 'motility' gives us 'an integrating concept that allows us to acknowledge the agent'. 'Motility' is different from the concept of mobility. What is important with the concept of 'motility' is the mobility potential of each agent, 'each agent has his or her own mobility potential, prior to movement, that may or may not be transformed into movement depending on the desire to do so and circumstances'. There are three components of 'motility': '. . . *context* [which] refers to the range of what is possible in a given place (...); *access* [which] refers to all of the conditions under which what is available becomes accessible (. . .); and *appropriation* [which] refers to an agent's abilities and internalization by that agent of his potential (opportunities) to move (. . .). [These] three dimensions (. . .) reflect the allocation of resources and skills and consequently social structure and its distribution in space, and as such they are necessarily associated to the issue of power'.

## REFERENCES

Assayag, J., *L'Inde, désir de nation*, Paris: Editions Odile Jacob, p. 348.

Begde, P.V., *Ancient and Medieval Town-Planning in India*, New Delhi: Sagar Publication, 1978.

Bénit, C., 'Johannesburg: déségrégation raciale, ségrégation sociale ? La banalisation des mobilités résidentielles dans la ville d'apartheid", in *Métropoles en mouvement. Une comparaison internationale*, ed. F. Dureau, V. Dupont, É. Lelièvre, J-P. Levy and Th. Lulle, Paris, IRD-Anthropos (Coll. Villes), 2000, pp. 69-80.

Bernard, C., 'Ségrégation et anthropologie, anthropologie de la ségrégation. Quelques éléments de réflexion', in *La ségrégation dans la ville*, ed. J. Brun and C. Rhein, Paris: L'Harmattan, 1994, pp. 73-84.

Berreman, G., 'Race, Caste and other Invidious Distinctions in Social Stratification', *Race*, 13, 1972, pp. 378-414.

———, *Caste and other Inequities: Essays on Inequality*, Meerut: Folklore Institute, 1979.

Béteille, A., 'Race and Caste', *The Hindu*, 10 March 2001.

Brun, J. 'Essai critique sur la notion de ségrégation et sur son usage en géographie urbaine', in *La ségregation dans la ville*, ed. J. Brun and C. Rhein, Paris: L'Harmattan, 1994, pp. 21-58.

Brun, J. and C. Rhein (eds.), *La ségrégation dans la ville*, Paris: L'Harmattan, 1994.

Brunet, R., et al., *Les mots de la géographie*, Reclus-La Documentation Française, 1992.

Bonnemaison, J., L. Cambrezy et al. (eds.), *Les territoires de l'identité*, t.1, *Le territoire, lien ou frontière ?*, Paris, L'Harmattan, 1999.

Castells, M., *La question urbaine*, Paris: Maspero, 1986 (1st edn. 1970).

Chamboredon J.C., M. Lemaire, 'Proximité spatiale et distance sociale. Les grands ensembles et leur peuplement', *Revue Française de Sociologie*, XI, 1, 1970, pp. 3-33.

Christopher A.J. (ed.), *The Atlas of Changing South Africa*, London: Routledge, 2001.

Deliege R., *The Untouchables of India*, tr. N. Scott, Oxford: Berg Publishers, 1999.

Dhavan, R., 'India's Apartheid', *The Hindu*, 24 August 2001.

*Dictionnaire de la Sociologie*, Paris: Larousse, 1989.

Di Méo, G., *Géographie sociale et territoire*, Paris: Nathan, 1998, p. 317.

Dumont, L. *Homo Hierarchicus, Le Système des castes et ses implications*, Paris: Gallimard, 1966.

———, *Homo Hierarchicus, The Caste System and Its Implications* (revd.), New Delhi: Oxford University Press, 1998.

Dupont, V., 'Delhi aujourd'hui: la ville des planificateurs et celle des habitants', in *Perception et organization de l'espace urbain: Une confrontation Orient-Occident*, ed. R. Hagelstein and P. Servais, Louvain-la-Neuve: Academia-Bruylant (série Rencontre Orient-Occident, no. 3), pp. 239-66.

———, 'Socio-spatial Differentiation and Residential Segregation in Delhi: A Question of Scale?', *Geoforum*, vol. 35, no. 2, March 2004, pp. 157-75.

Dupont, V. and A. Mitra, 'Population Distribution, Growth and Socio-Economic Spatial Patterns in Delhi: Findings from the 1991 Census Data', *Demography India*, 1995, vol. 24, nos. 1 & 2, 1995, pp. 101-32.

Evenson, N., *The Indian Metropolis, A View toward the West*, New Haven and London: Yale University Press, 1989.

Gandhi, R., 'Social Structure of Urban India: Continuities and Change', in

*Main Currents in Indian Sociology,* vol. VI: *Urban India*, ed. Giri Raj Gupta, New Delhi: Vikas, 1983.

George, P., 'Ségrégation', in *Dictionnaire de la Géographie*, Paris: PUF, 1970, p. 499.

Gervais-Lambony, Ph., *L'Afrique du Sud et les Etats voisins*, Paris: Armand Colin, 1997.

———, 'La ségrégation dans la grande ville, un essai de définition', in *Les très grandes villes dans le monde*, ed. M.-A. Gervais Lambony, Paris: Atlande, 2001, pp. 33-8.

Gilbert, A., 'Les territoires de la francophonie canadienne hors du Québec', in ed. J. Bonnemaison et al., 1999, pp. 173-81.

Grafmeyer, Y., 'Regards sociologiques sur la ségrégation', in *La ségrégation dans la ville*, ed. J. Brun and C. Rhein, Paris: L'Harmattan, 1994a, pp. 85-117.

———, *Sociologie urbaine*, Paris: Nathan, 1994b.

Herrenschmidt, O., 'Les intouchables et la Républiques indienne', in *L'Inde contemporaine. De 1950 à nos jours*, ed. Ch. Jaffrelot, Paris: Fayard, 1996.

Heuzé, G., 'Bombay: la Shiv Sena et le territoire urbain', *Hérodote*, 71, 'L'Inde et la question nationale', 1993, pp. 149-68.

———, *Bombay en flammes 1993. Le cri des deux mondes*, Paris: L'Harmattan, 2000.

Houssay-Holzschuch, M., *Le Cap ville sud-africaine. Ville blanche, vies noires*, Paris: L'Harmattan, Coll. Géographie et Culture, 1999.

Jaffrelot, C., 'Nationalisme hindou, territoire et société', in *Hérodote*, 71, 'L'Inde et la question nationale', 1993, pp. 93-111.

Joye, D. and M. Schuler 'Inégalités, territoires et mobilités: Une perspective renouvelée pour la sociologie urbaine?', in *Enjeux de la sociologie urbaine*, ed. M. Bassand, V. Kaufmann, D. Joye, Lausanne: Presses polytechniques et universitaires romanes (Coll. Sciences, Technique, Société), 2000, pp. 159-80.

Kaufmann, V., 'La mobilité : une notion clef pour revisiter l'urbain', in *Enjeux de la sociologie urbaine*, ed. M. Bassand, V. Kaufmann, D. Joye, Lausanne: Presses polytechniques et universitaires romanes (Coll. Sciences, Technique, Société), 2001, pp. 87-102.

Kaufmann, V. et al., 'Introduction', in *Enjeux de la sociologie urbaine*, ed. M. Bassand, V. Kaufmann, D. Joye, Lausanne: Presses polytechniques et universitaires romanes (Coll. Sciences, Technique, Société), 2001, pp. xi-xvii.

Lapeyronnie, D., B. Rouleau, 'Ségrégation', in *Dictionnaire de l'urbanisme et de l'aménagement*, ed. P. Merlin and Fr. Choay, Paris: PUF, pp. 611-12.

Le Bras, H., 'Echelle et ségrégation', in *La ségrégation dans la ville*, ed. J. Brun and C. Rhein, Paris: L'Harmattan, 1994, pp. 181-95.

Lemon, A., 'Post-Apartheid Cities: Planning for a New Society', in *Contemporary City Structuring*, ed. R.J. Davies, Cape Town: International Geographical Union: Commission on Urban Development, Society of South African Geographers, 1996, pp. 62-73.

Lévy J.-P. and J. Brun, 'De l'extension au renouvellement métropolitain: mosaïque sociale et mobilité', in *Métropoles en mouvement. Une comparaison internationale*, ed. Dureau et al., Paris: IRD-Anthropos (Coll. Villes), 2000, pp. 229-46.

Louiset, O., 'L'urbanité ailleurs', in *Logiques de l'espace, esprit des lieux. Géographie à Cerisy*, by J. Lévy et al., Paris: Belin, 2000, pp. 157-64.

Narang, A.S., 'World Conference Against Racism', *Economic and Political Weekly*, vol. 36, no. 27, 2001, pp. 2495-9.

Navez-Bouchanine F., 'Des villes entre fragmentation spatiale et fragmentation sociale: une approche critique de la notion de fragmentation', in *Vocabulaire de la ville*, ed. E. Dorier-Apprill, Paris: Editions du Temps, 2001, pp. 109-18.

Noble, A.G., and Dutt, A.K. (eds.), *Indian Urbanization and Planning: Vehicles of Modernization*, New Delhi: Tata McGraw-Hill, 1977.

Offner, J.M. and D. Pumain (eds.), *Réseaux et territoires. Significations croisées*, La Tour d'Aigues, Editions de l'Aube, Paris: LATTS, 1996.

Omvedt, G., 'The U.N., Racism and Caste', *The Hindu*, 9 and 10 April 2001.

Racine J.L. (ed.), *Peasant Moorings. Village Ties and Mobility Rationales in South India*, New Delhi: Sage, 1997.

Racine, Jean (ed.), *Calcutta 1981: The City, Its Crisis and the Debate on Urban Planning and Development*, New Delhi: Concept, 1990.

Ramachandran, R., 'The Genetics of Caste', *Frontline*, 22 June 2001, pp. 84-5.

Retaillé, D., *Le monde du géographe*, Paris: Presses de Sciences Politiques, 1997.

Rhein, C., 'La ségrégation et ses mesures', in *La ségrégation dans la ville*, ed. J. Brun and C. Rhein, Paris: L'Harmattan, 1994, pp. 121-62.

Roncayolo, M., *La ville et ses territoires*, Paris: Gallimard-Folio, 1990.

Sautter, G. and P. Pélissier, 'Pour un atlas des terroirs africains: structure-type d'une étude de terroir', *L'Homme*, vol. IV, no. 1, 1964, pp. 56-72.

Schelling, T.C., *Micromotives and Macrobehavior*, New York: Norton, 1978.

Schenk, H., *Views on Alleppey: Socio-historical and Socio-spatial Perspectives on an Industrial Port Town in Kerala, South India*, Amsterdam: University of Amsterdam, 1984.

Tarrius, A., 'Territoires circulatoires des migrants et espaces européens', in *La ville: agrégation et ségrégation sociales*, ed. N. Haumont, Paris: L'Harmattan, 1996, pp. 189-94.

———, *Les nouveaux cosmopolitismes. Mobilités, identités, territoires*, La Tour d'Aigues, Editions de l'Aube, Paris: LATTS, 2000.

Trivedi, H.R., 'Towards a General Theory of Urbanization and Social Change', in *Social Structure and Change*, vol 3: *Complex Organizations and Urban Communities*, ed. A.M. Shah, B.S. Baviskar and E.A. Ramaswami, New Delhi: Sage, 1996, pp. 237-8.

Vaguet, O., 'Ville indienne, ville hindoue? Facteurs et processus de ségrégation spatiale', *Espace, Populations, Sociétés*, 1997, vols. 2/3, pp. 211-24.

Watson, V., 'L'accès au logement en Afrique du Sud', in *La question urbaine en Afrique australe. Perspectives de recherche*, ed. Ph. Gervais-Lambony, S. Jaglin and A. Mabin, Paris: Karthala, 1999, pp. 227-42.

CHAPTER 3

# Identity, Space and Territory in India: An Anthropological Perspective

M.A. Kalam

What shapes an individual's identity? Is it language, religion, the culture of the group to which the individual belongs, the locale in which the individual is found, or a combination of all these? Can some other factors be added to this list, such as inhabited territory or space claimed or visualized by the group for domicile? When and why do these factors come into reckoning? Is it to define one's group in absolute terms, or *vis-à-vis* another, or to set one's group apart from another? In order to set one's group apart from the others what markers are used, how, why and in what different ways? Can a group draw boundaries in real physical terms around it and define the area as its territory in topological terms, or are such boundaries marked or visualized in cognitive (or even imaginary) terms?

According to Horowitz,

> [T]he symbols employed to differentiate group from group may be of widely divergent characteristics at different levels of identity. An over-arching identity may be indicated by language, while a lesser one may be evidenced by a behavioral trait and a still lesser one by a visual one. Finally, it almost goes without saying that a symbol of identity that is of the highest imperative in one society may be ignored or interpreted quite differently in the next, depending on the shape and significance of the underlying criteria of identity. (1976, pp. 120-1)

This paper examines how identities are shaped in spatial and territorial terms, and how space and territory impinge upon identity, and can even sharpen or blur and dilute identity. In this context, it is important to relate the discussion to questions of nationality and citizenship *vis-à-vis* the state and its role in *shaping* identities of those who are part of a country or nation state.

## IDENTITY, COUNTRY AND NATION STATE

A country, as a nation, is the ultimate in terms of territory; but a qualification needs to be made here: it is so in the realm of political science and international law as well as in physical terms. A country is bounded by its national borders, and at the same time separates and marks itself as different from other countries or nation-states. And the identity bestowed in such terms gives its inhabitants the 'we' feeling, whereby they become fellow countrymen. According to Isaacs, 'territory is, at the least, a critical factor in maintaining group separateness; without it a nationality has difficulty becoming a nation and a nation cannot become a state' (1976, p. 45).

The Bedouin are spread across a few countries of North Africa. From the Bedouin world-view, the post-colonial construction of modern states (and their territoriality in terms of national borders and boundaries) has very little meaning. The Bedouin conception of territory completely encompasses the colonial and post-colonial developments, which have given rise to national and international borders (perfect straight lines in many a case). The Bedouin concept of 'nationality' contrasts forcefully with forms of citizenship imposed on them. They do consider themselves as an ethnic group at one level, though during the colonial and post-colonial periods they have been divided as citizens of different countries (territories) by outside colonial powers occupying their lands. But they have ways of recognizing and reckoning internal differences among themselves, which sweep and cut across modern states. Barth's observation in such contexts is pertinent, 'ethnic boundaries are not merely or necessarily based on the occupation of exclusive territories; and the different ways in which they are maintained, not only by a once-and-for-all recruitment but by continual expression and validation need to be analysed' (1969, p. 15). Also, Horowitz's observation mentioned earlier fits in with the discussion here wherein he maintains, 'the symbols employed to differentiate group from group may be of widely divergent characteristics at different levels of identity' (1976, p. 120). Barth has further clarified the issue:

> (T)he ethnic boundary canalises social life—it entails a frequently quite complex organisation of behavior and social relations. The identification of another person as a fellow member of an ethnic group implies a sharing of criteria for evaluation and judgment. It thus entails the assumption that the two are fundamentally 'playing the same game', and this means that there is between them a potential for diversification and expansion of their social

relationship to cover eventually all different sectors and domains of activity. On the other hand, a dichotomisation of others as strangers, as members of another ethnic group, implies a recognition of limitations on shared understandings, differences in criteria for judgment of value and performance, and a restriction of interaction to sectors of assumed common understanding and mutual interest. (1969, p. 15)

Also, in the context of overseas migrations,[1] migrants construct their ethnic identities in their places of arrival and continued residence in terms of *boundaries vis-à-vis* the *others*, less in terms of territoriality of the physical kind than of the social and cognitive sort. Moreover, even if they do succeed in obtaining some sort of *territory* earmarked in residential terms, it still is a territory without any attempt or ambition aspiring to a state. Stated differently, in the ex-country context where some sort of territory of the kind mentioned earlier, that is, territoriality of the social and cognitive sort, is envisaged, it is without a country and as such has no boundary in real physical terms.

In the USSR, people from different states carried their nationality, territoriality in one sense, as a primary identification besides their ethnic identity. However, nationality apparently was subservient to citizenship (of the Soviet Union). For instance, inhabitants of Azerbaijan, Chechnya and Georgia were nationals of these respective provinces, and at the same time were Muslims, Christians, etc., but were also simultaneously citizens of the USSR. It is worthwhile to examine the context in the United States *vis-à-vis* Native Americans: prior to the 1924 Act of the US Congress that made them citizens, Native Americans were *noncitizen nationals* (LaFarge, 1956, p. 243)!

The two different cases of the Bedouins and the USSR can be construed as constructs of the opposite kind. While in the case of the Bedouins, nationality was much more spread out and wider than the factor of citizenship, in the latter case, citizenship was overarching compared to nationality. Though numerous examples of both kinds can be cited, suffice to point out that in real empirical terms there are different ways in which identity and territory impinge on each other at the highest level, at the level of the nation state. Nation states have to deal (and have been dealing) with these issues in various ways. There have been separatist movements and conflicts; wars have been waged and fought resulting in the partition of countries; and national and international boundaries have been redrawn many a time prior to colonization, during the colonial period, as also in the post-colonial context in various parts of the world.

Further, an identity in *nationality* terms can be constructed which could be *global* or *pan-world*, and not restricted to any particular people, country, nation-state or region, as in the case of the *Nation of Islam*, what has come to be known as the *Black Muslim Movement* in the USA. Besides, identity *sans* regional and country boundary is used in reference to the Christian *Community* or its Islamic equivalent of the Muslim *ummah*.

## IDENTITY, BOUNDARY AND TERRITORY

According to Alonso, 'despite Barth's proposal that anthropologists examine ethnic formation by focusing on the creation of social boundaries, which may have territorial counterparts, rather than on the unique "cultural stuff" that these boundaries are alleged to enclose, anthropological research on the role of space and place in boundary creation is scarce' (1994, p. 393). Traditionally, anthropologists dealt with small-scale societies which were more often than not territorial and when the social structure and organization of such societies was studied, the idea was to present a holistic and rounded picture of the societies concerned. The *cultural stuff* that Alonso refers to was what was covered in such holistic and rounded monographs. Invariably, these societies were territory-bound, that is, had a boundary, in the sense that their identification with the region they inhabited was taken for granted, and their dependence on resources in the given region was what made them inhabit the given territory. Of course, there were many groups at a very low socio-economic level which were nomadic or semi-nomadic or practised transhumance. But hardly any group was footloose in the sense of roaming around without any set pattern in terms of time and space in covering the ground. That is, even nomads and semi-nomads had notions of territory when it came to resource seeking, and nomadism to whatever degree it existed, had a nexus with seasonality. Thus, whether the groups were settled, or indulged in varying degrees of nomadism, the idea of territoriality, in terms of their own identity, was always present.

When anthropologists made forays into the uncharted territory of urban societies during the 1940s and moved into realms away from their erstwhile pursuit of tribal and small-scale rural societies, they borrowed research techniques mainly from sociology. The going was different, if not tough, but they did adapt to the new *terrain* and develop the field of urban anthropology. Yet Alonso's argument that 'anthropological research on the role of space and place in boundary creation is scarce' appears to be true. It is worthwhile to throw some light on what territory means in different cultural contexts. According to Gupta,

> [W]hen space is understood as locale of cultural practices, with memberships around root metaphors, it is easy to realise why the Native Americans and White settlers in the United States could not agree on a definition of territory. The native Indian population saw territory in terms of a distinct set of cultural practices, which did not include actual physical ownership of geography. For White settlers territory invoked a different kind of meaning—that which was based on exclusive possession and ownership of actual chunks of earth. (2000, p. 108)

There are examples from many ancient and not so ancient societies where only those who owned land or other forms of material assets were considered to be the real citizens. Even during the last century, in parts of north India, those who did not own land were referred to as *junglees*, that is, dwellers of the forest in the literal sense, but wild and uncivilized in a more derogative sense! Needless to say, there are societies even in the contemporary world, context, which believe in communal property or common property resources that are shared among members of particular societies without demarcating areas as private or individual property among themselves. The way they view identity is *vis-à-vis* what is common to the group in the larger sense of territory. 'The physical element in basic group identity', according to Isaacs, 'has to do not only with the body but also with place, the land, the soil to which the group is attached, literally, historically, mythically' (1976, p. 44; also see Kalam, 1997). The following discussion focuses on how issues of identity, space and territory operate at the sub-national level within a nation-state like India.

## IDENTITY, SPACE AND TERRITORY IN INDIA

Given its immense religious, regional, linguistic and cultural diversity, India presents a rich and profound field for studies on ethnicity, identity and territory. Also, two erstwhile regions of India—Pakistan and Bangladesh—became independent states thereby adding and contributing to the complexity of the subcontinent. Diversity of various forms enables people to construct their identity at various levels, and operate and organize their different activities at multiple levels, depending on the demands of the situation in the sub-national context. While it is generally possible that such identity constructs of people for themselves are recognized to be such by *others*, it is not uncommon to have labels foisted by *others* on groups; such labels can be, and mostly are, derogatory and the group concerned would be wary and resentful of such external constructs. Thus, there are regional, linguistic, state level, religious and other kinds of identity constructs. Within the sub-national context the linguistic and religious identity can be pan-national and across states, for instance, those who speak the same language but live in different states and similarly those who belong to the same religious group or caste but are spread out across the country.

In the contemporary context, most tribal societies in India do have specific locales and can be directly identified in terms of territoriality. Barring a few major tribal groups, which are spread over vast areas covering more than one state, most tribal societies are confined to more or less defined spaces and can be said to be relatively *static* (in terms of habitation patterns) in such spaces. Since tribal groups of the latter kind speak a common language, have a degree of homogeneity and a common name, their identity as a single group makes a lot of sense, and is much more acceptable compared to groups that claim a common identity in urban and more complex domains (because of heterogeneity).

Notions of territoriality between different tribal groups have existed for generations, and have had much to do with the availability of resources and control over those resources. Various neighbouring groups have been in conflict when boundaries that are either topological or cognitive have been trespassed. The fact that a single large group can be divided into small territorial groups and be spread out over a vast area in order to reduce the density of its population for better resource utilization implies that resource sharing can have an impact on, and can influence a group to limit its size. Ideas of space and territory among specific tribal groups in India have meaning, in the main, in the realm of their resource bases.

What has been said so far, however, is true only to an extent, and has a bearing on a small segment of the Indian population, as in 2001 the total tribal population of India is 8 per cent.

Moving from tribal moorings to more heterogeneous and relatively more complex human groups like villages, towns and finally cities, the element of caste enters the fray and alters the space and territoriality scene quite dramatically. Caste orders and ordains people to be apart not just in physical terms, but also in ritual and social terms. Hence, there is religious sanction for people belonging to different castes to be arranged hierarchically with respect to purity and pollution. Those who are more 'pure' are closer to temples, gods and their agents and functionaries, and those who are lower down on the purity heirarchy tend to be closer to the polluting polar opposite, which could be a residential colony for the lower castes, as is the case in most regions of India; or, to be more specific the *cheri* as in Tamil Nadu—a habitation exclusively for the Harijans/Dalits—a rather neat way of assigning people their territory and restraining them spatially as per their ritual/caste identity. This kind of layout is not just an academic or a mental construct, but is expressed in tangible, physical terms in settlement patterns in villages and towns in India. For instance, the *agraharam* (exclusive habitation for the Brahmins around and nearest to the temple) villages in Tamil Nadu exhibit this feature. One way of keeping those who pollute the upper caste groups, or their sacrosanct terrains (including water holes), or their gods, is to isolate them away from the ritually purer ones in fairly distinct spatial terms. This is achieved by segregation in physical terms and exclusion in religious and social terms, based entirely on the identity of some of the people as belonging or not belonging to certain groups in the ritual hierarchy. This is reflected in the settlement pattern of multi-caste habitations.

Segregation of the kind discussed earlier is just one form of the various aspects involved in such an exercise. Barring the access of the lower castes to water tanks, wells and taps is another way of defining the exclusivity of upper caste spaces. While exclusion is of a high order in the religious, social, cultural and territorial realms, it is ambivalent in economic terms. This ambivalence is due to the fact that the economic aspects seem to be, and are more complex and complicated as certain occupations, particularly the polluting ones, have to be performed in order to maintain a semblance of non-anarchy in multi-caste habitations. Also, labourers have to be hired for various manual jobs ranging from work in the agricultural fields to work in and around the patron's house. Hence, exclusion of the lower castes from the economic space is far more difficult than other kinds of exclusions, particularly in rural settings. It can be said that while the lower castes are partly included in certain economic spheres/activities—hence economic space—they are simultaneously excluded from other spaces, particularly ritual and social ones besides, of course, the physical. But one must hasten to add that mere *inclusion* in the economic space does not entail or guarantee upward economic mobility or bestow any upward social mobility on the lower castes. Denial of political space is part of the game here. Usually, upward economic mobility in clear and strong terms enables individuals and/or groups to gain a foothold in the political realm. Hence, economic exclusion in a telling way ensures denial of political leverage and space.

In urban settings, residential exclusiveness of the rural kind that is obtained in multi-caste areas is difficult to replicate mainly because modern spaces are not designed on the lines of caste-based segregation. However, many Indian cities and towns have vestiges, particularly in the original areas of development, which reflect territorialization based on the caste system. To revert again to the Tamil Nadu example, there are remnants of the *agraharam* village pattern in many towns/cities where the temple and its tank in the middle of the town/city and the streets around were earmarked for Brahmins. In terms of their standing in the ritual hierarchy, the other caste groups occupied places in increasing distance from the centrality of the temple and the god and the Brahmins in a concentric manner. Though such territorial markings are physically visible in many places, including various localities in the city of Chennai, the living spaces themselves have become *secular* as housing and property have entered the market, changing circulation and inheritance patterns formerly exclusively based on caste lines. Whether physical spatial changes have also influenced the thought and visual processes of different caste groups cognitively is an interesting research agenda that could be pursued further.

While caste operates predominantly in rural areas and smaller townships, it appears that the class aspect is more evident in urban and metropolitan areas in shaping settlement patterns and territoriality. Although purity factors maintain physical as well as social distance between different caste groups in the rural areas, in the cities the physical distance between different individuals (not always or necessarily between different caste groups) is reduced to the bare minimum (for instance, while travelling in packed buses/trains or interactions in crowded streets). At the same time, however, the social distance between them is quite large and marked. They do not know each other; that is, there is a high degree of anonymity between individuals in urban areas. People are in the midst of, and are by themselves, *lonely crowds* in the cities. As Peter Saunders put it, 'life in large settlements . . . is in general more anonymous than life in small ones, and people packed together in dense settlements (as in tower block flats, for example) may well respond to physical proximity through maintenance of social distance'

(1985, p. 72). The argument may be extended using Webber's assertion,

> [T]he physical becomes an extension of one's ego. The outer worlds of neighborhood-based peer groups, neighborhood-based family, and the *physical* neighborhood place itself, seem to become internalized in inseparable aspects of one's inner perception of self. . . . One's conception of himself and his place in society is thus subtly merged with his conceptions of the spatially limited territory of social interaction. (Webber, 1964 cited in Urry, 1985, p. 32)

In consequence, slums and lower class residential areas in large cities appear to be far more secular and cosmopolitan than poor and lower caste areas in rural areas. The sheer lack of space and constrained packing of humans in small areas leads to highly dense settlements and minimal choices in neighbours or living areas. Low incomes and job insecurity drives people to such places. How this density shapes and or alters identity is less well known as studies of ethnicity and identity in such areas have dealt with issues of poverty and housing in the main. Very little is known about the class construction of these types of settlements.

People have internal conceptions of themselves in all situations and contexts. Such conceptions come into play in interactions with others, but it is limited to situations wherein such knowledge exists. In other contexts, the non-knowledge of the identity of a person (an *other*) permits him/her to encroach upon certain territories. On the other hand, such knowledge on the part of an *other* acts as a barrier in more traditional settings of the village and restricts interaction to certain definite, confined spaces. Such restrictions are operative not just between humans, but are also extended to divine spaces and divine beings *vis-à-vis* certain individuals.

What is significant in this discussion is the fact that some religious groups, at least in theory, do not come under the ambit of caste hierarchy. For instance, Muslims and some Christian and tribal groups cut into, criss-cross and *encroach* upon spaces that are forbidden and prohibited to the lower caste groups in the Hindu pecking order. There are no clear-cut *rules* that are laid down to regulate such transgressions by those who are external to the Hindu hierarchy. The local context and the identity of the group concerned in such a locale and in some cases its economic status determine how and in what way such regulations operate. In the rural areas of Tamil Nadu, for example, Muslim groups, in general, have almost unhindered use of upper caste spaces (including water tanks, wells and taps, as also entry to tea shops and use of cups and saucers), which are vehemently denied to lower caste Hindus and lower rungs of Christians. Such differential treatment meted out to the latter two groups has had a wide ranging impact in different parts of the country including the Islamic conversion of lower caste Hindus and Dalits (see Kalam, 1984).

## CONCLUSION

None of the situations dealt with here are in any way static. Changes do occur at different levels and spheres in the lives and economic, social, cultural and linguistic dealings of a people. How do these reflect in terms of identity of the people? Do people construct a new identity in the wake of such changes? Normally, they do not as it is rather difficult to aspire for and achieve such paradigm shifts during an individual lifetime. An interesting empirical example is from the Palar Valley in northern Tamil Nadu where the Muslims have not only made territorial changes (by migrating to another part of the state) but have also gradually abandoned Tamil, their original mother tongue and adopted Urdu as their mother tongue. Over and above these linguistic shifts, they have also adopted a different school of Islamic jurisprudence and made changes in their kinship pattern by practising parallel cousin marriages that in the earlier Tamil context were avoided scrupulously. Despite these significant linguistic and social shifts, they still retain their former identity—that of *Labbai* Muslims, which in its normally understood form means Tamil-speaking Muslims (see Kalam, 2004).

## NOTE

1. I have consciously avoided using the term *diaspora*; for the reasons and discussion on this see Kalam (2002) and the contribution by Landy in this volume.

## REFERENCES

Alonso, Ana Maria, 'The Politics of Space, Time and Substance: State Formation, Nationalism and Ethnicity', *Annual Review of Anthropology*, vol. 233, 1994, pp. 379-405.

Barth, Fredrik, 'Introduction', in *Ethnic Groups and Boundaries: The Social Organization of Cultural Difference*, ed. Fredrik Barth, London: George Allen and Unwin, 1969.

Gupta, Dipankar, *Culture, Space and the Nation-State: From Sentiment to Structure*, New Delhi: Sage, 2000.

Horowitz, Donald L., 'Ethnic Identity', in *Ethnicity: Theory and Experience*, ed. Nathan Glazer and Daniel P. Moynihan, Cambridge: Harvard University Press, 1976.

Isaacs, Harold R., 'Basic Group Identity: The Idols of the Tribe', *Ethnicity: Theory and Experience*, ed. Nathan Glazer and Daniel P. Moynihan, Cambridge: Harvard University Press, 1976.

Kalam, M.A., 'Why the Harijan Convert to Islam Views Reservations with Reservation', *South Asia Research*, vol. 4, no. 2, 1984.

———, Moorings and Mobility in an Indian Context: An Anthropological Perspective', in: *Peasant Moorings: Village Ties and Mobility Rationales in South India*, ed. Jean-Luc Racine, New Delhi: Sage, 1997.

———, 'The Diaspora Bandwagon: Are Indians Part of the Journey?', in: *Indian Society: Continuity, Change and Development*, ed. P.S. Reddy and V. Gangadhar, New Delhi: Commonwealth, 2002.

———, 'Language, Ethnicity and Identity among the Muslims of Palar Valley', in *Industrialisation and Socio-cultural Change in the Tannery Belt of the Palar Valley (Tamil Nadu)*, ed. L. Kennedy, PPSS 32, Pondicherry: French Institute, 2004, pp. 19-29.

LaFarge, Oliver, *A Pictorial History of the American Indian*, New York: Crown Publishers, 1956.

Saunders, Peter, 'Space, the City and Urban Sociology', in *Social Relations and Spatial Structures*, ed. Derek Gregory and John Urry, London: Macmillan, 1985.

Urry, John, 'Social Relations, Space and Time', in *Social Relations and Spatial Structures*, ed. Derek Gregory and John Urry, London: Macmillan, 1985.

CHAPTER 4

# Re-inscribing Race and Ethnicity in Post-apartheid South Africa

JANE BATTERSBY

## INTRODUCTION

In the post-apartheid era race and ethnic identities have proven to be pervasive and, at the same time, flexible; identities to be overcome and reworked, yet, also celebrated in the 'new' South Africa. Over the past ten years, the state has re-inscribed race and ethnicity as central to discourses on socio-economic rights and cultural diversity, respectively. Race and ethnicity (as well as gender, class, geographical location and language) still shape the lived experiences of South Africans in complex ways, but their articulation in state policy, practice and politics has been reworked. I focus here on the re-inscription of race and ethnicity by the South African state in the contemporary period and on an examination of the initiatives to construct inclusive national identities that shift the role and place of racial and ethnic differentiation in the national imagination. I contextualize contemporary debates on the relationship between race, ethnic and national identities in theoretical literature on citizenship, hybridity and creolization that help move debates on identity beyond the classic race-class binary characteristic of much historical and contemporary analysis in South Africa (see Bond, 2000 and Wolpe, 1988).

## HISTORIES OF RACE AND ETHNICITY IN SOUTH AFRICA

There are considerable differences in the meanings ascribed to and the uses of race and ethnicity within the apartheid and post-apartheid contexts. The development of South African racial theory and practice under apartheid cannot be separated from its colonial legacy. Internationally, racial theory was developed for a specific purpose, as noted by Dubow, 'Social Darwinists, Spencerians, Lamarkians, craniologists and physical anthropologists all set themselves the task of classifying the world's races according to a natural hierarchy' (1987, p. 72). Through defining and ranking populations according to such phenotypic categories as the proportions of the pelvis and limbs, proportions of the skull, skin tone, texture of the hair and cranial capacity, population groups were classified and ranked according to their supposed evolutionary development (Finch, 1911, Keane 1908, Peschel, 1889, von Luschan, 1911).

As the international race debate moved from 'race as nature' to 'race as culture' (Goldberg, 1992, pp. 547-8), politicians increasingly utilized these debates in order to further their segregationist policies. In South Africa, where patterns of colonization and contact had already established differentiation on grounds of culture and colour, these theories were accepted and elaborated upon and claims of separate nations were promoted. It is from this context that the apartheid order developed. Under apartheid the concept of race imbued a physiological difference with cultural and intellectual characteristics. Within this framework a sliding hierarchy of status was adopted. Race was determined from above by a series of policies and practices that framed the lives and livelihoods of South Africans, defining access to political rights, location, education, employment and many other public and intimate aspects of life.

Where ethnicity was used, it served to fragment groups further for purposes of state control. For instance, the black African population was re-tribalized and assigned Homelands, and the people classed as coloured were subdivided into eight different categories of coloured groups under the Coloured Proclamation Act of 1959. Freire expressed this process as follows: 'As the oppressor minority subordinates and dominates the majority, it must divide and keep it divided in order to remain in power' (Freire, 1972, p. 111).

During apartheid there were many challenges to this racialization and theories of what would happen to the social order following the demise of the regime. The dominant Marxist idea argued that South Africa experienced 'colonialism of a special kind' (Wolpe, 1988). Race was 'not an independent factor but the manifestation of those underlying material conditions and class forces that made apartheid functional to the needs of capitalism' (Taylor, 1994, p. 91). In this literature 'race' was viewed solely as a social construction which attributed meaning to phenotypic variation. This attribution of meaning resulted in the reification of real social relations into ideological categories (Solomos, 1986, p. 98). The Marxist literature challenged the acceptance of race by declaring it to be 'false consciousness'. After establishing race as a construction that obscured the 'true' class differentials, many Marxist writers argued that the term race should not be recognized or used as adopting the term in research perpetuated and substantiated it as an idea. By using the term 'race' on the grounds that people *act* as if race exists, its construction is supported and enhanced (Phizacklea, 1984, p. 200 cited in Solomos, 1986, p. 98).

Other theorists challenged the dominance of race over class in social theory. 'Race', according to Stuart Hall, 'is the modality through which class is lived, the medium through which class relations are experienced' (Hall, 1982, p. 341 cited in Wolpe, 1988, p. 52). That is to say, race as a form of identity only exists as an expression of class relations. If this is the case, race should not be given primacy since it is only a constructed constituent element of the meta-structure of class. Therefore, it was predicted that in the post-apartheid era race and ethnicity would decline in importance as their masking effect of real social conditions was revealed (see Cohen, 1993, p. 1).

After ten years of democracy, race and ethnicity do not appear to be in terminal decline. Instead, there has been a conscious effort by the state to re-inscribe the meaning of race and ethnicity for South African citizens. Race now tends to be described as an economic and rights issue, and ethnicity as a cultural issue. The vision of state non-racialism is that the less race is a determining factor in access to social and economic goods and services the more diminished race consciousness will become. In order to achieve this, it is imperative to prioritize the needs of the most historically disadvantaged groups; therefore the state continues to recognize race and racial differentiation. Although there has been a general shift away from the use of race in its traditional understanding in policies, there is little evidence to suggest that outside of a few metropolitan enclaves race has ceased to have meaning for the general population.

The following discussion draws on the international literature on citizenship, hybridity and creolization to examine critically the reworking of race and ethnic identities in debates on socio-economic and cultural rights in the South African context.

## CITIZENSHIP, IDENTITY POLITICS AND IDENTITY THEORY

Notions of what it means to be a citizen of a country have undergone transformation as a result of developments in theory and in the lived experiences of the places one calls home. The debate has traditionally been couched in a polemic that contrasts two models of nationhood: the 'melting pot' of monoculturalism and the 'salad bowl' of ethnic particularism (Cross and Mkwanazi-Twala, 1998, p. 9). The issues of comparative inclusion and the terms of this inclusion have been understood through a range of ambiguous and at times interchangeable terms such as 'assimilation', 'integration', multiculturalism', 'pluralism' and 'separatism' (Grillo, 1998, p. 179). The extent to which those differing from the expected cultural norm have been accepted largely depends on the understanding of the notion used at the time.

These cultural understandings of citizenship and belonging have begun to be challenged. In the early 1990s there was a move towards considering citizenship as a contract between an enabling state and individuals who were free to choose and direct their own destinies (Mason, 1995, p. 115). The citizen ceased to be culturally directed and was instead constructed as a consumer with particular rights within a collective environment. Within this framework there was a mutual dependency between the state and the individual that was not so in the previous models. In this approach, the nation and the national identities encompassed within it were understood as built from both above and below.

Eisenstadt and Giesen (1995) suggested that collective identities (which include national identities) are constructed as primordial, civic or universalist. These constructions reveal the means by which inclusion can occur, and represent different understandings of the nature of identity. Under primordialism, inclusion is based on unchanging 'natural' features. As such, the boundaries to inclusion are very difficult to cross. In contrast, barriers to civic belonging are less difficult to cross, because they are based not so much on 'natural' characteristics, as on compliance to historically developed complexes of cultural and political rules which take time to learn and adapt to. The most inclusive form of collective identity is the universalist which aims to incorporate outsiders into the community on the basis of religious or secular institutions and ideas.

Parekh's engagement with civic multiculturalism, like many others, recognizes that national identities are constantly redefined by historically inherited characteristics, present needs and future aspirations (Parekh, 1995, p. 255). In his 2000 paper, Parekh identified eight conditions under which national identities and citizenship can be developed. These conditions address the purpose of such identities, their means of transfer and agents in their development. Although a national identity is deeply embedded in cultural practices, Parekh argued that it should be primarily an identity of a political community and have a political basis. The nation has long been recognized as a political construct, and national identity should accordingly be viewed in this light. Therefore, national (and I argue ethnic or racial identity) is 'located not in what its members personally like or dislike, but what constitutes and defines them as a political collectivity' (Parekh, 2000, p. 8). According to this view, national identity should, therefore, be defined in politico-institutional rather than ethno-cultural terms.

## IDENTITY POLITICS IN POST-APARTHEID SOUTH AFRICA

Under apartheid, South Africa had an exceptionally limited understanding of citizenship, restricted primarily on grounds of race, but also with severely restricted rights in terms of gender, ethnicity, disability and sexuality. The first post-apartheid government, the Government of National Unity, therefore sought to use a rhetoric of inclusion and to promote the kind of civic citizenship discussed earlier. A key indicator of this was the language of the Reconstruction and Development Programme (RDP), the government's statement of intent. Its introduction reads: 'The RDP is well aware that the birth of a transformed nation can only succeed if the people themselves are voluntary participants in the process towards the realisation of the goals that they themselves have helped to define' (Ministry of the Office of the President, 1994, p. 7).

In his inauguration speech Nelson Mandela made the often-quoted plea, 'Let there be justice for all.' He added, 'Let each know that for each the body, the mind and the soul have been freed to fulfil themselves' (Mandela, 1994). These statements reveal the conflict in the rhetoric of the RDP and that of the new citizenship between re-inscribing racial identities to promote economic justice (for instance through targeting particular sectors of the population as priorities for development) and, at the same time, facilitating freedom of identity within or outside of the boundaries of race and ethnicity. It is this conflict that fuels the fierce debate on the notions of Rainbow Nation (an inclusive identity spanning all groups in South Africa) *versus* the Two Nations thesis (an argument that the divide between 'black' and 'white' and 'poor' and 'rich' continues to splinter the nation). For the body to be freed to fulfil itself requires material redistribution, and freedom from restrictive economic practices and principles. This calls for strategic alliances to be made, and at times for essentialized notions of self to be adopted to achieve its objectives. This is the essence of the Two Nations rhetoric, in which the South African society is described in terms of a black/white, poor/rich binary.

Within this discourse, culture and intra-group differences are sidelined for political purposes. However, for the 'soul to be freed' to fulfil itself calls for a recognition and celebration of difference, of the many ways one is able to express one's multiple identities and one self. This is the essence of the Rainbow Nation rhetoric, which celebrated the diversity of South African society and sought ways to broaden understanding of what it meant to be a citizen of the country. Yet, in challenging essentialism and the existing categorization of individuals, the Rainbow Nation discourse blunted the opportunities to challenge the existing economic power structures. Within South Africa, this materialist versus differentialist debate (as outlined by Mac and Ghaill, 1999) does not just manifest itself at the national political level, but also the distinctions between the two ideologies in terms of purpose and practice have at times become blurred. Although the government has tended to adopt a materialist discourse about race (Two Nations) for the purposes of economic transformation, I argue that it has adopted a more inclusive differentialist discourse (Rainbow Nation) within education and other fields to meet these materialist ends.

South African experiences of re-inscribing racial and ethnic identities to address socio-economic and cultural goals provide a powerful illustration of the problems and politics of identities found in many other countries. In the United States, for instance, it has manifested itself in debates on the challenge of the politics of difference to affirmative action and the wider black struggle. As Sivananden noted, 'ethnicity blunts black struggle' (1983, p. 5). It is argued that race must be recognized, not because it is real, but because it still has power. The choice to mobilize oneself in terms of race is, therefore, an act of strategic essentialism (Spivak, 1987, p. 205). This contradiction led a leading academic in Afro-American studies to write, 'To relinquish the notion of race—even though it's a cruel hoax—at this particular time is to relinquish our fortress against the powers and principalities that still try to undermine us' (Spencer cited in Wright, 1994, p. 55).

The same debate continues in gay and lesbian politics. To what extent should gays and lesbians mobilize politically around a quasi-ethnicity? To what extent should they recognize that it is precisely these socially produced binaries that form the basis of oppression and that the key to liberation is the abolition of such categories (Gamson, 1995, pp. 390-1)? When these cases are considered together it becomes apparent that the issue is not simply about citizenship, but about the generation and politics of, as well as theorizing about, collective identities. These issues are discussed in the context of the South African government debates on the 'national project'.

## CHALLENGES TO CREATING A NATIONAL IDENTITY

Njabulo Ndebele, the Vice-Chancellor of the University of Cape Town, noted that South Africans still lack a national consciousness. According to him, 'we do not as yet have a common set of values as a people or nation in the country. Nor is there an overarching discourse to accommodate 'differences'. South Africa still lacks a central idea around which to mobilise its entire people' (Ndebele, 2001, p. 99).

The African National Congress identified this lack of a definable national identity as a critical problem in the process of transformation. They asserted that the formation of a national identity and consciousness is fundamental if the injustices of the past are to be overcome and the country is to move towards non-racial democracy. This new national identity has been conceptualized as the New Patriotism, based on the distinction between its national pride and the arrogance of the Old Patriotism. It is 'forged through an allegiance to the constitutional values of democracy, equality, social justice, non-sexism, non-racism, accountability, openness, ubuntu (human dignity), respect, reconciliation and the rule of law' (Department of Education, 2001b, pp. 77-8). The form of national identity being promoted is therefore clearly a form of civic national identity, as proposed by Parekh.

However, the actual meaning of this new nationalism has not been thoroughly or consistently articulated. The government recognizes that there are many identities in operation within the country, even within each citizen, and that these should not be devalued. This is a reaction against the devaluing of cultures by the apartheid regime. The validation of culture and difference is reflected in the inclusive nature of the 1996 Constitution and the 'Rainbow Nation' rhetoric.

Although difference is to be celebrated, the government proposes that national identity should become the defining identity, as revealed in the following. People should be given 'the space to express their multiple identities in ways that foster the evolution of a broader South Africanism as their primary identity' (ANC, 1997). This is in recognition of the divisive nature of the promotion of ethnic and racial identities under apartheid, which gave a boost to difference over commonality.

The nationalizing vision of the ANC has been most clearly articulated in the ANC's Nation-formation and Nation Building document, which states, 'Individuals will have multiple identities. These identities do not necessarily disappear into the melting pot of broad South Africanism. Rather, they can co-exist in healthy combination. The fundamental question that has to be asked is what identity assumes prominence, and under what circumstances' (ANC, 2001).

The government is, therefore, aspiring to a model that valorizes the identity choices of individuals and groups and allows them to persist, but only in relation to a broader national identity. Under apartheid, individuals were white, coloured or black African first and South African second, with nationality becoming increasingly less important in the eyes of the state as one moved down the racial hierarchy. The government's post-apartheid vision frames individuals as primarily South African but free to have many linked secondary identities that fit within this broader national identity.

Many attempts have been made to ground this vision in government policy development and implementation. This paper draws particular attention to education as it has been used by the government as one of the key areas for its nation-building projects and has been recognized as 'the nursery of values' (Department of Education, 2001b, p. 5). Used explicitly by the apartheid state to sustain notions of racial hierarchy and to determine the lived experiences of different races through education funding and content, education was one of the main tools used to ensure that people became socialized into the economic positions the state proposed for them. The following statement by H.F. Verwoerd in 1953 while Minister for Bantu Affairs illustrates this ideology: 'Education must train and teach people according to their opportunities in life, according to the sphere in which they live' (Verwoerd cited in Nkomo, 1990, p. 294).

In consequence, the restructuring of education is considered critical to post-apartheid social transformation, particularly as a tool for socialization and a way to counter the impact of apartheid on the construction of identities. The government introduced many changes in the education system to facilitate its role in the nation-building project, both generally and specifically. In 2000, the Department of Education appointed a working group on 'Values, Education and Democracy' to develop programmes to facilitate nation-building in schools. The group's report identified six key values that education should promote: equity, tolerance, multilingualism, openness, accountability and honour (Department of Education 2001a). These values reflect not only the government discourse on national identity, but also reflect an attempt to develop an identity based on these values.

This form of identity production, however, has many limitations reflecting the values that underpin the government's understanding of the relationship between cultures and identities as something that is static rather than fluid. These tensions are revealed in the following:

> These identities are not necessarily divisive. They have progressive aspects that can certainly be harnessed as part of our nation building project. (ANC, 1997)

> The main thrust of the [National Democratic Revolution] is not to promote fractured identities, but to encourage the emergence of a common South African identity. At the same time, it should be noted that some of the identities associated with 'culture' or 'ethnicity' or 'religion' could in fact be contradictory to the building of a new nation that is based on principles of equity. (ANC, 2001)

Although the state is seeking a multiplicity of identities, it also seeks to control or at least shape these identities. This is particularly evident in the way in which the government characterizes the diversity of the people of South Africa and the images adopted to promote the country, such as images of the Zulu warrior, the Cape Malay going to mosque, and the blond surfer. As emptied out bearers of culture each form of identity is considered of equal value and importance in its position below the national. They are linked to heritage and location but not to change and renegotiation of selfhood. An individual can assert any number of other identities, such as ethnicity, gender, location-based identity and sexuality, which may or may not be connected to each other, but these identities should only ever be secondary identities that contribute to a general South African national identity. Difference adds seasoning to the proposed national identity, but is not seen as a dynamic in the process of the reproduction of national identity.

## CONCLUSION

'The country sometimes feels like a ship winging wildly on a single anchor that is threatening to break loose. The passengers are fiercely proud of their vessel, but none of them really care about the others, or have bothered to find out their names' (Matshikiza, 2000, p. 30). The process of claiming and asserting an identity is inherently political, particularly in South Africa. Attempts to depoliticize non-national identities in the post-apartheid era have been fiercely resisted. Groups and individuals have challenged the primacy of a national identity by promoting localized identities that, at times conflict and, at others coalesce with the post-apartheid national project. Although in general, 'communities' accept the value of reworking apartheid period identities, the erasure of these identities through assimilation into a broader national identity has been problematized. The promotion of local identities could be understood as an attempt to promote stability. It involves the search for roots and often the production of histories. It represents the re-politicization of histories and identities in order to demonstrate resistance to a nationalizing agenda. Just as the nationalizing project has theoretical limitations with political outcomes, there are problems associated with the types of identities proposed by localizers. The identities created are dependent on the re-inscription of histories. Some have rejected this quest for 'roots' on the grounds that it offers not just a highly selective and value-laden conception of history, but also that it depends on the rewriting of histories. The re-casting of roots-based identities in the 'coloured' context,[1] for instance, was succinctly critiqued by Zoë Wicomb:

> Don't try to fob me off with nonsense about roots and ancestors. . . . Rubbish, it's all fashionable rubbish. Next thing you'll be off overseas to check out your roots in the rubbish dumps of Europe, but no, I forget, it's the African roots that count. What do you expect to find? Ours are all mixed up and tangled up; no chance of us being uprooted, because they're all in a neglected knot, stuck. And that, I'd have thought is the beauty of being coloured, that we need not worry about roots at all, that its altogether a good thing to start afresh. (Wicomb, 2000, pp. 27-8)

In attempting to valorize aspects of history and identity, local identities remain partial, built into the multiple identities that complexly structure people's lives. Nonetheless, such local expressions of racial and ethnic identities are subsumed in and overwritten by quests to construct an inclusive and unifying national South African identity.

## NOTE

1. For an extensive discussion on the historical construction of 'coloured' identities see Chapter 8 by Fauvelle-Aymar in this volume.

## REFERENCES

ANC, *ANC 50th National Conference Resolution of the National Question. Mafeking 1997* [Online]. Available FTP: http://www.anc.org.za/ancdocs/pubs/umrabulo/umrabulo8d.html, accessed 12 December 2003, 1997.

ANC, *Nation-formation and Nation Building: The National Question in South Africa* [Online]. Available FTP: http://www.anc.org.za/ancdocs/discussion/nation.html, accessed 12 December 2003, 2001.

Bond, P., *Elite Transition: From Apartheid to Neoliberalism in South Africa*, Pietermaritzburg: University of Natal Press, 2000.

Asmal, K., *Call to Action: Mobilising Citizens to Build a South African Education and Training System for the 21st Century* [Online]. Available FTP:http://education.pwv.gov.za/Media_Statements/July99/call_to_action.htm, accessed 12 December 2003, 1999.

Cohen, R., 'Race and Ethnicity in a Post-Apartheid South Africa: "Pluralism" Revisited', in *Knowledge Passion: Essays in Honour of John Rex*, ed. H. Martins, London: Tauris, 1993, pp. 1-22.

Cross, M. and Z. Mkwanazi-Twala, 'The Dialectic of Unity and Diversity in Education: Its Implications for a National Curriculum in South Africa', in *Dealing with Diversity in South African Education*, ed. M. Cross, Z. Mkwanazi-Twala and G. Klein, Kenwyn: Juta, 1998, pp. 3-34.

Department of Education, *Manifesto on Values, Education and Democracy* [Online]. Available FTP: http://education.pwv.gov.za/DoE_Sites/Curriculum/Values/manifesto_on_values.htm, accessed 12 December 2003, 2001a.

———, *Education in South Africa: Achievements since 1994*. http://education.pwv.gov.za/Policies%20and%20Reports/2001_Report/Achievements.htm, 2001b.

Dubow, S., 'Race, Civilisation and Culture: The Elaboration of Segregationist Discourse in the Inter-war Years', in *The Politics of Race, Class and Nationalism in Twentieth-Century South Africa*, ed. S. Marks and S. Trapido, London: Longman, 1987, pp. 71-94.

Eisenstadt, S.N. and B. Giesen, 'The Construction of Collective Identity', *European Journal of Sociology*, vol. 36, 1995, pp. 71-192.

Finch, E., 'The Effects of Racial Miscegenation', in *Inter-Racial Problems*, ed. G. Spiller, London: P.S. King and Son, 1911, pp. 108-12.

Freire, P., *Pedagogy of the Oppressed*, Harmondsworth: Penguin, 1972.

Gamson, J., 'Must Identity Movements Self-destruct? A Queer Dilemma', *Social Problems*, vol. 42, no. 3, 1995, pp. 390-408.

Goldberg, D.T., 'The Semantics of Race', *Ethnic and Racial Studies*, vol. 15, no. 4, 1992, pp. 543-69.

Grillo, R.D., *Pluralism and the Politics of Difference: State, Culture, and Ethnicity in Comparative Perspective*, Oxford: Clarendon Press, 1998.

Keane, D.H., *The World's Peoples: A Popular Account of their Bodily and Mental Characters, Beliefs, Traditions, Political and Social Institutions*; London: Hutchinson and Co., 1908.

Mac, M. and M. Ghaill, *Contemporary Racisms and Ethnicities: Social and Cultural Transformations*, Buckingham: Open University Press, 1999.

Mandela, N., Statement of the President of the African National Congress Nelson Rolihlahla Mandela, at His Inauguration as President of the Democratic Republic of South Africa. 10 May 1994 [Online]. Available FTP: http://www.polity.org.za/html/govdocs/speeches/1994/inaugpta.html?rebookmark=1, accessed 12 December 2003, 1994.

Mason, D., *Race and Ethnicity in Modern Britain*, Oxford: Oxford University Press, 1995.

Matshikiza, J., 'Aboard a Floundering Vessel', *Mail and Guardian*, 6 October 2000, p. 12.

Ministry of the Office of the President, 'White Paper on Reconstruction and Development', *Government Gazette*, vol. 353, no. 16085, 24 November 1994

Ndebele, N., 'The Social Bases or Values in South Africa: Prospects and Challenges. Keynote Speech by Njabulo Ndebele, University of Cape Town', in *Saamtrek: Values, Education and Democracy in the 21st Century. Conference Report*, ed. Department of Education, Pretoria: Department of Education, 2001, pp. 99-105.

Nkomo, M., 'Post-apartheid Education: Preliminary Reflections', in *Education: From Poverty to Liberty*, ed. B. Nasson and J. Samuel, Cape Town: David Philip, 1990, pp. 291-317.

Parekh, B., 'The Concept of National Identity', *New Community*, vol. 21, no. 2, 1995, pp. 255-68.

———, 'Defining British national identity', *Political Quarterly*, vol. 71, no. 1, 2000, pp. 4-14.

Peschel, O., *The Races of Man, and the Geographical Distribution*, London: Kegan Paul, Trench and Co., 1889.

Sivananden, A., 'Challenging Racism: Challenges for the '80s', *Race and Class*, vol. 20, no. 1, 1983, pp. 75-82.

Solomos, J., 'Varieties of Marxist Conceptions of "Race", Class and the State: A Critical Analysis', in *Theories of Race and Ethnic Relations*, ed. J. Rex and D. Mason, Cambridge: Cambridge University Press, 1986, pp. 86-109.

Spivak, G.C., *In Other Worlds: Essays in Cultural Politics*, New York: Methuen, 1987.

Taylor, R., 'South Africa: From 'Race' to Non-racialism', in *'Race', Ethnicity and Nation: International Perspectives on Social Conflict*, ed. P. Ratcliffe, London: University College London Press, 1994, pp. 91-107.

Von Luschan, F., 'Anthropological View of Race', in *Inter-Racial Problems*, ed. G. Spiller, London: P.S. King and Son, 1994, pp. 13-24.

Wicomb, Z., *David's Story*, Cape Town: Kwela Books, 2000.

Wolpe, H., *Race, Class and the Apartheid State*, London and Paris: Curry and UNESCO, 1988.

Wright, L., 'One Drop of Blood', *The New Yorker*, 24 July 1994, pp. 46-55.

# PART TWO

## Building Identities and Territories at National and Regional Scales

CHAPTER 5

# Reflections on British Imperial Geography: India and South Africa

A.J. CHRISTOPHER

The British Empire was one of the most extensive and complex political entities ever assembled. Yet as a subject of research it has been remarkably neglected by geographers. This is all the more surprising as the Royal Geographical Society was closely bound to the development of the imperial enterprise (Cameron, 1980). There was no school of British colonial geography akin to that which flourished in France (Harrison-Church, 1948). The Commonwealth Geographical Bureau offered inter-university assistance, rather than a directed programme (Steel, 1996).

In 1887, Sir Charles Lucas published the first part of his historical geography of the British colonies (Lucas, 1887). Lucas was a proponent of the Imperial Federation movement which viewed the British Empire as a single political unit securing a continuing place among the great powers. The theme was taken up by Sir Halford Mackinder but it failed to attract mass support (Parker, 1982). It was left to the Frenchman, Albert Demangeon, to produce a geography of the British Empire. He commented, 'no other subject yields richer or fuller material for the study of colonial geography, properly understood as an independent branch of knowledge' (Demangeon, 1925, p. 11). It was followed by Charles Fawcett's (1933) *A Political Geography of the British Empire*, which was concerned primarily with matters of imperial defence. However, these works had few successors and geographers have been slow to examine patterns within the British Empire (Christopher, 1988). They have preferred to compare elements of the imprints of different empires (Bell, Butlin and Heffernan, 1995; Godlewska and Smith, 1994).

The neglect is surprising as the imperial legacy in the post-colonial era has been profound in a host of ways, from the use of the English language as the *lingua franca* in international business and science, to the political state structures it bequeathed. This paper examines three spatial policies pursued in the colonial era which have had a profound impact on the modern world, with regard to the Indian and South African successor states. The first is the drawing of the international state boundaries, indeed the very existence of these two states today reflects the policies and priorities of the imperial power. Second, the internal state structures, associated with the concepts of federalism and indirect rule have survived decolonization. Third, the urban structures and networks, reflecting in large measure the requirements of the imperial power, rather than the indigenous peoples, have reinforced themselves in the post-colonial era. Finally, an examination of the census is presented as a significant colonial undertaking and a major source of information on the period.

## CREATING THE STATES

The outline of the modern state system within the Commonwealth is in many ways the outcome of decisions made in government offices in London for the better administration of the British Empire, which was an ongoing process (Christopher, 1999). As such, the boundaries of the present Indian and South African states are the fossilized result of decisions taken till the time of independence. In neither case were the outcomes deliberately sought and in neither was the outcome even considered to be desirable. Indeed, in both cases the present states are only a part of those envisaged in the colonial era. They did, however, reflect the British fascination with large federal structures and the recognition of human and physical diversity within the Empire, as within the United Kingdom. In any comparison of India and South Africa, it must be remembered that the former has twenty-five times the population of the latter and two and a half times the land area.

The British conquest of much of the Indian subcontinent in the eighteenth and nineteenth centuries was undertaken by the Honourable East India Company. Direct control by the British government was imposed only in 1858. At that time India extended from Aden in south Arabia, to Singapore on the Straits of Malacca, and from Kashmir in the north to Cape Cormarin in the south. It was subsequently expanded through the incorporation of Upper Burma and Baluchistan. However, even in the 1860s the imperial government recognized that the administrative structure was unwieldy and detached Straits Settlements, including Singapore, in 1867. In 1877, the Indian Empire was proclaimed, providing Queen Victoria with an imperial title, to rival those of continental Europe.

The governmental structures and bureaucracy established in the late eighteenth and early nineteenth centuries, during the period of rapid expansion, were crucial to the emergence of the modern Indian state. In territorial extent, it has been claimed, it was the maps produced by the Survey of India which gave physical and political shape to the country between 1765 and 1843 (Edney, 1997). Indeed, subsequent attempts to extend the state further north across the mountains into Afghanistan and Tibet proved to be unsuccessful (Hopkirk, 1990). The definition of India's northern boundary in Ladakh took a century (Mehra, 1992). The last significant advance was in Assam in 1913 following the chaos caused by the Chinese revolution, when the frontier was moved up to the crest line of the Himalayas (Mehra, 1974). Similarly, Indian military and diplomatic intervention in the Middle East failed to secure any permanent territorial advances (Tomlinson, 1979). The development of the Indian railway system provided the means of rapid communication which bound the different peoples of the subcontinent together in the second half of the nineteenth and twentieth century (*History of Indian Railways*, 1945). It is notable that the system was limited by the mountain barriers to the north, as the British army had been beforehand.

The introduction of self-government and the concept of India as a British dominion led to some reappraisal of the territorial extent of the state. India was a foundation member of the League of Nations in 1920 and the United Nations in 1945, although it lacked nominal independence. In 1937, the two most remote provinces, Aden and Burma, were detached and became separate colonies, with markedly distinct societies. The Second World War left the British government essentially bankrupt and unable to exert the degree of coercion that would have been necessary to retain control of the Indian Empire. The grant of independence and the transfer of power were therefore negotiated. The success of the Muslim League in persuading the British government of the necessity of creating a separate Muslim state, Pakistan, prevented preservation of the territorial extent of the Empire. The Partition of India in 1947 created a rump Indian state, from which the western provinces and half of the Punjab and much of Bengal had been excised. The problems associated with Partition are still evident in the confrontation between the two states more than fifty years later.

India extended its territory slightly between 1948 and 1961 with the incorporation of the French and Portuguese Indian possessions.

The creation of the South African state followed the Anglo-Boer War of 1899-1902 fought for supremacy in the subcontinent. The compromise settlement leading to the establishment of the Union of South Africa in 1910, was struck by the leaders of the two white communities to the exclusion of the indigenous Africans. The structure was prompted by the British government which viewed the creation of federal governments for Canada and Australia as successes in the restructuring of the Empire. The state included only the four colonies or ex-republics of White settlement. Other territories, notably Southern Rhodesia and the three High Commission territories of Basutoland, Bechuanaland Protectorate and Swaziland, were invited to join at some future date, and were included in the common customs area.

In a referendum the electorate of Southern Rhodesia rejected joining the Union in 1923 and became a separate self-governing colony (Lee, 1977). In South Africa the imperial government consistently resisted attempts by the South African government after 1910 to incorporate the three High Commission territories because of the country's repressive racial policies (Hyam, 1972). The transfer of the three High Commission territories was the subject of periodic negotiations until South Africa became a republic in 1961. Indeed the Tomlinson Commission report of 1955 explicitly included the three territories in its plans for African economic and political development. The High Commission Territories gained independence as separate states in the 1960s and remained outside the South African state. The peculiar position of Lesotho has been commented upon and the possibilities for incorporation once majority rule had been established in South Africa (Lemon, 1996). The South African conquest of (German) South-West Africa in 1915 presented a further opportunity for territorial expansion. However, the hostility of the United Nations in the post-1945 era eventually forced the South African government to abandon its plans for incorporation and grant the country independence in 1980. It may be claimed that the Southern African Development Community has the means to become South Africa's vehicle of projecting its power over the wider region (Gibb, 1998). The colonial railway system in this case exceeded the colonial state, extending into neighbouring countries including Mozambique and the (Belgian) Congo.

Thus, in both cases the imperial states were less extensive than anticipated, but represented a significant grouping of entities under the overall nominal control of the British Empire, later the Commonwealth. It may be noted that neither demonstrated any similarity to the pre-colonial states that had been conquered by the British. The legacy of such 'nation-state' creations in Africa has aptly been called 'The Black Man's Burden' (Davidson, 1992).

## INDIRECT RULE

The administration of the British Empire involved a high degree of delegation of authority to local rulers considered to be loyal to the Crown. Although Lord Lugard, systematized the concept, in the early twentieth century, it had been widely adopted throughout the Empire much before (Hailey, 1938). In India, approximately one-third of the country remained in the hands of indigenous rulers, with the remainder being under the direct rule of the British Indian government. In South Africa, only 6 per cent remained under indigenous control by the early twentieth century.

In India, the Indian princes preserved a varying degree of independence from the central government throughout the colonial era (Ashton, 1982). The imperial government assumed 'paramountcy', which ranged in practical form from the conduct of foreign affairs to the virtual entire administration of the princely state (Pruthi and Devi, 1998). However, the more important princes retained their own armies and legal systems intact, even with pretensions to separate independent statehood (Kibe, 1924). At the other end of the scale, rulers of small states owing allegiance to higher rulers retained their position of power. Policies towards the princely states changed. Lord Curzon, Viceroy 1899-1905, hoped to reproduce the English aristocracy, with the class system and landed estates, but not the administrative power (Gilmour, 1995). The princely states thus constituted a significant aspect of the colonial era. In addition, many of the aboriginal peoples were subject to special governmental oversight, notably the protection of their land rights, from internal colonization and often a high degree of self-government. The current importance of the 'tribal territories' of the North-West Frontier Province of Pakistan is an indication of the continuity of colonial and post-colonial policies. While the maintenance of the concept of 'scheduled tribes', requiring special protection remains in India.

Despite the wealth and prestige of the Indian princes at the end of the Second World War, they were forced to sign acts of accession to either India or Pakistan from 1947 (Menon, 1957). The religious differences between the rulers and the ruled, notably in Hyderabad and Kashmir, resulted in conflict, which in the case of the latter remains unresolved. Hyderabad, with its Muslim ruler, was occupied by the Indian army thereby preventing its accession to Pakistan. The same fate befell the states of Junagarh and Manavadar in the Kathiawar peninsula when the Muslim rulers of these Hindu populated states opted for Pakistan. Kashmir, with its Hindu ruler but predominantly Muslim population, was partitioned, with much of the state coming under Indian control and the temporary 'line of control' assuming the de facto status of an international boundary (Schofield, 1996).

The princely states were consolidated and amalgamated into larger units after 1947, and following the report of the Indian States Commission in 1955, they ceased to be recognizable on the map of India (*Report of the States Reorganization Commission*, 1955). Hyderabad, for example, was split between the three linguistically defined states in the region as language became the basis of state definition (Breton, 1997). In 1971, the government ceased to recognize formally the princes and their special position came to an end. The aboriginal lands were more problematic, with demands for separate statehood on the basis of language and culture (Corbridge, 1991). Other movements for separate states were formed while wishing to remain within the Indian Union (Mawdsley, 1997). The Indian state system was essentially federal in form, although under the supervision of the central government (Dikshit, 1975). It is notable that broadly national politics were based on national parties, rather than a series of regional entities, suggesting the development of an over-arching sense of Indian identity (Dikshit, 1997).

The Indian government initially sought to establish a series of large powerful states, which would be approximately equal in size without one dominating the others. Thus, the core Hindi area was divided on lines similar to the historic British administrative pattern. The largest, the United Provinces became Uttar Pradesh without any alteration. Elsewhere, linguistic states were defined. However, in the 1960s the fragmentation of Assam introduced a number of much smaller states which reflected the complex ethnography of the region (Gopalakrishnan, 1990).

In South Africa, the majority of the local kings and rulers were conquered and their lands greatly reduced in the interests of obtaining land for white settlement. If the most powerful monarchy in southern Africa is examined, its decline was dramatic. The Zulu state was defeated by the British in 1879, and after a period of continued separate existence, the remaining Zulu territories were incorporated into the colony of Natal in 1897. The lands were subsequently partitioned in 1905-7 between those earmarked for Zulu occupation, and those thrown open to European settlement. The Zulu king lost political power and was only nominally the custodian of Zulu occupied lands, under the control of the Governor, later Governor-General, then President, who assumed the position of paramount chief. Within the confines of the White colonies of settlement no equivalent of the princely states of India survived. Where they did, notably in Basutoland, Swaziland and Bechuanaland Protectorate, they were not incorporated into the South African polity.

In South Africa, the National Party government launched the reverse policy process of fragmenting its territory through the apartheid homeland policy after 1955 (Christopher, 2001a). The African rural reserves or locations became the territorial foundations of a set of ten ethno-linguistic homelands, which acquired in four cases all the trappings of sovereign independence. Aspects of pre-colonial polities were resurrected, in much constrained circumstances, and the duality of indirect rule accentuated. However, the pre-colonial patterns of kingdoms, paramountcies and chieftaincies could not be revived except in symbolic form. In 1994, the homelands were reincorporated into South Africa and the subsequent redrawing of the provincial boundaries erased them from the map, just as effectively as the princely states in India had been erased.

The transfer of power in South Africa in 1994 led to the redefinition of the provinces as a result of compromises reached in the political process of negotiation (Khosa and Muthien, 1997). They were based on the physical planning regions, although in most cases the amendments suggested a degree of linguistic definition, akin to India (Christopher, 1995). The contentious issues of an Afrikaner homeland and the status of the Zulu monarchy were left for future determination (Muthien and Khosa, 1995). As in India, elections were essentially conducted according to a national political agenda, rather than by a series of regional ethnic parties (Christopher, 1996).

## COLONIAL CITIES

Another outstanding British heritage is the colonial city. Sir Philip Mitchell, Governor of Uganda in 1936 commented, 'It is not as caretakers that we shall be judged in the eyes of posterity but as builders'

(Ehrlich, 1973, p. 649). This was true in many spheres, not least in the towns and cities bequeathed to later generations. Colonial town planning was imposed upon both countries, with the construction of towns and cities built in the image of England, and particularly London. Indeed the results, notably the capitals, were often on a grander scale than London, as befitted the different nature of the colonial state and the emphasis on state power symbolized in government buildings (Claval, 2000). The colonial city has a long history associated with the government and settlement of the English and later British conquests beginning with Wales under Edward I in the thirteenth century (Christopher, 1983). Thus it was possible for Nirad Chaudhuri (1959, p. 64) to write of Bombay and Calcutta: 'It was only after seeing London that I discovered the true lineage (of these cities). . . offspring of London. . . . London is the first and archetypical city of our age, created by modern government, bureaucracy, finance, world empire, international commerce and industrialism. . . . It is the Mother Megapolis of our era.'

The British built new cities and redeveloped old ones in a particular national style and with markedly spacious plans. Within the former British Empire there are similarities of architecture, monuments and even street furniture (postboxes, lamps, notices, etc.) to impart the feeling of familiarity which was desired by those who created the new environments. One of the objectives of colonial planning was residential segregation of the British and the indigenous inhabitants, indeed, the planning of complex multi-ethnic cities (Christopher, 1988). Town planning in the colonies could be more spacious and grander than the confines of England would allow and was considered to be necessary for the maintenance of health (King, 1976). As a result some of the most spectacular sequences of British architecture between the eighteenth and twentieth centuries were created in the Empire, particularly in India (Davies, 1985). Thus the plans of the pre-1911 capital, Calcutta, began as a fortified town (Fort William), surrounded by the open line of fire, the Maidan. However, a late eighteenth and early nineteenth classical styled city was subsequently built, with marked zonation between the European quarters and the area inhabited by the Indians. Similarly, Bombay, was substantially rebuilt in the later nineteenth century as industrialization progressed. This coincided with the creation of a distinctive Imperial 'Indo-Saracenic' architectural style, reminiscent of Venice, with layouts and plans resembling London. Although segregation was effected, it was not rigid, as the Parsee community and others with the requisite wealth and social standing were able to buy houses in the nominally European area (Christopher, 1992). Segregation was particularly marked in Madras where the Indian suburb, beyond Fort St George, was initially called 'Blacktown'.

The culmination of the British town planning in India was the construction of New Delhi between 1913 and 1931 (Irving, 1981). It has been described as 'the crowning achievement of British architecture in India' (Davies, 1985, pp. 15-16). This was achieved despite the 'congenital meanness and philistinism of British government and bureaucracy' (Stamp, 1981, 372). The main artery, Kingsway, was earmarked for administrative functions, notably the Viceroy's Lodge, flanked by the two Secretariat buildings, with their symbolic columns representing the four dominions, including South Africa. Significantly, the parliament building was added only as an afterthought, following the introduction of representative government. Zoning of the various functions was strict, while the residential areas were further designated for the various levels of the bureaucracy, which again effectively resulted in segregation, although the quarter for the Indian princes may have suggested otherwise. The architectural styles of the new capital aimed at a blending of Western, Hindu and Islamic tradition to produce a new distinctive British imperial style.

In plan, the low density British civil city, was often, as in the case of Delhi, built adjacent to an existing walled, high density Indian city with the rulers' citadel. The separate and extensive military cantonments, and railway settlements added to the physical and social complexity of the plan. The cities also reflected the fact that the British colonial population was essentially transient, living in housing provided by their positions. Officials, army officers, businessmen and their families worked in India for the length of their careers and then returned to retire in England. There was thus no permanent settler community to add to the problems of the country once the transfer of power had been achieved.

In South Africa, in contrast, the European population regarded itself as a permanent settler community, which controlled most of the land resources and administered the cities, although it did not constitute more than one-fifth of the total population. The cities were thus built, in the words of the Transvaal Local Government Commission of 1922, as 'the domain of the White man' (Transvaal, 1922, p. 42). Although most of the towns were British colonial foundations, there was little of the grand planning or architecture which seen in India (Haswell, 1979). The parliamentary buildings in both Cape Town and Pietermaritzburg were fitted into the basic town grid. In Pretoria, the republican government before 1900 attempted to produce an individual style to counter British influence, but it was short-lived (Picton-Seymour, 1977). Sir Herbert Baker's Union Buildings in Pretoria were the forerunner of his larger Secretariat Buildings in New Delhi, but there was no accompanying grand town planning (Keath, 1992). No equivalent of New Delhi, Ottawa or Canberra was built in South Africa to proclaim the identity of the new state.

As in India, South African cities were planned for multi-ethnic populations, with segregated residential areas. Colonial town plans included African 'locations', even Asiatic 'bazaars' in addition to the 'White town'. Similarly, colonial town planning was not inflexible and segregation was not complete (Christopher, 2001b; Davies, 1981). The separate quarters were accentuated in the apartheid era when an attempt was made to completely segregate between the different legally defined population groups. After the Second World War, the town planning controls introduced in England were copied in South Africa, with racial zoning just one of the many aspects of the planning process (Mabin and Smit, 1997). The government devoted forty years to this project, producing distinctive South African cities by the time of the transfer of power in 1994. The process has been described as akin to 'undoing the colonial city', recognizing the essential pragmatism of the colonial enterprise (Western, 1985).

In both India and South Africa post-colonial societies and governments have had to live within physical structures planned and built by the colonial power. The various sectors presented even after the racial connotations had been abolished. Thus the park-like landscapes of the former European suburbs are in marked contrast to the crowding of the poorer indigenous areas. The military cantonments remain one of the least changed urban landscapes of the colonial era. The imprint of segregation is clearly evident in the spatial layout of the cities. Subsequent extension has done little to obliterate the colonial form, although socio-economic class may have replaced race as the primary identifier.

## THE CENSUS

The bureaucracy established throughout the British Empire remains one of the monuments to colonial rule. The detailed recording and regulation of many aspects of people's lives as an act of government was entrenched and retained in post-colonial times. One of the most significant innovations was the introduction of detailed scientific censuses which remain an integral part of government control. Furthermore, the census was intended to be comprehensive, counting people throughout the Empire, whether directly ruled or subject to princely or indirect rule. The census was effectively part of the process of shaping the nation. In control were officials who sought to define an imperial identity, imparting wherever possible a sense of cohesion and uniformity to the Empirewide censuses (Newbury, 1984). Census taking was introduced comparatively late in the two countries. Censuses were taken in various parts of India from 1851 with the first comprehensive Indian census undertaken in 1872. In South Africa, colonial censuses began in 1865, but only in 1904 was the first comprehensive census covering the whole country completed.

Census commissioners were concerned with far more than simple headcounts. The diversity of population in the Empire was seen as an ethnographic challenge to record and describe and for the government to administer and exploit. The degree of diversity was a source of pride to census commissioners (Maheshwari, 1996). The Calcutta Commissioner noted 'It is no exaggeration of language to describe the population of Calcutta and suburbs as an agglomeration of races' (*Census of India, 1911*, 1913, p. 41).

However, as Barrier (1981, p. 75) observed, 'Individuals find themselves firmly fixed as members in various groups of a particular dimension and substance. Thus the census imposes order, and order of a statistical nature. In time the creation of a new ordering of society by the census will act to reshape that which the census sought to merely describe'. The Indian census of 1881 sought to disentangle the concept of caste, and define and order them. Some 11,645 castes and subcastes were distinguished, resulting in a reassessment of the nature of caste in Indian intellectual circles (Mohanty and Momin, 1996). It is notable that the Mandal Commission in the 1980s had to consult the 1931 colonial census data to distinguish caste as the post-Independence censuses considered the issue as too divisive (*Census of India, Volume VI Calcutta City*, 1954).

Colonial censuses were generally concerned with the enumeration of the European or White population, as representing the colonial power. In India and South Africa, the enumeration pursued different lines of enquiry reflecting the different positions of the communities involved. South Africa was viewed by the pre-1994 governments as an essentially white settler country. The number of whites or Europeans was, therefore, of prime concern to census takers. The Cape of Good Hope in 1865 and all subsequent censuses recorded the European population separately from indigenous peoples and those of mixed parentage. Subsequent enumerations introduced more complex classification systems, although none were as probing as those in India. The matter of who qualified as a European 'of pure descent' was central to the electoral process of the country (South Africa, 1923). Later provisions of the Population Registration Act (1950), administered by the Director of Census and Statistics, determined the race of everyone in the country and these were recorded in the censuses permitting the effects of government policies to be duly monitored. The four-fold racial classification survived the demise of apartheid and is recorded by the present government to monitor the effectiveness of the Employment Equity Act (1998).

In India the quest to record 'Europeans and Allied Races' in the 1901 census included the small Eurasian community (India, 1902). The attempt to determine the number of Europeans in the 1911 census was not repeated because of opposition from the mixed Anglo-Indian community (*Census of India, 1911*, 1913) There was an official acceptance of religion as the major identifier of the population. Detailed enumerations from small blocks to districts assumed greater significance as local political parties sought to gain advantage. Indeed, the figures of both Hindus and Muslims were believed to have been boosted by the two communities in the 1941 census for political purposes (*Census of India, Volume VI Calcutta City*, 1954). The census results were employed in the definition of the Partition lines between India and Pakistan in 1947.

The colonial and subsequent censuses provided the spatial information for government policy—in both the making and monitoring of those policies. The wealth of detail included in the questionnaires make the censuses the primary sources for understanding the diversity of the population of both countries. The retention of population classification though is a direct inheritance of the colonial era.

## CONCLUSION

British administrators, soldiers, merchants, and a host of others contributed to the development of a single polity prior to the 1930s. Within this political arena a wide range of similarities were developed loosely controlled by the centre in London. Although local conditions differed markedly, the education and training of the various players in the colonial enterprise resulted in an attempt to impose similar solutions in a wide variety of social and physical environments. Indeed, the experiences gained in one colony were applied to another as the imperial civil servants and others were transferred within the Empire. British products and preferences ensured a certain uniformity and resulted in the emergence of distinct imperial modes of operation and landscapes. This political edifice was dismantled more than forty years ago. It is hardly surprising that the memory of its existence has been blurred or erased. Nevertheless, it is necessary to remember the basic unity of the enterprise to appreciate why things were done the way they were and why places look the way they do. Here lies the essence of basic historical geography on a global scale.

## REFERENCES

Ashton, S.R., *British Policy towards the Indian States 1905-1939*, London: Curzon Press, 1982.

Barrier, N.G., *The Census in British India*, New Delhi: Manohar, 1981.

Bell, M., Butlin, R. and Heffernan, M., *Geography and Imperialism 1820-1940,* Manchester: Manchester University Press, 1995.

Breton, R. J.-L., *Atlas of the Languages and Ethnic Communities of South Asia*, New Delhi: Sage, 1997.

Cameron, I., *To the Farthest Ends of the Earth*, London: Macdonald, 1980.

*Census of India 1911: Volume VI Calcutta City*, Calcutta: Bengal Secretariat Book Depot, 1913.

*Census of India: Volume VI Calcutta City*, New Delhi: Manager of Publications, 1954.

Chaudhuri, N.C., *A Passage to England*, London: Macmillan, 1959.

Christopher, A.J., 'From Flint to Soweto: Reflections on the Colonial Origins of the Apartheid City', *Area*, vol. 15, 1983, pp. 145-9.

———, *The British Empire at its Zenith,* London: Croom Helm, 1988.

———, 'Urban Segregation Levels in the British Overseas Empire and Its Successors in the Twentieth Century', *Transactions of the Institute of British Geographers*, vol. 17, 1992, pp. 95-107.

———, 'Regionalisation and Ethnicity in South Africa 1990-1994', *Area*, vol. 27, pp. 1-11.

———, 'Regional Patterns in South Africa's Postapartheid Election in 1994', *Environment and Planning C: Government and Policy*, vol. 14, 1996, pp. 55-69.

———, *The Atlas of States: Global Change 1900-2000*, Chichester: John Wiley, 1999.

———, *The Atlas of Changing South Africa*, London: Routledge, 2001a.

———, 'Monitoring Segregation Levels in South African Cities 1911-1996', *South African Geographical Journal*, vol. 83, 2001b, pp. 249-57.

Claval, P., 'The European System of Capital Cities', *GeoJournal*, vol. 51, 2000, pp. 73-81.

Corbridge, S., 'Ousting Singbonga: The Struggle for India's Jharkhand', in *Colonialism and Development in the Contemporary World*, ed. C. Dixon, and M. Heffernan, London: Mansell, 1991, pp. 153-82.

Davidson, B., *The Black Man's Burden: Africa and the Curse of the Nation-State*, Oxford: James Currey, 1992.

Davies, P., *Splendours of the Raj: British Architecture in India, 1660 to 1947*, London: John Murray, 1985.

Davies, R.J., 'The Spatial Formation of the South African City', *Geojournal* (Supplementary Issue), vol. 2, 1981, pp. 59-72.

Demangeon, A., *The British Empire, A Study in Colonial Geography*, London: George Harrap, 1925.

Dikshit, R.D., *The Political Geography of Federalism: An Inquiry into Origins and Stability*, London: Macmillan, 1975.

———, 'The World Systems Theory of Elections and the Crucial Case of Liberal Democracy in India', in *Developments in Political Geography: A Century of Progress*, ed. R.D. Dikshit, New Delhi: Sage, 1997, 226-41.

Edney, M.H., *Mapping an Empire: The Geographical Construction of British India 1765-1843*, Chicago: University of Chicago Press, 1997.

Ehrlich, C., 'Building and Caretaking: Economic Policy in British Tropical Africa 1890-1960', *Economic History Review*, Second Series, vol. 26, 1973, pp. 649-67.

Fawcett, C.B., *A Political Geography of the British Empire*, London: University of London Press, 1933.

Gibb, R.A., 'Flexible integration in the "New" Southern Africa', *South African Geographical Journal*, vol. 80, 1998, pp. 43-51.

Gilmour, D., *Curzon*, London: Macmillan, 1995.

Godlewska, A. and N. Smith, *Geography and Empire*, Oxford: Blackwell, 1994.

Gopalakrishnan, R., *Political Geography of North-East India*, New York: Advent Books, 1990.

Hailey, Lord, *An African Survey*, London: Oxford University Press, 1938.

Harrison-Church, R., 'The Case for Colonial Geography', *Transactions of the Institute of British Geographers*, vol. 14, 1948, pp. 17-25.

Haswell, R.F., 'South African Towns on European Plans', *Geographical Magazine*, vol. 51, 1979, pp. 686-94.

*History of Indian Railways*, Simla: Government of India Press, 1945.

Hopkirk, P., *The Great Game: On Secret Service in High Asia*, Oxford: Oxford University Press, 1990.

Hyam, R., *The Failure of South African Expansion*, London: Macmillan, 1972.

Irving, R.G., *Indian Summer: Lutyens, Baker and Imperial Delhi*, New Haven: Yale University Press, 1981.

Keath, M., *Herbert Baker, Architecture and Idealism 1892-1913, The South African Years*, Gibraltar: Ashanti Publishing, 1992.

Khosa, M.M. and Muthien, Y.G., 'The Expert, the Public and the Politician: Regional Delimitation in South Africa', *South African Geographical Journal*, vol. 79, pp. 1-12.

Kibe, M.V., *The League of Nations and the Indian States*, Indore: Shree Gajanana, 1924.

King, A.D., *Colonial Urban Development: Culture, Social Power and Environment*, London: Routledge and Kegan Paul, 1976.

Lee, M.E., 'An Analysis of the Rhodesian Referendum 1922', *Rhodesian History*, vol. 8, 1977, pp. 71-98.

Lemon, A., 'Lesotho and the New South Africa: The Question of Incorporation', *Geographical Journal*, vol. 162, pp. 263-72.

Lucas, C.P., *Introduction to a Historical Geography of the British Colonies*, Oxford: Clarendon Press, 1887.

Mabin, A. and D. Smit, 'Reconstructing South Africa's Cities? The Making of Urban Planning 1900-2000', *Planning Perspectives*, vol. 12, 1997, pp. 193-223.

Maheshwari, S., *The Census Administration under the Raj and After*, New Delhi: Concept, 1996.

Mawdsley, E., 'Nonsecessionist Regionalism in India: The Uttarakhand Separate State Movement', *Environment and Planning*, vol. A 29, pp. 2217-35.

Mehra, P., *The McMahon Line and After: A Study of the Triangular Contest on India's North-eastern Frontier between Britain, China and Tibet*, London: Macmillan, 1974.

Mehra, P., *Agreed Frontier: Ladakh and India's Northernmost Borders 1846-1947*, New Delhi, South Asia Books, 1992.

Menon, V.P., *The Transfer of Power in India*, London: Longmans Green, 1957.

Mohanty, S.P. and A.R. Momin, *Census as Social Document*, Jaipur: Rawat Publications, 1996.

Muthien, Y.G. and Khosa, M.M., 'The Kingdom, the Volkstaat and the new South Africa, Drawing South Africa's New Regional Boundaries', *Journal of Southern African Studies*, vol. 21, 1995, pp. 303-22.

Newbury, C., 'The March of Everyman: Mobility and the Imperial Census of 1901', *Journal of Imperial and Commonwealth History*, vol. 12, pp. 80-101.

Parker, W.H., *Mackinder: Geography as an Aid to Statecraft*, Oxford: Clarendon Press, 1982.

Picton-Seymour, D., *Victorian Buildings in South Africa, Including Edwardian and Transvaal Republican Styles 1850-1910*, Cape Town: A.A. Balkema, 1977.

Pruthi, R. and R. Devi, *British Colonial Policy towards Indian States*, Jaipur: Pointer Publishers, 1998.

*Report of the States Reorganization Commission*, New Delhi: Manager of Publications, 1955.

Schofield, V., *Kashmir in the Crossfire*, London: I.B. Tauris, 1996.

South Africa, *Census of Population 1921*, Pretoria: Government Printer, 1923.

Stamp, G., 'British Architecture in India 1857-1947', *Journal of the Royal Society of Arts*, vol. 129, 1981, pp. 357-79.

Steel, R.W., 'Geography and the Commonwealth in a Changing World: A Silver Jubilee Overview', in *Global Change and the Commonwealth*, ed. Y.-M. Yeung, Hong Kong: Chinese University of Hong Kong, 1996, pp. 3-24.

Tomlinson, B.R., *The Political Economy of the Raj 1914-1947*, London: Macmillan, 1979.

Transvaal, *Report of the Transvaal Local Government Commission, TP1-1922*, Pretoria: Government Printer, 1922.

Western, J., 'Undoing the Colonial City?', *Geographical Review*, vol. 75, 1985, pp. 335-57.

CHAPTER 6

# From a Privileged to an Unwanted Minority: The Asian[1] Diaspora in Africa

BRIJ MAHARAJ

## INTRODUCTION

With a presence in more than 100 countries, the Indian diaspora may be regarded as a global phenomenon with roots in the colonial domination by the British (as well as the Dutch and the French to a lesser extent) and the exploitation of cheap indentured labour from the Asian subcontinent in different parts of the colonial empire. Tinker (1974) appropriately referred to this indentured labour as a 'new system of slavery'. In spite of such humble beginnings, Indians in the diaspora have prospered to the extent that they have been a sense of much envy, tension and conflict in their adopted countries. The Indian experience in Africa has been no different. Drawing from available published literature, this paper examines the social, economic and political dynamics associated with the Indian presence in East Africa.

This paper illustrates that in the colonial, post-colonial and contemporary eras, Asians in East Africa have primarily played the role of middleman minorities, often being portrayed as scapegoats and villains in times of economic and political crisis. Rather than engaging with the African majority, Asians tended to retreat into their cultural shells. This paper is divided into three major sections. The first section focuses on Asians in pre-colonial Africa. This is followed by an analysis of colonial dynamics with specific reference to pioneer traders, Asian-European conflicts, protest and resistance, socio-cultural isolation and racism. Post-colonial dynamics is the theme of the third section, including an analysis of Africanization of the economy, citizenship and expulsion, and economic liberalization and pragmatism.

## ASIANS IN PRE-COLONIAL AFRICA

The presence of Asians in Africa is commonly associated with the arrival of traders and indentured labour at the turn of the twentieth century. However, archaeological and documentary sources reveal that the Indian presence in Africa pre-dates the arrival of Europeans by almost 3,000 years (Hromnik, 1981). India had ancient commercial ties with East Africa through the Indian Ocean trading network. This was facilitated partly by geographical proximity and the monsoon winds. From their modest origins as 'seasonal traders they had developed a vast network of commerce throughout the region' (Desai, 1989, p. 38). They inhabited the coast after the Arabs established trading colonies during the AD 800 to 1500 period (Yambert, 1981).

Unlike Arab traders, they neither attempted to dominate the region politically nor married local women (Bujra, 1992). Furthermore, Indians did not 'appear to have established any comparable or permanent settlements in the region' (Mangat, 1969, p. 1). The majority of Asian immigrants to East Africa were Hindu and Muslim Gujaratis. In 1886 the apportionment of East Africa and the ensuing expansion into the interior under colonial government radically changed the traditional Asian connection in this region. It was only from the 1890s with the arrival of indentured labourers and voluntary migrants that Indians began to make a major social, economic and political impact in East Africa (Mangat, 1969).

## COLONIAL DYNAMICS

The British colonial government required efficient administrators in East Africa. A readily available pool of trained civil servants who were familiar with the British administrative system was available in colonial India. A significant number of Indian immigrants including administrative officials, customs officers and police were recruited from India and deployed to various locations in the interior and coast of East Africa (Desai, 1989; Gregory, 1993).

One of the first projects initiated by the English colonists was the construction of the East African Railway line. Between 1896 and 1903, 31,983 indentured labourers were recruited from India to construct the 562 mile long Ugandan railway line (Jain, 1989, p. 45). The indentured labourers came from Uttar Pradesh, Bihar and Madras. It has been 'estimated that for every mile of railroad built, four Asian labourers lost their lives' (Mampilly, 2000, p. 2). Only one-fourth of them remained after their period of indenture had expired.

The construction of the railway line was associated with 'the transplantation of the institutions of British India: British Indian laws, Indian police, Indian postal and currency systems and Indian administrative practices' (Jain, 1989, p. 45). The construction of the Ugandan railway line played a key role in encouraging voluntary immigration from India. The voluntary migrants, comprising traders, artisans and professionals, were Hindus, Muslims, Sikhs and Christians from Gujarat, Punjab and Goa. In 1896, the Protector of Emigrants reported in Bombay:

> The people are flocking to Africa of their own free will, at their own expense, and on the chance of doing better there . . . many classes and professions are represented in the exodus . . . numbers of Indians are going to East African ports, not as emigrants, but as adventurers. If I may venture to call them so . . . many have embarked for Mombasa . . . in the hope of finding work on the Uganda Railway, or in connection with the trade and wants that will spring up with the railway construction. (Mangat, 1969, p. 48)

The British colonial government, the expansion of the railways, as well as the labour demands of foreign industry undermined African traditional communal lifestyles through the introduction of a monetary economy. This was followed by the arrival of the 'legendary Indian dukawallahs' (Tandon and Raphael, 1973, p. 4).

## Pioneer Traders

Most of the Indians were pioneering merchants who followed the expansion of the railway lines or relocated to newly established trading centres in rural areas. In many ways they were the authentic initiators of Indian mercantile ventures in the interior of East Africa, pioneering the establishment and expansion of trading activities (Desai, 1989). Given the foreign, and sometimes hostile environment, this required extraordinary endurance and tenacity. Sir Winston Churchill, who was Under Secretary in the Colonial Office, aptly described the role of Asians in opening the rural hinterland of East Africa at the turn of the twentieth century,

> It was a Sikh soldier who bore an honourable part in the conquest and pacification of East African countries. It is the Indian trader, who is, penetrating and maintaining himself in all sorts of places to which no white man could

earn a living, has more than anyone else developed the early beginnings of trade and opened up the first slender means of communications. It was by Indian labour that one vital railway on which everything else depends was constructed. It is the Indian banker who supplies the large part of the capital yet available. (cited in Desai, 1989, p. 39)

The success of the Asian traders was phenomenal. This was attributed largely to their determination to work hard and succeeds business acumen and ability to identify markets. These markets ranged from the urban to rural trading outposts, maximizing connections with India, and utilizing family labour. Cumulatively, these factors, contributed significantly to the ability of Indians to compete successfully against white traders (Ghai and Ghai, 1965; Jain, 1989).

The general economic success and prosperity of the immigrants, as well as their ability to overcome almost impossible odds, generated a great deal of envy, bitterness and anti-Indian sentiments amongst whites. Whites were guilty of racial prejudice against Indians, feared economic competition from them, and were also concerned about their rapid population increase that was perceived as a political threat. This anti-Indian agitation began in the 1890s in Kenya.

That Indians were perceived to be an economic threat to Europeans was reflected in virtually pathological racial prejudices. In 1897, Indians were stereotyped racially as 'crafty, money-making, cunning, intensely polite, his soul bound to his body by one laudable and religious anxiety of its helping him to turn his coin to better advantage' (Mangat, 1969, p. 22).

## Asian-European Tensions

A conspicuous characteristic of colonial government in East Africa was the segmentation of society into three distinct racial groups—white, Asian and African. This division was 'reinforced by economic, social and political discrimination and segregation' (Ghai and Ghai, 1965, p. 35).

Colonial administrators emphasized racial separation between Whites, Indians and Africans. More specifically, the colonial racial hierarchy

> encouraged Asian merchants, traders and civil servants to occupy a middle rung in the social hierarchy, with Europeans at the top and Africans at the bottom. In the economic sphere Asians dominated commercial activity while Africans were discouraged from participating in commerce by the Credit to Natives Ordinance of 1931. (Nagar and Leitner, 1998, p. 231)

Colonial society was structured on racial lines and was characterized by segregation and discrimination. Whites had the best economic, educational and residential opportunities, followed by Asians, while Africans had the worst facilities. Asian traders purchased agricultural commodities from Africans and sold imported manufactured products to them. The civil service was staffed by a disproportionately large number of Asians (Nagar and Leitner, 1998).

The colonial authorities did little to encourage racial cooperation. As a result of residential segregation, the different groups were ignorant of each other's social and cultural values, and racial prejudices and stereotypes were entrenched (Spencer, 1981). Consequently, the 'legacy of British imperialism was thus one of racial suspicion and misunderstandings, of antagonism rather than co-operation' (Ghai and Ghai, 1971, p. 8).

In the first two decades of the twentieth century a new idea began to emerge that East Africa was European territory. The growing prosperity of the Asian communities posed a major challenge to the economic status of whites. Economic competition between the two communities began to increase, initially focusing on access to land (Duder, 1989). The white settlers often used 'political pressures to achieve economic ends and increasingly demanded restrictions on Indian immigration and imposition of various legal and administrative disabilities to restrict the Indian role' (Desai, 1989, p. 40).

The biggest European grouse about Asians included: their unsanitary habits; they reduced the value of their dwellings and neighbourhood; they engaged in unfair trading practices and were therefore able to undersell European traders and reduce their employment opportunities; and they sent their capital out of the country.

Basically, there was a conflict between white and Indian capital which was expressed in racial terms. During this period trade was not only the main economic activity of local whites, but was also a symbol of their social status. Indian merchants challenged white economic hegemony and status and the latter responded to this threat in racial terms.

These prejudices were transformed into policies, which limited their access to land as well as trading opportunities. There is little doubt that the various restrictions on Indian land tenure were ultimately conceived to curb their economic expansion. Associated with this were restrictions on trading licences. The basic aim was to inhibit the development of an Indian bourgeoisie. In Kenya, Indians were opposed to 'various colonial policies regarding immigration, segregation, education and political representation . . . Indians demanded racial equality in such matters as land ownership, immigration, accessibility to higher posts in the government, etc.' (Jain, 1989, p. 47).

As racial and ethnic tensions and conflict began to escalate in East Africa, the colonial administrators were initially compassionate towards the plight of the Asians. The view of Sir Winston Churchill from the Colonial Office was symptomatic:

> The Indian was here long before the British Official. He may point to many generations of useful industry on the coast and inland. . . . Is it possible for any government, with a scrap of respect for honest dealing between man and man, to embark on a policy of deliberately squeezing out the native of India from regions in which he established himself under every security of public faith. (Desai, 1989, p. 40)

In spite of these sentiments, white settlers continued to agitate against Indians and pressurized the colonial administration to restrict the land and trading opportunities of Asians in East Africa. Consequently, during the 1930s, the rights of Indians to engage in trade outside major urban centres were curtailed in East Africa. In the 1940s, unrestricted immigration from India to East Africa was no longer permitted (Twaddle, 1990, p. 156). Restrictions on Asian immigration were initially presented as an attempt to preserve white supremacy, and subsequently as an ostensible effort to protect the Africans (Ghai and Ghai, 1971).

Hostility toward Indian traders stemmed from economic grievances but was often expressed by exhibiting contempt for their social and cultural practices. Europeans and Africans frequently complained about the overcrowded and unsanitary conditions under which Indians lived (Power, 1993). The whites promulgated and gave credence to the conventional view of the Asians as a people who:

> exploited the illiterate Africans; who prevented their progress by occupying all the jobs to which the African aspired; whose social and religious influences were undesirable; and whose culture and religion were backward, obscurantist and unwholesome . . . many of these European attitudes were 'assimilated and internalised' by the Africans. (Desai, 1989, p. 40)

## Protest, Resistance and Acquiescence

Despite intermittent protests, Asians were generally inclined to comply with the colonial order for numerous reasons. The racial stratification of the colonial order (economic, social and spatial) enabled the Asians to identify their occupations and roles within the hierarchy. This was because as immigrants they were uncertain of their privileges and rank, and were presumably thankful to be spared the tensions associated with racial strife, especially competition from the local African population (Ghai and Ghai, 1965; 1970; Gregory, 1981).

Socially, the colonial segregated system suited the Asian character as they were very conservative, and preferred to be left alone to follow and maintain their own religion and culture (Desai, 1989; Ghai and Ghai, 1965). They were politically isolated in East Africa because of their tendency to be socially exclusive.

Another reason for their acquiescence to the colonial order was their low level of political awareness. There was also a realization that they were unable to exert any political influence in East Africa. Many Asians believed that there was 'safety in low visibility and that the absence of involvement in politics will serve to remove them from controversy and factionalism' (Ghai and Ghai, 1971, p. 33). However, 'the lack of a record of active, large-scale Asian opposition to the colonial system has been regarded by many African nationalist leaders as an instance of Asian complicity with the imperialists' (Ghai and Ghai, 1965, p. 36).

However, there were some attempts to forge alliances with African resistance movements in order to reduce the political isolation experienced by Asians. For example, M.A. Desai, editor of the *East African Chronicle*, regularly published African grievances relating to land, labour and wages. He also published articles in Swahili for Harry Thuku who, in many ways is regarded as the founder of African nationalism in Kenya. The *Muiguithano* edited by Jomo Kenyatta was also published with Indian support (Desai, 1989). Such initiatives emerged from the realization that 'if the Asians can integrate effectively at the political level, then many of their social and political problems will be dealt with more sympathetically and successfully' (Ghai and Ghai, 1965, p. 45).

There were also some radical Indian activists who played a key role in influencing the development of African nationalism. The most well known among them was Makhan Singh who founded the Labour Trade Union of East Africa in 1936 (Desai, 1989). He led the 1939 Mombasa dock workers' strike (Jain, 1989). However, there was hardly a close working relationship with African politicians and there was little strategic cooperation in terms of tactics to challenge imperial domination (Ghai and Ghai, 1970; 1971).

At the macro level, political relations between Africans and Indians were strained, and there was no evidence of mass-based support for

African nationalism from the Asian community. Their somewhat privileged class position did not allow them to fully identify with African nationalism and therefore did not earn them any significant degree of political legitimacy and respect in African eyes (Jain, 1989, p. 48). Also, African populations who courted Asian support were not popular with the indigenous people (Ghai and Ghai, 1971).

It is important to view the Asian political stance in perspective. While political organizations pledged solidarity with the African cause, the Asian community was ambivalent about the expectations of the new era. Asian leaders who emphasized the need to support the African majority were often unpopular amongst locals. Similarly, African politicians who courted Asian support were not popular with the indigenous people (Ghai and Ghai, 1971). However, as the negotiations for independence advanced in the early 1960s, the impact of Asian patronage became largely academic.

In the final analysis, the Asian contribution to the struggle for independence in East Asia 'may seem less in the support given to Africans than in the willingness to forego special minority provisions' (Ghai and Ghai, 1971, p. 13). As independence from colonial rule became imminent, there was an increasing realization among Asians that their position of relative privilege in the economic and social hierarchy could be threatened (Tandon and Raphael, 1973).

The growth of African nationalism simultaneously led to the decline of the political influence of Asians. Africans became increasingly bitter and angry because of the dominance of Indians in the economic sector. By the mid-1950s, the colonial authorities advocated 'measures to develop a class of African traders and entrepreneurs which inevitably began to compete with its Indian counterpart. However, this intra-class competition was not fully crystallised until after . . . independence' (Jain, 1989, p. 48).

As political independence became imminent, there were many misgivings and 'the Asians faced critical choices. The Asian community was ill-prepared to meet' (Desai, 1989, p. 41). By the time East Africa attained independence Indians were a dominant force in the economy but were insulated as a community and marginalized politically.

### Socio-cultural Isolation and Racism

The nature of colonial social organization in East Africa was based on strict racial lines. This inevitably generated practices and attitudes that were antagonistic, and opposed to any form of inter-racial interaction.

Asians were especially isolated from other races (Ghai and Ghai, 1965). Asian ethnic identities were influenced by segregation, economic competition and the need to preserve their culture in a hostile environment:

> A collective sense of ethnic identity has been cultivated by, and imposed on, communities of . . . Asians in their various colonial and post-colonial contexts. Competition for control over resources, geographical segregation, political organization, and efforts to maintain cultural traditions in an alien milieu are some of the important elements contributing to the migrant communities' development. (Clarke, Peach and Vertovec, 1990, p. 15)

While the colonial state fostered a collective Asian identity from above, this was reinforced by impulses emanating from within the Asian community itself. Caught between an antagonistic colonial minority government and the fear of the African masses, the Asians confirmed their cultural identity: 'Socio-cultural isolation, as the result of resistance to assimilation, is the common theme of almost all the histories. Indians because of their phobia of losing cultural identity tend to be over-religious, rigid, conservative, orthodox, close and restrictive . . . (Motwani and Motwani, 1989, p. 3).

This has been emphasized by other academic commentators on Asians in East Africa:

> The Asians wanted to be left alone to pursue their own traditional ways. Laws were enacted in East Africa for the application of personal, religious laws, e.g. marriage, divorce, succession, to the Asian religious communities. This helped not only to preserve the cultural identity of these communities, but also put obstacles in the way of inter-communal and inter-racial contacts. In addition, the Asians, by and large, continued to maintain links with their countries of origin . . . immigrants tended to come from certain specified regions of India, the Punjab and Gujarat . . . the effect of all this was to make the Asians a self-sufficient, ethnocentric community. (Ghai, 1975, p. 132 cited in Twaddle, 1990, p. 155)

As cultural dependence on India increased, there was an 'erosion of independent Asian will and initiative in Africa' (Gupta, 1975, p. 126).

African perceptions of Asians originated largely in the context of colonial society (Desai, 1989). For example, 'most Asian-African relationships have been at the shopkeeper-customer or master-servant level', which were unlikely to support interracial relations (Ghai and Ghai, 1965, p. 47). Also, many Asian cultural and social organizations were exclusive. Although Africans knew much about, and were often drawn to European culture, they were ignorant of the Asian way of life (Ghai and Ghai, 1965).

It is important to note that the Asian community was not homogeneous, but was fractured by religious, language and caste identities (Morris, 1957). As British domination came to an end, these divisions and 'communalist zealotry' were the 'despair of individual South Asians locally seeking to establish working relationships with the new African political leaders' (Twaddle, 1990, p. 155).

The negative perceptions of Asians were influenced by three considerations:

1. There is adequate evidence that the colonial rulers had orchestrated anti-Asian attitudes.
2. Asians were manipulated to act as middlemen and serve British interests. Inevitably, they became the scapegoats for colonial exploitation.
3. Their social and cultural customs generated anti-Asian attitudes amongst Africans (Desai, 1989).

The cultural pride of Asians and a 'sense of racial superiority *vis-à-vis* the Africans were at times as bad as that of the Europeans' (Tandon and Raphael, 1973, p. 15). This cultural detachment of Asians from the African mainstream has 'indirectly invited or contributed to racial discrimination by the natives against Indians, which has later turned into racial atrocity in several countries after their independence' (Motwani and Motwani, 1989, p. 3). In the post-colonial era Asians 'stood out as discordant, unassimilable citadels of exclusiveness' (Bhatia, 1973, p. 18). A major challenge facing the survival of Asians in Africa was to bridge and transcend this cultural divide (Bushan, 1989). An Asian leader commented that tensions in Indo-African relations must be seen in the national and regional contexts: 'I do not see resentment against Asian Africans out of the overall national context, that is, it is not any different from resentment of one tribe against another in the context of poverty, inequalities, power games, corruption and lack of pluralism' (Mampilly, 2000, p. 3).

## POST-COLONIAL TRENDS

After Independence, the colonial racial divisions and associated advantages accruing to Asians were challenged in various ways. There was large scale Africanization in the civil service and many Asians lost their positions, or their promotion opportunities were restricted. For example, in Kenya there was a decline to the tune of over 3,000 Indian civil servants from 11,900 in 1963, to 8,800 in 1964 (Jain, 1989, p. 49).

As East African states attained independence, the Asian minority found itself in a vulnerable predicament. Their former position of privilege under the colonial regime became a disadvantage as 'new nationalistic governments tried to put their colonial experience behind them and place political and economic power in the hands of native citizens' (Yambert, 1989, p. 189).

Following independence, ethnic tensions and conflict surfaced in East Africa. This was partly related to the characteristic exclusiveness of the Asian population: 'its wealth, urban concentration, retention of exotic cultural traits, and its physical distinctiveness' (Yambert, 1981, p. 189). Moreover, Asians were often ahead of the local African population in the occupational hierarchy.

However, the Asian supremacy in the private sector was as 'much thrust upon them as deliberately chosen because of restricted openings in the government sector' (Delf, 1963, p. 45). There were restrictions on their ability to invest in property. Their career options were confined to low-level jobs in the public sector and to 'reinvestment in their small businesses. In this way the Asians formed a middle class of white collar workers, traders, and urban merchants' (Yambert, 1981, p. 188). When the African's great expectations of upward mobility were frustrated, Asian 'middlemen' were identified as obstacles to the realization of their aspirations.

The Asian minority was blamed for the ills of East Africa and was periodically subjected to threats of violence, dispossession and expulsion:

> The former close association of alien merchants with colonial regimes, their continued identification with their homelands, the drain of resources represented by the money they ship abroad, and their defensive ethnicity under stress, all generate suspicion and hostility among the natives. . . . Aliens must chose from what are often undesirable choices: return to a homeland that many have never seen, having been born and raised in a host country; remain where they are as aliens subject to harassment; or apply, for citizenship in the new nation even though full citizenship rights are difficult to attain. (Yambert, 1981, p. 191)

The experience of East Africa reveals that as an aspiring indigenous bourgeoisie emerges, they often incite locals against foreign traders and benefit from the conflict. For example, the first significant boycott against Asian traders in Uganda occurred in 1959, and was influenced by a Muganda businessman, Augustine Kamya. The boycott continued for seven months. The emerging Baganda businessmen profited most from the boycott as they assumed control of Asian stores and transport. Nearly 10,000 workers who supported the boycott found to their dismay that they were unemployed once it was called off. Characteristically, the 'petty bourgeoisie was rising up on the backs of the workers and the peasant' (Tandon and Raphael, 1973, p. 9).

### Africanization of the Economy

Asians dominated the economy of East Africa and virtually monopolized the wholesale and retail trade. The economic power of Asians was seen as an obstacle to the upward mobility of Africans. It has been argued that Africans found it easier to accept the high salaries of whites compared to Indians because:

> it is European power and culture which attracts the African. European success is a target to emulate. The Asian is easily regarded as a foreign competitor who has nothing worthwhile to offer in return for his presence. In trade and in the public services it is the Asian who often occupies the job immediately ahead of the African. A picture is easily built up of a community, which uses its close-knit family and trading relationships to keep down competition. (Delf, 1963, p. 65)

There have been accusations that Asians have obstructed the economic progress of Africans. There is no doubt that the 'presence of a large, economically sophisticated community has had the effect of retarding African participation in the commercial sectors of the economy' (Ghai and Ghai, 1965, p. 41). However, the corollary that the absence of Asians would have ensured a higher income and better quality of life for Africans is not necessarily true. It is important to recognize that the 'Asians have made a vital contribution to economic development; it is difficult to believe that East Africa would have developed to anything like its present level without the full and active economic participation of Asians' (Ghai and Ghai, 1965, p. 41).

There has been some valid criticism that Asian businesses have not actively supported the policy of Africanization. This is because Asians were primarily concerned with their own economic survival, and did not focus on the issue of economic opportunities for Africans. While some Africans did acquire skills and experience from working for Asians, this was not the result of any deliberate strategy to empower Africans. This was mainly because Asian businesses were generally small and family owned. Invariably, the 'employment of Africans in "responsible" positions would have meant a loss of jobs for some members of the family—something very few Asians are prepared to accept' (Ghai and Ghai, 1965, p. 41).

However, as the pressure from African leaders increased, many Asians formed business partnerships with locals. Large Asian firms have also introduced Africanization policies. For example, in 1964, the (Asian) Dar es Salaam Merchants Chamber disclosed a far-reaching scheme to increase African participation in the economy. This included partnerships, provision of loans, commercial education and training, as well as the establishment of charitable trusts (Balachandran, 1981; King, 1975). Despite these progressive initiatives, there was a view that the 'Asian response to the need to increase the share of Africans in wholesale and retail trade has not been sufficiently swift or thoroughgoing' (Ghai and Ghai, 1965, p. 41). Also, such gestures were perceived as bribes intended to protect Asians after independence (Bharati, 1964).

While economic competition did adversely affect Asian-Africans relations, this would have been largely insignificant had there been an economic growth and expansion. This was because the competence and experience of the Asians would have been invaluable in an expanding economy. Delf emphasized:

> As ambition begins to founder in a stagnant economy that friction will develop . . . as wealth and employment contract, there forms an ebb tide in the social consciousness, exposing all the crude fears and eccentricities which are normally unseen. Societies which are confident can tolerate the existence in their midst of culturally distinct groups, but when things go wrong projected fear is quickly associated with any close and convenient scapegoat. (Delf, 1963, p. 65)

## Citizenship and Expulsion

A major issue following independence was that of citizenship. It has been argued that the 'independence constitutions made a generous provision for citizenship'. In terms of the scheme, Asians in Uganda, could automatically adopt local citizenship at the time of Independence, or had a choice to take citizenship within a specific period (two years), or retain the pre-Independence *status quo* (either Indian or British citizenship). The Asian response to the citizenship offer in the immediate post-Independence period was cautious, and most Asians adopted a 'wait and see' approach because of the political instability in the region, including army mutinies and civil wars (Table 6.1). Indians had also procrastinated over the issue because they were afraid that relinquishing British or Indian citizenship would mean that they would have no protection if there was confiscation or nationalization of property (Desai, 1989).

Towards the end of the two-year period of grace, there was a significant increase in applications for citizenship. Africans were concerned that Asians had been cogitating on the issue for too long and there was concern that 'many citizens were becoming citizens in order to avoid the adverse effects of Africanization; they were seen as opportunists and 'paper citizens' (Desai, 1989, p. 41).

Asian political organizations were keen to negotiate a special dispensation for Indians in the post-colonial era. For example, the Indian Congress in Kenya initially attempted to guarantee that the Asians would retain some elements of their privileged status after Independence. However, the younger members who were more radical forced the Indian Congress to extend total support to an African government 'based on

TABLE 6.1: ASIANS IN EAST AFRICA

| | | | | | |
|---|---|---|---|---|---|
| Kenya | Total Asian population | *c.* 1970 | 182,000 | *c.* 2000 | 100,000 |
| | Indian citizens | | 24,000 | | |
| | Kenyan citizens | | 70,000 | | |
| | British passport holders | | 82,000 | | |
| | Status to be determined | | 6,000 | | |
| Tanzania | Total Asian population | | 105,000 | | 90,000 |
| | Indian citizens | | 5,000 | | |
| | Tanzanian citizens | | 35,000 | | |
| | British passport holders | | 50,000 | | |
| | Stateless or status to be determined | | 12,000 | | |
| Uganda | Total Asian population | | 80,000 | | 7,500 |
| | Indian citizens | | 1,000 | | |
| | Uganda citizens | | 30,000 | | |
| | British passport holders | | 40,000 | | |
| | Stateless or status to be determined | | 9,000 | | |

*Sources*: Ghai and Ghai, 1971, p. 39, and High Level Committee on the Indian Diaspora, 2000 (www.indiaday.org/nri/singhvi.htm#1).

one man one vote, without any special provisions for minorities' (Ghai and Ghai, 1971, p. 12). In the critical phase of negotiations for Independence from Britain between 1960 and 1963, Asians supported the Africans. Although it initially vacillated, the Asian Association in Tanzania supported the Tanzania African National Union. The central councils of Indian and Muslim associations in Uganda backed the African nationalists led by the Uganda Action Group (Ghai and Ghai, 1971).

In December 1971, General Idi Amin of Uganda called a conference of Asians where he accused them of 'social exclusiveness, corruption and business malpractice of many kinds' (Tandon and Raphael, 1973, p. 13). On 4 August 1972, Amin ordered the expulsion of all 70,000 Asians from Uganda. The Asian community was shocked and the international community attempted to apply economic and political pressure on Amin to reverse his decision (Gupta, 1974; Mamdani, 1973; Patel, 1979; Twaddle, 1975).

Most African leaders did not publicly comment on Amin's actions, preferring the route of 'quiet diplomacy' to ameliorate the Asian problem. However, President Julius Nyerere of Tanzania and President Kenneth Kaunda of Zambia publicly condemned Amin's expulsion strategy:

> Within a few weeks of the first announcement of the expulsion in August, Nyerere called Amin a racist, and his Tanzanian government newspapers echoed him in defending the sacredness of citizenship regardless of race or tribe. Kenneth Kaunda . . . also denounced Amin's actions by saying 'what is happening in Uganda is terrible, horrible, abominable, and a shame to the whole human race'. (Melady and Melady, 1976, p. 15)

Amin distributed the businesses and other assets of Asians to his supporters. However, as pointed out by Mamdani (1993, p. 5) the expulsion of Indians and the acquisition of their property by Ugandans did not result in the creation of new wealth:

> By and large, wealth in post-1972 Uganda was more the result of 'falling into things' than investments. . . . Not only those with property, but even those without it, came to believe that you get rich not through creating new wealth but through political transfer of the already created wealth.

It has been argued that the expulsion of Asians from East Africa was inevitable because they had no power. The only concern was the way in which this mass exodus of Asians would take place. The African elite and the masses were keen to see their rapid departure. The only constraints were the international repercussions as well as the economic implications: 'Much as they wanted speedily to Africanise their economies, there were just not enough of the African middle class to take over from the Asians' (Tandon and Raphael, 1973, p. 15). The contradiction was that the 'economic development of East Africa depended very largely on the prosperity and satisfaction of the Indian trading population—a fact which necessarily made any government hesitant in carrying out a policy of restriction' (Morris, 1989, p. 57). This fact was clearly evident by the 1990s.

### 1990s: Economic Liberalization and Pragmatism

In 1989 the Kenyan government acknowledged that the: 'localization/Africanization/Kenyanization/indigenization policies had failed to achieve even modest success since 1964' (Himbara, 1993, p. 99). Not surprisingly, this was accompanied in the late 1980s and early 1990s by a gradual shift towards a more positive assessment and recognition of the role of the Asian community in East Africa. This shift in attitude was not based on philanthropic concerns. Against the background of a serious economic crisis, compounded by decades of corruption and mismanagement, governments were forced to develop partnerships with Asian business persons, in order to support reconstruction. This change in attitude towards Asians was significantly influenced by donor agencies, for example, the World Bank and the International Monetary Fund (IMF), which with their structural adjustment programmes (SAP), emphasized the importance of free market forces and the privatization of the public sector (Himbara, 1997; Himbara and Sultan, 1995). Consequently, Asian 'economic activity, ranging from small retail operations to large-scale industry has once again flourished in East Africa' (Himbara, 1997, p. 16).

This was most spectacularly illustrated in the case of Uganda, where the World Bank and the IMF insisted that a precondition for financial assistance was that businesses expropriated in 1972 be returned to the Asians. Furthermore, one of the important conditions influencing USAID policy towards Uganda was 'substantial progress on settling the Departed Asians' Property question (at least 50 percent of the property to be disposed off)' (Himbara, 1997, p. 16).

In Kenya, partnerships have been formed between the government, Asian and African businesses to assist in the process of economic reconstruction. The African urban elite benefits greatly from this coalition. However, this class coalition is opposed by the peasants, the working class and a small proportion of the commercial bourgeoisie:

> [T]he latter being particularly frustrated by the entrenched position of its Indian counterpart in the economy . . . (nevertheless) Indians in Kenya appear to be better placed than before. Their position in the given class structure of Kenya, however, continues to remain the source of their vulnerability as well as their strength. (Jain, 1989, p. 51)

This prosperity gave rise to yet another wave of anti-Asian sentiment in East Africa. Kenneth Matiba, an eminent Kenyan politician and entrepreneur, publicly declared that Kenya did not need the Asian commercial sector (Himbara, 1997, p. 2). In 1994 in Uganda, there was much debate about whether the properties expropriated from Asians in 1972 should be returned to them. There were allegations that the return of Asians to Uganda had increased the marginalization of Africans in cities. By 1996 there were reports of Asian businessmen being harassed by government officials. In Tanzania, Reverend Christopher Mtikila, leader of the Democratic Party asserted that the 'Tanzanian governing classes have given 98 per cent of the nation's cake to a mere 228,000 Asians and Arabs who turn around and loot the country' (Himbara, 1997, p. 3).

East Africa's development policy has tended to restrict the role of Asian capitalists of Indian ancestry, 'the most able domestic fraction of accumulators, on the mistaken notion that they constitute "Asian capital" of "Asians"' (Himbara, 1997, p. 1). The truth was that businessmen such as Madhvani were not 'out of India'; they were intrinsically African for two important reasons. First, they and their forefathers had lived in Africa for several generations. Second, most of their wealth was generated in East Africa (Himbara, 1993, p. 95).

While the economic worth of Asians has been recognized in an era of globalization and trade liberalization, Himbara concluded:

> [T]his does not constitute a lasting solution of the so-called 'Asian question'; the solution will have to be domestically derived, not only on the basis of economic value embodied in the East African Indian bourgeoisie. But on political and human rights grounds, given that the class in question and the community from which it comes are local or long-term residents. (Himbara, 1997, p. 2)

## CONCLUSION

The fortunes of Asians in East Africa have varied. While they were economically powerful, they had little or no political influence. They had no political ambitions and were passive. Although 'they have not lacked initiative and have sometimes resisted pressures, the history of the Asian communities is largely one of accommodation to the prevailing historical situation' (Ghai and Ghai, 1971, p. 5). As they attempted to adjust in an alien and hostile environment, they came into conflict initially with the colonial rulers and subsequently with the African majority. That their numbers in East Africa are dwindling is not surprising (see Table 6.1).

The nature of the colonial social formation in East Africa which resulted in the differential incorporation of the various racial groups, enjoying varying levels of rewards, set the stage for seeking a scapegoat and revenge for long-suffering misery. Africans perceived Asians as most obviously benefiting from this situation precisely because they played a 'middleman' role. These stereotypes provided a focal point for the rapid mobilization of Africans against Asians (Desai and Maharaj, 1996).

The distinguishing feature of middleman minorities is the economic role they play. Unlike most ethnic minorities, they occupy an intermediate rather than a low-status position. They are generally found in certain occupations, mainly trade and commerce, but also as labour contractors, rent collectors, moneylenders and brokers. They play the role of a middleman between producer and consumer, employer and employee, owner and tenant, elite and masses (Blalock, 1967).

Another important characteristic of middleman minorities is vulnerability. The role of a middleman is easily transformed into that of an 'economic villain' especially in times of economic crisis. As scapegoats, they often deflect hostility away from the superior status group. Raphael (1984, p. 19) observed that Asians in East Africa exist in a 'state of contained anxiety':

> They go about their daily lives with confidence and energy. But the old, nagging fears for the future remain. Prosperity has both eased and compounded their uncertainties. They may still be needed, yet are unwanted. And because they are unwanted, their loyalties are divided, which in turn makes them suspects in African eyes. It is a vicious cycle. Migration would break it, but that ultimate stage of despair has not been reached, assuming continued regional stability.

This argument continues to be relevant in the contemporary era.

NOTE

1. 'Asian' and 'Indian' are used interchangeably in the East African context and in this paper.

REFERENCES

Balachandran, P.K., 'An Embattled Community: Asians in East Africa Today', *African Affairs*, vol. 80, 1981, pp. 317-26.

Bharati, A., 'Political Pressures and Reactions in the Asian Minority in East Africa', paper presented at the African Studies Association Meeting, Chicago, 1964.

Bhatia, P., *Indian Ordeal in Africa*, Delhi: Vikas, 1973.

Bhushan, K., 'Indians in Kenya', in *Global Migration of Indians: Saga of Adventure, Enterprise, Identity and Integration*, ed. J.K. Motwani and J. Barot-Motwani, New York: First Global Convention of People of Indian Origin, 1989, pp. 53-5.

Blalock, H., *Toward a Theory of Minority Group Relations*, New York: John Wiley, 1967.

Bujra, J., 'Ethnicity and Class: The Case of the East African "Asians"', in *Poverty and Development in the 1990s*, ed. T. Allen and A. Thomas Oxford: Oxford University Press, 1992, pp. 347-61.

Clarke, C., C. Peach and S. Vertovec, 'Introduction: Themes in the Study of the South Asian Diaspora', in *South Asians Overseas - Migration and Ethnicity*, ed. C. Clarke, C. Peach and S. Vertovec, Cambridge: Cambridge University Press, 1990, pp. 1-29.

Desai, N., 'The Asian Influence in East Africa', in *Global Migration of Indians: Saga of Adventure, Enterprise, Identity and Integration*, ed. J.K. Motwani and J. Barot-Motwani, New York: First Global Convention of People of Indian Origin, 1989, pp. 37-43.

Delf, G., *Asians in East Africa*, London: Oxford University Press, 1963.

Desai, A. and B. Maharaj, 'Minorities in the Rainbow Nation: The Indian Vote in 1994', *South African Journal of Sociology*, 1996, 26: 118-25.

Duder, C., 'The Settler Response', *The Journal of Imperial and Commonwealth History*, 17, 1989: 349-73.

Ghai, D.P. and Y.P. Ghai, 'Asians in East Africa: Problems and Prospects', *The Journal of Modern African Studies*, 3, 1965: 35-51.

Ghai, D.P. and Y.P. Ghai (eds.), *Portrait of a Minority: Asians in East Africa.* Nairobi: Oxford University Press, 1970.

Ghai, D.P. and Y.P. Ghai, *The Asian Minorities of East and Cantral Africa.* London: Minority Rights Group, 1971.

Gregory, R.G., 'Co-operation and Collaboration in Colonial East Africa: The Asians' Political Role, 1890-1964', *African Affairs*, 80, 1981: 259-73.

———, *Quest for Equality: Asian Politics in East Africa, 1900-1967*, New Delhi: Orient Longman, 1993.

Gupta, A., 'Ugandan Asians, Britain, India and the Commonwealth, *African Affairs*, 73, 1974: 312-24.

———, 'India and the Asians in East Africa', in *Expulsion of a Minority: Essays on Ugandan Asians*, ed. M. Twaddle, London: Athlone, 1975, pp. 125-39.

Himbara, D., '"The Asian Question" in East Africa: The Continuing Controversy on the Role of Indian Capitalists in Accumulation and Development in Kenya, Uganda and Tanzania', *African Studies* 56, 1, 1997: 1-18.

———, 'Myths and Realities of Kenyan Capitalism', *The Journal of Modern African Studies* 31, 1, 1993: 93-107.

Himbara, D. and D. Sultan, 'Reconstructing the Ugandan State and Economy', *Review of African Political Economy*, 63, 1995: 85-93.

Hromnik, C.A., *Towards a New Understanding of the History of the Sub-Saharan Africa Indo-Africa*, Cape Town: Juta and Company Limited, 1981.

Jain, J.C., 'Socio-economic History of Indians in Kenya', in *Global Migration of Indians: Saga of Adventure, Enterprise, Identity and Integration*, ed. J.K. Motwani and J. Barot-Motwani, New York: First Global Convention of People of Indian Origin, 1989, pp. 44-52.

King, K., 'Indo-African Skill Transfer in an East African Economy', *African Affairs*, 74, 1975: 65-71.

Mamdani, M., *From Citizen to Refugee*, London: Francis Pinter, 1973.

———, 'The Ugandan Expulsion: Twenty Years After', *Economic and Political Weekly*, 16-23 January, 1993, p. 85.

Mampilly, Z., 'New Exhibit Highlights Kenyan Asians', 2002 (www.africana.com/Daily Articles/index_20000730.htm),.

Mangat, J.S., *A History of Asian East Africa c.1886 to 1945*, Oxford: Clarendon Press, 1969.

Melady, T.P. and M.B. Melady, *Uganda: The Asian Exiles*, New Delhi: Cosmo Publications, 1976.

Morris, H.S., 'Communal Rivalry among Indians in Uganda', *British Journal of Sociology*, 8, 1957: 306-17.

———, 'Indians in Uganda', in *Global Migration of Indians: Saga of Adventure, Enterprise, Identity and Integration*, ed. J.K. Motwani and J. Barot-Motwani, New York: First Global Convention of People of Indian Origin, 1989, pp. 56-9.

Motwani, J.K and J.B. Motwani, 'Introduction', in *Global Migration of Indians: Saga of Adventure, Enterprise, Identity and Integration*, ed. New York: First Global Convention of People of Indian Origin, 1989, pp. 1-5.

Nagar, R. and H. Leitner, 'Contesting Social Relations in Communcal Places—

Identity Politics among Asian Communities in Dar Es Salaam', in *Cities of Difference*, ed. R. Fincher and J.M. Jacobs, New York: The Guilford Press, 1998, pp. 226-51.

Patel, H.H., 'Power, Race, Class and Citizenship', *Zambezia–Journal of the University of Rhodesia* (Supplement), 1974, pp. 1-40.

Power, J., 'Race, Class, Ethnicity, and Anglo-Indian Trade Rivalry in Colonial Malawi, 1910-1945', *The International Journal of African Historical Studies*, 26, 1981: 575-607.

Raphael, A., *The East African Asians: The Situation in 1984*, London: Minority Rights Group, 1984.

Spencer, I.R.G., 'The First Assault on Indian Ascendancy: Indian Traders in the Kenya Reserves, 1895-1929', *African Affairs*, 80, 1981: 327-43.

Tandon, Y. and A. Raphael, *East Africa's Asians*, London: Minority Rights Group, 1973.

Tinker, H., *A New System of Slavery*, London: Oxford University Press, 1974.

Twaddle, M. (ed.), *Expulsion of a Minority: Essays on Ugandan Asians*, London: Athlone, 1975.

———, 'East African Asians through a Hundred Years', in *South Asians Overseas: Migration and Ethnicity*, ed. C. Clarke, C. Peach and S. Vertovec, Cambridge: Cambridge University Press, 1990.

Yambert, K.A., 'Alien Trading and Ruling', *Ethnic Groups* 3, 1981: 173-98.

CHAPTER 7

# Studying Urban Identities in South Africa

S. BEKKER, A. LEILDÉ and C. PUTTERGILL

## INTRODUCTION

Most societies at the beginning of the new millennium are caught up in seemingly never-ending processes of social transformation. One consequence for members of these societies seems to be increasing insecurity about 'fitting in' and about belonging. Debate and collective action on these issues has moved to the centre of politics and it is accordingly no surprise to observe that identity has become a key concern within the social sciences and humanities. Identity has become, in fact, 'the watchword of the times' (Shotter, 1993b, p. 188). In South Africa, identity, and more specifically ethnicity, have long been considered taboo subjects, either accepted unquestionably or dismissed *a priori* as an invention of the apartheid regime designed to preserve oppression. It was with the advent of democracy in the early 1990s that renewed interest in questions about identity emerged, as evidenced by five major conferences on this issue in South Africa at the time (Bekker, 1999).

We draw on our research on urban identities in South Africa to illustrate the complexities of studying identity and ethnicity in this chapter. We begin with general reflections on the notion of identity and then sketch the socio-historical context that frames issues of urban identity in South Africa. Subsequently we outline the method two of the authors have used to explore the notion of changing South African urban identities in Johannesburg and in Cape Town, drawing on selected research results in these two cities.

## THE NOTION OF IDENTITY

Different disciplines have addressed issues of identity in various ways and have produced a substantial albeit disparate body of theory and research. It appears in fact that the flexibility of this notion has enabled researchers to use it to frame questions that are of particular interest to them. This has led Goldberg and Solomos (2001, p. 5) to argue that the question of identity has 'taken on so many different connotations that sometimes it is obvious that people are not talking about the same phenomena'. Given the polysemic nature of the notion, and the complexities it refers to, it is clear that clarification is needed of how we intend using it here.

Conceptions of identity have changed dramatically over time. Identity in premodern (traditional) societies was perceived as undifferentiated, socially derived, fixed to a position and unproblematic. Change then took place from the absolute certitude of traditional or feudal forms of social and economic organization, culture and thought, to notions of autonomy, openness and questioning. The atomistic notion of self-contained, independent and rational individuals that emerged may be viewed as a product of modernity. In late or post-modernity, uncertainty resulting from accelerated social transformation brought to the fore notions of reflexivity and contingency (Calhoun, 1995; Giddens, 1991).

The Latin root of identity, 'idem' implies sameness. Such sameness in an individual or personal context points to continuity and coherence. Within a collective context, it implies similarity. However, whether referring to individual or collective identity, identifying or recognizing sameness requires considering difference. Hence, taking up an identity requires drawing boundaries, which in turn imply both inclusion and exclusion or similarity and difference. Recognition of 'difference' and 'similarity' depends on comparison and enables classification. Classification (which implies naming and the potential of regulating) depends on the marking of the boundary of one identity against another. Drawing a boundary delineates insiders from outsiders. An identity therefore relies on comparison and is relational. Both similarity and difference are socially constructed and therefore changeable even if they appear to be based on essential characteristics (Hall, 1996; Woodward, 2000).

These elements of similarity (the 'We') and of difference (the 'They' or the 'Other') are usually emotionally loaded. However, claiming an identity need not be conflictual. Todorov (1996, p. 298) argues that it is 'when one lacks positive elements (upon which) to build his or her identity (that) the temptation is to resort to negative elements and one's identity is then constructed around the rejection of the "Other"' [*our translation*]. Conversely, where the construction of an identity leads to experiences of pride and growing self-esteem, without denigrating an 'Other', the 'Other' may well be viewed in inclusive terms (Bekker and Leildé, 2000, 2002).

According to Castells (1997, p. 6) 'identity is people's source of meaning and experience'. It is neither essential nor immutable but a social construction open to change as circumstances, strategies and interactions fluctuate. It needs therefore to be situated historically and relationally since identity is a matter of social context. It is 'socially bestowed, socially sustained and socially transformed' according to Berger (1963, p. 116). Accordingly, identity is best viewed as a process rather than a property (Agger, 1998; Castells, 1997; Shotter 1993b). Viewing identity as a process therefore problematizes the notion of an already existing identity. Indeed, as a process, identity is emergent, never complete, finalized or fixed but rather always evolving. It is something we 'do' rather than something we 'are'.

Discourse plays a crucial role in this respect. It is because identities are constituted within discourse that they are historically specific and changeable. Meaning, cultural or otherwise, is not simplistically transmitted, it is continually recreated. Discourse is not a passive medium of representation, it is a form of social action through which social relations emerge and are maintained. Discourses work to produce, rather than merely reflect, the 'objects'. Discourses are historically constructed regimes of knowledge, they convey and articulate formal and informal knowledge and ideologies and are continually constituted and reproduced (Calhoun, 1995; Hall, 1992; Woodward, 2000). Such discourses have material effects through the social relations they sustain.

According to Shotter (1993a), there is a political economy of identity in the sense that opportunities to access resources and to construct identities are not equally spread within society. While it is generally agreed that identities are social constructs, Castells (1997, p. 7) argues that 'the real issue is how, from what, by whom and for what (are identities constructed)'. Broadly speaking, a distinction can be drawn between identity constructed or imposed from above and identity constructed from below. In the first instance—the macro-social level—attention is paid to structural processes and historical formations such as the nation state. The macro-social level is the context-bound world within which everyone works, the parameters of existing social relations, structures and cultural contexts. In the second instance, the focus is at the micro-social interpersonal level where meanings are negotiated in everyday social interaction. It is apparent that these levels are interrelated. According to Castells (1997, p. 7), identities that originate from dominant institutions 'become identities only when and if social actors internalize them, and construct their meaning around this internalization'. If the legitimacy of identities from above is questioned, meaning is derived from 'resistance identities', constructed 'around principles different from or opposed to those permeating the institutions of society'. Since identity can be seen as a construction of, on the one hand, government and other institutions in search of legitimacy (macro-social) and, on the other hand, of people wanting to give meaning to their day-to-day experience (micro-social), discourses on identity are shaped both from above and below (Weigert et al. 1986).

It is clear that individuals may draw meaning from belonging to more than one group, may construct and maintain multiple identities that emerge under different circumstances. This makes the idea of a single overarching social identity that 'fits' these diverse experiences, tenuous. Identities can overlap. The situation determines whether one identity is more salient than another (McAllister, 1999). In this respect Agger (1998, p. 53) contends that 'people are seen as dispersed into a wide variety of subject positions from which they speak polyvocally about their experiences and meanings . . . and multiple subject positions'. Castells (1997, p. 6) however argues that 'such a plurality is a source of stress and contradiction in both self-representation and social action' since these identities may be in internal tension with one another. Accordingly, under specific circumstances, a primary identity, one 'that frames the others' (Castells, 1997, p. 7), emerges to prevail over the others, thereby enabling collective action.

In our research we have argued that identity is 'a matter of social context' rather than a fixed entity. It emerges from and is sustained by the actions of people within the constraints of a historically and materially grounded context of lived social relations and interaction as a result of economic, political or cultural processes. Bradley (1996, p. 7) suggests that social reality, and by implication identity, reveals two faces, 'continuity within change; order within variability [and] fixity within fluidity'. Accordingly, in order to introduce the notion of urban identities in South African cities, we now turn to the changing socio-political context within which urban South Africans construct their identities.

## SOUTH AFRICA'S CHANGING SOCIO-POLITICAL CONTEXT

Let us begin with the issue of a primary South African national identity. Once the process of transition from apartheid toward a democratic state began, interest in this issue grew significantly. The questions underlying this interest derive from the ghosts of South Africa's past and the dreams of its future. Does race continue to carry deep meaning? Have the meanings attached to the ethnic and racial labels of the 'old' South Africa persisted, labels such as 'Zulu', or 'Afrikaner' or 'Coloured'? Have South Africans developed a new national identity? The implication appears to be that South Africans are able to make one choice only—to belong together to a new nation, or to remain divided by offensive cleavages inherited from an unjust past. The two choices stand in an inverse relationship to one another, according to a number of analysts (Alexander, 1999; Dexter, 1999; Tayob, 1999). If older racial and ethnic identities persist, a national identity cannot emerge and, conversely, if and when the former identities dissolve, pride in and identification with the South African nation will flourish.

This perspective obstructs the examination of new identities that may modify or even neutralize and supplant older ethno-racial identities while remaining compatible with an emergent national identity. Currently in South Africa a number of government policies aim at promoting 'from above' the construction of new identities. Fair distribution of resources to members of South Africa's historically discriminated groups is pursued through affirmative action policies and the standardization of welfare grants. The goal is to diminish the salience of these older racial identities. In addition, new identities are envisaged through the constitutionally embodied territorial dispersion of political power. The redrawing of provincial boundaries reflects the hope that new territorial communities at sub-national level may fashion new collective identities compatible with though differing from a new national South African identity (Bekker et al., 1999).

Similar hopes for the construction of identities from above flow from a series of national urban policies. A number of analysts have made the case that the manipulation of economic opportunity and of residential space under apartheid had a direct impact on how people constructed their identities (Sharp and Boonzaier, 1995; Houssay-Holschuch, 1999; Martin, 2000). More recently, Gervais-Lambony (2004) has argued that apartheid was 'a tool of identity construction based on the belief of the influence of space on identities', of the influence of space at a number of levels: nationally as it related to Bantustans, municipally as it related to Group Areas, and at the micro level as it related to the racial segregation of public places.

In similar ways, the scrapping of influx control policies that gave all South Africans equal right to urban residence and the repeal of the Group Areas Act in 1991 that gave urban residents the freedom to choose where they wanted to live within the city may be viewed as attempts through the manipulation of social space 'from above' to fashion urban identities. Further measures to this end include new government urban policies to integrate the city spatially, economically and socially. Equal distribution of resources across areas was envisaged through the redrawing of municipal boundaries and the election of single-tier metropolitan authorities with a single tax base. Parallel to these structural and financial changes to city government, planning strategies (such as the Metropolitan Spatial Development Framework in Cape Town and the Strategic Metropolitan Development Framework in Johannesburg) were designed and implemented to foster residential densification and sustainable urban development, to promote a 'compact' city.

The implementation of these urban policies aimed at the ideal of 'one city for all' have been constrained by three market-driven processes that are believed to lead toward continuing social and spatial polarization and fragmentation. The first process is located within the labour market: traditional manufacturing sectors in these cities have been shrinking as the services and financial sectors strengthen. This encourages an expansion of a highly skilled labour force whilst employment for blue-collar workers diminishes. As a consequence, wage differentials rise. The second process is located within the land market. The state appears unable or unwilling to intervene in the process of land acquisition. Well-orchestrated middle-class opposition to state interference in 'their' land market has accompanied rising land prices in middle class residential areas. As a consequence, most low-income housing development continues to be located in the periphery of cities where land is cheapest (Turok, 2000; Bremner, 2000). The third process is 'the suburbanization (. . .) of new economic activity' (Mabin, 2001), leading to the location of private sector investment in the northern sectors of both Cape Town (Blaauwberg, as an example) and Johannesburg (the edge cities of Sandton and Midrand, for example), thereby sidestepping employment demand in the populous but poorer

Cape Flats and Soweto areas of these cities. This general pattern of spatial development in these cities fuels the process of polarization both within the labour market as well as regarding residential segregation. It is far removed from the policy ideal of the 'compact' city. To quote Saff, 'racial segregation has been replaced by social segregation, in effect by "deracialized apartheid"' (1998).

The aim of the research we report on below was to investigate the extent to which this changing policy-related and market-related urban context influences collective identities constructed by rank-and-file urban South Africans.

## METHODOLOGY

Research in Cape Town and Johannesburg involved focus groups discussions with rank-and-file groupings selected on a wide range of criteria: residential area, religious affiliation, language, age and domain of activity. Each focus group was requested to discuss how they 'felt' about living in their local residential area, in Cape Town or Johannesburg and in general in South Africa. Discussions were conducted in the preferred language of each group and transcriptions were subsequently translated into English for analysis. The three research prompts and subsequent non-directive facilitation of discussion were deliberately chosen to enable groups freely to probe areas of shared interest, concern and meaning. Since focus groups were not asked to debate specific issues, identification and discussion of themes produced evidence of the relative importance of such shared sentiments and meanings.

Choice of a non-directive focus group methodology was based on the hypothesis that identity construction ought to be viewed as a process rather than a property and that this process is integrally related to discourse. Accordingly, people's narratives not only reveal which issues are chosen for discussion and the ways they are chosen but also play a role themselves in the construction of collective identities. In addition, focus group discussions identify and construct complex collective social representations that are shared by discussants. The identification of such representations, we believe, is not accessible by using quantitative research methods such as surveys (McAllister, 1999).

The advantages of this approach notwithstanding, it suffers from a number of limitations. Two will be mentioned here. The first points to issues of representativity and potential generalization. Since focus groups themselves and discussants within them are selected on the basis of convenience sampling, research outcomes at best illustrate trends and suggest conclusions. In the second place, a focus group interview—even when 'unstructured'—is a conversation with a purpose. It is initiated by the researcher and to a lesser or greater degree directed by his or her interventions. The focus group approach accordingly generates data, rather than merely collecting it. Bourdieu (1977) has argued that the interviewee is likely to provide the researcher with the 'official account'. In short, we need to consider not only the information gathered but also the relationship between how it was gathered and its nature (Bourdieu, 1977).

## CHANGING SOUTH AFRICAN URBAN IDENTITIES?

The interpretations of our qualitative focus-group (FG) data were guided by the extent to which such identities stand out in the narratives as primary identities, as identities that 'frame' others. After a preliminary scan of these data moreover, we decided to classify narratives into an 'urban middle class' and an 'urban poor' category and to analyse data in these two categories separately. This decision was based on results of the scan that revealed a wide range of similarities in both cities of narratives falling within each category and clear variance in both cities of narratives across categories. The urban middle class category is defined as comprising respondents in FGs that fall within a middle and higher income range within which residents live in suburbs and are formally employed in white collar (or established blue collar) positions; and the urban poor category is defined as comprising residents in FGs that fall within the ranks of the poor and unemployed and who reside in informal or low cost formal accommodation.

In both cities, middle class residents share a common pride in their choice of residence and such a choice is largely motivated by the socio-economic status of the area, rather than by racial issues. The neighbourhood rather than the city appears to give meaning to middle class urban residents. In such suburbs, class identities, constructed around shared values, a shared 'way of life', and common interests and concerns such as crime, property values and neighbourhood tidiness are widely asserted. Contrary to what is often claimed regarding middle class individualism, a close-knit community or a sense of 'neighbourliness' is actively sought out by middle class residents and appears to be the primary criterion for selecting a neighbourhood in which to live.

As one resident argues:

> I don't mind if my neighbour is black or coloured as long as we live in harmony, with the same standard. (That) I (may not) have decent people next to me, that (is) what bothers me. (Oranjezicht, German-speaking middle class, Cape Town)

Inversely, for the poor, place at local level is of little meaning as they appear to have little or no choice over where to stay. What matters to the poor and what shapes their identities is their ability to access jobs, housing and welfare benefits both at city and national levels. In both cities, competition over jobs and over scarce resources leads to widespread stigmatization and scape-goating of African immigrants who are seen as responsible for unemployment and crime. It also leads to lines of fragmentation within poor urban communities themselves (Bekker & Leildé 2004).

Given these similarities in the construction of class identities in Johannesburg and Cape Town, there are also striking differences. In Cape Town, where choice of residence is available as it is in better-off neighbourhoods, culture, language and religion enter into the equation —revealing Cape Town's middle and higher income neighbourhoods as culturally diverse and at times as deeply divided along cultural lines of cleavage. Neighbourhoods in Cape Town seem to be perceived in terms of both cultural as well as class terms and this appears to condition residential choice. Members of these neighbourhoods express pride and derive substantial self esteem not only from their class positions but also from their ethnic, linguistic and religious affiliations. For example, Afrikaans-speaking residents seek to live in neighbourhoods where their language and religion is majoritarian, middle class Xhosa-speakers and Muslim residents prefer to live together where they are free to express their beliefs and customs at neighbourhood level. As a consequence, cultural heterogeneity at neighbourhood level appears to engender a degree of conflict. One resident described this cultural compartmentalization of Cape Town in the following racial terms:

> Cape Town appears to be very white, that's what I think. And that's why they say we are very racist. We are very Europe-centric(sic). It's very white, unfortunately. It's so Eurocentric, it's almost like it's a separate place from SA in terms of its cultural mixing. But over and above the race, I think it's colour, creed and religion. I think we are also very intolerant about other races as well as religions. We are very polarised here, even within our inter-denominational communities, we tend to be very intolerant. (Pinelands, Coloured middle class, Cape Town)

Conversely, in Johannesburg, community at neighbourhood level seems to be based on a 'shared lifestyle' rather than on common cultural features. Cultural affiliation seems largely to be domesticated, practised in private within the immediate family or circle of friends but not playing an important role in the choice of neighbourhood. In the case of language, English as the *lingua franca* of Johannesburg seems to have been accepted by all urban residents.

The primary difference within narratives among the poor in Cape Town and in Johannesburg relates to the importance of a racial divide within the underclass. In Johannesburg, it is the shared experience of the divide in access to education, to the labour market and to political influence between the haves and the have-nots that appears to be most significant in this city, the divide between classes rather than between ethnic or racial groups.

> The people we have voted into power are turning (out) to be our enemies. Someone who loves you will not make your wife and children to suffer. You know I am working but this man is my best friend and he is not working. And I don't like it if I have R10.00 in my pocket (when) he does not have it. And so (for everything to) be wonderful, let everybody get equal opportunities. Let there be work. Let them not sing us a song that there will be jobs. And they . . . lie to us saying we got democracy. What is democracy if you are unemployed? What democracy do you enjoy if you are hungry? (Tsakane, African poor, Johannesburg)

In Cape Town, on the other hand, the perception—shared by different groupings of the urban poor—that there exists racialized privileged access to resources such as jobs, services and housing adds race to the dominant underclass identity in this city.

> There are a lot of places where I would not go in Cape Town, because apartheid is still around. Africans who live in Cape Town don't get jobs. Our people in our society are isolated. This province is different to other provinces. Our people come from other provinces where Apartheid is gone. . . . Gauteng is better. Here African people have problems. Here in Cape Town, only coloureds and whites get better jobs. But if you are African, it's like in apartheid a long time ago. (Khayelitsha, African poor, Cape Town)

Though race appears to be an important line of cleavage, an important boundary between 'us' and 'them' in Cape Town's underclass, there appears to be little pride or self-esteem in this ethnic or racial identity. It appears to be carried as an imposed identity, as a stigma, rather than as a badge of pride (Bekker and Leildé, 2004).

## CONCLUSION

Identities in Cape Town and Johannesburg reflect continuity and change. It is apparent from the narratives in both cities that polarization between the middle classes and the poor both in terms of labour market access and in terms of residential space is something residents worry about. Sentiments expressing social distance and the need for residential separation between these classes suggest strongly that living in these cities—thinking of oneself as a Capetonian or a Johannesburg resident —carries very different meanings for middle class and poor residents. And these meanings that range from pride in neighbourhood and self-esteem in career achievement to frustration about exclusion and anger about stigmatization appear be at odds with the lofty post-apartheid ideals of 'one city for all'.

Urban middle class identities in both cities appear to be constructed around shared middle class values that in turn are significantly related to living in neighbourhoods where notions of a close-knit community and of neighbourliness ought to be shared. In contradistinction, though the poor in both cities are trapped in racially homogeneous low-cost formal and informal residential areas, it is not the nature of this residential space but rather economic and social exclusion as well as fierce competition over local resources that shape the identities of the urban poor.

Simultaneously, significant differences emerge between such urban identities in Cape Town and in Johannesburg. In the first place, where choice of residence in better-off neighbourhoods is available, shared culture, language and religion appear to play a significant role in the decision-making process in Cape Town. This in turn suggests that residents in middle and higher income neighbourhoods perceive themselves at both neighbourhood and city level to be culturally diverse and at times deeply divided along cultural lines of cleavage. Such a trend appears to be much less pronounced in Johannesburg where cultural identities are domesticated and accordingly lived out in the private domain.

In the second place, whilst community solidarity among the urban poor appears to fragment as residents compete over access to scarce resources, the lines of fragmentation are not always the same in Cape Town and in Johannesburg. Xenophobia and stigmatization of the foreign African is a shared narrative among the urban poor in both cities. In Johannesburg, it appears that shared sentiments of suffering at the hands of employers and of the new political elite as well as emotionally-loaded responses to competition and conflict over local turf fashion the identities of the underclass. In Cape Town, on the other hand, the perception—shared by different groupings of the urban poor—that there exists racialized privileged access to resources such as jobs, services and housing adds race to the dominant underclass identity in this city.

## REFERENCES

Agger, B., *Critical Social Theories: An Introduction*, Boulder: Westview Press, 1998.

Alexander, N., *Prospects for a Non-racial Future in South Africa*, Cape Town: University of Cape Town, 1999.

Bekker, S. 'Introduction: Recent Developments in Identity Studies in South Africa', in *Identity: Theory, Politics, History*, ed. S. Bekker and R. Prinsloo, Pretoria: HSRC, 1999, pp. 1-9.

Bekker, S. and A. Leildé, 'New Urban Identities in a New South Africa? Class, Culture and Race in Cape Town and Johannesburg,' unpublished paper presented at a workshop on Urbanization, Local Government, Space and Identity in Selected African Cities, Stellenbosch, 2004.

Bekker, S. and A. Leildé, 'New Urban Identities in a New South Africa? Class, Culture and Race in Cape Town', in *Transforming South Africa*, ed. A. Osmanovic, Hamburg: Hamburg African Studies, 2002, pp. 243-71.

Bekker, S. and A. Leildé, 'Residents' Perceptions of Developmental Local Government: Exit, Voice and Loyalty in South African Towns', 1995, *Politea*, 22 (1), pp. 144-65.

Bekker, S., A. Leildé, S. Cornelissen, and S. Horstmeier, 'The Emergence of New Identities in the Western Cape', *Politikon*, 27 (2), 2000, pp. 221-37.

Berger, P.L., *Invitation to Sociology: A Humanistic Perspective*, Harmondsworh: Penguin, 1963.

Bradley, H., *Fractured Identities: Changing Patterns of Inequality*, Cambridge: Polity, 1996.

Bourdieu, P., *Towards a Theory of Practice*, Cambridge: Cambridge University Press, 1977.

Bremner, L.J., 'Post-apartheid Urban Geography: A Case Study of Greater Johannesburg's Rapid Land Development Programme', *Development Southern Africa* 17 (1), 2000, pp. 87-104.

Calhoun, C., *Critical Social Theory: Culture, History, and the Challenge of Difference*, Oxford: Basil Blackwell, 1995.

Castells, M., *The Information Age: Economy, Society and Culture,* volume I: *The Power of Identity*, Oxford: Blackwell, 1997.

Dexter, P., 'Perceptions, Imaginings, and Practices of Collective Identities in the Transition: National Identities and Ethnicity in the Western Cape', in *Religion and Politics in South Africa: From Apartheid to Democracy*, ed. A. Tayob and W. Weisse, vol. 1, Berlin and New York: Waxmann Publishing, 1999.

Gervais-Lambony, P., 'Space and Identities: Reflections on South African Examples', unpublished paper presented at a workshop on Urbanization, Local Government, Space and Identity in Selected African Cities, Stellenbosch, 2004.

Giddens, A., *Modernity and Self Identity: Self and Society in the Late Modern Age,* Cambridge: Polity Press, 1993.

Goldberg, D.T. and J. Solomos, 'General introduction', in *A Companion to Racial and Ethnic Studies*, ed. D.T. Goldberg and J. Solomos, Oxford: Blackwell, 2001, pp. 1-12.

Hall, S., 'The Question of Cultural Identity', in *Modernity and Its Futures,* ed. S. Hall, D. Held and T. McGrew, Cambridge: Polity, 1992, pp. 273-316.

———, 'Introduction: Who Needs Identity?', in *Questions of Cultural Identity,* ed. S. Hall and P. du Gay, London: Sage, 1996, pp. 1-17.

Mabin, A., 'Suburbs and Segregation in the Urbanising Cities of the South: A Challenge for Metropolitan Governance in the Early Twenty-First Century', paper presented at the Lincoln Institute of Land Policy, Cambridge (MA, USA), 2001.

McAllister, P., 'Can We Measure Ethnicity?', in *Identity: Theory, Politics, History*, ed. S. Bekker, and R. Prinsloo, Pretoria: HSRC, 1999, pp. 181-6.

Saff, G., *Changing Cape Town: Urban Dynamics, Policy, and Planning During the Political Transition in South Africa*, Lanham (Md.): University Press of America, 1998.

Shotter, J., *Conversational Realities: Constructing Life through Language*, London: Sage, 1993a.

———, *Cultural Politics of Everyday Life: Social Constructionism and Knowing of the Third Kind*. Buckingham: Open University Press, 1993b.

Tayob, A., 'Managing Cultural Diversity in a Democratic South Africa: Is there a Surplus Value to the National Project?', in *Religion and Politics in South Africa: From Apartheid to Democracy*, ed. A. Tayob and W. Weisse, vol. 1, Berlin and New York: Waxmann Publishing, 1999.

Todorov, T., 'La Coexistence des Cultures', in *L'Autre. Etudes réunies pour Alfred Grosser*, ed. B. Badie and M. Sadoun, Paris: Presses de Sciences Po, 1996.

Turok, I., 'Persistent Polarization Post-Apartheid? Progress Towards Urban

Integration in Cape Town', Discussion paper UCAP 1, Urban Change and Policy Research Group, Department of Urban Studies, University of Glasgow, 2000.

Van den Berghe, P., 'South Africa after thirty years' *Social Dynamics*, 16 (2), 1990.

Weigert, A.J., J.S. Teitge and D.W., Teitge, *Society and Identity*, Cambridge: Cambridge University Press, 1986.

Woodward, K., *Questioning Identity: Gender, Class, Nation*, London: Routledge, 2000.

CHAPTER 8

# Entangled Isolation: Construction and Articulation of Naga Ethnicity in Indian Policy

SURANJAN DAS

It is an unfortunate reality that average Indians tend to be unbelievably ignorant of the north-east which has emerged as a complex site of ethnic insurgency in South Asia and the most durable theatre of, what has been called, 'insurgent crossfire'.[1] An understanding of this ethnic imbroglio in the north-eastern region of India calls for a contextualization of the construction of ethnic identities in the region and identification of historical conjunctures, which have determined the nature of the area's identity politics. To a large extent ethnic politics in the north-eastern hills is an outcome of 'entangled territorial identities', a combination of territorial awareness and collective identity. This generated amongst the hill tribes a feeling of separatism from the Indian mainstream. Neither the Indian national movement nor the nation-building process in the immediate aftermath of independence could effectively overcome the isolation of the north-east. The current situation in the region is largely a result of this failure. My concern here is with the problematic of Naga ethnicity. The Nagas, a generic term applied to denote at least thirty-six tribal groups[2]—most of whom inhabit the province of Nagaland, while others are scattered in the neighbouring provinces of Arunachal Pradesh, Assam and Manipur and in the north-western part of Myanmar—were the first effective ethnic challenge from the north-east to the post-colonial Indian state. An examination of the construction and assertion of Naga ethnic identity, therefore, is an important entry point for a study of the ethnic challenge in north-eastern India.

## COLONIZATION OF THE NAGA HILLS

Contrary to some western perceptions, the Nagas in India had close interactions with the plains people during the pre-colonial period.[3] Although the plains were subject to occasional Naga raids, the

Brahmaputra, Barak, Surma valleys and the Himalayan foothills were regular centres for trade between the Nagas and plains people. It was the British who brought the Nagas under alien control for the first time and rudely shattered the traditional political economy.

The penetration of colonialism into the Naga Hills can be traced to the end of the first Anglo-Burmese War of 1825, especially in the wake of the British search for a route from Assam to Manipur. British interest in the region was initially dictated by the need to use it as a buffer for the Assam tea plantations and the plains. By 1888 centres of British administration for the Naga Hills were established in Kohima, Wokha and Mokochung. Nevertheless, at a popular level the acceptance of British hegemony over the Naga Hills was never unquestioned.

The British, however, chose not to impose direct administration over the Naga Hills. This was in continuation of the Ahom claim of sovereignty over the area coinciding with the independence of Naga villages. But, unlike the Ahoms, the British imposed a regulated tax structure and created for the Nagas new geographic, political and administrative boundaries, without the 'consent and knowledge of concerned Nagas'.[4] Moreover, this demarcated area was considered as a 'protected area' from outside influence. Subsequently, the Government of India Act of 1935 categorized the area as 'excluded' and 'partially excluded', placed it under the direct administration of the Assam Governor, and kept it outside the ambit of either the federal or Assam legislature. The only formal channel of contact with the outside world was the local officer, responsible to the Governor of Assam. Consequently, the delineation of an ethnic boundary of the Nagas became coterminous with colonialism. The administrative cost was kept to a minimum and the sole colonial concern was maintenance of peace and taxation. No developmental measures were undertaken. The colonial administration thus imposed an insular existence upon the Nagas.

## COLONIALISM AND THE CONSTRUCTION OF NAGA IDENTITY

### The Colonial Discourse

The British—civil servants, missionaries and anthropologists alike—were unsure of how to define the Naga community. However, all of them shared a common perception that with their Mongoloid physical features and Indo-Tibetan language, culture, food and dress the Nagas had no synonymity with the Indo-Aryan ethos of the plains. The Nagas were informed that their acceptance of Christianity had alienated them from the Indian way of life. Not unnaturally, in their depositions before the Simon Commission in 1929 British officials of the Assam government asserted the 'separateness' of the Naga tribes.[5] The colonial discourse on Naga incompatibility with mainstream Indian identity led the tribal leaders to perceive Indians as 'babus' of the plains. The segregationist feeling amongst the Nagas was imparted a political content when colonial sociology viewed all Naga tribes as belonging to one administrative structure. Traditionally, the Nagas did not constitute a united people. The primary referral point for the Nagas was their village or local group. But the British mistook it for some larger combination into which villages could be classified. They categorized as tribes, what were essentially clans, villages and *khels* (territorial divisions within a village usually containing several clans). Although a Naga viewed himself or herself as a member of a particular group rather than a Naga[6] and the pattern of governance varied from group to group—from hereditary chieftainship to councils, autocracy and clan democracy[7]—the colonial officials clubbed together these different groups in official communications and private tour diaries under the broad generic term 'Nagas'. Once the census reports classified the different tribes as subtribes of one generic tribe—the Nagas—there occurred for the Nagas a transmutation of village and subtribe-based identity to a generic identity.[8]

This process of affixing an administrative notion to the term 'Nagas' has been characterized by many scholars as 'detribalization'.[9] Increasing monetization of the hill economy, an offshoot of colonialism, led to the concentration of wealth amongst the tribals, which in turn gave rise to widespread indebtedness and the emergence of a landless class. The presence of alien officials and missionaries also diminished the prestige of tribal chiefs. Colonial rule thus destroyed the 'traditional moorings' of the Naga society and imposed upon it an identity which generated amongst the Nagas both a spirit of separateness from the Indian mainstream and fostered loyalty to their new-found British patrons.

## Christian Missionaries and the Construction of Naga Ethnicity

The colonial administrative policy of imposing territorial isolation upon the Nagas was reinforced by Christian missionaries, the most active among them were the American Baptists who begin to effectively function in the Naga Hills in 1876.[10] Despite initial opposition, the Christian conversion movement amongst the Nagas became 'one of the large mass movements to Christianity in Asia'.[11] The size of Christian converts rose from 0,18 of the total Naga population in 1901 to 17.9 per cent in 1941, 45.7 per cent in 1951 and 66.76 per cent in 1971.[12]

The social impact of Christian missionary activities in Nagaland was significant. The missionaries perceived the Nagas as 'uncivilized, barbaric and savage' who were to be made 'worthy' and 'civilized' through Christianity. They condemned Naga customs like feasts of merit through which wealthy sections of the community customarily improved their social position. Such Naga practices as headhunting, premised on the belief that the capture of a human head was necessary for ensuring the fertility of the land and the community's economic well-being, were denounced.[13] Simultaneously, medical work of the missionaries sought to substitute the 'essentially supernaturalistic' tribal healing practices with Western medicine. Credit goes to the missionaries for spreading primary education in the Naga Hills. They introduced Roman script for the unwritten tribal languages, primarily to enable the tribals to read the Bible. Christian missionaries in the Naga Hills assumed the status of 'official educationists'.[14]

Such missionary activities, however, eroded the traditional code of conduct of the Nagas. The suppression of traditional customs deprived the Naga life of its vibrancy and 'dynamism'. Contemporary observers testified to how the colonial suppression of status-feasting was contemporaneous with increasing inequalities within the Naga villages.[15] Besides, exposure to Western knowledge through missionary education resulted in the emergence of a first generation of educated elite amongst the Nagas who not only questioned the hitherto undisputed authority of tribal chieftains, but also became carriers of modern politics. Conversion to an alien religion tended to distance the Naga Christian converts from the plains people, most of whom were either Hindus or Muslims. Due to the Romanization of tribal dialects, the tribals forgot the plains languages—Assamese in the case of the Nagas and Bengali in the case of the Khasis and Garos. This estrangement of the Nagas from the plains in turn generated a sense of groupness amongst the Christian Nagas.[16]

## ARTICULATION OF A NAGA IDENTITY

### THE COLONIAL PHASE

The assertion of a constructed Naga identity is usually traced back to the period following the return of the survivors of the 2,000 odd Nagas—mostly from the Sema clan—who went to France to work as labourers during the First World War. One of the first Naga groups to be exposed to the outside world, these returnees helped Charles Pawsey, the British Deputy Commissioner of the Naga Hills, to establish the Naga Club in Kohima, which functioned as the British administrative centre for the Naga Hill District. Modelled on Western lines, it was to be a tribal pressure group within the colonial administrative framework. The Club's separatist stance from mainstream nationalism was demonstrated when, with the support of local colonial officials, it submitted a memorandum to the Simon Commission demanding the non-incorporation of the Naga Hills within the province of Assam.[17] The Naga internalization of a constructed separatist identity was again evident when the Naga leadership demanded the exclusion of the Hills from the ambit of the Government of India Act of 1935.

The Second World War was the next turning point in the articulation of a separate Naga ethnic identity. Although some Nagas, including Angame Zapu Phizo, the future leader of Naga ethnic politics, joined Subhas Chandra Bose's Indian National Army, a considerable number of Naga tribes rallied around the British war-effort primarily 'as intelligence behind the Japanese lines, [and] as interpreters, scouts and porters'.[18] If the British benefited from Naga loyalty during the War, the Nagas, too, gained from their participation in the War. It accustomed the Nagas to modern armaments; the rapid improvement in communication between India and Burma brought to an end much of the traditional isolation of the Nagas from the Indian mainstream. Besides, the Naga leadership hoped that their loyalty would be rewarded by the British support for Naga autonomy or independence in a decolonized South Asia.[19]

### PRELUDE TO AUGUST 1947

The legacy left behind by the British rule over the Naga Hills was both destructive and constructive—destructive because it disrupted the traditional tribal economy and insulated the Nagas from the Indian mainstream, and constructive because colonialism brought in its trail, although for its own administrative interest, modern political ideas and institutions. But, it was the negative impact of colonialism which generated a sense of political uncertainty amongst the Nagas. While the British politics of Naga isolation deprived the Hills of economic growth and development of its own administrative manpower, the failure of the departing British to secure for the Nagas self-determination for the tribal areas'[20] had not been anticipated by the dominant sections of the Naga society.

Unfortunately, the Congress leaders failed to dispel the political confusion afflicting the Naga leadership. The 1936 Faizpur session of the Indian National Congress had unequivocally rejected the system of 'excluded' and 'partially excluded areas' for the Hills as 'another attempt to divide the people of India into different groups'. Further, the Congress failed to formulate an alternative blueprint to protect the distinct Naga identity that had been constructed under British colonialism. Instead, once Nehru became the Prime Minister, he took a rigid stance on the Naga issue. Nehru hurt Naga sentiments when he referred to Assamese or Hindustani as the most useful language for the Hills, and even advised the Nagas to learn Hindustani for better integration with mainstream Indian life. Because of such integrationist sentiments, the Naga politicians lost faith in the Congress as a protector of the Naga cause.

However, not all segments of Naga political opinion initially favoured an 'outright severance of ties with India'.[21] On 19 June 1946 even the Naga National Council (NNC) accepted the retention of the Naga Hills within Assam, although with local autonomy and proper safeguards for Naga interests. Yet, by the beginning of 1947, the NNC's political stance began to change. It is difficult to document with direct evidence the possibility of any British encouragement for the adoption of this NNC resolution. Sir Andrew Clow, the Governor of Assam, visited Mokokchong in January 1947 where he appreciated the Naga claim for local authority and advised the tribal leaders to think about their political future and 'form their own conclusions'.[22] Other civilians like Sir Henry Knight also thought that the outright integration of the Naga Hills with the Indian province of Assam ran the risk of outbreak of famines and resurgence of headhunting in the Naga Hills.

In this context Akbar Hydari, the first Indian Governor of Assam, reached a compromise with the Naga leadership on 29 June 1947. The Agreement forbade automatic applicability of the Central and Provincial

Acts in the Hills whose natural resources were made inalienable to non-Nagas. The ninth clause of the Agreement also stipulated a ten-year operation period after which 'the Naga National Council will be asked whether (. . .) a new agreement (. . .) (would be) arrived at'.[23]

Unfortunately, the Constituent Assembly refused to ratify this clause, which reduced the Hydari Agreement to nothing more than a piece of paper.

The breakdown of the Hydari Agreement heralded the emergence of an extremist section within the NNC. Led by Zapu Phizo they formed the People's Independence League to struggle for a sovereign Nagaland. Interestingly, at this juncture on 19 July 1947 a seven-member Naga delegation had a favourable audience with Mahatma Gandhi who assured 'Nagas have every right to be independent . . . I believe in brotherhood of man [and not] . . . in force or forced union'.[24]

The Naga leaders drew solace from their meeting with Gandhi, affirming later to the President of India: 'We took his [Gandhi's] word as final as far as Nagaland and India were concerned.'[25]

## Independence and Its Aftermath

The construction and initial articulation of Naga ethnicity—as the discussion so far demonstrates—had occurred in the context of and within the framework of colonialism. Unfortunately, the Nehruvian strategy of imposing a pan-Indian unity from above by undermining local diversities in the interest of creating a national market for the rising indigenous bourgeoisie failed to reconcile the Naga ethnic aspirations within the centrist federal framework of the post-colonial Indian state. Jawaharlal Nehru chose not to extend the principle of linguistic states to the north-east. Instead, the Naga Hills, along with other parts of the region except the princely states of Manipur and Tripura, because a part of the province of Assam. On the eve of India's Independence, posters proclaiming 'outsiders (Indians) let us separate as friends and live like good neighbours', 'Indians, it is better to go from Nagaland without delay' and 'Nagaland is for the Nagas' were pasted all over Kohima. In post-Independent India the Nagas became victims of a dual process: commercialization of their resources and the hegemonizing dictum of 'one state, one nation'.[26] In July 1948, the NNC supremo Angami Zapu Phizo was arrested on charges of 'anti-Indian manoeuvres'. The intensity of Naga animosity to the new regime in New Delhi was demonstrated by a plebiscite organized on 16 May

1951 by the NNC in which 99 per cent of the Nagas reportedly endorsed the demand of independence. Subsequently, the Nagas overwhelmingly boycotted the first Indian general election of 1952.

Meanwhile, the Assam administration found itself in a quandary in administrating the Naga territory. This was partly because of the Naga groups' differential experience of colonial rule since the extent of British hegemony over the Naga tribes varied greatly. Faced with such a variegated situation, the Assam government viewed the Naga Hills as an area that required a tough administration. In September 1953 the Assam government enacted a law empowering it to requisition the services of porters in the Naga Hills on emergency grounds. The Assam Disturbed Act of 1955 entrusted the Assam Armed Police and the Assam Rifles with extraordinary powers to 'contain insurgency'. In 1962, the Assam Legislature proposed Assamese as the official language of the province and the Nagas, who had primarily gained literacy through English and had about thirty languages and innumerable dialects, found themselves disadvantaged in the race for joining provincial schools, universities and government jobs.

The line of division between New Delhi and the NNC surfaced in March 1953 when Jawaharlal Nehru refused an audience with the NNC leaders whilst on a visit to the Naga Hills accompanied by Indira Gandhi and U Nu of Burma. During this visit Nehru had a taste of Naga dissension when virtually the entire gathering walked out of a mass meeting upon his arrival. This incident was prelude to a period of Naga non-cooperation with the Indian state. Yet another expression of Naga dissent was protest against the continuous alienation of their customary rights over the commons. In March 1956, the NNC announced the formation of a Federal Government of Nagaland and its standing army, signalling the first powerful insurgency in post-colonial India.[27]

The Indian state's response to this situation was fast and brutal. It was widely believed that 'there was nearly one security troop for every adult male Naga'.[28] By 1956, the size of Indian security forces in the Naga Hills increased to two divisions of the Indian Army and thirty-five battalions of the Assam Rifles. Between 1956 and 1958, 1,400 Naga insurgents were killed and 162 Indian soldiers also lost their lives in these operations.[29]

As in Kashmir and Sindh, ethnic politics in Nagaland had external ramifications. This has been largely facilitated by a decolonization process, which resulted in non-convergence between the state and ethnic identity that consequently left the Nagas on both sides of the Indo-Burmese border with divided loyalties to the two successor states. This geographical fact has enabled the rebels to seek refuge in Bhutan, China, Bangladesh and Myanmar. According to the Indian government's claims, at the height of insurgency the Naga rebels were supported by the Pakistani intelligence agency, the ISI. The United Kingdom offered another safe haven for Naga politicians waging a war against the Indian state. A perusal of the Charles Pawsey papers preserved in the South Asian Studies Centre at Cambridge University reveals that at one point some people in the United States administration were favourably disposed towards the cause of the Naga insurgents.

A split within the rebels, however, facilitated the Indian effort to deal with handling of the Naga insurgency. New Delhi readily rallied around the moderates to foment a permanent dissension between the overground and underground Naga political groups. To bolster up the former, Nehru created in December 1963 a separate province of Nagaland, encompassing approximately 6,366 square miles with an aggregate population of 3.7 lakhs spread over 700 villages.

This step of the Indian government could not stem the tide of violence in the Hills since the Federal Nagas remained steadfast in their demand for a sovereign state and condemned the Nagas who cooperated with the Indian state. Repressive measures of the Indian state, however, yielded fruits when in 1975 the outlawed Naga Federal Government signed the Shillong Accord with New Delhi by which the former ratified the formation of the state of Nagaland, undertook to surrender their arms and agreed to enter into a dialogue with the Indian government for a political resolution of the Naga issue. Significantly, the Accord was concluded when a national emergency was declared in the country, abrogating all democratic rights of the citizens.

The Shillong Accord was, however, not an unmitigated success. It injected a new life into Naga militants who formed in June 1980 the National Socialist Council of Nagaland or the Naga National Socialist Council (NSCN) with S.S. Khaplang as chairman, Isaak Chisi Swu as vice-chairman and Thiungelang Muivah as general secretary. However, differences soon raised their head between the Khaplang and the Swu-Muivah factions, the latter alleging the former to be 'the equivalent of an Indian puppet'.[30] The Indian state successfully adopted a carrot and stick policy: the Swu-Muivah faction was persuaded to accept a ceasefire agreement in 1997 while the Khaplang group reconciled itself to a formal truce in April 2001.

The creation of the province of Nagaland and the peace accords between the Indian state and Naga rebels did not guarantee political democracy since the province was subjected to doses of central rule. Besides, Nagaland has not derived much advantage from Indian economic planning. While the First and Second Five Year Plans for Nagaland were substantially shelved because of insurgency, lack of adequate economic growth made the Nagas a victim of 'relative under-development'. The north-eastern region contributes a little more than 2 per cent to the country's GNP and Nagaland's share in the national industrial investment is only 0.01 per cent.[31] Like other states of the north-east, Nagaland also suffers from the lack of adequate economic infrastructure at a time when the province is experiencing 6.44 per cent of demographic growth as against the national average of 2.13 per cent (2001 census). Not unnaturally, the purchasing power in the north-east is also lower than the national average—in 1994 the estimated per capita expenditure per month is Rs. 260.3 in the north-east compared to the national figure of Rs. 287.1.[32] National policy planners have generally failed to appreciate regional specificities and requirements which have denied the Nagas the benefits of public investment. For instance, technical developments introduced at the behest of New Delhi are proving to be out of tune with the region's 'consumption habits and management practices' since the production process in Nagaland is still largely dependent on communal ownership and management.[33] Besides, as revealed by studies conducted by the Centre for Monitoring of the Indian Economy, most of the developmental funds pumped into the area were misused to create a *nouveau riche* comprising of politicians, contractors, bureaucrats and police officers.

## THE WAY OUT

The roots of the current Naga imbroglio are twofold. On the one hand, colonial social engineering gave the Nagas a spatial identity that generally tends to make the concerned people 'personalize the territory, while simultaneously (. . .) (defining) their own identity on the basis of anthropomorphism'.[34] At the same, the failure to strike a balance between Naga ethnic aspirations and Indian mainstream politics both during the freedom struggle and in the post-colonial period accelerated a crisis. The current ceasefire between the Indian state and the two major insurgent Naga groups—the Naga National Socialist Council of Nagalim led by Isak and Muivah, and the National Socialist Council of Nagaland under Khaplang—has, however, thrown up new opportunities for the reconciliation of the Naga and mainstream Indian identities. The province has a respite from continuous violence.[35] Unlike the older tribal leaders who had a vested interest in the traditional system, the new generation of Naga elite prefers to 'be an integral part of India while retaining their identity and control over their livelihood'.[36] Increasing participation in general elections also demonstrates a growing adjustment of the Nagas with the reality of the Indian Union. New Delhi should utilize the current ceasefire to provide a platform for dialogue with the various political forces in Nagaland. The Naga civil society groups like the Naga Students' Federation, the Naga People's Movement for Human Rights, the Naga Mothers' Association, the Naga Women's Union of Manipur and Naga Hoho also need to use the ceasefire as a political entry point in search of new democratic alternatives. After all, a ceasefire cannot be an end in itself, it has to be a precursor of a new and better phase. Unless New Delhi realizes this, the current peace in the north-east will remain elusive.

NOTES

1. Subir Bhaumik, *Insurgent Crosssfire: North-East India*, New Delhi: Lancer Books, 1996.
2. Andrew West, 'The Most Dangerous Legacy: The Development of Identity, Power and Marginality in the British Transfer to India and the Nagas', The University of Hull, Centre for South-East Asian Studies, Occasional Paper No. 34, 1999.
3. S.K. Chaube, *Hill Politics in Northeast India,* Calcutta: Orient Longman, 1973; David Syiemlieh, 'Socio-Cultural Background of the Peoples of North-East India (19th-20th Centuries),' in *The Impact of Christianity in North East India*, ed. J. Puthenpurakal, Shillong: Sacred Heart Theological College, 1996.
4. Asoso Yonuo, *The Rising Nagas: A Historical and Political Study*, Delhi: Vivek Publishing House, 1974.
5. See Hutton's typescript on the effect of Simon Commission on the Hill tribes, Hutton Papers, Centre for South Asian Studies, Cambridge, India Microfilm No. 47B. D. Syiemlieh, 'The Future of the Hills of North-East India 1928-1947: Some British Views', in *Reorganization of North-East India Since 1947*, ed. B. Datta Ray and S.P. Agarwal, New Delhi: Concept, 2000.
6. A. Yonuo, *The Rising Nagas.*
7. J. Jacobs et al., *The Nagas: Society, Culture and the Colonial Encounter*, Stuttgart, Thames & Hudson, 1990, Chap. 7.

8. Captain Brodie, 'Narrative of a Tour Over that Part of the Naga Hills Lying Between the Diko and Dyang River', *Journal of the Asiatic Society of Bengal*, vol. 167, 1845, pp. 828-44; J. Avery, 'The Ao Naga Language of Southern Assam', *American Journal of Philology*, vol. 8, 1886, pp. 334-6.
9. S. Nag, *India And North-East India: Mind, Politics and the Process of Integration*, New Delhi: Regency Publ., 1998.
10. R. Gopalakrishnan, *North-east India: From a Geographical Expression to Regional Accommodation*, Delhi: Har Anand Publ., 1995, p.117. Other missionary groups in the north-east were the Welsh Calvinistic Methodists' Foreign Mission Society, the Baptist Missionary Society, the London Missionary Society and the American Baptist Foreign Mission Society.
11. Richard M. Eaton, 'Conversion to Christianity among the Nagas, 1876-1971', *Indian Economic and Social History Review*, vol. 21, no. 1, 1984, p. 7.
12. Eaton, 'Conversion to Christianity among the Nagas', pp. 18, 43.
13. Lal Denga, *Christian Missions and Colonialism: A Study of Missionary Movement in Northeast India With Particular Reference to Manipur and Lushai Hills 1894-1947*, Shillong, Vendrane Institute, 1998, pp. 105-6.
14. *Missionary Herald*, 1935, p. 268.
15. J.P. Mills, ed., *The Ao Nagas*, London: Macmillan, 1926.
16. P. Moasosang, 'The Naga Search for Self-Identity', in *A Common Perspective for North-East India*, ed. Rathin Mitra and Barun Dasgupta, Calcutta: Pannalal Dasgupta, 1969.
17. Neville Maxwell, *India, the Nagas and the North-East*, London: Minority Rights Group, 1980.
18. Louanne Richards, *A Journey into Nagaland*, Chicago: Abzu Bibliography, 1995, p. 5.
19. A. Yonuo, *The Rising Nagas*, p. 150.
20. Typescript of Hutton's analysis of Simon Commission's impact on the Nagas, Hutton Papers, Centre for South Asian Studies, Cambridge, Microfilm No. 47B.
21. S. Nag, *India and North-East India*, p. 11.
22. Cited in A. Yonuo, *The Rising Nagas*, p. 169.
23. S. Nag, *India and North-East India*, p. 74.
24. *Collected Works of Mahatma Gandhi*, vol. LXXXVIII, 25 May 1947 to 31 July 1947, New Delhi, 1983, p. 373.
25. See Phizo's communication to the President of India of 1 November 1957; Girija Kumar and V.K. Arora, eds., *Documents on Indian Affairs*, New Delhi: Asia Publ., 1965, p. 108.
26. Brijendranath Datta, 'Ethnicity, Nationalism and Sub-Nationalism with reference to North-East India', in *Nationality, Ethnicity and Cultural Identity in North-East India*, ed. D. Pakem, New Delhi: Osmos Publ., 1990.

27. S. Bhaumik, *Insurgent Crossfire*, p. 42.
28. B.N. Mullick, *My Years with Nehru: The Chinese Betrayal*, Bombay: Allied Publ., 1971, cited in Bhaumik, *Insurgent Crossfire*, p. 42.
29. Maxwell, *India, the Nagas and the North-East*, p. 6.
30. Sanjoy Hazarika, 'Nagas: The Long March', *Asian Age*, 8 May 2001. The comment was made by Muivah to Hazarika in an interview at Bangkok.
31. Ministry of Industry, Government of India, *SIA Statistics*, April 2001.
32. Abusaleh Shariff, *India Human Development Report: A Profile of Indian States in the 1990s*, New Delhi: Oxford University Press, 1999, p. 257.
33. Many commentators had indicated as early as the 1980s the pitfalls of introducing modern production system in the north-east without changing the pattern of landownership. See, for instance, B.K. Ray Burman, 'Points and Counter-points in North-East India', in *Multi-Ethnicity and National Integration: A Politico Anthropological View*, ed. A.D. Pant and Shiva K. Gupta, Allahabad, 1985.
34. Izhak Schnell, *Perceptions of Israeli Arabs: Territoriality and Identity*, Aldershot, Avebury: Ashgate, 1994, p. 33.
35. But a crisis ensued when New Delhi accepted the Naga demand not to limit the ambit of the ceasefire to Nagaland alone but to bring within it those Nagas living outside Nagaland. This step produced a hostile reaction in states like Manipur having a sizeable Naga population since they feared it would boost the slogan of Greater Nagaland. Faced with the angry outburst, New Delhi abandoned its project of extending the territorial limits of the ceasefire.
36. Walter Fernandes, 'Conflict in North-East: A Historical Perspective', *Economic and Political Weekly*, 34, 51, 18-24 December 1999, p. 3581.

# PART THREE

# Reconfiguring Minority Identities and Territories

CHAPTER 9

# From Conquest to Enclosure: South African Coloured Minorities and Their Territories[1]

FRANÇOIS-XAVIER FAUVELLE-AYMAR

The geographical backdrop to this paper is the old 'frontier' region of present-day South Africa: an area that is bordered by the lower stretches of the Orange River on its southern flank, at the level of its border with Namibia. Today this region is part of the Northern Cape Province, carved from the former Cape Colony (later Cape Province), and divided into three separated entities in 1994. It is a semi-desert, with the Namib and Kalahari deserts bordering its northern limits. This region is sparsely populated with a density of generally less than one inhabitant per square kilometre, suitable only for extensive livestock farming or semi-nomadic pastoralism. It is an area where Afrikaans is spoken practically exclusively and almost all people are Christian. Despite this geographical and cultural unity, this region is marked by profound spatial and identity fractures, rooted in its historical context. On the basis of an analysis of critical periods in the last two centuries, this paper examines the sedimentation of new group identities through miscegenation and geographical and identity polarization. I argue that in the process, places have become critically important, as forms of remembrance (the starting point of migration, of itineraries taken, for instance) or in their expression of economic and religious realities. They represent conflicting geographies where it is possible to define, claim and assign territories in order to differentiate between natives and foreigners to establish a hierarchy of identity.

## RESTRUCTURING OF IDENTITY IN A FRONTIER SOCIETY

Before colonization, the region was dominated by Khoisan-speaking herders who set up camp seasonally on grasslands hugging the river front or around waterholes. Some of these semi-nomadic communities were referred to as Namaqua or Nama by their southern neighhbours and by the colonial authorities, even before the first official European expedition. According to later ethnographic data, these peoples were collectively known as Kham-Naman,[2] or Little Namaqua, a subdivision of a larger Nama group, native to the southern half of Namibia. The Kham-Naman comprised a number of communities regrouped around a central lineage, interconnected by vassalage or alliances (Barnard, 1992, pp. 179-93). Following colonization, the Nama names of these lineages acquired a second Dutch name, and their camps were called *kraals* and their chiefs *kapteins*. Apart from these herders, who together with the Khoikhoi from the Cape and the Korana came to be known as 'Hottentots' in colonial jargon, the region also included groups which depended exclusively on hunting, gathering and conducting raids against the herding communities, designated as 'Bosjesmans' or Bushmen in English terminology.[3]

Often linguistically distinct from the neighbouring herding communities, these groups were named 'San' (robbers or bandits) by the Namaqua, a term whose value alternated between an ethnic designation (which has been retained in the current anthropology literature) and a social designation applicable just as much to the proletarianized herders (those excluded from the Namaqua) as to whites or blacks considered as predators (Barnard, 1992, p. 8). Nigel Penn argues that (1995, pp. 25-7) the more arid zone situated to the east was probably almost exclusively inhabited by the Bushmen, the latter delimiting a buffer zone between the Little Namaqua and another herding community, the Einiqua, settled near the central stretch of the Orange River. To the west of the region, the Bushmen were at loggerheads with the Little Namaquas because both wanted to exploit the best grasslands or hunting grounds. This spatial expression of ethnic and socio-economic polarization, of which the earliest adventurers and colonists were aware, has been expressed and preserved in the names of two districts in the region, Namaqualand and Bushmanland.

The earliest recorded division of space rested on competition between shepherds and hunters over territory and exploitation of resources, in particular the same waterholes and seasonal pastures. These conflicts conditioned identities of and perceptions of groups living in these respective zones, at times resulting in the assimilation and socialization into Bushmen groups of many marginalized individuals forced to live in the arid and remote zones of Bushmanland.

Initially situated outside the nominal boundaries of the colony, the first foreigners who ventured into these regions were not only white farmers, but also farmers of mixed-descent born to Khoisan concubines (called *Bastaards*, later *Basters* in colonial terminology[4]). The latter, Christians, Dutch-speaking and with Afrikaner names, could not however aspire to the farms of their white fathers, and had to move further north (Legassick, 1989, p. 363; Marais, 1957, p. 12). However, some of the families of Bastaard farmers, who had settled in the region as early as the mid-eighteenth century, were able to benefit from the right of possession until the end of the nineteenth century.

Another way of penetrating these areas was as 'commandos'. In the early eighteenth century commandeering was a colonial institution created for the purpose of conducting punitive or preventive raids against attacks perpetrated by the Khoisan. Composed of colonial officers, colonists, men of mixed descent and Khoisan dependents, these vigilante squads killed thousands during the eighteenth century, in the process liberating the land for farmers to expand their holdings as well as supplying the latter a relatively servile labour force comprising captured or isolated Khoisan (Elphick and Malherbe, 1989, pp. 25-8). The process continued for decades and forced the colonial authorities to take note of the *de facto* expansion of the colony, transformed by successive stages into a *de jure* extension. By 1856, the regions bordering the Orange had all been integrated into the Cape Colony. The commando system became a way of life, of survival, even a mode of social organization for some of the groups living in these open and savage frontier tracts. These composite groups depended on hunting, trade and plunder for their livelihood. At the end of the eighteenth century, they were led by charismatic and unscrupulous chiefs, in particular whites who had rejected society, deserters, Bastaards, Khoisan chiefs or free slaves, whose power depended on their capacity to provide their respective groups with horses, arms and ammunition necessary for their protection (Legassick, 1989, pp. 368-72). Another element of this frontier society was the *Oorlams*, a term generally used to designate the Namaqua who lived as clients or dependents of white farmers, and who were, therefore, under the influence of Afrikaner culture. At the dawn of the nineteenth century, the Oorlams first organized themselves into a social category, then into partly restructured autonomous groups (speaking Nama as well as Dutch), at times absorbing a few individuals from outside.

A second critical point in the history of the region was marked by social chaos, the dilution of identity and a relative cultural fusion, processes which took place far from the colonial centres of power, yet set the moral and social norms in the region. In the first few decades of the nineteenth century, the Namaqualand region gradually began to lose its pioneering character because of the rampant colonization of lands by farmers and the consequent imposition of colonial order. Itinerant bands operating in the region responded in two ways, both aimed to maintain the status that some communities had acquired by deliberately placing themselves outside the colonial order.

In the first case, Bastaard communities organized into commandos or bands of trekkers converted their low social status and the uncertain conditions prevailing in the colony by penetrating these open zones. When peace was gradually restored in these regions, village communities grew next to missionary outposts. Away from zones directly or exclusively controlled by whites, the term 'Bastaard' required a positive connotation and was gradually given an autonomous ethnic meaning. But, as mentioned earlier, by the middle of the century these communities found themselves within the boundaries of the colony. Some of them, composed of a few hundred individuals, responded by setting themselves up as separate Republics, complete with a constitution. They demanded to be considered an integral part of the British Empire. Among them were the inhabitants of Kommagas (1857), Steinkopf (1870) and Concordia (1888) (Carsten, 1983, pp. 144-50). This two-phased process (departure from the colony and the formation of an independent political entity within a larger colony) was a dual strategy aimed at preserving a status, which, away from the centre of power, had been transformed and acquired a positive value. In this new environment, these communities were able to consolidate themselves as the new centres of power and to set a norm, as well as to get the support of various Khoisan elements and persons of mixed descent. These processes led to an internal polarization, still evident today.

In the second case, the response to the imposition of the colonial order in this old frontier zone took the form of a new trek. This was the strategy adopted by some groups or commandos who guaranteed their economic survival by going up the Orange River or crossing it, distancing themselves from the centres of power and thereby continuing to live in 'frontier' conditions. Archival sources reveal the emergence, between 1800 and 1830, of the Bastaard state of the Griquas in central Transorangia (Legassick, 1989, pp. 376-95; Schoeman, 1996). At the instigation of missionaries, who had been invited by the Bastaards, this state also drew up its own constitution (1813); it remained in place until 1861, when a new trek to the east was undertaken. Similarly, diverse Nama and Oorlam groups operated along the southern banks of the Orange for some time before crossing into present-day Namibia, where their colonial culture ensured their hegemony during the major part of the nineteenth century (Legassick, 1989, p. 375). In fact even today some Namibian communities claim a specifically Oorlam identity, distinct from the Nama identity.[5] Certain village communities also found themselves forced to trek northwards, for example, the Bastaards from De Tuin in Bushmanland, who abandoned camp in 1868, stayed briefly in Pella, then left the colony by crossing the Orange River. They stayed for a while in the Nama mission in Warmbad, where they, too, adopted a Republican Constitution (Carstens, 1983, pp. 138-44). Later, they continued their trek till Rehoboth (1870) in central Namibia. Incorporated into the German colony, then into South-West Africa, the vast territory of the Rehobothers enjoyed a degree of political autonomy for a long time.

The discussion here points to a relatively long and effective resistance to the restoration of the colonial order. The third 'high point' marks the transformation of particular social groups from an individual to a communal identity, which then became the basis for the formation of a sense of community (for example, groups of individuals, the 'bastards', were transformed into 'Bastaard' communities). Such transformations were part of a process of ethnicization of the frontier identity.

Integrated into the Crown lands in the mid-nineteenth century, the missions responsible for the communities settled around their stations were granted 'tickets of occupation', the equivalent of land deeds conferred on individuals. These certificates had been introduced in order to give these communities a juridical existence and a legal foundation for their territorial possessions to protect them from prospective claims by neighbouring farmers. Once this status had come into force, individual deeds were increasingly withheld from non-whites on the pretext that they could settle instead within village communities. This step had an additional outcome: the concretization of social and spatial identities that had been fluid (until the beginning of the twentieth century)—into two distinct statuses that resulted in the 'introduction of an institutionalised form of racial classification' (Sharp and West, 1984, p. 3). Spatially and socially it separated whites from 'natives' and 'Bastaards with native ancestry'. The segregationist, and later apartheid, laws reinforced this tendency further by prohibiting whites from settling on mission stations, renamed 'communal reserves',[6] while designating still vacant Crown lands for occasional herding exclusively for whites (Land Settlement Act, 1912), and last, permanently prohibiting the purchase of farms by non-whites (Group Areas Act, 1950).

The effect of these waves of segregation constitutes the fourth high point that put the finishing touches to the freezing of racial groups around the categories 'white' and 'coloured', the latter category[7] the only one that the central apartheid government used to contain the multiple communities born in the context of the frontier society described earlier. Although the institutionalization of segregation incorporated a number of processes, it is important to understand the specifics of the application of this racial policy in the region. Its application in the old frontier region perhaps 'preserved' the 'purity' of the white race from 'pollution' by other ethnic groups—its ideological goal—but also resulted in a 'de-mixing' of people of mixed descent. The classification of diverse ethnic groups into categories of 'coloured' and 'white' forced these groups to conform to the racial categories applied to the rest of the country. Thus, all those who had succeeded in acquiring and maintaining the economic status of farmers were by definition white, whereas all individuals living on the reserves, were by definition '*coloured*' (even if they could have been classified as 'poor whites' living in missionary establishments). The threat of the absorption of '*poor whites*' by native elements became an important issue for the government in the 1930s. Commissions were appointed to neutralize the threat, but they mainly employed criteria that were sociological rather than racial in nature. An ethnologist revealed the irrelevance of phenotypic characters in an interview conducted in the 1930s with one of the members of the Carnegie Poor Whites Commission. The Commission member confessed that it was 'difficult to distinguish between some impoverished Bastards and poor Whites. The difficulty was solved by the fact that the Bastaards always addressed them [the Whites] as "*Baas*" [master]' (Marais, 1957, p. 96, n. 3).

The effect of the gradual closure of the space of the reserves and the confinement of their inhabitants valorized the Bastaard status within reserves. Through genealogical manipulations or 'bricolages' and preferential marriage alliances many people began to identify themselves as Bastaards. As early as 1913, anthropologist Winifred Hoernlé, who travelled through Namaqualand, expressed disappointment at meeting people all claiming to be Bastaards, whereas she was looking for 'authentic' Hottentots (Hoernlé, 1985). But, as will be discussed later, this terminological homogenization did not eliminate differences in identity.

The twentieth century history of communities generalized as 'coloured' is one of the enclaves, encircled by 'white' farms and mining concessions, whose space in consequence was gradually encroached upon by the parceling out of lands to whites. Between the 1960s and the 1980s, the government made attempts to transform reserves, where the land tenure was communal, into farms that could be allocated to the more affluent members of the community. With some exceptions this policy failed because it met with stiff resistance.

In the contemporary period, approximately 27,000 inhabitants live on the six reserves in Namaqualand. But in the democratic context and with the repeal of racially-based legislation, the politics of identity has changed quite radically. Some segments of groups which were classified 'coloured' tend to valorize their African rather than white origins. Baster identity, now redundant, is being supplanted by an indigenous identity. In fact, the authenticity attached to being 'indigenous' has been capitalized on both for attracting tourists and as a basis of land claims. The fifth and last high point, characterized by the resurgence of indigenous identities, is based on the concept of autochthomy. A case, studied by J. Sharp (1994), clearly illustrates how identity and claims on land are closely interwoven. The Komaggas reserve, created by an 1843 'certificate of occupation', covers an area of approximately 69,000 hectares. Since the beginning of the twentieth century, the area has been hemmed in by private lands belonging to White farmers or mining companies. However, the inhabitants never gave up their claim of a much bigger area than the present reserve, affirming either that the original certificate had in fact allotted 369,000 hectares, or that it had been preceded by another land grant personally ractified by Queen Victoria. In both cases, their claims were based on a juridical deed presumably executed between the colonial authorities and the Bastaards who were occupying the site. In the early 1990s, local developments prompted the inhabitants of Komaggas to put forward their claim once more. Their claim failed however. In the process some Komaggas realized the unfounded nature of their reasoning and that their 'certificate of occupation' (the only existing juridical act that marked their legal right to land) had in reality been the instrument of their dispossession. This reformulation implied a complete reinterpretation of the history of their community. Until then, it was believed that the community had descended from a Bastaard colonist, Jasper Cloete, who had settled in Komaggas in the early nineteenth century, and whose name is borne by more than half the population. Over the past few years another interpretation has been put forward, which lays stress on the fact that Cloete's wife, a Namaqua, belonged to the community that was living on the site before his arrival. No less legitimate than the previous one, this interpretation had been dismissed earlier because it called into question the 'white' ancestry of the community. In the contemporary period, it has the advantage of binding the community's territorial claims not to a colonial juridical act but to the rights of the indigenous as the land's first occupants.

## RELATIONSHIP TO TERRITORY: COLOURED 'MINORITIES' AND THE AFRIKANER 'MAJORITY'?

Here I will not discuss the allotment of the status of colonizer and colonized in the context of a frontier in a perpetual state of flux due to the continuous restructuring of groups and identities. But over and above the unequal relationships among the various social entities, I will highlight the points of convergence, on the one hand, between the numerous coloured communities and/or the 'natives' that manifest a somewhat high degree of ethnic identity within localized territories, and on the other, a specific pioneering group that proclaimed a proud pan-South African nationalism.

The commando technique, the custom of treks, the presence of real dynasties led by charismatic chiefs, the republican form of organization of communities, unquestionably originated in frontier life structured mainly by violence, patriarchy and an unwavering resolve to defy the colonial order, seen as the emanation of the British monarchy. Moreover, determination to escape the colonial stranglehold by leaving the colony juridically and/or geographically is similar to the Great Afrikaner Trek of the 1930s, motivated specifically by the rejection of English dominance, which ultimately resulted in the formation of several Boer Republics (such as Natalia, Orange Free State and Transvaal). It is therefore useful to study the Afrikaner example in the same historical context, even though it exceeds the geographical framework of the northern frontier of the Colony. This comparison is appropriate because both treks were part of the same process of avoiding English colonial rule. After all the Bastaards did not see themselves as anything other than 'Brown Dutchmen' or 'brown *voortrekkers*', rather than Afrikaner 'white *voortrekkers*'.

Another point of convergence lies in the emergence, in the context outlined earlier, of strong identities, in some cases bordering on quasi-national sentiments (for example with the Afrikaners or Rehobothers)—sentiments based on political ideologies that, despite being republican, were no less rooted in race. In practically all the cases mentioned earlier, the community's identity was shaped in a context of isolation and persecution in a socially chaotic environment. Attitudes aimed at preserving, and if possible, amplifying a 'racial' or 'ethnic' status acquired at great cost were the basis of communal identities that were organized to combat the absorption of groups and individuals whose blood was not so pure through, for instance, marriage with lighter skinned people. Many attitudes revealed the importance of racial distinctions inherited from living in the colony, ideas that were internalized and exported through the process of trekking and establishing claim over lands. Systems of social differentiation built on different characterizations of 'pedigree' thus cast citizens (***burghers***) against non-citizens (***bywoners***, co-residents, or ***bediendes***, servants), the ***inkommers*** (incomers) against the ***boorlinges*** (natives), the Oorlams against the Namas, the Basters against the others, and even within a community, one family against another. Although some missionaries, operating in central Transorangia in the beginning of the nineteenth century, for instance, attempted to abolish the differences between the Basters, the Oorlams and the Koranas, in order to forge a new Griqua identity (Legassick, 1989, p. 382), such attempts were infrequent as well as indicative of the general social milieu of the period. The formidable sensitivity that still pervades the Little and Great Namaqualand communities on such issues as the vintage of the mixed ancestry, the anteriority of the lineage, the origin of the family name, skin colour, or hair texture[8] has produced an entire 'casuistry of bastardization'. A casuistry, which makes it possible to refine *ad infinitum* the racial hierarchy between groups and within groups, could explain the absence of Oorlam and Baster nationalism, and also the absence of a 'true' Oorlam or Baster identity that works in favour of multiple local identities associated with specific places. One is not simply an Oorlam but an Oorlam from Vaalgras or from elsewhere; one is not Baster but Rehobother, Griqua or Pellanaar. This is symptomatic of the genesis of identity rooted in linkages to specific land, which although originally imposed have been reinterpreted today in terms of autochthony.

This powerful bonding with land is only one of the modalities of the relationship with space, which evolved in the frontier and trek historical periods. Religious symbolism interweaves with representations of the land, an area analysed extensively in the context of Afrikaner ideology and its theological foundations. In an excellent article, André du Toit (1983) criticized the myth of Afrikaner nationalism's Calvinist origin. Du Toit demonstrated that nothing of what characterized Afrikaner ideology is specifically related to Calvinism and that the 'Calvinist paradigm' is nothing more than the fruit of a reinterpretation of history by English missionaries from the second half of the nineteenth century. This reinterpretation attempted to confer theological legitimacy on the twin expansion of European dominance and Christianity. It is on the basis of this rather late interpretation, one external to the Afrikaner milieu, that the idea of a 'divine mandate' finds its way into the literature of the late nineteenth century and is re-appropriated by the Afrikaners at the dawn of the twentieth century. The 'Calvinist paradigm', therefore, could be understood as both a key to the interpretation of history as well as an ideological fact whose history can be followed in contemporary discourse.

This critical reading of the 'Calvinist paradigm' throws light on the role of certain religious agents in the second half of the nineteenth century as producers and mediators of a legitimizing discourse. But, in the wider context, it seems to me, that just like the entire debate on the theological foundations of Afrikaner ideology, it ignores the role that other frontier communities may have played in this domain. The latter included 'specialists' in the Biblical texts. Missionaries, for example, settled among the non-white Christian populations who, even more than the whites, were determined to distance themselves ideologically from the pagan natives, and were prone to seeking topographic references and behaviour patterns in the Scriptures to impart some meaning to the repeated wanderings and treks.

A study of the toponyms adopted by missionaries in the frontier zones indicates which biblical episodes were used more often, and how they contributed to making the chaotic space of the frontier more intelligible. In texts that record the presence of Christians in the *veld*, one can find among many others, Berea (Acts 17, 10-11), Berseba (Genesis 21, 31), Bethany (Mark 11, 1), Bethlehem, Bethulia (Judith 4, 6-7) and Rehoboth (Genesis 26, 22).[9] Another example, Pella, exemplifies the memorial significance of religion-inspired toponyms. In 1805, the missionaries of the London Missionary Society settled in Warmbad which lay to the south of present-day Namibia. The mission was destroyed in 1811 in an attack by an Oorlam *kaptein.* Some inhabitants took refuge with their pastor near a waterhole situated to the south of the Orange River, which was thereafter christened Pella.

This toponym is not from a purely Biblical source, but derives from an ancient Christian tradition, which can be traced to the *History of the Church* (3, 5, 3) by Eusebius of Caesarea. The passage relates how Jerusalem Christians, forewarned by a revelation (probably the one recounted in Matthew 24, 1-25; Mark 13, 1-23) announcing the destruction of Jerusalem, fled the town and gathered at Pella,[10] to the east of the Jordan, from where they witnessed the capture of Jerusalem by Titus' troops in the year 70. The re-enactment of this Act by Nama families, who, accompanied by their pastor like the primitive Christians of antiquity, migrated to safer lands by crossing a river, provides a good example of the role of missionary activity in a formative space and time.

Groups living in a pioneering environment situated outside or on the fringes of the colony shared a feeling of evolving in a world without a centre, uncharted and without limits. The formation and restructuring of identities thus became a more subterranean process structured through the invention of territory, of the projection by each community of remote referents that transformed a chaotic space into an organized or familiar one. The internalization of territorial moorings and exact frontiers by each itinerant group created a sense of familiarity which defined, in turn, territoriality. Forcibly conflict ridden, always controversial, faced with the constant possibility of renegotiation, the formation of territory gave meaning to each community's wanderings and existence, engendering a sentiment of common destiny.

White Dutch-speaking communities leaving the British colony at the beginning of the nineteenth century were not exempt from this process. If there was a special case, it was that of pioneering Afrikaner communities that in the specific political context at the dawn of the twentieth century managed to federate their numerous territorialities, generating for themselves a common attachment to an 'Afrikaner' identity. The combination provided a framework for a new society, which made it possible to affirm its primacy and exceptional character. The minorities present in South Africa today are thus not the predictable outcome of a preconceived historical project. On the contrary, they are products of historical engineering, born from the complex distinctions that fractured an originally more fluid set of frontier identities into 'white' and 'coloured' 'minorities'. Having undergone the same experience and shared the same culture, the 'white' minority has been able to impose a dominant historical discourse from which the Afrikaner 'nation' emerges as 'major' and as 'majority'.

This discourse is officially outdated today, the Afrikaners have been reduced to a minority in contrast to the new black 'majority'; but the unravelling of frontier identities sheds light on the distinction between white and coloured minorities, a distinction that persists in contiguous juxtaposition in the idealized 'rainbow' of democratic South Africa. Contiguous and distinct means that researchers cannot pass imperceptibly from the one to the other; they have to leap over a divide, which although less physical and more symbolic is not less structured.[11]

NOTES

1. This paper is based on bibliographical and various archival research as well as on field studies. I am grateful to P. Gervais-Lambony, Georges Hérault, Len and Elzette Hansen, Benoît and Elizabeth Antheaume and Philippe Guillaume.
2. The Khoisan languages comprise a certain number of aspirated sounds (clicks), marked as /, //, ! and ≠.
3. On the origin of the terms 'Hottentot' and 'Bushman', see Fauvelle-Aymar, 2002, *passim*.
4. In Dutch and Afrikaans respectively.
5. According to oral tradition recorded in 1997, through interviews of inhabitants of Vaalgras in Namibia, not far from Keetmanshoop—originally the Oorlams in this region were probably Herero (Bantu-speaking people from central Namibia). A war against the Nama is believed to be the reason these Hereros migrated southwards, where they settled south of the Orange, in Namaqualand, before crossing the river in the opposite direction during the 1870-1880 period. Probably assimilated during this period with Nama-speaking groups, the Oorlams of Vaalgras are quick to point out their superiority *vis-à-vis* the 'true' Nama.
6. Mission Stations and Communal Reserves Act, 1909. For the coloureds, the 'reserves' were the equivalent of the 'Bantustans' or the 'Homelands', reserved for the blacks.
7. The term 'coloured' is defined by the 1928 Pensions Act as: 'a Coloured is neither a White, nor an Asian, neither a member of an African aboriginal race or tribe, nor a Hottentot, neither a Bushman, nor a Koranna . . .'.
8. Investigation conducted in Pella, June 1997: long and smooth hair is deemed typical of the 'Coloureds', whose ancestry is servile, whereas short, thin hair is said to be typical of the Bastaards.
9. Examples and references are taken from RAPER, 1989, *passim*.
10. A town founded at the end of the fourth century BC by veterans from Alexander's army, and which was named after Philip's Macedonian capital.

11. A general comparison with India is useful: it shows how the promotion of nationalist icons and the re-writing of history have, in recent times, participated in a race for autochthony and purity which has resulted in dividing the common history of Hindu Indians and Muslim Indians and consolidating the 'barrier' between these religious communities (Assayag, 2001, p. 90 and *passim*). That this barrier was reinforced by the 1947 Partition between India and Pakistan and the relocation of populations which followed, and that apartheid precisely consisted of spatially preventing contamination, are illustrations of the same underlying principle as examined in this chapter: the transformation of the self or the known into a stranger.

## REFERENCES


Assayag, J., *L'Inde. Désir de nation*, Paris: Odile Jacob, 2001.

Barnard, A., *Hunters and Herders of Southern Africa: A Comparative Ethnography of the Khoisan Peoples*, Cambridge: Cambridge University Press, 1992.

Carstens, P., 'Opting out of Colonial Rule: The Brown Voortrekkes of South Africa and Their Constitution, *African Studies*, 42 (2), 1983, pp. 135-52; and 43 (1), 1984, pp. 19-30.

Du Toit, A., 'No Chosen People: The Myth of the Calvinist Origins of Afrikaner Nationalism and Racial Ideology, *American Historical Review*, 88, 1983, pp. 920-52.

Elphick R., and V.C. Malherbe, 'The Khoisan to 1828', in *The Shaping of South African Society, 1652-1840*, ed. R. Elphick and H. Giliomee, Cape Town: Maskew Miller Longman, 1989, pp. 3-65.

Fauvelle-Aymar, F.-X., *L'invention du Hottentot. Histoire du regard occidental sur les Khoisan (XV^e-XIX^e siècle)*, Paris: Publications de la Sorbonne, 2002.

Hoernlé, A.W., 'Richterveld: The Land and its People, in *The Social Organisation of the Nama, and Other Essays*, ed. P. Carstens, Johannesburg: Witwatersrand University Press, 1985.

Legassick, M., 'The Northern Frontier to *c.* 1840: The Rise and Decline of the Griqua People', in *The Shaping of South African Society, 1652-1840*, ed. R. Elphick and H. Giliomee, Cape Town: Maskew Miller Longman, 1989, pp. 358-420.

Marais, J.S., *The Cape Coloured People*, Johannesburg: Witwatersrand University Press, rpt., 1957 (1939).

Raper, P.E., *Dictionary of South African Place Names*, Johannesburg: J. Ball, 1989.

Saunders, C. and N. Southey, *A Dictionary of South African History*, Cape Town and Johannesburg: David Philip, 2001.

Schoeman, K. (ed.), *Griqua Records: The Philippolis Captaincy, 1825-1861*, Cape Town: Van Riebeeck Society, 1996.

Sharp, J., 'Land Claims in Namaqualand: The Komaggas Reserve', *Review of African Political Economy*, 61, 1994, pp. 403-14.

Sharp, J. and E. Boonzaier, 'Ethnic Identity as Performance: Lessons from Namaqualand', *Journal of Southern African Studies*, 20 (3), 1994, pp. 405-15.

Sharp, J. and M. West, 'Controls and Constraints: Land, Labour and Mobility in Namaqualand', communication présentée à la *Second Carnegie Inquiry into Poverty and Development in Southern Africa*, Carnegie conference paper no. 71, University of Cape Town, April 1984.

CHAPTER 10

# Contextualizing 'Territorial' and 'Social' Identities: Historical Regions and a Minority Community in North India

ATIYA HABEEB KIDWAI

Places, regions or 'territories' represent the dynamism and the discontinuities of human aspirations as they historically evolve and intersect with contextual forces. They are the active construction of social groups. Social groups, in their turn, acquire their identity and circumscribe their potential through the 'territories' they construct. 'Territories' and social groups are always in a flux since socio-economic contexts, which govern them, change and new political exigencies become manifest. Responding to this flux, 'territorial' and 'social' identities are formed and dissolved and the factors which bring them into existence change in their relative importance. The intensity of the connection between people's sense of identity with particular 'territories' also waxes and wanes.

In plural and multilayered societies like India the formation of 'identities' is a multifaceted process and is governed by several factors. This paper aims to understand this multifaceted process and to pinpoint the factors which have historically been instrumental in forming identities at different territorial levels and in various social realms in societies characterized by a range of diversities.

The paper is divided into three sections: In the first section, some theoretical issues and concepts which frame discussions on 'identities' are addressed and the specific context in which they are used in this paper is delineated.

The next section examines the concept of territorial identities and indicates the politico-economic and social factors and processes which are integral to their formation at the macro and micro levels in towns and cities. My approach is historical, drawing on past restructuring to demonstrate the ways in which elements of the past have been continually present and influential in the creation and perpetuation of identities today. The case studies demonstrate territorial identity in two regions in north India—Awadh and Rohilkhand (Uttar Pradesh), which have considerable historical significance and represent microcosms of the Indian regional and social amalgam.

The last section sheds light on the process of formation of 'social' identities and focuses on the minority community of Muslims in Awadh and Rohilkhand. This diverse group of different sects and ethnicities has gone through the manifold processes of social assimilation and differentiation over several centuries. They are, therefore, also an *historical* community with their own identity framework. Throughout the medieval period Muslims in both regions were politically and socially, and at times even a numerically, dominant social group. They were, however, fractured and reduced to a minority at the time of the Partition of the country in 1947. During this period many members willingly or unwillingly migrated to Pakistan. The Muslims of Awadh and Rohilkhand have since adopted several strategies to regain some coherence they lost as a community in the wake of the Partition.

## I

## THEORETICAL FRAMEWORK AND CONCEPTUAL PROPOSITIONS: HOW IS 'TERRITORIAL IDENTITY' CONSTRUCTED?

Each place, region, or 'territory' (local languages use the term *desa* in Hindi or *ilaqa* in Urdu), is an 'object for a subject', in fact, for a 'plurality of subjects' (Eyles, 1988, p. 121). These spatial units are hence socially produced and are both abstract (imagined and mental) and concrete (physical and geographical) (Deshpande, 2000, p. 169). They represent different units of 'space' as conceptualized in contemporary critical social theory. A 'territory', as Eyles argued, is not constructed by a 'collective human response, an undifferentiated regional man' but is the product of a regional history and a regional sociology which, through a historically carved social stratification, represents 'class, status, power, lifestyle and interest group cleavages to the intersection of people and place' (Eyles, 1988, p. 121). One may add a necessary rider to this statement—regional history and regional sociology not only introduce 'cleavages', but also 'cohesiveness' which is manifested through the construction of territorial and social identities. Territorial identities are created by 'territorial organization'; i.e. the social construction of space, and through a territorial blend of language, religion, race, caste and ethnicity. These factors can create territorial identities independent of each other but such identities are very simplistic and not always clear-cut since ethnic, linguistic and caste regions do not always correspond to and are invariably cut across by religion (Spate, 1967, p. 150). Language, religion, race, caste and ethnicity also are instrumental in the formation of social identities.

The 'traditional' pre-modern organization of territorial identities existed at two levels of articulation of space. First, the higher order homogeneous divisions which divided a territory into 'a number of vast coherent sectors' based on 'major contrasts in cultures, landscapes and social development, great dissecting forces which produce cracks across the entire edifice' of a country (de Planhol and Claval, 1994, p. 121). Second, the lower level of smaller regional units, 'areas of close communication, mostly constituted on the basis of complementary natural elements interacting to a greater or lesser degree within the framework of feudal political institutions and dominated by the urban centres to which they were linked' (de Planhol and Claval, 1994, p. 121).

The process of territorialization in India began in the proto-historic times following the formation of a large number of petty states carved out by the innumerable Vedic tribes. These small states existed at three levels ranging from micro to macro. They were *janapadas* inhabited by specific tribes; *mahajanapada*, i.e. 'confederations of several tribes' differentiated by dialect/language and local culture; and, *rashtras* or 'kingdoms'. 'Territorial' loyalty was to the politico-cultural regions or *janapadas*, which continued to exist and provided the edifice on which the Mughal provincial structure was established in the sixteenth century. The British administrative organization followed in the nineteenth century, and the Indian states in the twentieth century (Keay, 2000, p. 50). Within this territorial formation of *janapadas* there existed the micro level *desa* or *ilaqa*, a coherent cultural-ecological space wherein inhabitants had some awareness of an identity that was derived from belonging to that territory/region (Sopher, 1977, p. 281). These 'subjective regions', perceived by the folk as unique and belonging to them, are in many ways historically analogous to the French folk region, the *pays*.

Like the *desa*, the *pays* have been territorially stable from the time they were formed as Gaulish tribal territories, converted into *pagus*, the Roman administrative district and then transformed into ecclesiastical units of the Roman Catholic Church (Sopher, 1997, p. 283). The differences between the *desa* and the *pays*, however, are also significant and suggest caution in using the *pays* as a model in India. Given the level of communication technology at the time, the range of social contacts with the outside world which reinforce or dilute the sense of identity may have been small in the case of the *pays*. This preserved their identity whereas the *desa* subjected to customs, allowed marriage links to cut across their perceived boundaries as well as specialized long distance trade routes which strongly linked them. Moreover, in pre-modern France the political order did not affect the underlying tier of smaller regions and imparted a more effective identity to aggregates of them, i.e. the province. In India's tumultuous history the *desa* boundaries were often significantly disturbed.

## WHAT FORMS A 'SOCIAL IDENTITY'?

The creation of a social identity is a complex historical process. At any time it is conditioned by continuities from the past as well as reactions to the present. Religion, caste, ethnicity and community structure social identities. These terms are so loosely used in common parlance, in so many contexts and with so much conceptual blurring that it is important to discuss their specific utility and connotation in this study to facilitate debate.

A social identity is a component of human consciousness and is created by the process of socialization which takes place at two levels. Primary socialization takes place within the confines of the family and is based on the family's religious, caste and ethnic affiliations. Secondary socialization takes place through interaction with one's kin and community. Secondary socialization may or may not reinforce an individual's perception of his or her social identity imbibed during primary socialization.

It is worthwhile to begin with the most problematic of these concepts, i.e. the 'community'. In contemporary social science research the term has been used as an omnibus loaded with diverse associations. There are, however, two main arguments about 'community' in the literature: community as a type of *collectivity*, a social unit; or as a type of social *relationship* wherein cohesion occurs through a 'sentimental' sense of belonging to a collectivity. These two threads were combined in the concept of *Gemeinschaft* by Tonnies and later by Nisbet (1953).

Communities are also differentiated *via* two approaches: the *territorial* approach wherein a community is interpreted as a group sharing a defined physical space or geographical area; and the *non-territorial* approach wherein the community is considered as a group sharing common traits, a cultural distinctiveness, the perception that people within it are alike, a sense of belonging and/or maintaining social ties and interactions which shape it into a distinct social entity, such as an ethnic, religious, racial or professional community. Since this paper, analyses a minority community in the quest of a lost identity, I will consider it both as a type of 'collectivity' as well as an aggregate of social relations bound by sentiment. I will employ the territorial approach to understand the construction of territorial identities and the non-territorial approach to address the formation of social identities.

Since the Muslim community (*qaum*) in India is divided in terms of social, rather than religious, practice into ethnic and caste groups, it is in order to briefly discuss the contending approaches to the analysis of ethnicity and caste. Ethnic groups are defined either through the 'ascriptive' or 'primordialist' approach as a people bound together by their common descent and 'attachments' derived from it (Geertz, 1967, p. 108); or, through the 'situational' or 'subjectivist' approach as people who consider themselves as culturally and physically distinct from others. In the context of this paper, I agree with Blumer who combined these approaches and suggested that an ethnic group is a 'collectivity within a larger society having real or putative common ancestry, memories of a shared past and cultural focus on one or more symbolic elements which define the group's identity such as kinship, religion, language, shared territory, nationality or physical appearance' (Blumer, 1998, p. 193). The cultural focus and the employment of cultural markers makes an ethnic group a 'subjectively self-conscious com-munity' which has claims to status and recognition *vis-à-vis* other groups (Brass, 1991, p. 19).

Caste is of some concern here because, influenced by the indigenous Hindu society, Indian Muslims structured a hierarchical social structure for themselves based on several criteria (see Ahmad, 1978). This hierarchy in the upper strata of Muslim society was defined by lineage and social status, while the lower classes and converts adapted the Hindu caste system. This system was particularly prevalent in rural areas.

Religion has probably been the most visible factor in the formation of community identities in India where all the major religions of the world are practised. Muslims are considered in this paper both as a religious community as well as a '*community of culture*'. I consider their own world of social life, social relations and social identity because Islam, as defined by the Koran and *Sunnna* (the teachings of the Prophet), is a 'way of life'. 'Culture' defined in the social sense is also 'a particular way of life' expressed in ordinary behaviour as well as in the totality of life experience and social relations.

II

## THE HISTORICAL ROOTS OF REGIONAL OR TERRITORIAL IDENTITIES: THE CASE OF AWADH AND ROHILKHAND

Since the ancient times Awadh and Rohilkhand, located in the upper-Gangetic plains (state of Uttar Pradesh, see Map 10.1), have been nuclear regions that were significant bases of power in the historical geography of the subcontinent.

The existing structure and identity of Awadh and Rohilkhand emerged in the thirteenth century following the advent of Islam when a new period of relative prosperity was ushered in and the regions attracted families of substantial *zamindars* (landlords) as well as clans and Muslim *sufi* saints from Central Asia, Arabia, Afghanistan and Iran. However, with the decline of the Mughal Empire towards the end of the seventeenth century, Awadh was taken over by Iranian Nawabs and Rohilkhand by the Rohilla and Afghan Pathans who came to north India around 1720 to serve the Mughal Empire as mercenary soldiers (Bayly, 1983, p. 17). Though created by the same political environment, Awadh and Rohilkhand proceeded on different political trajectories, structured different regional societies and acquired distinct regional identities.

These trajectories are traversed from the time of the decline of the Mughal Empire to the establishment of the British imperial rule in the two regions. Sa'adat Khan, an influential Iranian Shia at the Mughal court, established the dynastic rule of the Nawabs of Awadh in 1722. The main components of Awadh society at that time were the rural Hindu (Brahmins and Rajputs) chieftains, the Muslim and Hindu (Kayastha and Khatri) urban elite, the *qazis* (Islamic judges), the *taluqdars* (holders of revenue subdivisions), the *jagirdars* (assignees of land revenue), and the smaller landholders. To consolidate himself, Sa'adat Khan adopted a non-sectarian policy of accommodation and appeasement of local social groups which brought political stability

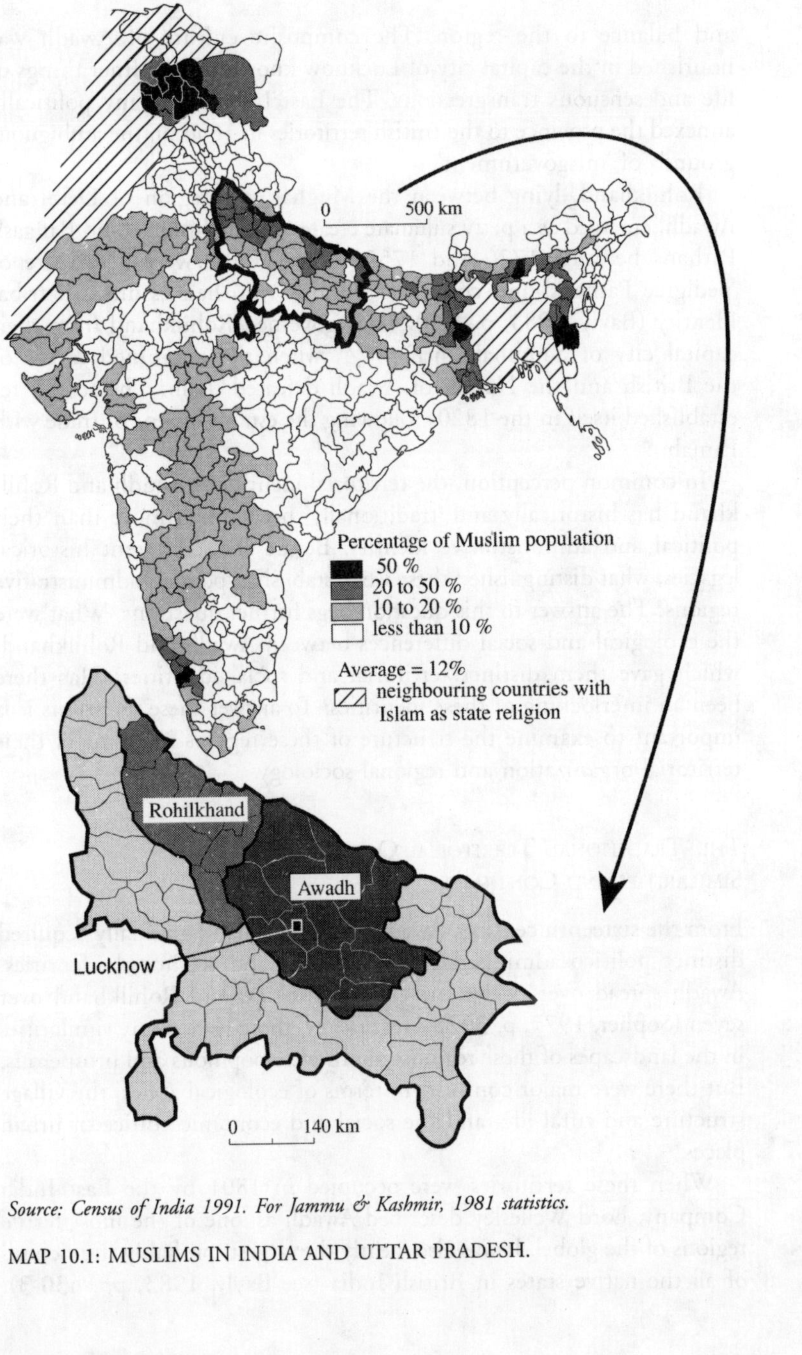


*Source: Census of India 1991. For Jammu & Kashmir, 1981 statistics.*

MAP 10.1: MUSLIMS IN INDIA AND UTTAR PRADESH.

and balance to the region. The composite culture of Awadh was nourished in the capital city of Lucknow known for the finer things of life and sensuous transgressions. The East India Company politically annexed the province to the British territories in 1856 on the ambiguous grounds of 'misgovernment'.

Rohilkhand, lying between the Mughal core region of Delhi and Awadh, emerged as a petty sultanate created by the Rohillas and Bangash Pathans between 1720 and 1750. The Rohillas were a mixture of 'pedigree Pathans' and converted Hindus who had assumed a tribal identity (Bayly, 1983, p. 120). They governed Rohilkhand from their capital city of Sambhal until 1774, when the combined forces of the British and the Nawab of Awadh defeated them. The region re-established itself in the 1820s following the establishment of trade with Panjab.

In common perception, the territorial identity of Awadh and Rohilkhand has historically and 'traditionally' been much more than their political and administrative identity. Beside their different historical legacies, what distinguished these well-established politico-administrative regions? The answer to this question begs further questions. What were the ecological and social differences between Awadh and Rohilkhand, which gave them distinct territorial and social identities? Has there been an interlocking of these identities? To answer these questions it is important to examine the structure of these regions in terms of their territorial organization and regional sociology.

## The 'Traditional' Territorial Organization—Similarities and Contrasts

From the sixteenth century, Awadh and Rohilkhand gradually acquired distinct politico-administrative boundaries and territorial identities. Awadh spread over twelve present-day districts and Rohilkhand over seven (Sopher, 1977, p. 302). Historically, there were many similarities in the landscapes of these regions—both were populous and prosperous. But there were major contrasts in terms of ecological zones, the village structure and rural life, and the social and economic edifice of urban places.

When these territories were occupied in 1801 by the East India Company, Lord Wellesley described Awadh as 'one of the most fertile regions of the globe'. It was also 'nearly the largest, probably the richest' of all the native states in British India (see Bayly, 1983, pp. 430-3).

The population growth was considerable and most of the cultivable land was reclaimed. The situation in Rohilkhand was not as favourable. It was very sparsely populated and lacked agricultural labour required both for cultivation of poor lands and for developing new cultivable lands. These ecological and demographic differences between the two regions were gradually obliterated by the end of the nineteenth century when the agricultural growth in Rohilkhand improved and Awadh reached a plateau (Bayley, 1983).

The pattern of villages in medieval Awadh and Rohilkhand was linked to their varying needs for security. The Rohilkhand villages were open to constant disturbances and were often grouped around a petty fort (Spate, 1967, p. 199), whereas in Awadh one site was as good as another. Even today, there is not much variation in the everyday social life of the villagers, which in both regions was defined by the 'grueling round of the seasons' (Spate, 1962, p. 203); endless toil; 'narrow horizons for a full life', peppered with the *bonhommie* around the village well or under the shade of the banyan tree; occasionally relieved by the recitation and dramatization of the great epics; the seasonal festivals and feasts.

## The Historical Edifice of 'Places' and 'Place Identities'

The villages in the area had a tiered structure of places, i.e. the *ganjs* (rural markets), the *qasbahs* (country towns) and the *shahars* (cities). Rohilkhand had a higher density of urban centres than Awadh. The Pathans were, by nature, town dwellers. Originating from humbler martial families and being 'outsiders' in the region, they had to establish their legitimacy to build a base from which they could assert their power. Hence, the Rohilla nobleman did not seek land grants from the rulers but only status through representation at the court, an elephant, a drum and a 'place of his own' for his horses and clan. Towns provided this place, a *durbar* (court) as well as the security they needed (Bayly, 1983, pp. 122, 199).

Awadh and Rohilkhand were dotted with *ganjs* along the arterial and cross-country routes and developed an indigenous economy based on the specialization of handicrafts. Next in the hierarchy of places were the *qasbahs* or country towns, many of which originated during the Mughal period as the home of the service gentry from Hindu warrior castes, pedigree Muslim lineages and bodies of craftsmen (Bayly, 1983, p. 111). These places acquired a distinct urban status which was usually symbolized by a mosque, a public bath and a judicial officer (*kazi*). Though small in size with a population ranging from 3,000 to 10,000, their importance was due to social, legal and economic functions and status. By the mid-nineteenth century there was a well-developed base of such towns, with each region having approximately the same number of *qasbahs*. The *qasbahs,* however, lost their significance when the social and economic power of the landed and service gentry which supported them, was denuded after the Great Rebellion. At the top of the 'traditional' urban hierarchy were the *shahars* with a population of over 10,000. They were the seats of regional and local political and administrative power, transit points for long distance trade and managers of religious practice if they happened to have a shrine or a pilgrimage point. There were eighteen cities in Awadh and twenty-two in Rohilkhand.

Place identities in Awadh and Rohilkhand were important, they were established with reference to *qasbahs* and *shahars*. Notable families, poets and writers adopted the names of their towns as their titles and took pride in this affiliation. The most distinct among the places in these two regions was Lucknow which emerged as a rival to Mughal Delhi and British Calcutta. It combined the 'monumental magnificence of Shah Jahan's Delhi with the scented allure of Scheherzade's Baghdad' (Ahmad Shah Abdali cited in Keay, 2000, p. 435). The Nawabs endowed their city with palaces, gateways, halls and mosques of 'riotous profile' in a final outburst of what was known as 'Indo-Sarcenic' architecture. No less sensational was Lucknow's lavish and distinct lifestyle so vividly described by Keay,

> As connoisseurs of the exquisite and the exotic, the Nawabs supported the most celebrated Urdu poets, Persian calligraphers and Shi'ite divines. In the royal employ, Hindu minstrels, dancers and impersonators mingled with English barbers, Scottish bagpipers and European clock masters. Closer still to the royal person moved a swarm of eunuchs, courtesans, concubines and catamites. In short to the best of their limited abilities the last Nawabs fulfilled to the bejeweled hilt their role as the dissipated Oriental despots of European imagining. (2000, p. 435)

Out of this eclectic extravaganza, 'debilitating, decadent, Orientalism' as the British described it, a culture specific to Lucknow was created by the Nawabs, their gentry and the common people. This culture was elegant, refined, leisurely, gracious, peaceful and pervasive. Its charm was due to its variety. The elite patronized and nurtured it and the common man made his living from it by servicing it (see Sharar, 1913, still considered a classic description of the elite culture of Lucknow). This culture was also insular and chauvinistic. However, this did not create a conflict between the rich and the poor but spiced life with life cycle rituals; food, festivals and sports; saints and shrines; dance and music; architecture and the arts in which all classes and religious groups participated at different levels. Though greatly transformed, Lucknow still represents elements of the composite culture, the social diversity and cultural eclecticism of north India.

In contrast, the towns in Rohilkhand were bland. The Pathan urban gentry were 'completely devoid of any taste for learning or for the niceties of society . . . their tastes were purely military. . . . Their attitude towards polite society and the embellishments and etiquette of cultured life did not allow them to appreciate poets, men of letters and other accomplished persons' (Sharar, 1913, p. 79). This unpretentious simplicity and 'blandness' of the Rohilla gentry was, however, not bred out of religious orthodoxy and was not antagonistic to the local Hindu culture and social practice.

This survey of 'places' and the territorial organization in these two regions has shed light on many similarities as well as territorial differences. But can it be concluded that these territorial differences, both political and ecological, gave Awadh and Rohilkhand distinct 'territorial' identities in popular perception? The answer has to be both 'yes' and 'no' because such ecological contrasts have little or no impact upon popular consciousness (see de Planhol and Claval, 1988, p. 159). It is quite plausible to assume that purely as *political* and *ecological* units Awadh and Rohilkhand could not have been symbols of identity for the common man, both urban and rural. Two reasons can be given for this. First, political and administrative identities, for the commoner, existed historically only at the local level of revenue tract in the rural areas and the jurisprudence limits in the urban areas. In the minds of the more 'aware' segments of the urban population, a sharp focused politico-administrative identity did not develop, because systematic maps, which become mental referents when frequently encountered, did not exist in these regions until the nineteenth century. The mental maps of these regions would have been vague as they were delineated by zonal frontiers and not linear boundaries (Embree, 1977). Second, these regions had a long-term correspondence between a politico-administrative identity and a cultural identity (Sopher, 1977, p. 283). Between these two identities, the cultural character emerged as the stronger referent since it was based on the experience of everyday living and was perceptible. The cultural identities in these regions were a reflection of their historically determined regional sociology.

## III

### HISTORICAL REGIONAL SOCIOLOGY— AWADH AND ROHILKHAND

Earlier discussion has indicated that an identifiable physical territory is a necessary, though not a sufficient, condition for the emergence of a sense of identity or oneness and 'functions at a meta-physical level' (Deshpande, 2000, p. 168). For an identity to emerge and be perceived, the people within a given 'territory' or 'place' should be of the opinion that they are similar. What has given a sense of social identity, an impression of 'being alike' to the Muslims, the minority community that is the case study in this paper? Is it religion, caste, ethnicity, language, material culture or the framework of daily life?

Muslims constituted slightly less than 50 per cent of the total population in the towns of Rohilkhand and approximately 30 per cent in the towns of Awadh throughout the twentieth century (see Map 10.1). However, in the rural areas their share in the total population has been around 20 per cent only.

### THE AWADH AND ROHILKHAND MUSLIMS— A DIFFERENTIATED 'COMMUNITY'

The Muslim community in Awadh and Rohilkhand was gradually constituted. Originally it was differentiated by religious beliefs, practices and levels of orthodoxy (see Ahmad, 1983). The forces that held its diverse elements together and gave it a community identity were rooted in this gradual evolution. The Muslims were, to a great extent, not immigrants but 'people of the land', with beliefs and customs that were deeply influenced by fellow inhabitants of another faith. They adopted 'a catechism which rejected many of the things which would identify them with non-Muslims' (Mujeeb, 1967, p. 527).

The Muslims of Awadh were divided in terms of religion into Shia and Sunni sects. The Sunnis comprised three distinct and 'subtly hierarchical' sub-communities of Sayyid, Mughal and Shaikh, who prayed and ate together but had reservations about intermarrying. The Muslim Pathans in Rohilkhand were a more varied group. The census of 1891 counted twenty-six identifiable ethnic groups of Pathans, the most numerous being the Rohillas, Afridis, Ghoris, Kakars, Lodhis and Yusufzais.

The urban Muslims in these two regions came from several strata and were divided internally by region, sect, ethnicity and class (see Ahmad, 1983). An undifferentiated toiling class of menial workers and petty craftsmen were at the base. Above them were the dominant groups differentiated in terms of the hierarchy of 'places' they inhabited. In the cities the Muslim elite consisted of *zamindars*, *taluqdars* and the higher order service gentry; whereas, in the *qasbahs* they belonged to the 'more obscure' Muslim landed families or those who served in the local administration as undermanagers and collectors of rural revenue (Bayly, 1983, 166-9). It is important to note here that the Hindu community in the cities was composed of the commercial families of big merchants, 'middling' traders and moneylenders. In the *qasbahs* the Hindu urban elite came from the Kayasthas who, like the *qasbah* Muslim gentry, served in the local administration (Bayly, 1983, pp. 166-9).

Muslims became aware of the importance of an inward sense of cohesion only when their hold on land rights and on markets gradually increased with the consolidation of the rule of the Nawabs. With more resources at their command, they traced back their genealogy to 'great Islamic ethnicities' (*qaum*) but, at the same time, had a sense of belonging to 'their land' (*watan*). This feeling of *qaum* had been instrumental in creating and buttressing the 'place' identity both at the *qasbah* as well as the city level discussed earlier. It was these groups that evolved a distinct culture that acquired its specific quality from Islam, literacy and a lifestyle dependent on the agrarian economy but which was not rustic. It was these groups that also encouraged the evolution of a composite culture in Awadh and Rohilkhand.

Muslims did not have a common language or a language of their own. In Awadh and Rohilkhand, the common people and the gentry spoke Awadhi and Khari Boli respectively. Both were dialects of Hindustani, the regional language. The language of the court was Persian and the language of religious orthodoxy was Arabic. Gradually, several regional languages and local dialects emerged which included words from Persian as well as Sanskrit. Urdu, the new language, was soon patronized and refined by the court and since it cut across religious boundaries, became the language of the nobility, the gentry, poets and scholars throughout north India. Urdu did not acquire its Muslim identity until the last few decades of the nineteenth century (Mujeeb, 1967, p. 169). Muslims did not consider that they had a 'language of the Muslims' until the divisive politics of the British compelled them to use it as an instrument to assert their rights *vis-à-vis* other communities.

Political interest was also not a unifying force in the Muslim community, but according to the history of Awadh and Rohilkhand, bound the ruling classes and cliques together until 1857. An economic interest was not evident either. The religion of the rulers seldom disturbed the prevailing economic order. Tradition and custom, professional ethics and the system of *biradari* or 'brotherhood' provided the cohesive force within the professional and the productive classes regardless of their religion.

It has been noted that the Muslims of Awadh and Rohilkhand were historically divided into sects and classes and had no common language or political and economic interests. As a religious community, they were 'unified at best by a few common rituals and by the beliefs and aspirations of a majority—not the totality—of its scholars' (Hardy, 1972, p. 2; Hasan, 2000, pp. 142-3). What gave the Muslims a sense of community identity? According to Mujeeb, 'the only unifying factor among Indian Muslims was common allegiance to Islam.' This allegiance 'created the sentiment of belonging to a community and this sentiment has been the point at which religion, the instinct for self-preservation, political interest and social traditions can be said to meet' (Mujeeb, 1967, pp. 22-3). But has this been, historically speaking, the only factor?

## The Awadh and Rohilkhand Muslims as a 'Religious Community'

What was the Islam of Indian Muslims? Was it conducive to the emergence of a religious community? Two versions of Islam have historically been practised in India. The Islam of the common Indian Muslims, i.e. the uneducated urban and rural lower classes, that has strands of non-Islamic ritual practices and 'caste' distinctions adopted from Hinduism or invented by Muslims themselves. On the other hand, the Islam of the educated, i.e. 'orthodox' Islam—one which endeavours to maintain uniformity in belief and practice by enforcing conformity through social and legal sanctions (Mujeeb, 1962, pp. 13, 18, 20). This Islam existed in pockets—in urban areas and among the Muslim elite who encouraged religious thought, patronised the *ulema* (learned men) and set up centres of Islamic education. The common man was touched by 'orthodox' Islam only in the public domain because urban life since the Mughal period had been 'encompassed by city-wide Islamic institutions' (Bayly, 1983, p. 176). These institutions were obliterated only after the establishment of colonial rule in India in the mid-nineteenth century. The private as well as the public lives of the majority of Muslims were, therefore, dictated by Islam in a limited way. It provided a religious identity but one that was latent and overlaid by other identities.

The Islam of the Muslims of Awadh, as already noted, was differentiated in terms of Shia and Sunni sects. The religious identity of the Pathans was superimposed by their ethnic as well as territorial identities in Rohilkhand. As a religious community they did not practise the 'universal brotherhood' that Islam professed. It is said that they fought more wars among themselves than with the Hindus (Schermerhorn, 1978, p. 181). As Brass pointed out, 'in the early nineteenth century . . . there was at most a Muslim community of believers, with only a limited set of beliefs and religious practices held in common' (Brass, 1991, p. 87). It was only later that they attempted to preserve their distinct religious identity by establishing religious seminaries (Deoband and Nadwa) to keep alive the observance of the *Shari'ah* which would make them both a religious as well as a 'legal', i.e. largely self-governing community (Brass, 1991, p. 89; Hardy, 1971, p. 41). The Muslims of Awadh and Rohilkhand were, therefore, not an amorphous '*religious community*' until well into the twentieth century. Their diversity added layers to their sense of identity.

## The Awadh and Rohilkhand Muslims as a Community of Culture

Are the Muslims of Awadh and Rohilkhand a community of culture? Are they a type of community akin to the 'historical-political community' suggested by Brass (1971, p. 90)? Till the last decades of the nineteenth century, Muslims were much more than a religious community and were recognized more as a historical-political community. In practice they did not use the *Shari'ah* as a symbol of their identity and did not adhere to it rigorously. Ethnic, cultural and linguistic diversity was accepted and encouraged. It has been discussed how this diversity created a distinct culture, a *tehzeeb*, that sprang from the normative and everyday practice of Islam, social and institutional relationships, family structure, life cycle rituals and a social hierarchy—inherited or adopted from the larger Hindu society. The defining parameters of the Muslim identity had, therefore, been a religion or '*mazhab*' as well as a 'culture' or '*tehzeeb*'.

This identity, however, changed along with the context that framed their lives. The foundations of the life and thought of Muslims in these two regions were shaken after 1857 when they acquired new masters who were antagonistic to them. They lost their privileged social status as well as their land and revenue rights. The Urdu and Persian gentry was unable to compete for government jobs with men from Bengal and Bihar who had some education in English, the new language of the administrators. What did they do to protect their identity?

The Muslims attempted to preserve their religious identity by establishing religious seminaries. However, they quickly realized that they also needed to strengthen their grip on the limited political and economic opportunities. Some projected a secular image; others adopted a 'communal spirit' and openly opposed the government policies 'to extract rights and status for the Muslims as a community, more specifically as a 'minority' community' (Mujeeb, 1967, pp. 525-8). These attempts at self-preservation were an acknowledgement that they could not regain their lost identity on the basis of religion alone.

The dissipation of the Muslims of Awadh and Rohilkhand as a 'community of culture' was almost complete by the middle of the nineteenth century since the means to support their material culture was greatly reduced. India was divided into Hindu-majority India and Muslim-majority Pakistan in 1947. The Muslims of Awadh and Rohilkhand who did not migrate to Pakistan were a demoralized group. Their families had been truncated, their lands lost after the abolition of *zamindari* and the tinselled images of their bygone culture were extant only in commercial cinema. Their identity as a community of culture had lost its legitimacy. Their pride in their territorial identity was destroyed as Awadh and Rohilkhand became like any other region in north India and no longer a boast of their urban culture. The cities have been cosmopolitanized and their material culture vandalized. Rifts between religious communities are vast and increasing. Muslims consider themselves extremely marginalized and in such circumstances all they are capable of nurturing and articulating is a sense of identity pegged to religion, a 'minority' religion, which is the only identity that represents them as a collective. And it is in this context that they usually make efforts to create a territorial identity for themselves in secular India.

## CONCLUSION

This analysis has led to certain propositions about the formation of identities in the context of 'territories', 'culture', 'religion' and 'ethnicity' i.e. '*ilaqa*', '*tehzeeb*', '*mazhab*' and '*qaum*' which may be tested in historical regions and communities that have travelled on parallel trajectories of territorial organization and socio-political change:

1. Micro level politico-administrative units, even when they have been historically significant, form weak 'territorial' identities which have little impact on popular consciousness. They acquire a sentimental value only when a long enduring correspondence exists between a politico-administrative identity and a 'social' identity as is demonstrated by the case of Awadh and Rohilkhand.
2. A 'social-cultural' identity is historically determined and is a reflection of regional sociology. It becomes a powerful referent and acquires its significance from the fact that it is based on everyday experience and is perceptible. Such an identity emerges not only in communities which are in the majority and in a position of power, but is also tenaciously preserved by the 'weaker' minority communities when they feel threatened or alternative identities fail to develop. The Muslim community in Awadh and Rohilkhand lived through both these situations.
3. An identity based on religion alone is usually possible at the level of the individual. It can be constructed at the level of a collectivity only when religion is made to operate in a broader context and is 'used' by social agencies for collective gains. A religious identity is most potent when it is counterpoised against a competing religious identity. The post-1857 Muslim community in Awadh and Rohilkhand acquired this collective identity and tried to use it for community gains.
4. A 'community' identity becomes strong when it has several layers of 'identities' overlapping, signifying commonness as well as diversity. 'Culture' makes this possible when 'culture' is contextualized in the 'social sense', i.e. 'as a particular way of life' that springs from the normative and everyday practice of religion, social and institutional relationships, life cycle rituals and a social hierarchy—integral to

the community or adopted from the larger society. The Muslims as a 'community of culture' in Awadh and Rohilkhand could absorb their internal diversity and adopt much from the Hindu culture to create the *tehzeeb* of Awadh, which was a composite culture *par excellence.* This essentially was their identity and, in spite of historical forces sometimes operating against them, they were able to sustain themselves as a 'community of culture' for almost a century.

5. There may or may not be a correspondence between 'private-religious' and 'public-cultural' identities in multi-religious societies. Communities may have separate religious identities but a common composite cultural identity where religious antagonism is absent or latent as was the case in the Hindu and Muslim communities in Awadh and Rohilkhand until a certain juncture in their history.
6. The edges of any single identity may become blurred or focused when communities have a 'manifold frame of identification' and a perception of privileged or preferred identities. The Muslims of Awadh and Rohilkhand changed their identity from 'a community of culture' to that of a 'religious community' when the latter seemed to them to be the 'preferred' identity in post-Partition India.
7. An integral and fundamental identity of a community such as a religious or a linguistic one may be subdued or, in extreme cases, may be disowned when it is perceived as a threat to a preferred identity. Many Muslim elite families in Awadh and Rohilkhand became 'secular' and anglicized to fit into the mould of the preferred 'modern-liberal-western' identity in British India.
8. A sense of identity may remain latent or dormant for long periods but can be roused within an incredibly short time. The communal conflict which gradually surfaced in Awadh and Rohilkhand, and which took the extreme form of riots between the Hindus and Muslims or even between Shia-Sunni sects, substantiates the destructive potential of identities in plural, multilayered societies.

These propositions and their validation in the context of two historical regions and communities in India, indicate that 'territorial identities' can become as important and as forceful in manipulating privileges and fermenting conflict between communities as they can be in achieving a synthesis that is sustained over generations. Identities can unite; identities can divide.

REFERENCES

Ahmad, Imtiaz, *Caste and Social Strafication among Muslims in India*, New Delhi: Manohar, 1978.

Ahmad, Imtiaz, ed., *Modernization and Social Change among Muslims in India*, New Delhi, Manohar, 1983.

Bayly, C.A., *Rulers, Townsmen and Bazaars, North Indian Society in the Age of British Expansion, 1770-1870*, Cambridge: Cambridge University Press, 1983.

Blumer, H., 'Ethnicity and the Welfare State', *International Social Science Journal*, 1998, p. 193.

Brass, Paul, *Ethnicity and Nationalism, Theory and Comparison*, New Delhi: Sage, 1991.

Deshpande, Satish, 'Hegemonic Spatial Strategies: The Nation-space and Hindu Communalism in Twentieth Century India', in *Community, Gender and Violence*, ed. Partha Chatterjeee and Pradeep Jaganathan, Subaltern Studies XI, New Delhi: Ravi Dayal Publisher, 2000.

Embree, A.T., 'Frontiers and Boundaries: From the Traditional to the Modern State', in *Realm and Region in Traditional India*, ed. Richard G. Fox, New Delhi, Vikas Publishing House, 1977.

Eyles, John, ed., *Research in Human Geography: Introduction and Investigations*, Oxford: Basil Blackwell, 1988..

Fisher, M.H., 'Áwadh and the English East India Company', in *Lucknow - Memories of a City*, ed. Violette Graff, New Delhi: Oxford University Press, 1997..

Geertz, Clifford, *Old Societies and New States: The Quest for Modernity in Asia and Africa*, New York: Free Press, 1967.

Hardy, Peter, *The Muslims of British India*, Cambridge: Cambridge University Press, 1972.

———, *Partners in Freedom and True Muslims: The Political Thought of Some Muslim Scholars British India, 1912-1947*, Lund: Studentlitteratur, 1971.

Hasan, Mushirul, '"Majorities" and "Minorities", in Modern South Asian Islam: A Historian's Perspective', in *Pluralism and Equality, Values in Indian Society and Politics*, ed. Imtiaz Ahmad et al., New Delhi: Sage, 2000.

Keay, John, *India—A History*, London: Harper Collins Publishers, 2000.

Mujeeb, M., *The Indian Muslims*, London: George Allen and Unwin Ltd., 1967.

Nisbet, R.A, *The Quest for Community*, Oxford: Oxford University Press, 1953.

de Planhol, Xavier and Paul Claval, *An Historical Geography of France*, Cambridge: Cambridge University Press, 1994.

Schermerhorn, R.A., *Ethnic Plurality in India*, Tucson: University of Arizona Press, 1978.

Sharar, A.H., *Lucknow: The Last Phase of an Oriental Culture*, 1913; rpt.', New Delhi: Oxford University Press, 1999.

Sopher, David E., 'Rohilkhand and Oudh: An Exploration of Social Gradients Across a Political Frontier', in *Realm and Region in Traditional India*, ed. Richard G. Fox, New Delhi: Vikas Publishing House, 1977.

Spate, O.H.K. and A.T.A. Learmonth, *India and Pakistan*, London: Methuen and Company Limited, 1967.

CHAPTER 11

# Land of the Ancestors and Territory of the Diaspora: The Example of the 'Indian' South Africans

FRÉDÉRIC LANDY

> The India where Gandhi and Nehru and the others operated was historical and real. The India from where we had come was impossibly remote, almost as imaginary as the land of the Ramayana. . . . I lived easily with that darkness, that lack of knowledge. I never thought to inquire further.
>
> V.S. Naipaul, *Finding the Centre*, London: André Deutsch, 1984

In the context of theoretical preoccupation with 'globalization', 'post-modernism' and 'cultural hybridization', 'diasporas' of many different types and forms have been the subject of extensive study. No longer are groups in a diaspora perceived as exceptional (or disturbing) in relation to the once-thought normality of fixed citizenship and belonging to nation-states. Instead, they are read as premonitory signs or indicators of what a 'global' civilization, founded on mobility and on fundamental trans- or multi-cultural references could be (Schnapper, 2001). Understood initially as the *result* of centuries of globalization, today they are considered as, and consider themselves as, true *agents* of this globalization, and as such are able to reinforce its dissemination across the globe through the circulation of people, goods and ideas. A discussion on the validity or invalidity of such an approach is not the aim of this paper. More modestly, drawing on the example of 'Indian' South Africans, I reflect on the significance of country of origin within the South African Indian diaspora experience, focusing in particular on its role in shaping the identities of individuals, now often fifth generation migrants.[1]

To what extent is India still a part of the identity of South Africans of Indian origin? Although the question suggests many angles, I focus here on its political and economic aspects. The concept of 'territory', considered the result of the projection of identity on space and the domain of symbolic appropriation (cf. Dupont and Landy's contribution in this volume), is critical to understanding the relationship between 'Indian' South Africans and India. Does the territory of 'Indian' South Africans still include India? The question is not an easy one. In South Africa some 'Indians' are wary of having strong ties with India because they feel that this could provide an excuse to black extremists to demand their expulsion from the country. In India the question is of special relevance to the economy, as foreign investments are currently being wooed, especially those from the Indian diaspora. If ties between Indians and 'Indian' South Africans were severed a long time ago, can one expect a big improvement in trade and investments? The issue is also important to Hindu nationalist movements, which receive part of their funds from the Indian diaspora. Not only do facts have to be discussed in detail, but also the concepts. First, one has to ask if Indians abroad really form a diaspora and whether 'Indian' South Africans are part of it. Next, the definition of the ethnicity of these South Africans has to be investigated in relation to the place occupied by 'Indianness' in their identity. Then the limits of their territory have to be defined to reach the conclusion that, except as a play on words, it cannot be said that India is part of the territory of 'Indian' South Africans: the economic effect on Indian growth can, therefore, be only a limited one.

## DO 'OVERSEAS INDIANS' FORM A DIASPORA?

Approximately 20 million people of Indian origin live outside India, although estimations vary greatly. There is obviously an enumeration problem which is not only physical but also due to conceptual vagueness: how many generations can one count—in terms of ancestry or degree of interbreeding—and still be considered of Indian origin? Can one include descendants of present-day Pakistanis, Bangladeshis and Sri Lankan Tamils in this count?

Roughly four types of Indian migration can be distinguished (see Map 11.1):

1. Traders who, often as early as the sixteenth century, came to East Africa or South-East Asia from Gujarat (Muslims) or from Tamil Nadu (Chettiars).

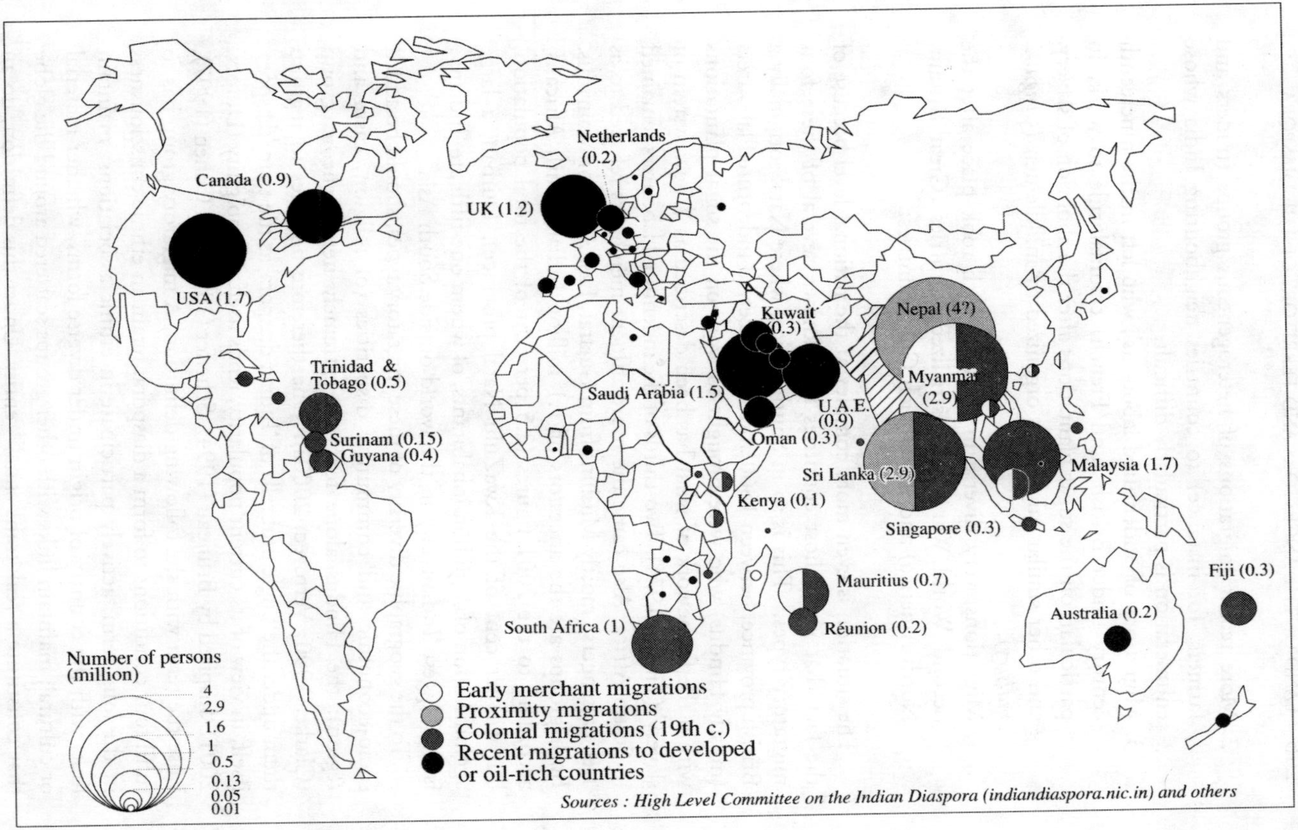


MAP 11.1: THE INDIAN 'DIASPORA' (*c.* 2001).

2. More recent migrations of heterogeneous groups (traders and farmers, for instance) to countries neighbouring India whose enumeration is particularly difficult.
3. Migrations of 'indentured labourers', who left in the nineteenth century under British (and French) colonial rule to work, in particular, on the sugar plantations after the abolition of slavery, and other similar migrations organized by middlemen (*kangani*, *maistry*).
4. Migrations, very diverse in nature, which took place after the Second World War to industrialized countries (Great Britain, North America) and the oil-rich Gulf countries.

The situation is even more complex at the national level because of the fact that many host countries have known several of these four migratory types.[2] This is so in South Africa, where Natal, originally a British province, between 1860 and 1911 received indentured labourers (mostly Hindus) who were brought to work on the sugar plantations within the framework of what has been described as 'a new system of slavery' (Tinker, 1974). Two-thirds of the indentured labourers remained in South Africa. Also came the more affluent merchants referred to as 'free passengers', mostly Muslims from Gujarat, East Africa or Mauritius. Both groups are the ancestors of 1.1 million Indian South Africans, according to the 2001 figures (2.5 per cent of the total population, but 14 per cent of the KwaZulu Natal province). Durban, a large agglomeration of 3 million inhabitants, of whom one-fifth are 'Indians', is the biggest 'Indian' city in the world outside South Asia.

To the geographic diversity of these migratory types, should be added socio-economic and community disparities (of religion, caste and region): the Hindus alone form an extremely heterogeneous group (Clarke, 1990; Vertovec, 2000a). One therefore hesitates to regroup them under the single umbrella of 'Indian diaspora' as the term 'diaspora' itself, in view of its current popularity, lends itself to ambiguity (Dufoix, 2001). Inspired by Bruneau (1994), Scheffer (1996) and Cohen (1997), I use the term with the following definition. A migratory group has to fulfil four conditions to form a diaspora: retain an ethnic consciousness in the long term; actively participate in ethnic associations; maintain links with the country of origin under diverse forms, whether material or cultural; maintain links with other groups scattered around the globe that constitute a real 'trans-statal'[3] entity. Under this definition, do all overseas Indians belong to such a diaspora?

Diasporas are not merely dual entities, composed of migrant groups and the country of origin. A diaspora in reality corresponds to three focal points: the host country, in this case South Africa; the country of origin—India; as well as the diasporic network that unites all migrant groups across the world.[4] In the South African context, relatively poor relations between South Africa and India can be related to these three focal points: (a) South African segregation, (b) Indian policy, and (c) the dynamism of the diasporic network. These issues are elaborated in the following:

1. Very early on, *segregation* was a factor which motivated Gandhi to spend 21 years in South Africa (1893-1914). Early segregatory policies culminated in apartheid. In consequence, Indian identity and the internal identities of the different Indian subgroups were simultaneously subjected to:

   Spatial segregation that tended to break up old neighbourhood communities by forcing 'Indians' to dwell in purely 'Indian' townships.

   Discrimination that helped to cement Indian identity, administratively classified under one single racial category.

   A break with India due to its embargo of South Africa after 1946 which radically reduced economic relations and travel between the two countries.

   At the time of the creation of the South African Republic and its expulsion from the Commonwealth in 1961, South African citizenship was officially granted to 'Indians'. No longer faced with the threat of expulsion, for some this was a factor of integration that also widened the breach between India and South Africa and reduced ties with the country of their ancestors. Gradually 'Indians' came to be considered by the whites in power as an intermediary group that could act as a political buffer. Some 'Indians' accepted the regime's ideology, but some others joined the anti-apartheid movement.
2. At the same time, the Government of India's attitude *vis-à-vis* South African immigrants, and the diaspora in general, was not very consistent. During the colonial era, the Indian government agreed to export indentured labour, but soon protested against the ill-treatment meted out to indentured labourers. Moreover, in 1946 the Indian government imposed a trade boycott and

appealed to the United Nations which in consequence, condemned South Africa. With the attainment of Independence in 1947, the Indian government's policy of considering Indians living abroad as part of India was abruptly discontinued.[5] From that time whenever India criticized South Africa internationally, it was done in the name of human rights rather than from a specific desire to protect people of Indian origin. The diaspora was no longer seen as the spearhead of the struggle against British repression, but as a group of individuals who had chosen to leave India to seek their fortunes abroad rather than participate in the national effort. In many instances, expatriates were portrayed as traitors to the cause. For Nehru, it was from then on that soil and not birth determined nationality. In South Africa as in the rest of the Third World, the Indian diaspora was encouraged to integrate with local populations to fight what remained from colonialism to create young independent nations.

3. Last, the diverse character of the South African Indian diasporic network does not favour relations solely with India. Due to the antiquity of the migration, the links of 'free passenger' traders with India were mostly indirect from the start, with many generations born in Mauritius or East Africa rather than in India. In the contemporary period, trans-statal exchanges have multiplied with the ease of new information technologies. The success of certain segments of the diaspora, especially in the United Kingdom and North America, fuels 'Indian' South African fantasies much more than the economic potential of India, where they have no intention of migrating.[6] Although they are fully integrated in the South African national fabric, increasing number of Indian South Africans are members in their own right of global networks constituted by the Indian diaspora—at least those who have the financial and cultural means. Others, especially those from the poorer classes, often Hindus, have few dealings outside South Africa. In consequence, many do not meet the fourth criterion of my definition and thus cannot be considered part of the global Indian 'diaspora'.

## An infinitely variable Indianness

'Indianness' is immediately visible in Durban. Still isolated from the new industries and recently constructed neighbourhoods largely for the underprivileged Blacks, the Shiva temple in Cato Manor has limewashed walls in the shadow of an enormous *pipal* tree under which some old men greet each other, hands joined, intoning 'Vanakam': the visitor has the impression of being somewhere in Tamil Nadu. Durban 'Indians' watch Zee TV and Bollywood films. When I asked the manager of an 'Indian' department store, whether he was not worried that the demand for saris, incense sticks, copper utensils and other largely 'Indian' products would decline and if he did not think it advisable to diversify his products and clientele, he replied smiling, 'Indian Indians are Westernised, but not Durban Indians'. In line with this, religious festivals that vanished from India some decades ago are still celebrated in Durban, and the Tamils' new fashion of venerating popular Dravidian festivals appears quite remarkable (Diesel, 2000). Durban is however not 'Little India'. Another department store, Haribhai, sells basmati rice from the Punjab, *dal*, tobacco for *hookah*, posters of Shiva and Mecca, but does not stock *idli* (flattened rice balls) ingredients common in big cities in India. Many young girls wear a *tilak* (*chandho*) on their foreheads, but wear jeans. Men often support moustaches but rarely wear *chappals* (sandals). Some traces still remain of the 'original' 'Indianness' that disembarked from the ships in the nineteenth century, whereas others have been effaced (cf. Ebr.-Vally's contribution in this volume).

As in most countries of the world to which Indian indentured labour migrated, the caste structure was probably the first aspect to disappear, primarily because migrants of different geographical origins were thrown together in plantations where they could not reproduce the socio-religious hierarchy typical of their region. Another structure that, if not rendered completely obsolete, has been greatly diluted is the original class structure. Simply put, indentured labourers corresponded to the working class, whereas 'free passengers' came from the middle class and sometimes even the elite (Freund, 1995). KwaZulu Natal's Indian group was initially so highly stratified and hierarchical that at the dawn of the twentieth century only a fraction of the indentured labourers really belonged to the 'diaspora' because in this proletarian and rootless environment it was practically impossible to find either network or ethnic consciousness. Only the 'passengers' had developed relationships of any depth with others in similar circumstances in South Africa, with other Indian diasporic groups across the world, as well as between themselves and with family and friends based in India. It was only later, when the difficulties of the initial years were partly overcome, and when some second generation indentured labourers joined the ranks of the middle class, that an ethnic consciousness truly developed. Today, socio-economic disparities have been completely restructured. This does not mean that 'Indians' constitute a homogeneous social group, quite the opposite: even if Indian standards of living are comparable to those of whites in South Africa, the South African Indian community includes working class people and even the impoverished—no doubt an exception in the African context (Desai, 1996).

The attachment to Indianness is due less to the peculiarities of this culture, than to a need to forge an identity in relation to other South African groups. Ethnicity is never bestowed *per se* (Barth, 1969; Bayard, 1996), and in this instance the strength of Indianness comes less from India than from the situation in South Africa. Even today, despite the end of apartheid, internal disparities within the Indian community stay in the background, in view of the fact that the policy of black empowerment, based on communitarian logic, has probably contributed to the reinforcement of Indianness. However, all these indicators of identity act as factors of heterogeneity within the group, which has given rise to a 'foliated identity' (Mainet-Valleix, 2002) within Indianness itself. In consequence, the common denominators between all 'Indians' are finally very few: films, music, some culinary preparations and dress codes—not much in the final analysis. This must be placed in the context India itself has had in defining its own unity: is not political India officially designated as the 'Indian Union', i.e. a union of different cultures and states? Under the appellation of nation-state lies hidden a much more disparate notion, 'civilization-State' (Kumar, 1989). It comes as no surprise then that Indianness in South Africa is difficult to define since Indianness in India is such a complex reference.

## What are the Links with India?

Although India definitely represents the roots of 'Indian' South Africans, does it form part of their 'territory? The two terms must not be confused. Roots are as unique, defined precisely spatially and culturally, as 'territories' are exportable: new ones can be reconstituted and extended after migration to include a new territory and identity. Or, conversely, roots eventually disappear from territory, the latter ultimately defined by the boundaries of the host country. Another difficulty arises from the fact that there are two ways of looking at 'territory'. One is cultural, according to which territory is considered in abstraction: India is present practically everywhere as a cultural referent in the domestic space of Durban 'Indians'; it is therefore part of their 'territory'. The other more material approach, which I retain, recognizes India as a country in its geographical reality. In this form, India is not part of the territory of Durban 'Indians'.

*India, a Transcendent Country*

For many 'Indian' Durbanites India forms only a cultural entity. They have never been there, or if they have, it has been as almost ordinary tourists. No efforts were made, therefore, to visit ancestral regions. India, as an imagined country, is used as a marker of differentiation on two counts. First, in the South African context of 'ethnic frontiers' (Barth, 1969) it demarcates that: 'I am Indian, that is to say I am neither an Afrikaner nor a Zulu'. Second, it is also used, to distinguish oneself within the Indian group in order to signal a 'micro-identity' and define oneself as, for instance, 'Hindi', 'Gujarati' or 'Tamil'. This resilient regional culture does not correspond, however, to a local geographical identity. Durban's South Indian Forum, for example, has not forged any links with South India! Indian identity is based, therefore, on a culture, not on a geographical region.

In consequence, the Asian referent of some Durban Muslims is more likely to be Pakistan, although their ancestors were from present-day India (Gujarat). Their connection to identity is based on a religious referent, not a geographic and even less so a familial one. As for the 'Hyderabadees', they are not considered 'south Indians' in Durban despite the southern origin of their forebears; in Durban, they are Urdu-speaking Muslims. This does not prevent these descendants of labourers (from the south!) from sometimes being looked down upon by 'north Indian' Muslims, with whom marriage alliances are rare. Such communities, situated at the intersection of groups, suffer from an ambiguous and conflicting identity.

All Durban groups, however, have two images of India, both very 'Western'. The first is of Gandhi and of peace, tolerance and wisdom. The other is a negative image built on the idea of India as poverty-stricken, as a place of beggars. An employee in a sari shop in Durban asked me, for instance: 'Are these stories of infants true, that they have their legs broken to force them to beg on the streets? And are baby girls killed at birth?'

*An Economic India More or Less Restricted to Mumbai*

The breakdown of diplomatic and commercial relations between India and apartheid South Africa did not bring a complete halt to economic exchanges. Many intermediary places such as Singapore and Maputo were used for more or less official transactions. The restoring of normal relations in 1993 facilitated the expansion of this exchange. These surface in Durban as four types of 'ethnic economies'. The first corresponds to informal activity: the 21,000 'Indian' South Africans who visit India each year and return loaded with goods that they sell or present to their relatives and friends. The second, seen especially in the Grey Street area, the old Indian quarter near the Durban central business district, includes small shops selling clothes, whose proprietors stock up during visits to Delhi or Mumbai two or three times a year. Their low prices are attractive to a black clientele when the products are not obviously Indian, say in the sale of t-shirts. The third type corresponds to big retailers, sometimes situated outside the central Indian quarter, such as the Roopanands chain of stores. In this case, most firms get their supplies via exporters from Mumbai or other big cities. There do not seem to be any particular ties uniting the entrepreneurs to their ancestral region, thus the relationships of 'Indian' South Africans often stop at the doorstep of the Mumbai brokers. As for the fourth type of business, it involves some big firms working with India in 'non ethnic' activities, capitalizing on a cultural asset that allows a Durban businessman of Indian origin easier access to India than other South African business people.

In sum, 'Indian' South Africans' business relations with India are diversified and stratified. It seems that the heritage of the pre-embargo era, when the business world was dominated by the descendants of the 'passengers', has largely vanished. This heritage is, in fact, even less visible in the case of trade without links with India, where one finds new types of business initiatives. For example, E., a carpenter initially now owns four hotels (totalling 5,000 rooms) in the central business district of Durban. This Tamil gentleman is a fourth generation migrant, but he represents the first generation in his family to go into business.

Most Indian businessmen interviewed in Durban were wary of investing in India. They commented: 'The Indians in India are too sharp', 'too shrewd', 'when I go there, for me it is like going to business university'. Not to mention the 'RBI bureaucracy',[7] and the 'red tape rather than the red carpet'. Another reason for the negligible number of investments is the lack of capital. But a last factor needs to be mentioned. Non-Resident Indians (NRI) living in the Gulf countries have restricted rights to invest there and therefore repatriate some of their money to India; on the other hand NRIs living in more liberal countries, such as the United States, habitually do business with India because of their strong sentimental relationship with their home country. None of these situations apply to 'Indian' South Africans. Segregation no longer exists to prevent them from investing in South Africa, whereas links with the country of their forebears have become tenuous because of apartheid and the antiquity of the migration. As far as trade is concerned, South Africa was one of India's important partners before the embargo (5 per cent of Indian exports in 1946). In 2000, however, India ranked nineteenth in the category of most significant commercial partners of South Africa.[8]

In comparison, capital from India has been invested in South Africa, as in the case of the clothing giant, Nalli's, with an outlet in Chatsworth, a Durban 'Indian' township. The shop's origin is not visible anywhere in the store's display window. Nalli's offers the ultimate in Indian fashion and considers this enough to attract a clientele looking for the latest in clothes, discovered through Bollywood films and the country's opening-up. The made-in-India factor has other importance, particularly because prices are competitive relative to goods made in South Africa with high labour costs and taxes. But it is also a matter of 'class'. 'You would not buy a perfume that was not made in France, would you? So, Indian clothes must also be made in India', affirmed another sari vendor in Chatsworth Centre. This is also the reason why good Indian restaurants in Durban hire Indian nationals as chefs and waiters (which incidentally proves that in this case coming from Indian *territory* remains important).

Indian South Africans' regional heritage does not explain investments and business from India in the contemporary period. The biggest investor from India in South Africa is United Breweries (UB), whose founder and CEO belonged to Mangalore in Karnataka, a region that did not supply indentured labour to Africa at all. UB executives posted in South Africa are from all over India. The majority of South African UB workers are black, and the beer produced is for a black clientele. In this industry, any ethnic, Indian-oriented factor is clearly absent. Indian firms are drawn more to Johannesburg and the Gauteng region than to Durban, a smaller city with few company headquarters and a more limited market. Sentimental attachment to Durban's 'Indianness' neither attracts entrepreneurs from India nor influences their choices of sites for business.

It is clear that the current economic liberalization and political uncertainty favour exchanges between India and South Africa. In 2001, however, the latter ranked twentieth (with an investment of Rs. 19.1 billion in India) with regard to total direct foreign investments approved by the Indian government since the 1991 liberalization. 'Indian' South Africans are noticeable for their absence rather than presence. Independent India's decision to slacken its ties with the international diaspora partly explains why it does not count for much in the economic development of the country. As a result it has only a small share in trade and NRI's percentage of direct foreign investments has never touched 10 per cent. It is debatable whether this has been a case of 'missed opportunity' (Lall, 2001). On the whole, with a few exceptions, South Africa finds itself in a defensive and inferior position in relation to the Indian economy. The latter, therefore, cannot rely on South Africa for its revitalization.

## Between Indian Hindu nationalists and South African Black extremists

Political issues also enter into the poor economic relations between India and South Africa. In particular, some 'Indian' South Africans fear being identified with India and as such being suspected of distancing themselves from South Africa. In 1994, the first democratic elections saw half of the people classified 'Indian' vote for the National Party, and only 22 per cent for the African National Congress. Many 'Indians' close to the ANC believe that the Minority Front as also the Arya Samaj and the South African Hindu Maha Sabha ('Indian' South African movements) have discredited Indianness because of their earlier relations with the racist apartheid government: they, therefore, prefer to call themselves 'non-whites' rather than 'Indians'. The situation is even more delicate in KwaZulu Natal, where 'Indians' find themselves sandwiched between the ANC, the national majority party, and the Inkatha Freedom Party, an aggressive Zulu party that controls the province and the Durban metropolitan area. Oppressed in the apartheid period by segregation, some feel oppressed today by policies of affirmative action and Black empowerment.

How is this malaise expressed in relations with other groups of the international diaspora, and with the Hindu nationalist movements in

India itself? A good many nationalisms in the world are largely financed by diasporas (for instance, the Sikh, Kurdish and Jewish). On the one hand, migrants generally have enough funds in their host country to enable them to transfer money to their country of origin. On the other hand, and perhaps above all, many members of the diaspora harbour a feeling of guilt *vis-à-vis* their country of origin, and remorse for having 'abandoned' it. At the same time, they are able to reinforce their ethnic identity through contact with foreign cultures. 'The experience of migration is thus not by accident formative in the nationalist career of Mahatma Gandhi. But it also plays a crucial role in the construction of Hindu nationalism in general' (van der Veer, 1994, p. 118). As a result, it is from the diaspora that the Sangh Parivar, the umbrella organization of the Hindu nationalist movements, receives a large part of its funds.

One can, however, doubt the importance for 'Indian' South Africans of what Anderson (1998) called 'long distance nationalism'. Despite its origins (its founder tried to convince Hindus not to celebrate the Muslim festival of Moharram), the South African Hindu Maha Sabha—which has no connection with the Hindu Mahasabha in India—is trying to revitalize Hinduism while taking care not to offend the sensibilities of other religions. It is relative to these sensitivities that it expressed its fears when the VHP (Vishva Hindu Parishad—Universal Hindu Association) announced that it was setting up a branch in South Africa, all the more as the RSS (Rashtriya Swayamsevak Sangh—Association of National Volunteers) has been in Durban since 1996 under the name of Hindu Swayamsevak Sangh (HSS).[9] These movements are known in India for their extremism bordering on violence.

The economic global diasporic network has a relatively constrained and limited presence in Durban. The Global Organization of People of Indian Origin (GOPIO), created in 1989 in Montreal, has operated in South Africa since 1996. There is only one Muslim, on its 40-member board, perhaps because the GOPIO is linked, so it is said, with the Sangh Parivar via the VHP. Another reason is that few 'Indian' South Africans, Muslims in particular, who were descendants of the 'free passengers' are interested in these types of associations because they have access to other global networks that make the GOPIO superfluous (for instance, the Memon and Konkani networks). Although the GOPIO, in effect, has a very limited following in South Africa, its existence and that of other associations are proof that 'Indian' South Africans, in particular Hindus, are conscious of the need to play the international card. The aim of most of their members is to belong to as many diasporic associations as possible: the discourse and the actions of these associations on political and religious issues in India is not of much import. To belong to the World Hindu Conference is to become a member of a powerful association that links numerous Hindus across the world. The chance to link globally through the Conference is more important than its role in domestic Indian politics, particular its fight to practise a Hinduism that is antagonistic towards Islam. Also, membership of the HSS is less offensive (fight the enemies of *Hindutva*) than defensive as a possible cushion in the case of radical political change in South Africa. Although inter-religious relations in Durban are relatively harmonious, access to the diasporic network is sometimes articulated as a safety net.

One can understand the reaction of 'Indian' South Africans to the creation in 1999 of 'PIO cards' by New Delhi. This option for all Persons of Indian Origin (PIO), excepting Pakistanis and Bangladeshis, did not find favour with NRIs[10] around the world, first because of its cost (US $1000), and second, because of the minimal additional advantages it offered relative to what NRIs already had. It met with even less approval from 'Indian' South Africans. It was feared that black extremists could use this formal identification as a pretext to demand the expulsion of 'Indians', whom they might consider foreigners. After all, had not the Indian Home Affairs Minister, L.K. Advani, declared on presenting the measure: 'Although the PIO card does not confer upon its holder any political rights, it would bring him very close to dual citizenship.'[11] Such a declaration was tactless in the extreme as far as the South African situation is concerned, and eventually the Government of India realized it. The great majority of 'Indian' South Africans do not want dual nationality, considering themselves full-fledged South African citizens.

## CONCLUSION

Many South Africans of Indian origin find themselves excluded from the 'diaspora' as soon as its definition is tightened. Some were unable to maintain links with other diasporic groups across the world (such as poor descendants of Hindu indentured labourers). Sometimes for religious reasons, the country of reference became Pakistan and not India. All South African Indians, however, continued to maintain a strong 'Indianness' in the course of South Africa's greatly troubled political history. For most, because migration occurred many generations ago and apartheid caused a break in relations with India, India is nothing more than an ideal, in essence a de-territorialized referent (Sinha-Kerkhoff and Bal, 2003). This referent has changed scales in the course of generations, from the village, where the migrant's roots were found, to the region, the linguistic area and religion, to the point where for some today it is nothing more than a symbolic entity (Ebr.-Valley, 2001 and contributions by Mainet-Valleix and Ebr.-Vally in this volume). It is important to highlight the nuances further by differentiating 'Indian' identities according to generations, age, gender, social class and communities. In doing so, we cannot say that India still belongs to the territory of 'Indian' South Africans, except by removing spatial reference from the word 'territory' and understanding it as rooted in 'nostalgias without memory.'[12]

NOTES

1. The primary data was collected during a three-week visit to Durban in 1999. The initial results were published in Landy et al., 'Are People of Indian Origin (PIO) "Indian"? A Case Study of South Africa', *Geoforum*, vol. 387, 2004.
2. Also note that in the industrialized countries a major portion of the migratory flux correspond to 'double migrations', such as 'Indians' having fled the Fiji islands or Uganda to settle in Great Britain or the United States.
3. Instead of 'transnational', the adjective preferred by researchers. 'Transnational' has, one drawback, namely of taking away the cultural and 'ethnic' connotations from 'nation': can one say that the Kurdish nation, scattered across several countries, is 'transnational'? 'Trans-statal' or 'trans-bordering' are more appropriate.
4. Kliot (1966) added a fourth pole specific to the Indian diaspora: Great Britain.
5. At least such is Lall's opinion (2001). According to Tinker (1977), Nehru's efforts to create a common citizenship within the Commonwealth were on the contrary an indication of his interest in Indians living abroad.
6. That there is no 'myth of return' is one of the reason why Kalam (2002) refuses to use the term 'diaspora'.
7. RBI or Reserve Bank of India.
8. Department of Trade and Industry, Durban.
9. There are eight *shakhas* (units) in Durban (Hansen, 2000).
10. The definition of NRI, dating from 1973, implies that they have Indian nationality (they are recent migrants, many going to industrialized

countries), in contrast to the PIOs, whose Indian origin may go very far back, as is the case of those in South Africa. Nevertheless, it is important to specify that an individual is considered a PIO if (to make it simple) at least a great-grandparent was Indian (Singhvi, 2000); with a definition historically so restricted, many young Indian South Africans cannot theoretically subscribe to the title of PIO.

11. *Economic Times*, 1 April 1999.
12. An expression coined by Appadurai (1990) and quoted by Aisha Khan in van der Veer, ed., 1995, p. 96.

## REFERENCES

Anderson, B., *The Spectre of Comparisons*, London: Verso, 1998.

Appadurai, A., 'Disjuncture and Difference in the Global Cultural Economy', *Public Culture*, vol. 2, no. 2, 1990, pp. 1-24.

Barth, F., ed., *Ethnic Groups and Boundaries. The Social Organization of Culture Difference*, Bergen-Oslo: Universitetsforlaget, 1969.

Bayard, J.F., *L'illusion identitaire*, Paris: Fayard, 1996.

Bruneau, M., 'Espaces et territoires de diasporas', *L'Espace géographique*, vol. 1, 1994, pp. 5-18.

Clarke, C., C. Peach, S. Vertovec (eds), *South Asian Overseas: Migration and Ethnicity*, Cambridge University Press, 1990.

Cohen, R., *Global Diasporas. An Introduction*, Seattle: University of Washington Press, 1997.

Desai, A., *Arise Ye Coolies: Apartheid and the Indians 1960-1995*, Johannesburg: Impact Africa Publishing Co., 1996.

Diesel, A., 'Hinduism in KwaZulu-Natal, South Africa', in *Culture and Economy in the Indian Diaspora*, ed. B. Parekh et al., London: Routledge, 2003, pp. 33-50.

Dufoix, S., 'Chronique bibliographique: l'objet diaspora en questions', *Cultures et conflits*, vol. 44, 2001 (www.revues.org/conflits).

Ebrahim-Vally, R., *Kala Pani—Caste and Colour in South Africa*, Cape Town: Kwela Books, 2001.

Freud, B., *Insiders and Outsiders: The Indian Working Class of Durban 1910-1990*, Portsmouth, Heinemann-James Currey-University of Natal Press, 1995.

Hansen, T.B., 'Going Global, Going Hindu. Hindu Nationalism, Diasporic Politics and Hindu Practices in Contemporary South Africa', paper presented at CERI, Paris, 25 April 2000 (to be published by *Modern Asian Studies*).

Kalam, M.A., 'The *Diaspora* Bandwagon: Are Indians Overseas Part of the Journey?', in P. Sudhakar Reddy, V. Gangadhar, *Indian Society:*

*Continuity, Change and Development*, Commonwealth Publ., New Delhi, 2002, pp. 102-11.

Kliot, N., 'Asian Diaspora's Role in International Politics: Features and Evolution', in ed. G. Prevelakis, *Les Réseaux Des Diasporas*, Paris: L'Harmattan, 1996, pp. 69-80.

Kumar, R., 'India: A "Nation-State" or a Civilisation-State?', *Occassional Papers on Perspectives in Indian Development*, no. 8, Centre for Contemporary Studies, New Delhi: Nehru Memorial Museum & Library, 1989.

Lall, M.C., *India's Missed Opportuninty. India's Relationship with the Non Resident Indians*, Aldershot: Ashgate, 2001.

Landy, F., B. Maharaj, H. Mainet-Valleix, 'Are People of Indian Origin (PIO) "Indian"? A Case Study of South Africa', *Geoforum*, vol. 387, 2004.

Mainet-Valleix, H., *Durban. Les Indiens, leurs territoires, leur identité*, Paris: Ifas-Karthala, 2002.

Schnapper, D., 'De l'Etat-nation au monde transnational. Du sens et de l'utilité du concept de diaspora', *Revue Européenne des Migrations Internationales*, vol. 17, 2001, pp. 9-34.

Seffer, G., 'Wither the Study of Ethnic Diasporas? Some Theoretical, Definitional, Analytical and Comparative Considerations', in ed. G. Prevelakis, *Les Réseaux Des Diasporas*, Paris: L'Harmattan, 1996, pp. 37-46.

Singhvi, L.M., ed., *Report on the High Level Committee on the Indian Diaspora*, 2000, http://www.indiaday.org/nri/singhvi.htm#1.

Sinha-Kerkhoff, K., E. Bal, 'Eternal Call of the Ganga: Reconnecting with People of Indian Origin in Surinam', *Economic and Political Weekly*, 38, 38, 20 September 2003, pp. 4008-21.

Tunker, H., *A New System of Slavery. The Export of Indian Labour Overseas*, London: Oxford University Press, 1974.

———, *The Banyan Tree. Overseas Emigrants from India, Pakistan and Bangladesh*, Oxford: Oxford University Press, 1977.

van der Veer, P., *Religious Nationalism: Hindus and Muslims in India*, Berkeley: University of California Press, 1994.

van der Veer, P., ed., *Nation and Migration. The Politics of Space in the South Asian Diaspora*, Pennsylvania: University of Pennsylvania Press, 1995.

Vertovec, S., 'Comparative Patterns in the Hindu Diaspora', seminar *Culture and Economy in the Indian Diaspora*, ESRC Transnational Communities Programme, 8-10 April 2000a, New Delhi, mimeo.

———, *The Hindu Diaspora*, London: Routledge, 2000.

CHAPTER 12

# Migration of an Identity: South Africans of Indian Descent

REHANA EBR.-VALLY

The first Indians as indentured labourers arrived in South Africa in 1860. They were mainly Hindus from Madras and were imported to work on the sugar cane plantations of Natal. The decision to import Indian labour was backed by Act 14 of 1859. The first indenture contracts were for a period of three years at a wage of ten shillings a month. An increase of one shilling per month was granted for each year worked. It was stipulated that the employer would provide accommodation and one meal. This contract was considered to be one of the cheapest in the world. Throughout the 1860-1910 period, before Indians were formally prevented from entering the country under any circumstances, South Africa witnessed different waves of Indian immigrants. These can be divided into 'indentured contract workers' and 'Passenger Indians'.

As Indians came after 1860, they represented the last wave of immigrants which chose to settle in South Africa. They brought with them a *Weltanschauung* that was different from that of the settled populations and the most salient criterion that instantly set them apart was their phenotype. Their dress, food, belief system was different and, most important of all, they looked different. In short, they were instantaneously recognizable as the 'Other'. They were neither black nor white and as immigrants in South Africa, they could not be assimilated into a black or white culture. The mysterious image of the Indian was, as Calpin explained, an incomprehensible person: '[. . .] the Indian was an intruder from the mysterious East, with a centuries old tradition behind him, possessed a civilisation, a religion incomprehensible for the stolid *Burgher*'.[1]

This should not detract from the fact that black, white and Indian did mix, albeit on an insignificant level, as such experiences are documented as part of the South African experience of racial and cultural mixing. Yet, it needs to be assumed that the phenotype of the Indian was a factor that influenced both blacks and whites to consider them as inassimilable. They were constantly required to take into account the perceptions they created in society. Which of these perceptions could they control and influence or change to their advantage and which not?

## THE FAILURE OF REPATRIATION POLICIES AND ANTI-IMMIGRATION LAWS

The presence of Indians in South Africa was fraught with problems from the beginning. The colonial administration desired their presence, as they represented a solution to the labour-intensive sugar cane farming. The indenture system almost immediately became a 'problem' when the issue of re-indenture did not proceed according to plan.

In 1865, the Indian government decided to ban emigration to Natal because of the ill-treatment of Indians. Labour shortage in Natal worsened when the discovery of diamonds and the prospects of wealth enticed workers out of Natal. In 1874, an agreement was reached which not only stipulated the extension of the indenture period to five years, but also an obligation to remain in Natal for another five years. In sum, the Natal government negotiated the ten-year clause to acquire a cheap labour force for the construction of harbours, railways and public buildings. To ensure the availability of a cheap workforce, the Natal authorities agreed to encourage an Indian settlement in the colony.

In contrast the 'Passenger Indians' arriving from 1875 included merchants and other professionals who arrived as independent Indians, having paid their own fare. As subjects of the British Empire there was little the Natal authorities could do to stem the flow of Passenger Indians to Natal, since this was concomitant to the idea of encouraging the development of an Indian community in Natal. The situation in Natal was further complicated by the fact that, in the case of difficulties, Indians could appeal to either the Indian government or invoke their rights as British subjects.

The independent Boer Republics tried to quell or prohibit the entry of Indians into their jurisdictions. The Orange Free State prohibited all Indians from settling there whilst the ZAR (better known as the Transvaal) sought to stem the flow of Indians by introducing preventative measures in the form of legislation and the imposition of taxes. Nonetheless, Indians migrated to these areas in small numbers.

Since 1910 and with the formation of the Union of South Africa, the presence of Indians became a thorny problem and was perceived by the government as in need of a resolution. The Union government tried to address the Indian problem on a national scale but could not legislate against Indians, as they were British subjects. At all times, the Union government was guided by its fervent desire to rid itself of the Indian problem and the logical solution was to ensure that the Indians left South Africa.

By the time the Union government addressed the presence of Indians on South African soil, many families had been in the country for almost five decades. During this period they had ample time to set themselves up as merchants and had become redoubtable competitors in the business community. The Union government used the business acumen of Indians as a ploy to introduce legislation that would directly affect them. The legislation, couched in terms that had direct implications for Indians, was general, directed at all and done in a manner to introduce a measure of uniformity to business in the Union.

Thus, the regulations demanding that all accounting be done in English and that stringent hygienic standards be maintained were in practice used against Indians. Indians responded to these measures by using the services of English bookkeepers or learning to do their bookkeeping in English. The Union inspectors responsible for the enforcement of these measures were merciless to the extent that even a few figures jotted in an Indian language was enough ground for them to revoke the license of an Indian businessmen. White business that feared competition from Indian merchants resorted to using the law as well. The popular perception among whites of Indians as unhygienic people was used indiscriminately. A disgruntled white could complain to the licensing authorities about the unhygienic conditions of an Indian's premises and have it shut and the license revoked. Indians, however, did not have the same recourse.

Despite legislation indirectly targeting the Indians and designed to induce them to leave the country, they stayed. The object of such legislation in the words of P.S. Aiyar was to ruin Indian traders and farmers by declaring them aliens and by segregating them on grounds of unsanitary premises and unfair competition.[2]

G.F. Cronjé in *Righteous Apartheid between Races*[3] stated that Indians were a problem and a foreign element in South Africa who had no right to the land. Reiterating the formal apartheid ideology, he described Indians as an ungrateful people who thought nothing of tarnishing the good name of South Africa and found their idea of seeking equality with the white race despicable. To him, Indians were a threat to the white race and using the examples of welfare, economy and politics, he portrayed them as parasites guided by greed. A greed manifested in their desire to compete with white business instead of accepting the superiority of the white race. In his opinion the only solution to the Indian problem was repatriation to India.

> The Indians are an economic threat. They have pushed out White trade in the Transvaal rural districts (*Platteland*). . . . On the Witwatersrand their trade thrives. . . . In Natal their economic value would soon overshadow the economic might of the White. . . . The Indians are not only a threat to the White but to the Coloureds and Natives as well. For as long as the Indian is allowed to trade, the Coloured and the Native would not stand a chance to even trade among their own. . . . The role of the Indian in the economy of the country is that of a parasite. Thus their idea to influence Coloureds and Natives to denounce apartheid is proof of this.[4]

The attempts to repatriate Indians failed but the independence of India in 1947 solved one part of the Indian problem for the Union government. It no longer had to recognize Indians in the Union as British subjects as they had become citizens of the independent state of India. Indians, however, refused to leave and in 1961, a century after the arrival of the first immigrants, the government under Prime Minister H.F. Verwoerd granted permanent status to Indians in the country. This decision was not a sign of an enlightened gesture on the part of the state but rather a means of preventing the Indian government from interfering in the affairs of South Africa.

## WHO ARE THE SOUTH AFRICANS OF INDIAN DESCENT?

Between 1860 and 1911, 152,184 indentured migrants arrived in Natal from India.[5] According to the first democratic census of 1996, they constituted 2.6 per cent population of South African. The figure represented 1,045,596 South Africans who defined themselves as 'Indian'.[6] The use of the term 'Indian' to designate a specific segment of the South African population remains problematic however. Should one use the qualifier 'so-called' to distinguish them from the citizens of India? Should one use the various forms of hyphenated identities that some politicians and members within this population segment use? Should one use inverted commas to indicate the difficulties in using the term? After considering the various options, I have decided to use the term 'Indian' to indicate the difference between South Africans of

Indian origin and citizens of India. Moreover the use of 'Indian' problematizes affiliation to the subcontinent of India and indicates that South Africans use the adjective Indian as a means of self-designation and, therefore, as a marker of differentiation within the South African nation.

'Indians' were seen as a homogenous entity by the apartheid state, anti-apartheid organizations and non-'Indian' South Africans. The only understood common denominator of the 'Indian' segment of the South African population was their phenotype attaching them to their land of origin, India. The 'Indian' community perceived itself as various sub-communities within the larger entity called 'Indian'. To understand how 'Indians' manoeuvre in and out of the generic idea of being 'Indian' and the sub-communities they belong to calls for the deconstruction of the 'Indian' identity to consider the way in which different markers intertwine to form what I call a horizontally constructed and stratified world-view. This horizontally structured identity combines in complex ways elements of caste, regional background, linguistic and religious characteristics.

## Migration and Caste

Caste was a fundamental criterion that underpinned all Indian immigrants' life experiences. They arrived in South Africa with a consciousness of differentiation and of accepted and unaccepted norms and associations defined by their rank within—or—outside of the caste system.[7] The (re)establishment of a system of differentiation allowed Indian immigrants to make sense of their new adopted world. The first marker of Indians in South Africa was linked to the Indian port of embarkment from which families departed. Thus, *Madrassi* and *Calcuttie* became labels that were the first functional and tangible sign of separation of the indentured migrants. Having had no choice of regrouping themselves along socialized affinities, they resorted to the most obvious difference to reproduce a world they understood.

The Passenger Indians did not experience the same constraints as their indentured counterparts, for they did not have to endure the promiscuity of the plantations or ill-treatment by farmers and other employers. They could settle freely and form groups along the lines of caste or fraternity membership. Their migratory patterns were considerably different from those of the indentured Indians. Where the Indentured Indian was recruited by an agent in India, and sent as an isolated individual or, in rare cases, with his immediate family, the Passenger Indian usually came on an exploratory mission, almost always with the consent of his family, clan or village. Family members, co-villagers, friends or acquaintances from surrounding villages then usually joined him. As a second migratory wave from India, Passenger migrants' first concern was to differentiate themselves from the 'indentured stock'. Migrant identities reflected immediate concerns such as this, but also regional Indian north/south politics, as well as deeper issues related to the caste principles of purity and impurity. Passenger Indians originating from north India considered themselves purer than the indentured Indians who, in the main, hailed from south India. Passenger Indians and their descendents continued to consider the indentured Indians and their descendents as 'inferior' because those families which came as indentured labour had to sever their ties with India, to transgress caste rules because of their indentured status, and thus, had to reconstitute a community that did not follow the basic precepts of the caste system of fraternity.

## The Sub-caste and Fraternity Strata

In South Africa, the use of sub-communities referring to caste type organizations evolved over the decades to include the socio-political changes 'Indians' experienced constantly reinventing themselves to face and find answers to the challenges before them. Among the descendents of Passenger Indians, *jat* or *kutumb* and increasingly the term 'community' was used as a euphemism for membership to a caste-type community.

Given the different conditions of migration and the relatively diminished size of immigrant groups in South Africa, the religious dimension of the caste system collapsed. In South Africa's different social and political structure, both the indentured and Passenger Indians had the task of reinventing a social order that was familiar to them. An important dimension of the caste system that required replication was its ability to mark the rites of passage of its constituent members to regulate marriage and determine which rituals a particular *jati* (sub-caste and the visible form of the caste system) could perform or officiate. In the absence of a social system that replicated the familiar Indian one, Indian migrants drew on specific elements that allowed them to create a social order that was familiar and connected them to their land of origin. Stratification became the most important marker in establishing sub-communities that resembled the *jati* families hailed from in India.

To institute social stratification, it became necessary to recreate sub-communities. Through a carefully planned network of immigration and regrouping, Passenger Indians were able to create sub-communities that allowed them to observe some of the cardinal operating rules of the caste system. Marriage and other rituals could be performed according to rules that were manipulated to resemble the religiously ordained mechanism of social organization. For indentured migrants, however, it was not easy. On the ship, migrants shared the confined space, resulting in touching and living, albeit temporarily, with others of a lower sub-caste. The security of knowing one's place and acting accordingly was disrupted, calling for initial manoeuvring of the rules that were to continue on the South African *terra firma*.

### Linguistic and Religious Stratification

Although some researchers have argued that linguistic differentiation replaced the caste system in the South African context,[8] its significance was transformed rather than eradicated. Regrouping into linguistic communities also seemed as a means of survival for the indentured Indians particularly in an unknown and inhospitable land.

Reworking linguistic boundaries allowed 'Indians' to reinvent the borders of their communities to include larger districts from India rather than the narrow village links which language had previously represented. The subsumption of Indian village identities reflected the need for more tangible markers of identity acceptable to the youth who had few links with India itself. However, the transformation of the village link into a larger linguistic community (such as Gujarati, Hindi, Mehmon, Tamil, Telugu and Urdu) was not synonymous with proficiency in that language nor was it static. Within linguistic communities, 'Indians' continued to redefine themselves, with language being less cohesive as an identity marker. Education in either English or Afrikaans rather than in Indian languages and the shedding of Indian attire for western clothes can be understood as reflective of the fading memory of India in the minds of South African born 'Indians'.[9]

The ability to constantly reinvent themselves required 'Indians' to use those parameters of their identity they considered most salient to either create larger or smaller sub-communities. As a fundamental marker of identity, religion became the symbol of rejuvenation of different sub-communities. In the process, religious markers supplanted linguistic distinctions. This relatively recent shift from language to religion as a dominant and determining marker of identity has produced a fundamental distinction between Hindu and Muslim South African Indians. Although there are Christian and Buddhist communities among the 'Indian' population, they are relatively insignificant in number. Within this quasi-homogeneity of the Hindu and Muslim communities, sub-communities continue to proliferate. Yet, to a large extent the merging of the linguistic sub-communities points to India as a guiding principle.

## THE RESURGENCE OF THE 'INDIAN' QUESTION IN THE POST-APARTHEID PERIOD

In the first democratic elections in 1994 many 'Indians' voted for the National Party (NP) supposedly out of fear of a *swart gevaar* (black peril) and of being swamped by a black majority. Large numbers of 'Indians' in KwaZulu Natal voted for the NP at the national level and for the Minority Front (MF) of Amichand Rajbansi at the provincial level. The MF led by Rajbansi campaigned on an ethnic ticket. The inability of other political parties to address the immediate concerns of the poor 'Indians' in impoverished areas like Chatsworth and Phoenix, paved the way for Rajbansi and the MF to present his party as a viable alternative to the Democratic Alliance and the New National Party which he branded as 'white parties'. The MF, it should be noted, did not have any illusions about ruling. This was made clear at a meeting in Chatsworth in May 1999 when Rajbansi is quoted as saying: 'It (is) the policy of the MF to work with the ruling parties, whoever they were.'[10]

Fears persisted in the 1999 election period, exacerbating a public discourse on 'Indian' political indecisiveness. *The Post*, the 'Indian' weekly owned by Independent Newspapers, highlighted this issue in the *Comment and Opinion* column. Columnist Satish Jaggernath asked: *Will our children look back with pride?* He virulently criticized the readership of their intention to vote for parties other than the African National Congress (ANC): 'If the predictions are correct, the Indian community is about to commit its most deplorable act of political suicide'. Citing Indian leadership who fought all forms of tyranny in India and in South Africa, he warned the fence sitters: '[The] Indians who dare to vote NNP or DP will effectively be spitting on the graves of their forefathers'. Although the ANC was poised to win the elections, it nonetheless desired to expand its base among all citizens. The 'Indian' vote and its underlying 'Indian' question were thus placed at the centre of the debate, particularly in KwaZulu Natal, the region with the largest proportion of 'Indian' voters (9.4 per cent) at that time ruled by the Inkartha Freedom Party (IFP) with the ANC coming in a close second.

Thabo Mbeki, as presidential candidate and president of the ANC, considered it appropriate to write an open letter to 'Indians' telling them that they have a 'long walk' to the socio-economic and political transformation of South Africa. Addressing them as *African-Indians* he praised them for their talent, achievement and commitment to the country.[11] By his use of the term *African-Indian*, Mbeki highlighted the politics of an 'Indian' identity, alluding that some 'Indians' had one foot in Africa and the other in India. At the same time, the ANC's campaign tried to embrace the 'Indian' population by calling on their sense of responsibility and contribution to *one* nation. Within 'Indian' circles, this argument raised many eyebrows. Some 'Indians' conveyed their dismay at Mbeki's reference to them as African-Indians to the then Minister of Constitutional Development, Mohammed Valli Moosa. They argued that they were *Indian-Africans* rather than *African-Indians*. In consequence, the wording was reversed.[12]

In contrast, Kader Asmal, a member of the ANC Executive and the then Minister of Water Affairs and Forestry, challenged the notion of hyphenated identity used by his colleagues in the ANC. At a meeting in Laudium (23 May 1999), an 'Indian' township outside Pretoria, he opened his speech by challenging the audience on their identity: 'Indians? What Indians? There are no Indians here, except for His Excellency (the Indian High Commissioner sitting in the hall). Indians are in India. There are no Indians. There are South Africans.' The ANC and other political parties needed to address the fears of the people. This was aggravated by an editorial that appeared in the *Ilanga*, the IFP mouthpiece in KwaZulu Natal. Despite the apologies that were printed following the editorial that gave Idi Amin reason for having ousted the Indians, the suspended editor Amos Maphumulo insisted: 'I believed I was stating a point held valid by most of our readers'. Whilst the editorial spawned a national debate around hate speech and the dangers of singling out a minority, it did fuel racial fears among 'Indians' of KwaZulu Natal.

The fears were tangible fears that the ANC and its prominent and respected members like Nelson Mandela, Thabo Mbeki, Valli Moosa and Kader Asmal tried to address. The saliency of the 'Indian' vote was further emphasized in the way the ANC leaders (the president included) made reference to individuals like Mahatma Gandhi, Monty Naicker, Yusuf Dadoo, Nana Sita and others who had dedicated their lives to the struggle. The reference to 'Indians' in the struggle was intended to emphasize the space for 'Indians' in the ANC. In an attempt to draw 'Indians' away from pure ethnic politics, prominent figures in the 'Indian' community, like sociologist Fatima Meer, film producer Anant Singh, sports executive Sam Ramsamy and playwright Ronnie Govender formed The Concerned Citizens Group. Their aim was to canvas votes away from the MF of Amichand Rajbansi, the Democratic Alliance, the IFP or the New National Party and for the ANC. This is reflected in the statement: 'Your single vote can either condemn us as a people who side with our former oppressors, or it can redeem our reputation, established by our forefathers, as a people who stand with the oppressed and the poor: Let us reaffirm our loyalties to the country of our birth and to the vast majority of her people.'[13]

## EMERGENCE OF A DIASPORA CONSCIOUSNESS

Efforts to allay the fears of 'Indians' underline that 'Indians' remain a visible minority in South Africa, despite accounting for only 2.6 per cent of the national population. Since their arrival in South Africa, 'Indians' have constantly sought to reconstitute themselves into different communities of various dimensions. In the contemporary context, their visibility as a minority has posed a new challenge and has led some to seek affiliation with the broader global Indian diaspora (cf. Landy's contribution in this volume). For 'Indians' belonging to an Indian diaspora is a decision that gained relevance in democratic South Africa. This membership allows people of Indian origin to situate themselves in a larger entity that often supports and does not necessarily conflict with local and regional communal value systems. At the same time, although India remains a key referent in the lives of 'Indians', its force as a rallying point often acts as a point of divergence. Collective memory of and connection to India has acquired a religious rather than secular significance with 'Indian' Muslims disassociating, even purging, the connection and 'Indian' Hindus emphasizing India as the source of their religion and spirituality.

Such connections and disconnections can be seen in negotiations pertaining to marriage in particular. Among Gujarati-speaking Hindu 'Indians', for example, arranging a marriage in India has become increasingly common. During the tricameral apartheid period, 'Indian' members of parliament lobbied the state to allow brides to be imported from India. Their argument was based on upholding Indian culture. In the period before the formal demise of apartheid, many families used this option to find spouses for their children. 'Indian' Muslims inclined to use this option figured among those who consider perpetuating their religious idea of *Baap dada ka Islam*, India as the *land of the ancestors*, and seek to keep the memory and the bond alive. 'Indian' Muslims who seek to purge India from their collective memory are inclined to look for spouses within the *Umma.* Arguing that Muslims in India are not 'pure' enough, they turn to the Arab-speaking world to arrange marriages. Marriages between South African men and Moroccan women, for example, are becoming common.

Connections to the diaspora appear segmented when one considers the desire to learn the ancestral and religious languages and the ways in which these choices reflect the particular diaspora connection that is made. Thus, an 'Indian' Muslim wishing to learn Arabic, would seek affiliation to the *Umma* while the learning of Gujarati, Tamil or Telugu would point towards a connection to an Indian diaspora. Belonging to the diaspora is not a homogeneous concept among 'Indians'. It, in fact, allows different groups to reinforce communal ideas and identities. Membership of a diaspora functions on two levels: on the one hand, it acts as a reassuring mechanism for it allows entry into a larger entity and, on the other, it reflects South African patterns of stratification within the 'Indian community'.

## CONCLUSION

The 'Indian' community has constantly reinvented itself. These reinventions have been closely linked to minority status in South Africa as well as to a desire to maintain their distinctness, oscillating between and fusing different parameters of identity. Thus, some subgroups decide to affix 'Indian', Muslim or Hindu to their South African identity and others decide to adopt a non-hyphenated identity as South African. Such affiliations and choices facilitate entry into larger diasporas that operate beyond an obvious attachment to India as the land of their ancestors.

NOTES

1. G.H. Calpin, *Indians in South Africa,* Pietermaritzburg: Shuter and Shooter, 1949, p. 22.
2. P. S. Aiyar, *The Indian Problem in South Africa*, Durban: African Chronicle Printing Works, 1925, pp. 16-17.
3. G. Cronjé, *Regverdige Rasse-Apartheid, Die Christen Studentevereenigingmaatskappy van Suid Afrika*, Stellenbosch, 1947, pp. 203-6.
4. Ibid., p. 205.
5. S. Bhana and J. Brain, *Setting down Roots: Indian Migrants in South Africa, 1860-1911*, Johannesburg: Wits University Press, 1990, p. 15.
6. *Census in Brief,* Report No. 03-01-11, Pretoria: Statistics South Africa, July 1999.
7. For details see R. Ebr.-Vally, *Kala Pani: Caste and Colour in South Africa,* Cape Town: Kwela, 2001.
8. Frene N. Ginwala, 'Class Consciousness and Control: Indian South Africans 1860-1946', doctoral dissertation, Department of Philosophy, Oxford University, 1974.
9. For a fuller discussion, see Landy's contribution in this volume.
10. A. Rajbansi, Letter to *The Post,* 19-22 May 1999, 'It's Making Mischief to Link MF with ANC.'
11. Thabo Mbeki, President of the ANC, open letter and speech in Phoenix ('Indian' township, Durban district), 25 May 1999.
12. Marlan Padayachee, 'Mbeki Engages in Battle of Words to Secure Indian Vote', *Sunday Independent*, 30 May 1999.
13. Quoted in the *Mail* and *Guardian*, N. Moodley, 'Parties Appealed to Indian Fears', 28 May-3 June 1999, p. 6.

CHAPTER 13

# Indian Territories in Durban

HÉLÈNE MAINET-VALLEIX

The concept of territory relates to the idea of a social space, appropriated by its inhabitants. The latter have memories, customs, and representations of space, which form into a territory.

> For a specific group, [territories] are the link in the social relationships taking place within it; they give it substance and a contextual physicality. In consequence, the territory becomes part of the identity package of the 'spatialised' social group that shapes it. It makes it more tangible, more intelligible, more alive and more decipherable. (Di Méo, 1998, p. 9)

Similarly, territory is a fundamental element shaping relationships with the external world, i.e. with those who do not belong to the group. Collective and individual representations are integral elements in the social construction of space. These territorial representations articulate and strengthen the sentiments of collective identities and 'give [them] space and place, that indispensable base, that substance without which the symbolic markers of a representation and a shared memory would not be able to exist' (Di Méo, 1998, p. 10).

Indians account for presently 30 per cent of Durban's population. They have lived there since the city was founded and have been witness to the successive policies of segregation during the British era of colonization and apartheid. Imposed spaces have been appropriated and claimed as representations of specific identities. The study of Indian residents' day-to-day urban practices and representations undertaken in this paper permits an exploration of residents' relationships with the city and the ways in which spaces have been appropriated and consolidated as territory.[1] To understand such processes, it is necessary to examine Indian residents' territoriality, specifically the different ways of referring to geographical space in order to construct personal and social relationships with the city.

In this paper I draw on three basic, interlinking territorial categories: housing, locality and agglomeration. At each scale, I will demonstrate the extent to and the function for which each category is socially invested and appropriated by Durban-based Indians.

## DOMESTIC SPACES: CRUCIBLES OF DIVERSE IDENTITIES

### FROM MUNICIPAL HOUSING TO A PLACE OF ONE'S OWN

The residential geography of Durban's Indian population dates from apartheid. The municipal townships constructed in the 1960s and 1970s (Chatsworth and Phoenix among the most important) house the majority of the population (Map 13.1). Original pre-apartheid neighbourhoods still exist, like Clairwood, but only house a minority. For the most part Indians were given no choice with regard to the allocation of housing. Despite this lack of choice, there are numerous obvious signs of appropriation that reveal the ways in which residents have invested in their homes and neighbourhoods.

The municipal housing models were relatively varied according to socio-economic criteria at the scale of the township (especially compared to black townships), but uniform within subunits. If one takes the example of Chatsworth, the oldest and largest of the Indian townships (with more than 200,000 residents), there is great diversity between apartment blocks, semi-detached houses of Bayview, two-storied semi-detached houses of Havenside, and the self-built housing of Mobeni. Despite this relative heterogeneity, municipal construction was uniform, particularly in one choice of materials as well as design. This uniformity reflected in part a Victorian ideal of 'hearth and family life' that served as the model for the apartheid city. Houssay-Holzschuch argued that the apartheid project was about modernizing African families: 'It was necessary to domesticate African space. African houses, the extended family, polygamy, seemed the very antithesis of the bourgeois ideal of family life' (Houssay-Holzschuch, 1999, p. 155). These concerns about the family and living standards applied equally to Indian extended families and to housing practices in predominantly Indian pre-apartheid localities in Durban as well.

Although residential urbanscapes found in townships appear monotonous, there are increasing signs of personalization, evidence of a physical and symbolic resolve to appropriate an imposed space. Housing has been physically transformed and adapted to suit its inhabitants.

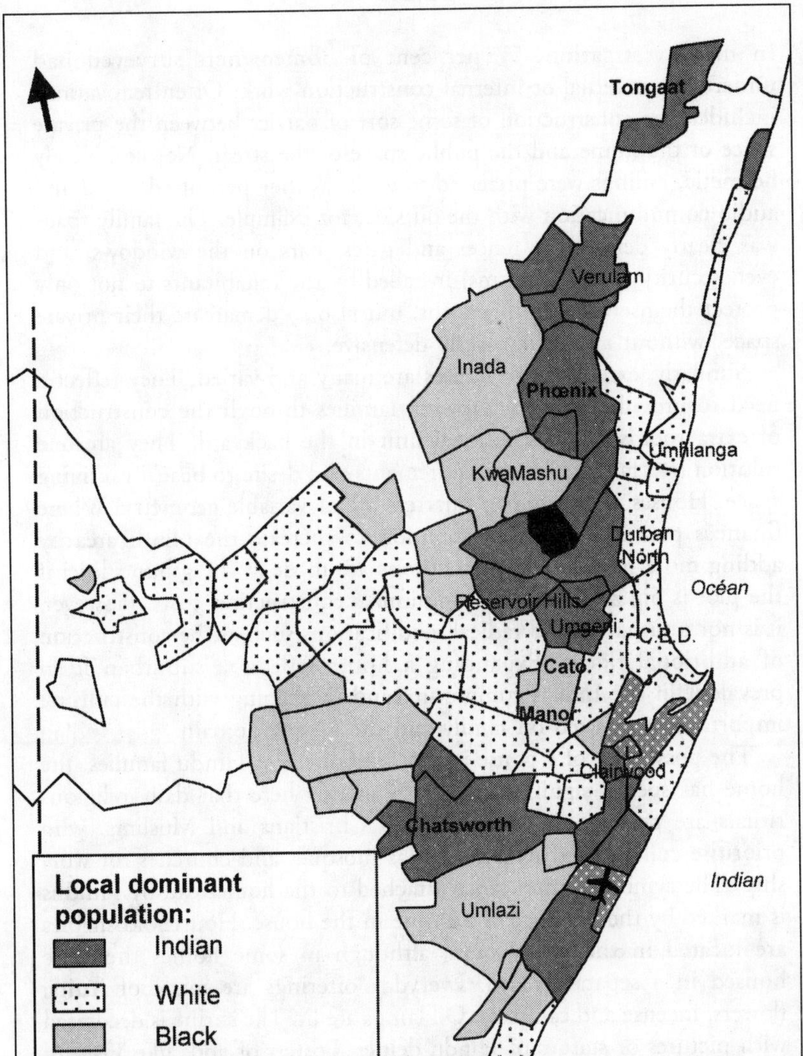


*Sources:* Population Census 1991-7; HMV, 2000.

MAP 13.1: POPULATION GROUPS IN DURBAN AGGLOMERATION.

In my investigation, 57 per cent of homeowners surveyed had undertaken external or internal construction work. Often renovations included the construction of some sort of barrier between the private space of the home and the public space of the street. Not completely hermetic, railings were preferred to walls, as they permitted visual and audio communication with the outside, for example. The family space was clearly defined by fences and gates, bars on the windows, and even security systems (alarms) installed by the inhabitants to not only protect themselves from break-ins, but also to demarcate their private space, without appearing overly defensive.

Similarly, extensions to houses are many and varied. They reflect a need to provide space for growing families through the construction of extra rooms or an additional unit in the backyard. They are one solution to a family's space requirements and desire to beautify a living space. Houses in the Indian quarters are of variable geometry. Where finances permit, it is quite common to increase the plinth area by adding more rooms. These extensions are made at the ground level if the plot is big enough as this minimizes construction costs. However, it is not unusual to find radical modifications such as the construction of additional floors. Expanding a home reflects a suburban ideal prevalent in the Indian community and in keeping with the cultural importance conferred on family and the private domain.

The possession of a house is also symbolic. For Hindu families, the home has special significance as it is mainly here that daily religious rituals are performed, in contrast to Christians and Muslims, who prioritise collective structures such as mosques and churches for worship. The symbolic importance attached to the homestead by Hindus is marked by the presence of a shrine in the house. Household shrines are located in the main room, although in some homes these are housed in a separate room. Everyday offerings are made of fruits, flowers, incense and camphor. Oil lamps are lit. The shrine is decorated with pictures or statues of Hindu deities. Posters of gods like Vishnu, Krishna and Ganesha are hung on the walls of the drawing room. Families with a garden or a courtyard often construct a more permanent edifice in brick or stone to house a bigger shrine. Some almost have the appearance of temples. Flags are hung outside to protect the family. The spatiality of a Hindu home is thus symbolically marked by religious beliefs. Muslim and Christian beliefs are less visible in the home; although mural decorations, polychrome posters of Christ, a crucifix, pictures of the Kaaba or religious images from calendars are quite common. These examples of religious practice not only demonstrate group affiliation, but also illustrate attachment to a plot of land, a house, and a neighbourhood.

Similarly, the desire to become a homeowner reflects an expectation that is associated with living in the city. For some years now the Municipality has been gradually disengaging itself from its housing stock and schemes by selling homes to residents. Owning a property is a lifelong dream of all residents. It is considered a sign of social success. These personal and familial aspirations explain the current evolution of localities. Townships gradually cease being municipal housing estates and increasingly become private housing estates. This desire to become owners can be interpreted as an expression of economic security, having not only fixed assets but also urban security. After witnessing a troubled and violent urban history, to own a house is a sentiment shared by many. The desire to provide one's children a roof over their heads is important for people who have suffered from the politics of segregation and the uncertainty of living under the constant threat of eviction. Houses are a financial, affective and patrimonial investment, transferable to one's heirs and a potential source of profit.

Property is thus a multidimensional matrix expressing individual and family identities. It fosters familial and matrimonial practices, both proof of the group's cultural diversity. As a haven and crucible of family life, it is the cornerstone of Indian identity, a place in which the cultural diversity of Indians is given its fullest expression.

## Preservation of Familial and Cultural Identities

Identities of Indians have evolved since their arrival in Durban at the end of the nineteenth century. Identities have adapted gradually to an urban context marked by strict segregation. In the process, some referents have vanished, while others have become stronger in the process of modification (Freund, 1995). Although outsiders have often characterized the Indian community as highly economically differentiated, its extreme social, linguistic and religious diversity should be stressed. Differences between various subgroups are no doubt linked to social position, but above all, they are related to cultural, religious and linguistic factors.

Although caste has ceased to be relevant as a cultural identifier, reference to a person's original religion has replaced it as the most significant marker of identity. Indians no longer think of themselves in terms of caste but rather as north Indians or south Indians. The distinction between the north and the south is visible during religious festivals. Diwali, the festival of lights for north Indians, Deepavali for south Indians, is celebrated one day apart. There are many examples that reveal internal disparities in everyday life, even if relations remain entirely cordial between north and south Indians.

As memories of origins fade, geographical origin has replaced language as a cultural referent. In response to this issue, someone may say, for instance, 'I am Hindi or Tamil' rather than 'I am from the north or the south of India'. Thus, it is the original mother tongue, even if it is no longer spoken, which remains the criterion of cultural identification, designating the name of a communal group rather than a language. In this sense there exists a strong 'linguistic endogamy', especially seen during marriages between Indians. The linguistic referent has replaced geographical origin and the bond with the village or region as the indicator of identity.

The other critical source of identity is religion (Landy, Maharaj and Mainet, 2004). It constitutes a broader frame of reference because it incorporates other identities to some extent (for example, one can be a Hindi-speaking Hindu or a Tamil-speaking Hindu). Other customs and beliefs have evolved in comparison to practices in India, while remaining pillars of identity for Indians in Durban. In the contemporary period, Hindus represent 62 per cent, Muslims 19 per cent and Christians 12 per cent of Indians in Durban, shifts that reflect a minor erosion of Hinduism, stabilization of Islam, and increased adoption of Christianity.

Religious distinctions have a bearing mainly in the private sphere. They become important during marriages; marriages between persons from different religions are rare. In the daily life of Indians, however, they barely count. In the business sphere, for instance, Indian shops are patronized without the proprietor's religion being of any consequence: Hindus buy from Muslims or from Christians, children attend the same public schools and everyone lives in the same Indian 'townships'. The construction and perpetuation of personal cultural referents have reinforced cohesion in the face of discriminatory policies. The family, along with the cultural practices that it sustains, served as the refuge of identity during the period of segregation. It continues to fulfil this function in the present context of profound political and economic transformation.

## NEIGHBOURHOODS: THE NUCLEUS OF INDIAN SOCIABILITY

Beyond the primary unit, i.e. the home, neighbourhoods have become a second space in which social identities are produced. The diversity and density of amenities available in the Indian neighbourhoods/townships are remarkable: each big township has a well-developed commercial shopping complex; stalls and cottage industries flourish at every street corner; and each locality has places of worship and community centres, which were constructed and funded by the residents themselves. There are numerous and varied associations such as: sports and cultural activities, women's clubs and taxpayers associations are common structures. This neighbourhood sociability encompasses and transcends individual cultural divisions to make way for a second casing of identity, namely, 'Indianness', which finds expression at the level of the locality.

### The Township Transformed into a Neighbourhood

The unvarying landscapes of the townships have been radically altered by their residents. The variety and density of the amenities are one of the factors that structure Indian localities (Mainet, 1999). Social linkages are woven around developed, built-up areas for commercial, political, religious and communal reasons. The density of communal amenities is a sign of the adaptation of inhabitants to experiences of and the constraints of segregation.

Religious edifices abound and reflect the cultural diversity of the residents. The task of construction falls on the residents' association. Hindu temples, mosques and Christian churches juxtapose each other in localities. In Chatsworth, the diversity and density of the buildings is striking, demonstrating the importance attached to religious practice by the people, as well as the harmonious coexistence of various religions. A sub-locality of Chatsworth, Havenside has, among others, the Pentecostal Protestant Church, the Chatsworth Baptist Church, the Islamia Musjid Mosque, Saint John's Catholic Church and the Shri Vishnu Temple. There are numerous community halls, often located close to a religious building when the same association manages them. They are rented to individuals or to associations for weddings, festivals and public meetings. Along with religious monuments and business establishments, they are among the most vital social spaces, representing meeting places and social landmarks in the neighborhood's urbanscape.

Some territories lie in the other parts of the city, areas from which Indian communities were forcibly evicted. Areas destroyed during the apartheid period occupy a unique place in the memory and customs of Indians. Even in areas completely razed to the ground, individual and collective practices continue, especially connected to religious festivals and remaining religious buildings. The names of Cato Manor, Sea Cow Lake, Umgeni and Clairwood resonate in the vacuum created by the total or partial destruction of these places by the apartheid government. Even though some religious edifices have been destroyed, most are still intact, even where entire neighbourhoods have been deserted. Association with and practices in these structures continue to perpetuate the memory of bygone days. Several temples organize the annual festivals of Kavady and Draupadi, attracting many believers, participants and spectators. The temples on Jacobs Road in Clairwood and the Shree Draupadiamman Alayam in Cato Manor organize the Draupadi celebrations every year during which participants walk on red hot coals. Apart from these annual special occasions, temples remain open although regular attendance is often minimal.

Graveyards are also important places in former Indian neighbourhoods. To recall where the dead are buried is a way of maintaining a symbolic attachment to the past, to family, and to urban space. The sites where Indian families inhume and incinerate their dead are primarily situated in neighbourhoods where Indians once lived before the imposition of apartheid segregation. Apart from the Indian cemetery in the centre of the city, which is largely for Muslim burials, the rest have areas reserved for other religions. The residents of Clairwood and Tongaat do not generally use other cemeteries as they have their own and also because people from these two localities have been less geographically mobile. On the other hand, diversity is greater in the case of the township residents. The principal cemeteries used by the people of Phoenix are Chatsworth and Umgeni, as well as Merebank, Clairwood and Cato Manor. The old family ties explain this localization more than actual geographical proximity. Many Phoenix residents formerly lived in Chatsworth or have family there, whereas the Umgeni and Merebank zones, 'swept' by apartheid, have partly populated the township. Whenever religious ceremonies are held in memory of the dead or during new burials and cremations, people get an opportunity to visit these old areas. For the younger generations, they are a reminder of Indian spaces across Durban, and reinforce the families' attachments to land where their ancestors are buried.

The uses of space in areas of Durban where Indian residents previously lived are emotionally charged and strengthen the feeling of belonging to a territory. For Indians, the city is a place of memory and veneration, a territory common to all the endogroups. In this sense, the old inhabited localities and isolated temples are like 'geo-symbols', identity-conferring places. For Indians, Durban is therefore not only the place where they live, but also a receptacle of memories of their ancestors. These types of places and practices facilitate a tangible re-imagination of 'the invisible city, the one that existed before the great destruction of the 1960s, past landscapes, places of memory' (Gervais-Lambony, 1999, p. 9).

### Assuming an Imposed Identity

Neighbourhood networks, woven around everyday exchanges and a well-developed network of associations, create social linkages between Indians from different cultural groups, encompassing and moving beyond individual distinctions. The adoption of an 'Indianness' common to all South African Indians is a rejoinder to the politics of segregation, which confined people by assigning to them a stipulated identity.

Community habits and social networks are strong. There exist important kinship, friendship and economic relationships between members of different groups. The concept of community also embraces and masks conflicts and inequalities. Associations play an important role in helping inhabitants adapt to the urban context, as they constitute urban networks whose importance in daily life represents much more than a simple group membership. Joining an association is normal for many Indians: 37 per cent of adults and 69 per cent of youth questioned were members of an association. Religious associations have the highest number of members, especially Christian churches (33 per cent) and Hindu temple associations (20 per cent). Neighbourhood associations such as sports clubs (29 per cent) and neighbourhood clubs (25 per cent) are other important groups.

In well-to-do localities inhabitants have a greater propensity to become members of neighbourhood associations, for instance 65 per cent membership in Woodview, a higher income area, relative to 17 per cent in Mobeni, a lower income area. Woodview has a Neighbourhood Watch surveillance association which was established on the initiative of the residents after a series of attacks and break-ins. Its aim is to ensure the security of persons and property in the locality.

Members take turns, depending on the time they can spare, to watch over children on their way to and from school and guard the houses in the surrounding area. In the case of a problem the association is expected to contact the local authorities for greater police surveillance. Signboards announcing the association's presence signal a warning to would-be burglars. Sports clubs are another key association in the local life of the community. The most popular sports are football and cricket which are played in the local clubs with nearly every area of the township boasting its own club. Regular meetings and inter-area competitions are held which encourage social interaction and engender familiarity with different areas and parts of the city. Forty per cent of the youth questioned belonged to religious associations in particular. These groups organize tuition classes after school and leisure activities at weekends and during school vacations, practically free of cost. Parents use them to channel their children's energies and to keep them off the streets.

In these townships, traditional patterns of sociability and membership in associations act as a bulwark against possible humiliations outside the geographical confines of the locality. Associations provide a fertile ground for community to take root, thus forming the bedrock of Indian neighbourhood sociability. In the process, attachment to places becomes real, generating local identities.

## THE CITY: UNCERTAIN TERRITORIES

Home and neighbourhood-based identities do not exclude engagement with other areas and social practices that cross and extend in and beyond the city. Identity and territory at a citywide, metropolitan scale are examined in the following discussion.

### Territories as Archipelagos

Since mobility so critically shapes identity formation at the city scale, I will discuss territories as archipelagos to describe territorialization at the city level. Personal transport is a necessity for city dwellers, especially in the case of a metropolitan area the size of Durban, stretching 50 km east to west and 70 km north to south over undulating terrain. Of the surveyed Indian residents, 74 per cent of adults and 89 per cent students' families owned at least one personal vehicle, which enabled families to move around relatively easily within zones which do not have a public transport system or after service hours. Apart from the mandatory urban commuting in connection with work or with the use of specific urban services, the study of recreational practices helps analyse the nature of voluntary mobility around the city. Beaches, cinemas and other places of recreation in the metropolitan area are regularly frequented. The same is true of commercial complexes. In addition to the facilities found in Indian townships, facilities in the former white areas are used by more affluent Indians, such as the *Pavilion* in Westville, the biggest and most 'chic' commercial complex, and Musgrave Centre. These American-style malls are more expensive but also better stocked with high quality products. Moreover, shopping in the former white neighbourhoods is indicative of a certain lifestyle and in some cases, even snobbery.

However, my research revealed that visiting family and friends was one of the most common reasons for travelling outside of a family's immediate residential area. Visits to Chatsworth were the most common (71 per cent), followed by Phoenix (59 per cent), Tongaat (28 per cent), Verulam (25 per cent) and Merebank (21 per cent) (see Map 13.1). Although these locations are spread over a wide area within the city, they are mainly concentrated in areas formerly reserved for Indians and still largely inhabited by them. Other non-Indian neighbourhoods mentioned were all former white areas (Westville, Durban North and Umhlanga), reflecting a highly anecdotal but common Indian aspiration to move into these areas. Durban's town centre is well connected by different public transport routes. It is popular with the young and less affluent families for purposes of accessing commercial facilities, leisure activities and beaches. In general, former white areas are visited for recreational and commercial purposes (cinemas, restaurants, shopping complexes and up-market shops, for instance). Facilities are more numerous and of better quality, which attracts more affluent families who visit these areas regularly. African neighbourhoods are rarely frequented, except in connection with work.

The city lived and experienced by Indians, individually or collectively, is thus amputated in the sense that mobility is highly circumscribed. This way of functioning, however, is not unique to Indians, but common to all urban groups living in Durban (see Map 13.2). Broadly speaking, such habits are specific to large cities where objective or subjective criteria result in the segmentation and compartmentalization of urban perception and movement.

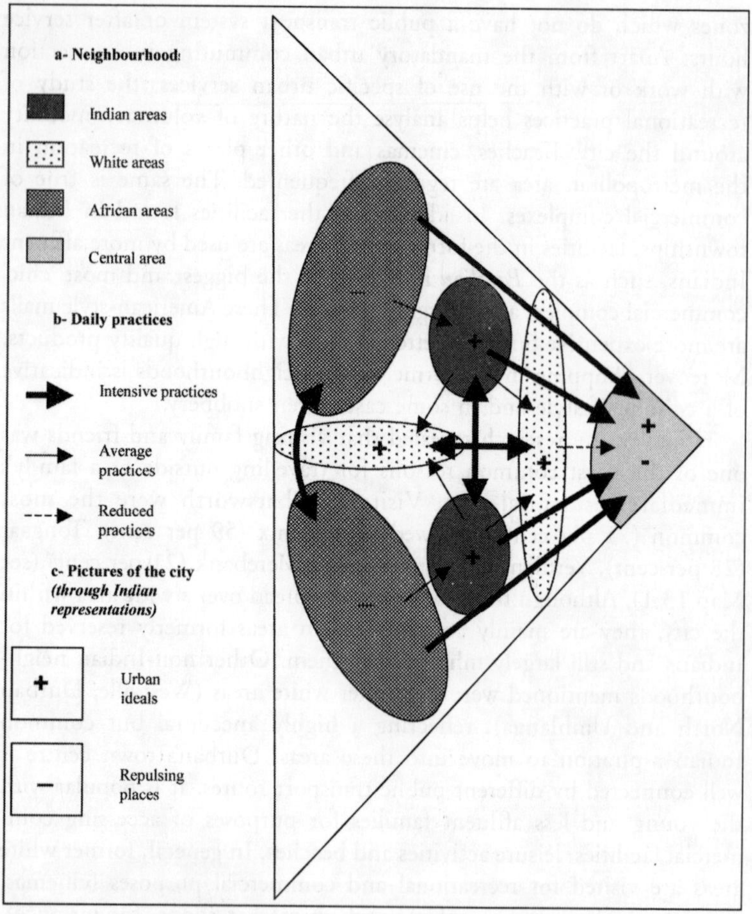


MAP 13.2: SYNTHESIS MAP OF POST-APARTHEID DURBAN.

## The Identity Issue

The function assigned to this truncated or archipelago territorialization of urban space is of primary importance. It enables Indians to reinforce their identity in the current context, a phenomenon that some people find distressing. The representations that Indians have of the city and of their urban identity oscillates between openness and isolation and between confidence and frustration.

These perceptions filter into the Indian understanding of other urban spaces. For instance, African townships are commonly symbolic of urban ghettos, associated with very negative images (filth, danger and poverty). White residential areas are perceived as the urban ideal (clean, safe and opulent). The image of Indian neighbourhoods has more nuance. To the extent that they are better known, they present more contrasts and have both positive (social cohesion and security) as well as some negative aspects (lack of amenities and distance).

These urban perceptions reflect a specific urbanness, still marked by ignorance, if not fear, of other urban groups after fifty years of apartheid 'separate development'. This urban reticence is, however, not confined to Indians alone. It is characteristic of all urban groups living in Durban, substantiating my survey results that the racial question is still pervasive and profoundly affects social relations. Communalism figures strongly in Durban's social relationships. On the geographical front, this reinforces the dichotomy between the central and suburban/township areas on the one hand, and the more remote peripheral areas on the other. The former are much better known and frequented, whereas the latter remain practically unacknowledged. The poorer areas, predominantly former African areas, are relegated to the urban fringes and neglected. It is striking to note that a zone such as Inanda, which has a population of several hundred thousand, was not once mentioned by any of the Indians interviewed, even as a poor or unpopular area. It is an antagonistic territory that remains cut-off from a considerable part of the city.

Indian territories for the most part have been appropriated for the purpose of urban recognition: to recognize oneself and be recognized as an urban resident and citizen. The territorialization of areas proclaimed Indian in the apartheid zone helped the preservation and even adoption of specifically Indian identities. These identities reflect internal specificities drawn from the home and family and assume an imposed Indianness at the scale of the locality and neighbourhood. At a city scale, such identities appear more ambiguous and uncertain, simultaneously appropriated and rejected, adopted and denied. At the same time, at the city scale, such identities and social practices confront other spaces, urban groups and broader territorial issues bound up with questions of urban legitimacy. Yet, despite these complexities, after more than a century in Durban, Indians perceive themselves as and unequivocally claim to be Durbanites and South Africans, first and last.

## NOTE

1. This work is based on a survey of a sample of 492 persons conducted in 1998 in the Indian localities of Durban (Chatsworth, Phoenix, Clairwood, Isipingo) (see Mainet, 2000).

## REFERENCES

Bonnemaison, J., L. Cambrézy, L. Quinty-Bourgeois (eds.), *Les territoires de l'identité. Le territoire, lien ou frontière ?*, vol. 1, Paris, L'Harmattan, 1999.

Christopher, A.J., 'Towards the Post-Apartheid City', *L'espace géographique*, 4, 1999, pp. 300-8.

Di Méo, G., *Géographie sociale et territoires*, Paris: Nathan Université, 1998.

Ebrahim-Vally, R., 'La stratification interne de la communauté dite indienne d'Afrique du Sud', Ph.D. thesis, University Paris I, 1995.

Freund, B., *Insiders and Outsiders : the Indian Working Class of Durban 1910-1990*, Pietermaritzburg: University of Natal Press, 1995.

Gervais-Lambony, P., *De Lomé à Harare : le fait citadin*, Paris: Karthala, 1994.

———, 'Villes d'Afrique du Sud, paysages, violences', in *La recherche sur la ville en Afrique du Sud*, ed. J.M. Rennes, Paris: Anthropos, 1999, pp. v-xiii.

Houssay-Holzschuch, M., *Le Cap ville sud-africaine, ville blanche, vies noires*, Paris: L'Harmattan, 1999.

Landy, F., B. Maharaj, H. Mainet, 'Are People of Indian Origin (PIO) "Indian"? The Case of South Africa', *Geoforum* 35 (2), 2004, pp. 203-15.

Maharaj, B., 'The Group Areas Act and Community Destruction in South Africa: the Struggle for Cato Manor in Durban', *Urban Forum*, 5, 2, 1994, pp. 1-25.

Mainet, H., 'Vivre à Phœnix, township indien de Durban', *Espaces, populations, société*, 1, 1999, pp. 107-17.

Mainet-Valleix, H., 'Les Indiens dans la ville post-apartheid, l'exemple de Durban', Ph.D. thesis, University Paris X, Nanterre, 2000.

CHAPTER 14

# Building White Spaces, Making White Minds: Space and Formation of 'White' Identity in South African former 'Poor White' Areas

ANNIKA TEPPO and PHILIPPE GUILLAUME

The object of this paper is to analyse the relationship between South African 'white' identity and urban space. We argue that for the study of the formation of a South African 'white' identity, the changing position of marginal whites, the so-called 'poor whites', is a key phenomenon. In the twentieth century, 'poor whites' were subject to extensive social engineering, which was partly achieved through urban planning. To this end, the paper examines the process of identity building of 'poor whites' in two 'poor white' suburbs—Jan Hofmeyr in Johannesburg and Ruyterwacht (formerly known as Epping Garden Village) in Cape Town. These suburbs were established in the 1930s for the betterment of 'poor whites' in their poverty-stricken circumstances and to 'rehabilitate' them.

We begin our analysis by examining the fears and ideologies underlying these attempts by the elite to make 'good whites'. The central idea of this process of 'rehabilitation' was to fortify the racial boundaries between 'whites' and 'non-whites', and thus construct a 'proper' 'white' identity for the residents of these 'poor white' areas. Thereafter, we examine the way in which urban space was used to achieve these goals, and the fate of these attempts with the demise of apartheid.

Although we draw attention to the differences between these two areas by comparing them with each other, their similarities are considered more essential. It is noteworthy, however, that today an outsider would have difficulty guessing that the two suburbs were built for the same purpose.[1]

Outwardly Ruyterwacht is improving by the day. Previously owned by a private housing company, Communicare (formerly the Citizens' Housing League), in the 1990s half of the houses were sold to private buyers. A process of gentrification occurred, and although some houses are still poorly maintained, newly installed satellite dishes dot the roofs of many. House prices have increased continuously since the beginning of the 1990s. The residents include both 'white' and 'coloured',[2] but there are no overt racial tensions between them.

In sharp contrast to Ruyterwacht, Jan Hofmeyr is decaying. Its white residents are angry and disillusioned, they foresee a grim future for themselves, and perceive the new African residents of the suburb as invaders. Residents continue to rent from the municipality because the process of selling houses to private owners has been delayed. Racial relations are more tense than in Ruyterwacht, and poverty is visible everywhere. Despite contemporary differences, the ideological premise underlying the establishment of these two suburbs was identical.

## 'WHITE' IDENTITY IN SOUTH AFRICA

Admittedly, white South African identity was never constructed as a unified category as was done in the United States where the category 'Caucasian' was developed in the twentieth century to refer to immigrants from all over Europe (Jacobson, 1998). Also, the existence of one unified 'white' identity in South Africa has often been disputed, since the white population has traditionally been split into English-speaking and Afrikaans-speaking groups. This division has in itself functioned as part of the identity building of both factions. Despite the eagerness of English- and Afrikaans-speaking white South Africans to emphasize their different identities, the two groups have much in common.

The most important factor for these groups in their everyday life has been their mutual whiteness, and the vast advantages acquiring from it. In practice, the differences brought about by their differing mother tongues, or wars (the Anglo-Boer Wars and the Second World War) in which they were on opposite sides, are of secondary importance. Emphasizing these differences has functioned as a diversion that has undermined the similarities between the two groups, and their interconnectedness. This diversion was particularly useful to Afrikaners, for it helped them to build a separate identity.

Despite their internal differences, in South Africa 'whites' or 'Europeans' were always treated as a separate category that was perceived as opposite to the category 'natives' or 'non-whites'. There are certain discourses concerning racial identity, class and self-other division that were of importance to all 'whites' in South Africa. One of these discourses was the 'poor white problem' that emerged after the second Anglo-Boer War (1899-1902). This problem was brought on by the new phenomena of urbanization, economic depression and the emergence of a white landless class.

In Europe, the fear of urbanization was a typical feature of the moral panic at the end of the nineteenth century. The city was seen as dangerous, dirty and morally corrupting, while the countryside represented the pure, sound and innocent lifestyle of hard-working people. In South Africa, urbanization and poverty[3] led 'whites' and 'non-whites' to become spatially and socially closer to one another as 'poor whites', 'coloureds' and Africans shared quarters and the daily struggle for survival.

The elite feared the dangers of racial and cultural miscegenation and the dissolving of the racial hierarchy that would occur without social and economic barriers. Afrikaners—who were also considered a 'lower race' by British eugenicists—were considered particularly vulnerable to this perceived threat. The church, welfare organizations and English-speaking and Afrikaans intellectuals were all keen to deal with the problem, particularly in the 1930s and 1940s. Their efforts to uplift the 'poor whites' became a symbol of national unity and the reconstruction of the post-War Afrikaner *volk* (Groenewald, 1987, pp. 62-3; Dubow, 1995, pp. 284-91; Freund, 1992, p. xvii; Parnell, 1992, pp. 126-9.)

Eugenic thinking was central in attempts to make 'poor whites' racially worthy. In the 1930s, eugenic ideas were popular throughout the Western world. Eugenic thinking—also known as 'racial hygiene' in German-speaking countries before the Second World War—believed in the possibility of controlling and improving the quality of human populations. The advocators of eugenics emphasized a need for 'purity' of races and feared the degeneration of 'superior races'. These ideas also reached South Africa, where the English-speaking and Afrikaner elite was particularly concerned about the racial status of 'poor whites' (Dubow, 1995, p. 172).

This was an era in which the revolution had swept away the Russian aristocracy, and the fear of Marxism (which the Nazis considered as the 'poison of race') was rampant. The social hierarchies based on class, gender and race were increasingly questioned throughout the Western world, and were no longer self-evident. New means and institutions were needed to keep old hierarchies alive.

In South Africa, the transformation to industrial capitalism was a recent event. The 'poor whites' originated from farms, and needed training if they were to be engaged as wage labour. It was important to train 'poor whites' to suit the capitalist regime, and transform them into hard-working, God-fearing, obedient citizens. The rehabilitative goals of racial hygiene concurred with the ideas of capitalism. For both it was important to separate working-class whites from blacks, and to ensure that class-based alliances did not develop between them.

The experience of uplifting 'poor whites' focused on various areas of life: work, family, appearance of bodies and homes and behaviour were areas in which 'poor whites' had to be guided. The use of urban space and the areas allocated to 'poor whites' were crucial to this exercise. They would have to be functional in order to be effective. The rationale underlying the establishment of 'poor white' suburbs can be summarized into three main themes:

1. Racial degeneration was seen as imminent. Some whites were impoverished to the same extent as Africans. Some Afrikaners were even employed as domestic or farm workers for blacks or coloureds. Afrikaners who were originally farmers were in particular considered culturally 'backward', and needed to be trained for capitalist production.
2. Racial degeneration was seen as contagious. It was feared that 'poor whites' would introduce racial degeneration into the white race, both genetically and culturally (in Afrikaans—*die swart gevaar, the black fear*).
3. It was feared that a racially degenerated white working class would become class conscious and ally themselves with Africans. This would lead to a Marxist revolution with the elite itself losing its privileged position (in Afrikaans—*die rooi gevaar, the red fear*).

A 'poor white' person did not fit into a society built on the presumed supremacy of the white man. He was in danger of losing his own self: he had to be guided back to civilization. To ensure the purity of the 'white' race, to create a sense of self-value and social distance, a spatial isolation from the 'natives' (as Africans were called) was critical. A 'white' man needed a 'white' identity. Their social and racial mixing with the natives, which was perceived as potential physical and cultural degeneration, had to be stopped. Thus, distance had to be maintained, be it social, economic or spatial. The urbanized and impoverished South African whites had to be integrated into a racial class. These efforts to sustain and increase racial distance characterized much of the political history of South Africa in the twentieth century and laid the foundation for the creation and implementation of apartheid after 1948.

It was to achieve these ends that suburbs for 'poor whites' were established. In the apartheid era, they became places where those who were unable to comply with the ideals of middle class whiteness were sent, or to which they drifted. Simultaneously, a process of social and spatial distancing between middle class whites and 'poor whites' began.

## HOUSING FOR THE REHABILITATION OF 'POOR WHITES'

In 1934, during a *Volkskongres*,[4] Afrikaner leaders noted the urgent need for social housing programmes. These projects unified the South African elite. Males and females, English and Afrikaners participated in planning, building and managing these areas. In the 'poor white' areas, the similarities between the English and the Afrikaners were obvious: everyone was poor and lived under similar conditions. It was primarily about being white, not about being English or an Afrikaner, since there were no separate areas for English-speaking or Afrikaans-speaking 'poor whites'.

In 1936, Jan Hofmeyr was the first South African 'poor white' area to be established in the immediate vicinity of central Johannesburg. Shortly after, Ruyterwacht was created on the vast Cape Flats near Cape Town in 1938. The ideas underlying the development of both these suburbs were similar, since they served the same purpose: to accommodate and racially uplift suitable whites, both English and Afrikaners.

As Cape Town and Johannesburg differed, life in the 'poor white' suburbs also evolved in different ways. Cape Town was markedly more English, while Johannesburg was more Afrikaans. This was reflected in the differences in the construction of identities. In Cape Town, this process focused more on building a 'white' rather than a purely Afrikaner identity, while in and around Johannesburg attempts to build an exclusively Afrikaner identity were more prominent, and also more visible in the urban space. The socio-economic history of the two cities differs greatly. Since the discovery of gold in the Witwatersrand in 1886, Johannesburg had grown into a large, industrial metropolis by the 1930s. It had a larger white working class population than Cape Town and was more cosmopolitan. Africans offered tough competition to white workers, who soon learnt to take advantage of their superior racial position (van Onselen, 1982).

In contrast, Cape Town remained a laid-back, provincial town. It had fewer white workers and consequently poverty was less visible. Manufacturing and services were the key areas of production since the industrial boom in Cape Town began only after the First World War (Bickford-Smith et al., 1999). Competition in Cape Town was against 'coloureds' rather than against Africans. Whites and 'coloureds' shared a language, a culture and, to some extent, a genetic heritage, which made it difficult sometimes to discern the physical difference between a white and a coloured. Despite these differences between the two cities, there were some common underlying principles in the planning of the physical location and layout of 'poor white' areas. They logically followed from the reasons for the establishment of the suburbs. These principles set certain standards, affecting their spatial and social planning.

1. It was important that the areas had a pleasant appearance, as they were designed to offer healthy, countryside-like experiences to 'poor white' families in rehabilitation. A lush, green environment was essential. Both areas were reasonably spacious compared to European and American cities. The ideals of garden cities—such as those seen by Ebenezer Howard in his utopian visions—and American suburbs were applied.
2. In order to discourage class-based alliances, all the 'poor white' areas were spread across both Johannesburg and Cape Town, far away from one another. The planners also had to ensure that the races were kept apart. The twin challenges facing the planners were therefore not only to create areas that would prevent the working-class whites from forming alliances with one another, but also to ensure that they did not form alliances with other races. Simultaneously, the suburbs had to be included in, or, at least, ensure contact with the middle class white areas. The logic of exclusion was thus completely different from that of African townships, which were totally separate from the white areas. Jan Hofmeyr was built near the city centre, while Ruyterwacht was connected to central Cape Town with a railroad that simultaneously formed the northern border of the suburb.
3. The suburbs had to be such as to ensure ease in control socially and spatially. This meant the establishment of social services and a particular spatial planning at the street level. In Ruyterwacht, the original layout included houses for schoolteachers who would be allotted corner houses so that they would be able to observe

the suburb. Both the areas were characterized by openness of spaces, and a lack of private gardens with yards enclosed by low fences, if any.

In 1948, Ruyterwacht was praised for its exemplary planning and successful influence on the rehabilitation of its residents. The Afrikaner authors emphasized the Afrikanerness of the suburb, while many residents were, in fact, at least bilingual.

> There is a real need for model villages or residential areas near our cities. An example of this is the village of Epping Garden [Ruyterwacht] near Cape Town. . . . Most of the houses are inhabited by less affluent Afrikaners . . . with a true Afrikaans spirit ruling in the village . . . in spite of all the men working in the city, the home atmosphere is Christian-Afrikaans. The new situation, created by the influx into towns, necessitates the church to strive for the construction of similar villages or residential areas in future. Not only in the countryside, as has been the case this far, but particularly near the cities. In this way newly arrived congregation members can acquire healthy and affordable housing, and the church can maintain its influence over them. (Albertyn et al., 1948, pp. 39-40, original in Afrikaans)

Although they were similar to local black townships in terms of building materials and housing design, in both cases houses were more spacious and comfortable than in the townships, endowed for instance, with small luxuries such as verandas. From the beginning the physical appearance of both areas seemed to be much less oppressed than that of African or 'coloured' townships.

## SELECTING RESIDENTS

After the spatial organization had created the basic structure for effective rehabilitation, efforts had to be made to ensure that the social environment was both supportive and well managed. The emphasis was on choosing families and rehabilitating the family life of 'poor whites'. Families were easiest to police: it was the most effective unit of rehabilitation. This process of rehabilitation was strongly reminiscent of the process that had begun in Europe a century earlier: in order to govern citizens and ensure the existence of freely moving labour power, families had been educated to become economically autonomous. 'Poor white' families in South Africa were not trusted to bring up healthy offspring independently. They had to be prompted and educated to do this. The ideal of a chaste and hard-working *Volksmoeder* (mother of the people) was a perfect fit in these attempts (du Toit, 2002; McClintock, 1995). Mothers were the gateway to the otherwise closed family unit, and the key to its racial betterment.

In the 1930s, utmost care was taken to select residents for these suburbs. They were subjected to stringent selection procedures (Parnell, 1991). The uplifters wanted to make sure that they selected the best young people: the most deserving ones, those who had jobs and a stable family life. Such families only needed a fair chance to be able to join the ranks of the white middle class. At that time the definition of 'race' was not as precise as during the apartheid era. In Ruyterwacht, approximately 80 per cent of the first residents were Afrikaners. Since the beginning, however, there was a deep suspicion that some of them were 'pass-whites', in other words, people of 'coloured' origin attempting to be reclassified as whites. Particularly around Cape Town, where it was often almost impossible to distinguish between a 'coloured' and a white person, poor white areas gained a reputation as areas where people 'passed for white'. A darkish white person could still be considered white, if he had a decent lifestyle and proved himself worthy in his everyday life (Teppo, 1999). The founders of 'poor white' suburbs wanted ordinary, proper, *ordentlik* respectable families who *looked* white.

To create these conditions, residents were given education, and provided health care and social services. Social workers tried to improve every aspect of their lives, their free time and family lives were supervised, with a particular focus on mothers. Through these interventions, many 'poor white' families were able to save, buy their own houses, and shift to more middle class suburbs in the 1940s and 1950s.

The construction of 'poor white' suburbs ended in the early years of apartheid, as the emphasis shifted to the ideal of providing every white person a home of his own. The rise in the standards of living during the 'miracle decade' of the 1960s almost eradicated white poverty. In 1996, for instance, only 1 per cent of white South Africans were classified 'poor' (Statistics South Africa, 1996). Areas such as Ruyterwacht and Jan Hofmeyr were not rendered obsolete, they were forced to accept just about anyone who could officially prove he was white, instead of accommodating carefully selected families. Consequently, the areas accommodated many persons with disabilities and problems, those who could not have made it anywhere else. Increasing numbers of single parents and families with problems such as alcoholism, disabilities or unemployment moved to these areas (Teppo, 2000).

Gradually, Jan Hofmeyr and Ruyterwacht became places where the white society sent those whites it rejected, and those it wanted to correct. Residents became increasingly institutionalized. For eample, in Ruyterwacht dependency ratios rose from near zero in the first years to two-thirds in the contemporary period. Social workers became disillusioned and had doubts about the purpose of their work (Teppo, 2000). An ex-social worker in a 'poor white' area reflected, 'I still do not know whether they [residents] were there to be isolated from the rest of the (white) society, or whether they were there to be helped' (Cobus, personal communication, 1999).

While poor whites were reduced to a minority, the stigma of being a 'poor white' grew more severe. They were white, and yet they had not made it in a society that had harnessed all its resources for their benefit. The general perception was that there was clearly something wrong with them.

Views on how a white person should dress and behave, and what a white lifestyle should be, were firmly instilled into the minds of South Africans. The true success story of the apartheid government was an internalized idea of a white person being *naturally* connected to a certain habitus. This view made the existence of 'poor whites' both unnatural and wrong.

Middle-class feelings of pity and amusement were mixed with suspicion and contempt. A stigma was attached to being born or living in a poor white suburb. Those who had ascended to the ranks of middle class whites from the 'poor white' areas—and they were many—often hid their origins.

## 'POOR WHITE' AREAS TODAY

After the end of the apartheid era, the mere existence of 'poor whites' became an embarrassment surrounded by silence for many white South Africans. The 'degenerate' label adheres more firmly than ever before. In Jan Hofmeyr and Ruyterwacht,[5] white residents are once again in the same situation: isolated from middle-class whites, losing the fight for social benefits, and stigmatized. Yet, in the contemporary era there are differences.

The process of desegregation has altered racial demographics in both the suburbs. In the 1996 census, Jan Hofmeyr had mostly white residents, while in 2000 they accounted for an estimated half of the population.[6] In Ruyterwacht, this change has been slower, but nonetheless a substantial one. The process of desegregation began in the early 1990s with the repeal of the Group Areas Act. According to census data, in 1996 approximately 40 per cent of the residents in Ruyterwacht were 'coloured'. In this respect the process of desegregation has been fairly similar in both suburbs.

The reason for the difference between the suburbs is to be found in the change in the class structure. In Ruyterwacht, the new 'coloured' residents bought their houses when the previous owner, a private housing company, sold half of the houses to them in the 1990s. These 'coloured' home owners are young, well educated and ambitious. They not only upgrade their homes, but also strive towards middle class prosperity and status. The area no longer appears outwardly homogeneous. The new residents redesigned the houses, painted them or clad them with bricks and built fences to wipe out the memory of the 'poor whites' who once inhabited these buildings.

This has not been the case in Jan Hofmeyr where the houses still belong to the municipality of Johannesburg. In consequence, Jan Hofmeyr has not changed much. Residents are poor, although they now represent all the racial groups of South Africa. Residents are insecure and unwilling to invest in renovations because they do not own their houses. There are no visible signs of the great consumerist ethos that stimulates the 'coloured' residents of Ruyterwacht. Consequently, Ruyterwacht has become a more upmarket residential area, whereas Jan Hofmeyr is sinking into decay.

With increasing poverty, racial tensions have escalated. Jan Hofmeyr is poorer, more depressed and much more tense. The ethos seems to be: 'We defend ourselves, or else we die.'

There is poverty in Ruyterwacht no doubt, but a large percentage of the residents are doing better than before. It is also racially more relaxed. The ethos seems to be: 'We adapt, we get along'.

## CONCLUSION

The 'poor white project' aimed to create an image of whiteness through a series of social and material interventions. In South Africa, the elite managed to create an impression that there was, indeed, a fixed white identity. 'Poor whites' were artificially uplifted in order to solidify this impression. In reality, these identities were fragile constructions that were likely to disintegrate at the first blow. The changing character of cultural identities became obvious after the end of the apartheid era when deep social stagnation lifted.

In 'poor white' suburbs, the uplifters created mimetic spaces, which were stage settings or imitations to bring about the 'real' thing. Ruyterwacht and Jan Hofmeyr were designed to imitate white middle class spaces and thus produce white identities. At the very least they would make the poor whites *appear* more middle class. In the eyes of the middle-class South Africans, these suburbs failed in this task.

Along with this perceived failure, the white middle class lost its contact with the remaining 'poor whites'. Today, few middle-class whites even know where these areas are located; most 'poor white' suburbs are sinking into oblivion. This process is particularly visible in Jan Hofmeyr. As the informal spaza shops replace the big supermarkets, the residents witness the shifting of services to wealthier suburbs. This is part of the overall change occurring in central Johannesburg.

In Ruyterwacht, the process of gentrification is rapidly overtaking the previous 'poor white' stigma of the suburb. Instead of services disappearing, new investments are being made. The new Grand West Casino has been built on the western border of the suburb. It has brought wealth and some glamour to the suburb, while in Jan Hofmeyr the harsh realities of everyday life persist.

The new casino creates these spaces of mimesis in Ruyterwacht. In the casino, tourists do not see traces of the embarrassing apartheid past of South Africa. Instead, they can dine in the restaurant zone inside the casino, called the District. Its multiple ethnic restaurants are placed in corridors that imitate the long lost alleys of the legendary District Six. Even the most commercial of enterprises has seen it apt to revive the multicultural past of Cape Town and to elevate it to the pedestal of mythology. Separate cultures and fixed identities have been promptly forgotten as they are not good for business.

In Jan Hofmeyr, there have been no such pressures to appear fashionably hybrid. The identities and positions there seem more set, but in fact, they are just one end of a continuum. At that end very few chances are given to those who were once told they would inherit the land, since it was theirs. In consequence, a middle aged resident concluded, 'It is not the white man who makes apartheid now. It is the black man, and the coloured man. I do not see a future for this place. This is going to be a hateful place. The future is going to be hateful' (Schalk, 45, personal communication, Jan Hofmeyr).

## NOTES

1. The fieldwork in these suburbs was conducted for our doctoral theses between 1997 and 2000.
2. Coloured people are the offspring of Europeans, the original Khoi-San people and Indonesian and East African slaves. Their first language tends to be Afrikaans. Most South African coloureds (80 per cent) live in the Western Cape (Statistics South Africa, 1996).
3. In the 1920s, one-third of the Afrikaners were considered as living below the poverty line.
4. People's conference. An annual gathering of Afrikaner leaders in the 1930s. Each year the conference had a new theme, and in 1934 the theme was 'the poor white problem'.
5. Ruyterwacht reached international fame in 1995 when racial riots broke out while the residents demonstrated against the placing of African students in an empty school building in the suburb. Consequently, the whole community was labelled as thoroughly racist.
6. This estimation is based on a combination of fieldwork and the election results of the 2000 municipal elections.

## REFERENCES

Bickford-Smith, V., E. van Heyningen, N. Worden (eds.), *Csape Town in the Twentieth Century: A Illustrated Social History*, Cape Town: David Philip, 1999.

Bourdieu, P., *Distinction: A Social Critique of the Judgement of Taste*, London: Routledge, 1984.

Coquerel, P., *L'Afrique du Sud des Afrikaners*, Brussels: Complexe, 1992.

Daloz, J.P., 'Le phénomène des pauvres Blancs en Afrique australe: l'exemple d'Harare', *Politique Africaine*, no. 51, 1993, pp. 160-5.

Guillaume, P., 'Du blanc au noir . . . Essai sue une nouvelle ségrégation dans le centre de Johannesburg', *L'Espace Géographique*, vol. 26, no. 1, 1997, pp. 21-33.

———, 'Johannesburg. Géographies de l'exclusion', Ph.D. thesis, University of Reims, 2000 (P. Guillaume, 2002, Paris: Karthala/IFAS).

Guillaume, P., M. Houssay-Holzschuch, 'Du township à la ville . . . Nouveaux chemins de l'identité urbaine des Noirs sud-africains', *Géographie et Cultures*, no. 28, 1998, pp. 47-60.

Hannerz, U., 'Sophiatown: a View from Afar' in *Readings in African Popular Culture*, ed. K. Barber, Bloomington: Indiana University Press, 1997.

Houssay-Holzschuch, M., 'Les Métis au cap: étude de deux problèmes identitiaires', *L'Espace Géographique*, vol. 28, no. 2, 1999, pp. 135-47.

Jacobson, F., *Whiteness of a Different Color: European Immigrants in the Alchemy of Race*, Cambridge: Harvard University Press, 1998.

Moerdijk, D., 'La nouvelle culture des Afrikaners? (autour de *Triomf*, de Marlene Van Niekerk)', *Travaux de l'Institut de Géographie de Reims*, nos. 99-100, 1999, pp. 121-7.

Parnell, S., 'Sanitation, Segregation and the Native (Urban Areas) Act: African Exclusion from Johannesburg's Malay Location, 1897-1925', *Journal of Historical Geography*, vol. 17, no. 3, 1991, pp. 271-88.

Proctor, A., 'Class Struggle Segregation and the City: A History of Sophiatown, 1905-1940', in *Labour, Township and Protest: Studies in the Social History of the Witwatersrand*, ed. B.B. Bozzoli, Johannesburg: Ravan Press, 1979, pp. 49-89.

Salazar, P.-J., *L'intrigue raciale. Essai de critique anthropologique*, Paris: Méridiens Klincksiek, 1989.

South African Institute of Race Relations, *1997/1998 Surveys*, Johannesburg: South African Institute of Race Relations, 1998.

Teppo, A., 'Reproducing Diversity: Aspects of a Process of Racial/Spatial Desegregation on a Former "Poor White" Area', workshop paper, University of Cape Town, 1999.

———, 'The Whitewashers: Struggles Concerning the Body Politics in a "Poor White" Community in the "Old" and "New" South Aftrica', workshop paper, University of Cape Town, 2000.

van Niekerk, M., *Triomf*, London: Little Brown & Co., 1999. (Original edition in Afrikaans, *Triomf*, Pretoria: Queillerie Publishers, 1994.)

van Onselen, C., *Studies in the Social and Economic History of the Witwatersrand 1886-1914*, vol. 2: *New Nineveh*, Johannesburg: Ravan Press, 1982.

# PART FOUR

## Urban Territory and the Politics of Identity

CHAPTER 15

# Segregation and Fragmentation in South African Cities

PHILIPPE GERVAIS-LAMBONY

Current urban literature increasingly refers to cities as fragmented urban spaces (see especially Balbo, 1993; Bénit, 2001; Donzelot, 1998, 1999; Jaglin, 2001; Navez-Bouchanine, 2002; Prevot-Schapira, 1999). Yet, in this literature fragmentation has been employed in various ways, encompassing diverse realities and processes that rarely connect. For instance, some authors draw on ideas of dispersion and spatial fragmentation to explain pockets of urban exclusion; others highlight the breakdown or disappearance of links between urban social groups; those with an economic interest focus on economic fracturing and division of the city; whereas others concentrate on the political separation of urban territories and the creation of communitarian exclusion anchored in micro territories. Despite such divergence, authors concur on the utility of the concept of fragmentation. The tendency for large cities to fragment is empirically visible in North and South America (although it can be questioned, see Baby-Collin, 2000), and in some Asian and African cities (notably in cities where there has been civil war). Elsewhere, including Indian cities (Shaw, 1999), premonitory signs of fragmentation can be discerned (Jaillet, 1999).

Fragmentation is clearly different from the more traditional concept of segregation. In short, what differentiates segregation from fragmentation is the fact that the former divides urban groups but does not prevent them from being part of the same urban system, whereas the second splinters the city as a system in itself. The relationship between segregation and fragmentation needs to be further investigated to better understand the temporal aspect of the fragmentation process; to grasp the role of political and economic players in this process; to determine which new political players and social networks emerge in 'fragmented' cities to facilitate urban survival; and to consider the ways in which processes of fragmentation may re-establish other sets of 'urbanness' and connections to the city.

What does the study of South African cities add to this debate? I argue that South African cities constitute a special case for two reasons. First, during apartheid, cities were subjected to urban policies that tried to divide space racially and socially by endorsing the fabrication of urban territories and, therefore, urban identities. Second, since 1994, major South African cities have implemented administrative and political urban policies that counter fragmentation, tending on the contrary to regroup diverse territories. An examination of the concepts of segregation and fragmentation in South African cities in these two periods thus proves useful.

## SEGREGATION AND FRAGMENTATION IN THE APARTHEID AND POST-APARTHEID PERIODS

In the apartheid period, apartheid cities formed coherent and unified systems of management and exploitation of labour, despite their spatial fragmentation. To explain this context many South African writers applied the word fragmentation to apartheid cities in the 1990s, even though this concept was not yet used elsewhere (Bénit, 2001). Fragmentation was defined, however, as an extreme form of segregation.[1] In the post-apartheid period, South African urban studies have focused largely on city governments and the ways in which state-driven processes have attempted to reunify urban bodies and spaces formerly institutionally separated. In other words, the post-apartheid project has worked towards unification rather than fragmentation of urban space. The shift from institutional segregation in the post-apartheid period could be conceptualized as a shift to 'normal' fragmentation, i.e. South African cities have now joined the league of major inter-national cities facing the challenges of fragmentation evident in patterns of social and economic polarization and exclusion.

Researchers working in South African cities must grapple with the relationship between segregation and fragmentation and the conceptualization of their linkages in the apartheid and post-apartheid periods. Often arguments about these processes build on a normative assumption that fragmentation is a negative process. For most writers, the concept of fragmentation thus has a pejorative connotation, demonstrating the limits of the city as an entity and a reduction in urban residents' mobility and opportunities. By portraying contemporary South African urban fragmentation in a similar way, as a process that exacerbates the legacies of apartheid segregation, one runs the risk of assuming that all forms of fragmentation are negative.[2] One needs, instead, to unpack and analyse the various processes that generate fragmentation. It cannot be assumed that socio-spatial segregation—which allows residential separation but authorizes contact between communities in specific public places and through economic ties—is immediately comparable with processes of fragmentation that operate at the city and global scale and that arguably 'destroy' the city itself. In the South African context, we cannot conceptualize fragmentation and segregation as by definition negative, dichotomous, and mutually exclusive, but as contextual, interdependent and contingent processes.

The concept of fragmentation is limited if used as the primary and exclusive lens for understanding political and economic evolution in major cities (see Agier, 1999; Baby-Collin, 2000; Davis, 1997; Guillaume, 2001). Most definitions of fragmentation depend on 'top-down' approaches that analyse fragmentation (and segregation for that matter) at a city scale. Yves Grafmeyer (1994) argued in contrast that segregation should be understood at the individual scale of 'urbanites', i.e. city dwellers themselves. In his argument, segregation exists when there is a feeling of exclusion among concerned individuals and groups. Although Grafmeyer's definition is not sufficient (as it fails to account for forms of segregation that are supported by people or which are so obscure that urbanites do not perceive themselves as excluded), he rightly asserted the micro local scale at which processes of social fragmentation in particular operate.

Social fragmentation has been frequently studied in particular political, economic and spatial forms. Although social processes are not independent of political, economic and spatial change, they cannot be reduced to these other processes because they have their own logic and existence. On this issue South African cities are illustrative. Do social linkages or a common political 'citizenship' disappear because they have been legally prohibited as in the apartheid period? Do social processes cease when economic relationships between fragments of the city are formally broken? The South African experience clearly negates such simplistic arguments. Although social, political and economic dimensions are not absolutely independent of each other, they also cannot be reduced to each other. Cities continue to function even in the context of extreme forms of segregation and fragmentation (Agier,

2000) because these processes themselves generate new urban networks and players.

Is a conceptual distinction between fragmentation and segregation useful at the level of urban representation and practice? Do the customs and representations of the apartheid years in South Africa, for instance, enable one to assume the existence of a collective urban identity (because the city was 'simply' segregated)? Have these practices and representations changed today and thus altered the collective identity (because the city is 'fragmented')? In concrete terms, for an unemployed resident of an 'illegal' squatter camp—now a citizen with formal rights—is the fragmented city different from the segregated city? By posing this provocative example, I argue for the importance of urban experience in normative conceptualization and empirical analysis of segregation and fragmentation. The right to vote, the democratic reform of local government, the implementation of policies for economic redistribution, the delivery of urban services, for instance, cannot be understood as processes that represent a shift from a 'bad' system of segregation to a 'worse' system of fragmentation, despite the challenges (defects and failures in many cases) of political and economic reform in South Africa. I consider the apartheid city, therefore, as a segregated political and economic system and the post-apartheid city, in contrast, as fragmented, constituted by processes that correspond increasingly less to a previously existing urban system. The following discussion examines this argument in detail in the context of the East Rand, the Ekurhuleni Metropolitan area,[3] in the apartheid period (1948-94) and in the contemporary democratic period.

## A HISTORICAL APPROACH TO THE ISSUES OF APARTHEID AND URBAN FRAGMENTATION ON THE EAST RAND

An industrial conurbation of 2 million inhabitants, the East Rand was formed following the merger of eight former municipalities situated to the east of Johannesburg. It is spatially discontinuous and encompasses major socio-spatial differences. The spatial structure of the region is represented in Map 15.1. The eight municipalities that together form the East Rand were constituted into a metropolitan authority in 2000.

The core of the apartheid city and system was institutionalized between the mid-1940s and the late 1960s. During this period, commencing before the National Party came to power in 1948, older non-white neighbourhoods were destroyed and massive construction

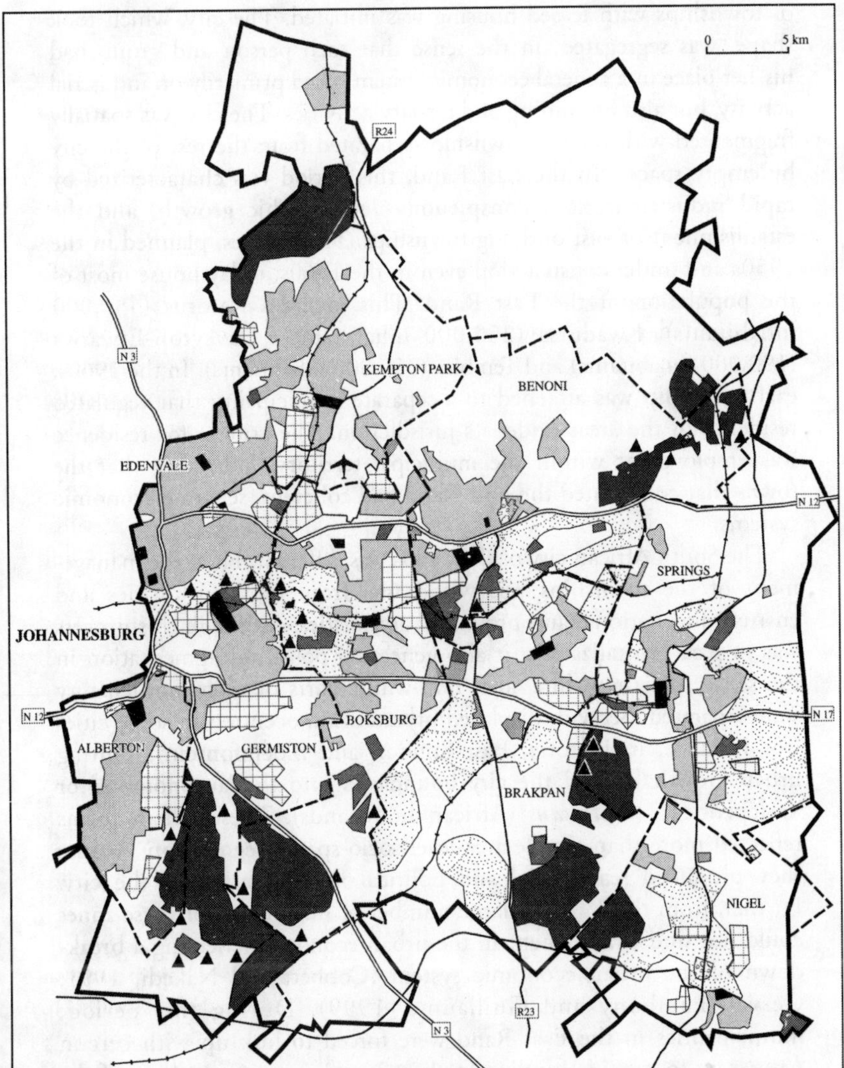


MAP 15.1: LAND USE IN EAST RAND.

of townships with leased housing was initiated. The city, which took shape, was segregated, in the sense that each person and group had his/her place in a general economic system based primarily on industrial activity, but also on mining and tertiary activities. The city was spatially fragmented with remote townships separated from the rest of the city by empty spaces. In the East Rand, this period was characterized by rapid industrialization, conspicuous demographic growth, and the establishment of vast outlying townships. These zones, planned in the 1950s and under construction even in the 1960s, today house most of the population of the East Rand. This includes Katorus (430,000 inhabitants), Kwadutsa (250,000 inhabitants), Daveyton-Etwatwa (190,000 inhabitants) and Tembisa (250,000 inhabitants). In the 1960s, each township was attached to a separate municipality that regulated residence in the areas under its jurisdiction. The criteria for residence was employment within the municipal territory, indicating that the towns that constituted the East Rand had coherent, separate economic systems.

The South African city of the 1970s was different. First, the management of the townships was withdrawn from local authorities and entrusted to national and provincial authorities. Although this process was in part centralization, it also generated political fragmentation in the sense that the 'white' and 'non-white' parts of each municipality were separated. Second, displaced urbanization occurred in some cities (for instance, in Pretoria, East London and Bloemfontein), shifting urban growth beyond the city boundaries into the 'autonomous' or 'independent' *bantustans* (African homelands). These urban forms reflected more than simple area-level socio-spatial segregation because they produced real spatial and political fragmentation of the city. Further, from the 1970s, a large number of inhabitants of these zones could not find employment in the urban economy, reflecting a breakdown of the urban economic system (Cobbett and Nakedi, 1991; Gervais-Lambony and Guillaume, 1999). During this period, municipalities in the East Rand were forced to link up with certain *bantustans* to provide funding for housing projects. Consulates of the *bantustans* of Ciskei and Transkei were established in townships. The construction of huge hostels to provide accommodation for single migrant workers was a product of these relationships. Beyond the segregation of whites from Africans within the urban area, African workers were temporally regulated; the length of their stay in the city was determined by the tenure of their work.

The South African city of the 1980s was again different. In 1982, Black Local Authorities were created as local elected governments in townships. Through a circumscribed system of elections, the government further politically fragmented cities. In reality this process was to some extent cosmetic, as the powers of these municipalities were linked directly to the central government. Even more importantly, civic and political associations, developed in resistance to the apartheid state, assumed progressively greater control of entire sections of black areas of cities. Representing highly localized sets of social linkages, townships became territories of resistance, where the formal city system was rejected and alternative political strategies developed to demolish the system. Finally, the economic crisis and the lay-offs in the mining and industrial sectors completed the process by throwing a great number of the cities' inhabitants out of work and thus out of the urban system.

This periodization of the apartheid city demonstrates progressive and sustained processes of spatial, social as well as economic and political fragmentation. At the end of the 1980s, the East Rand had nineteen different municipal authorities (nine 'black' local authorities and ten 'white' municipalities). Further, from 1990, the 'East Rand war' set the big townships ablaze, with battle lines drawn in earnest. It began as a local conflict between hostel dwellers and a squatter camp, probably about access to the hostel facilities. The predominantly Zulu Inkhata Freedom Party associated the defence of the hostels with the defence of Zulu culture. The conflict thereafter took on a political and ethnic complexion and spread across the entire zone, integrating territorial and identity politics. The conflict became all the more violent, as in the other townships of the country, the youth took on the adult migrant workers living in the hostels in what was a clash of generations and cultures (Chipkin, 1998).

I argue that fragmentation is a useful conceptual tool, to understand the ways in which the state and organizations in civil society negotiated segregation at the 'micro' scale and at a citywide 'macro' scale in the South African urban context. Political struggles of the apartheid period were not concerned solely with tensions at the level of local identities, but also coalesced around political demands at the level of the entire city. At the time, it was the political involvement in a collective struggle that created the social linkages, which demonstrated that claiming urban citizenship (urbanness) signified resistance to fragmentation imposed by the apartheid state.

The example of the Boksburg boycott illustrates this mix. In Boksburg, a small town in the East Rand, the Conservative Party, which had campaigned for a return to the 1950s principles of apartheid won the municipal elections in 1988. The newly elected leaders decided to revive all the regulations which were in force during the apartheid period, i.e. public benches, toilets and buses were re-segregated; and non-whites were barred from the promenade around the lake in the town centre. In protest against this municipal policy, urban associations from the 'coloured' township of Reiger Park and the 'African' township of Vosloorus launched a collective movement. The commercial boycott of businesses in the Boksburg town centre was successfully organized, forcing the elected members of the Conservative Party to resign. This series of protests was clearly an urban struggle for the right to the city and the use of public space at a city scale (Gervais-Lambony, 2001). The success of the struggle also revealed that the urban system could not function without its black citizens, despite the city's fragmentation at multiple scales.

## FRAGMENTATION AFTER APARTHEID?

Today, the post-apartheid city is characterized by a contradiction between an integrative urban policy and a 'fragmenting' reality. On the one hand, metropolitan local government institutions and policies attempt to limit fragmentation. On the other, within these same metropolitan spaces, old tendencies have become more pronounced: the exclusion of entire sections of the population, the elitist attitude of the well-to-do classes which keep to themselves (living in splendid isolation in private new or old exclusive neighbourhoods with restricted access), and strong territorialization at the level of the neighbourhood. In the contemporary context, there are a few united collective struggles, for instance, for the 'right to the city'. One can ask whether metropolization is an instrument of resistance to fragmentation, or whether it is a cosmetic policy that promotes fragmentation under the guise of an integrative discourse.

Why was the local government set up at the metropolitan scale in large South African cities? External influences and special national considerations led, on the one hand, to the promotion of large-scale metropolitan local government institutions. The more specific problems of South African cities also justified the setting up of metropolitan authorities to generate political willingness and an economy of scale to redistribute assets and services among urban territories that had earlier received unequal treatment; to manage the political imperative to deracialize segregated cities; and more specifically to harness and give expression to the political control of the African National Congress of municipal administrations inherited as racially segregated former municipalities. This last point explains the case of the East Rand, an urban context with few elements to indicate that it would or should become a metropolitan authority. A sole authority was installed at the metropolitan scale not because a city existed but because there was a political imperative for one to exist. Territorial identities are central to this debate, at least as much as the question of functionality.

To what extent did the setting up of a sole metropolitan authority facilitate the emergence of a metropolitan identity? Identification with former municipalities on the East Rand seems to be disappearing, officially at least. Although the original territorial bases of the East Rand, the municipalities of the region have strong 'personalities' that have always served as the basis for discourses on identity, even more so today because the powers of municipalities within the metropolitan area have been seriously curtailed. As elsewhere in South Africa (see Cameron, 1999, for Johannesburg, Durban and Cape Town examples), the administrative division of the East Rand between 1994 and 2000 was the outcome of negotiations that generated local racially integrated municipalities rather than metropolitan structures. In 1993, the Local Government Transition Act, pertaining to local government reforms, came into force. Its intent was to help prepare for the 1995 local government elections.

This Act facilitated the setting up of interim local authorities prior to the promulgation of the 1996 Constitution. It made mandatory the setting up of local negotiating bodies, Local Government Negotiating Forums. The text specified that the forums must be created at the level of the municipal territories established prior to 1971 (i.e. before townships were administratively separated from 'white' cities), but also at a 'functional' level so that zones of the city were linked economically. Within these forums, municipal choices had to be made through negotiations with 'statutory' participants (former municipal authorities from the 'white' cities but also from the 'black' local authorities where they still existed), 'non-statutory' participants (political parties, civics, and civil society), with observation by key economic players. In large urban areas, forums originally had the choice of either Transitional Local Councils (TLC, municipalities combining townships and the 'white' city) or a transitional metropolitan council, i.e. a metropolitan authority encompassing several former municipalities.

In the East Rand case, municipalities were opposed to the setting up of a metropolitan authority, arguing that their local identities were too strong. The underlying argument was evidently guided by politics (the creation of a metropolitan authority would deprive them of their powers) and budgets (the rich municipalities, especially Germiston, wished to retain control of their budget considerations as well). The 1994-2000 period was marked by a return to the logic of municipalities, as revealed by the convergence of interests of 'white' ex-municipalities and regional bodies and the power of various discourses on territorial identity operating at the municipal level. Other territorial levels were also in competition with each other: new electoral constituencies (wards), townships and neighbourhoods (formerly 'white' suburbs, parts of townships, and squatter camps). In contrast to the municipal level, territoriality was contested and reinforced at all scales.

The institutionalization of metropolitan government thus obliterated one of the dimensions of socio-spatial division but appeared to reinforce others. For instance, economic ties between 'white' sections of the agglomeration and other parts were fractured through industrial lay-offs and the closure of mines. Unemployment rates in some areas affected 60 per cent of the workers, delinking many households from employment and particular parts of the city. Particularly acute on the East Rand, criminal violence increased, exacerbating the existing patterns of fragmentation in neighbourhoods and in town centres. At the same time, however, more resources for urban infrastructure projects and housing programmes revealed the underlying vested interests and strategies in this urban setting, which sometimes came into conflict with one another and ended up deepening local territorial identities. These diverse processes signify that political fragmentation is distinct from other forms of fragmentation. I would argue, however, that fragmentation is also incipient in urban policy, which constantly refers to and claims to depend on the 'community'. Community implies identity, therefore alterity and hence conflict with other groups. The process of metropolization has created a new level of identity at the metropolitan scale, at the same time as it has developed additional layers of small-scale territories within the metropole. It may be argued that despite attempts of integration in policy, by recognizing territorialized communities the metropolitan authority has helped increase fragmentation rather than prevent it. Paradoxically, under apartheid an urban policy that tried to fragment the city as an entity (in its own way) contributed to the emergence of the city as an entity through urban struggle, whereas post-apartheid urban policy which aims to pull the parts of the city together again has been unable to halt the process of fragmentation. Underlying these observations are deeper questions about the efficacy of political action in relation to cities, the role of economic changes and external influences, and also the roles and agency of various urban actors.

## CONCLUSION

In conclusion, I propose another avenue of research on the basis of the East Rand example. I hypothesize that to be able to talk of the city there has to be a collective urban subject/entity. This collective subject is the outcome of a complex and permanent interaction between the materiality and the social relations of the city (Berque, 1993). In other words, urban residents create territory from the dense and diverse spaces of the city. Contacts between groups, the sharing of the same symbolic territorial referents, but also a unifying urban policy and economic exchange facilitate these processes and relationships. These processes and exchanges are situated temporally, and are also constitutive of a singular geographical subject, a city, i.e. a place united by a shared history and characterized by an aesthetic quality, an atmosphere and customs. Is it therefore possible to search for an identity unique to a metropolitan area that would transcend others and remain present despite manifold changes?

The most striking impression that one has when moving about the East Rand is that of a journey, which over short distances also takes one through time. The past, which keeps resurrecting, mingles with the present. In a region with only recent holistic management, successive economic cycles have structured space: mines, industries, the tertiary sector, and their various crises, have succeeded each other in time, but have occupied different spaces. In the heart of the East Rand, the marks left by the gold mining industry make sure that the past is eternally present: mine dumps, debris, vacant lots, abandoned buildings burn this bygone activity onto the landscape. They are symbols of a past full of conflict but nevertheless shared by residents on the East Rand.

Many inhabitants of the townships are still nostalgic about the old *locations*, areas destroyed in the 1950s from which residents were shifted to the townships. Driven away, old and young, they remember and idealize the memory. As elsewhere in South Africa, the *location* era has given birth to an urban myth, that of a lost African urbanness. Under this form, *locations* are always present in the urban culture. It is an 'archelandscape', in the words of Augustin Berque, an essential urban referent that is well and truly part of the collective representation of the city, and so contributes towards keeping the city alive. The 'war' years (1990-4) in Black parts of the East Rand are memorialized through demarcating territorialization: residents still talk about and continue to interpret places through this geography. Today, pre-war nostalgia and even a yearning for the mining era compound the nostalgia for the location. These images constitute the kaleidoscope that forms the city and its collective subjectivity.

The residents of the East Rand do not necessarily need to share a common identity; rather it is important for all citizens to be able to refer to their city as a space that contains their diverse identities. I argue, therefore, that it is important to understand and theorize what binds together different parts of the city and their inhabitants and what constitutes the city, despite forceful processes of fragmentation.

## NOTES

1. Although as early as 1981 Davies argued that the apartheid city formed a system, I would add that it could be understood to represent one of the earliest forms of a fragmented city.
2. In practice, however, segregation and fragmentation have been drawn on by some urban groups as a source and expression of communitarian ideology that in effect has preserved communitarian identities (e.g. see Mainet-Valleix's contribution in this volume).
3. East Rand is the historical name of this urban region, which designates it as being the eastern periphery of Witwatersrand, centred around Johannesburg; Ekurhuleni is the African name given to the new metropolitan zone in 2001.

## REFERENCES

Agier, M., *L'invention de la ville, banlieues,* townships, *invasions et* favelas, Paris: Editions des Archives contemporaines, 1999.

Baby-Collin, V., 'Marginaux et citadins. Construire une urbanité métisse en Amérique latine. Etude comparée des barrios de Caracas (Venezuela) et des villas d'El Alto de La Paz (Bolivie)', Ph.D. thesis, University of Toulouse II-Le Mirail, 2000.

Balbo, M., 'Urban Planning and the Fragmented City of Developing Countries', *Third World Planning Review,* vol. 15, no. 1, 1993.

Benit, C., 'La fragmentation urbaine à Johannesburg', Ph.D. thesis, University of Poitiers, 2001.

Berque, A., *Du geste à la cité. Formes urbaines et lien social au Japon*, Paris: Gallimard, 1993.

Cameron, R., ed., *Democratization of South African Local Government, a Tale of Three Cities*, Pretoria: JL van Schaik, 1999.

Chipkin, I., 'Un processus d'identification territoriale: le conflit de l'East Rand', *Géographie et Cultures*, no. 28, ed. P. Gervais-Lambony, 1998, pp. 77-88.

Cobbett, W. and B. Nakedi, 'Marchés et déchets du travail à Botshabelo', in *Génie social et manipulations culturelles en Afrique du Sud*, ed. C. Meillassoux and C. Messiant, Paris: Arcantère, 1991, pp. 73-97.

Davies, R.J., 'The Spatial Formation of the South African City', *Géojournal*, supplementary issue 2, 1981, pp. 59-72.

Davis, M., *City of quartz, Los Angeles, capitale du futur*, Paris, La Découverte, 1997.

Donzelot, J., 'La ville éclatée', in *France : les révolutions invisibles*, Paris : Calman-Levy, 1998.

———, 'La nouvelle question urbaine', *Esprit*, no. 258, 1999, pp. 87-114.

Gervais-Lambony P. and P. Guillaume, 'Odi-Moretele (ex-Bophuthatswana): urbanization déplacée et ré-intégration territoriale', *L'Espace Géographique*, no. 2, 1999, pp. 159-69.

Gervais-Lambony, P., 'Petite histoire d'espace et d'identité dans une ville sud-africaine', *Champs Psychosomatiques*, no. 21, 2001, pp. 119-32.

Grafmeyer, Y., 'Regards sociologiques sur la ségrégation', in *La ségrégation dans la ville*, ed. J. Brun, C. Rhein, Paris, L'Harmattan, 1994, pp. 85-118.

Guillaume, P., *Johannesburg. Géographies de l'exclusion*, Paris: Karthala, 2001.

Jaglin, S., 'Villes disloquées ? Ségrégations et fragmentation urbaine en Afrique australe', *Annales de géographie*, no. 619, May-June 2001, pp. 243-65.

Jaillet, M.-C., 'Peut-on parler de sécession urbaine à propos des villes européennes ?', *Esprit*, no. 258, 1999, pp. 145-67.

Navez-Bouchanine, F., ed., *La fragmentation en question: des villles entre fragmentation spatiale et fragmentation sociale?*, Paris: l'Harmattan, 2002.

Prevot-Schapira, M.-F., 'Amérique Latine: la ville fragmentée', *Esprit*, no. 258, 1999, pp. 128-44.

Shaw A., 'Emerging Patterns of Urban Growth in India', *Economic and Political Weekly*, 17-24 April 1999, pp. 969-78.

CHAPTER 16

# Fragmentation and Access to the City: Cape Town and Delhi in Comparative Perspective

VÉRONIQUE DUPONT and MYRIAM HOUSSAY-HOLZSCHUCH

## INTRODUCTION

This comparative paper investigates access to the city by underprivileged social groups in the context of two spatially and socially segmented metropolises, Cape Town and Delhi, and reflects on the question of urban fragmentation and urbanity.

The notion of urban *fragmentation* has been debated in the social sciences since the 1980s. In its most extreme form, urban fragmentation implies an 'absolute break between the different parts of the city, in its social, economic and political dimensions' (Gervais-Lambony, 2001, p. 35).[1] As highlighted by Navez-Bouchanine, the implicit understanding of fragmentation in urban situations:

> [E]stablishes a link between, on the one hand, the spatial dynamics related to the process of metropolization and globalization (urban sprawl, mobility), and, on the other, the process of breaking up of urban social unity, as the result of an extreme diversification of urban practices and references, the increasing social inequalities, the socio-economic mechanism of exclusion and modes of social solidarity dissociation which are favoured by spatial break up. (2001, p. 109)

Yet, she concludes her review with a caveat that: a broken up urban landscape does not necessarily imply a fragmented urban society (p. 114). In the late 1960s Henri Lefèvbre (1968) and the French neo-Marxist school (Castells, 1981; Lipietz, 1977) argued that the spatial organization of the city was the projection on the ground of social and class relationships. This analysis has been refined in order to interpret better the complexity of socio-spatial urban structures and divisions, and to take into account the influence of new contexts such as globalization (Préteceille, 1998). We should also use the more recent concept of fragmentation cautiously to avoid a mechanistic approach that would, conversely, read the social landscape from the city's spatial structure.

We begin this comparative study of Cape Town and Delhi with a preliminary analysis of the characteristics of the functional and physical organization of urban space, on the one hand, and the spatial structuring of urban society and its residential segregation pattern, on the other. We then consider the linkages between them to appraise to what extent these two metropolises should be considered as spatially and/or socially fragmented.

We draw on methods of analysing urban integration (such as measuring different groups' mobility and accessibility to places and urban amenities in the city) to investigate fragmentation as its opposite form. In the process we need to differentiate processes of fragmentation from specific dimensions of segregation. Here, Castells' argument that urban segregation has to be explored not only as difference in residential places, but also, more dynamically, as a capacity to move and access strategic points of the urban transport network (1981, p. 232) proves a starting point. Grafmeyer (1994) also identified 'the unequal access by different social groups to material and symbolic goods supplied by the city' as a dimension of residential segregation.

Yet, how do we distinguish urban fragmentation from urban segregation? Navez-Bouchanine (2001, p. 113) usefully separates the two concepts in the following way: segregation is based on a hierarchical sorting of social groups, not on their autonomy to separate from each other; in contrast, fragmentation implies that different groups have autonomy to withdraw in major spheres and fields such as politics and city management. Obviously, segregation and fragmentation are not exclusive from one another: the two processes can coexist in the same city (Jaglin, 2001). But what is at risk in a fragmented city is its specific social integrating function, in other words, its *urbanity*, the 'system of representation' and 'collective construction that enables conviviality among different groups, among different populations using common spaces' (Navez-Bouchanine, 2001: 114).[2] Navez-Bouchanine proposes that to verify (or nullify) hypotheses of fragmentation calls for questioning 'urbanity' or 'opposing urbanities' in cities to look for possible convergence or divergence.

In this paper we analyse issues of fragmentation and urbanity through a focus on underprivileged social groups and their residential contexts. We have chosen this focus because these groups are the most visible victims of exclusion processes linked to urban fragmentation. Owing to stringent financial limitations, residential choices and access to urban resources are severely constrained. At the same time, due to social ostracism, legal policies and urban planning, segregation has been more often than not imposed on these groups.[3] Nevertheless, economic and/or social deprivation does not mean that people lack residential or economic strategies—as illustrated in our cases studies.[4] We analyse specific neighbourhood contexts and group agency without, however, obliterating the structural interdependence that shape urban areas. Our investigation of specific local situations will thus be linked to the analysis of the whole urban structure and its relationship with global processes (Préteceille, 1998, pp. 42-3).

Access to the city by underprivileged groups is examined in terms of residential location, access to housing and urban amenities, in relation to access to places of work, education, shopping and socializing. Everyday urban practices and daily journeys of underprivileged groups are, as far as possible, compared with those of better off groups. This paper thus examines the *motility* of these social groups, defined by the capacity to move spatially or virtually, with reference to the context, the access and the appropriation, and therefore to 'the allocation of resources and abilities, hence to the social structure and its spatial distribution' (Kaufmann, 2001, pp. 94-6). The notion of motility provides a relevant analytical framework to bring to the fore social inequalities in access to the city.

Our comparative approach is a preliminary exploration of fragmentation in Delhi and Cape Town. We follow Détienne's (2000) methodology outlined in *Comparer l'incomparable* (Comparing the incomparable). Rather than justifying the relevance of a comparison between Cape Town and Delhi by a few similarities in the development of these two metropolises, we put forward the heuristic value of the comparative approach, and even 'the heuristic violence of what arises as incomparable' (p. 45). However, to produce 'spaces of intelligibility' out of a comparative perspective of several experiences requires the explicit construction of the comparison and the *comparable*. Thus, as proposed by Détienne, 'the comparative approach continually applies two or three questions as a beam in order to scan widely the investigation field whose limits are not fixed yet' (p. 47). Then, 'the comparative approach conducts a logical deconstruction in order to decipher articulations between two or three elements, and to isolate micro-configurations opening onto differences more and more refined and contiguous. (. . .) The work of the analyst consists of identifying the constraints of the configurations put into perspective. (. . .) The comparable are these sets or 'plaques' of chain relationships engendered by an initial choice' (pp. 50-2). Our analysis will highlight the following questions: What kind of access to the city do underprivileged groups have in a segregated or fragmented city? To what extent are their mobility and urban practices shaped by the social and economic organization of urban space? Beforehand, we identify the constraints linked to the metropolitan spatial configuration, the functional specialization of urban space and its spatial organization.

## TWO FRAGMENTED METROPOLISES?

Although Cape Town and Delhi differ widely in terms of population size, socio-cultural context and history, they present certain common characteristics: both are cities of the South, having undergone major changes and growth in the second half of the twentieth century. For both cities, the organization of space and society is examined in order to investigate their degree of fragmentation or segmentation. Moreover, socio-spatial structuring is a key factor to understand their functioning as cities and their potential for urban and social integration.

### Metropolitan Contexts: Urban Growth and Spatial Configuration

Since its foundation by Dutch settlers in 1652, Cape Town has continually expanded, gradually acquiring more diversified functions. The harbour and refuelling station became a popular stopover on the sea route to Asia. Its strategic situation controlling the Cape of Good Hope—and the route to India before the construction of the Suez Canal—attracted the attention of the British from the beginning of the nineteenth century, eventually leading to their effective colonization of the Cape. As the first European settlement in South Africa and its biggest city before the development of mining in Johannesburg, Cape Town played a double role: a base from which to occupy and colonize southern Africa and an exit point from which to export its riches. Cape Town underwent several phases of development leading to the construction of an important road and railway system linking the city to the interior, and to the creation of local industries (Bickford-Smith, van Heyningen and Worden, 1998 and 1999; Whittingdale, 1973 and 1982).

Extreme diversity characterized the population of early Cape Town (Saunders, 1979) and continues to this day, reflected in residents' diverse geographical origins, languages, religions and cultures. During the twentieth century and especially since the Second World War, population growth accelerated. Cape Town has approximately 3.1 million inhabitants. In 1996, the majority of the population (about 48 per cent) was constituted by the 'coloured'[5] group followed by 'whites' and 'Africans' (about 25 and 21 per cent respectively). Since the beginning of the twentieth century, African migration to the cities and especially to Cape Town was severely controlled and limited by segregation and apartheid laws that were only repealed in 1986. As in other cities, recent demographic growth has occurred more in the periphery of the city, in areas included in the Cape Town municipality since the post-apartheid delimitation in 1996.

Cape Town's spatial organization reveals a great deal of fragmentation, owing to natural, historical and planning elements (Map 16.1). The city has developed on a peninsula between two large bays, later sprawling on to the sandy plains of the Cape Flats. Steep mountains such as the 1,087 m high Table Mountain dominate the Cape landscape. Table Mountain isolates the city centre—also known as the City Bowl—in a natural amphitheatre of great aesthetic value and practical inconvenience: access to the Central Business District (CBD) from the suburbs negotiates a way between the mountain and the ocean. Other areas declared as natural reserves segment the urban fabric further.

Urban planning and historical developments have also favoured social, functional and landscape differentiation: the old, isolated, city centre, whose architecture has been either preserved or demolished for the construction of the CBD, is in itself fragmented, first by transport networks: the motorway system divides it from the ocean and the waterfront; the railway is a major barrier (or 'edge' in Kevin Lynch's terminology). Industrial areas as well as airports add to the urban partition. This structuring of space can also be found in the twentieth-century suburbs on the Cape Flats where transport, industry, residence, preserved natural spaces such as dunes or wetlands, and empty spaces set aside for further development all contribute to spatial fragmentation.

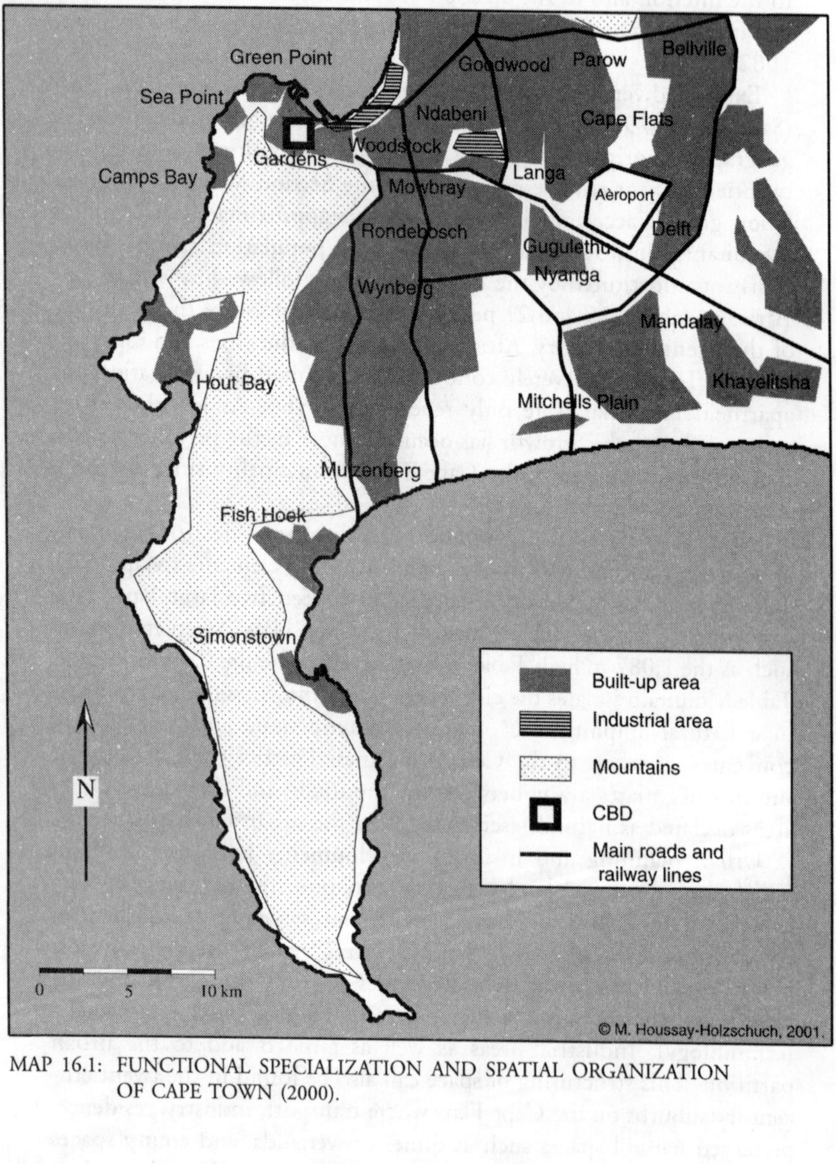


MAP 16.1: FUNCTIONAL SPECIALIZATION AND SPATIAL ORGANIZATION OF CAPE TOWN (2000).

In contrast, the foundation of the first urban settlement on the site of present-day Delhi is dated around tenth century BC (Frykenberg, 1986). In order to understand the pattern of urban growth as well as the present socio-spatial organization of this capital city, it is necessary to discuss the establishment of New Delhi by the British at the beginning of the twentieth century as an urban entity radically different and separate from Shahjahanabad, the old city built in the seventeenth century by the Mughal emperor Shahjahan.

The evolution of Delhi during the twentieth century is deeply marked by the history of the country. Following the promotion of Delhi as the capital of the British Indian Empire in 1911, the population of the city rose from 238,000 in 1911 to 696,000 in 1947, with an increasing rate of growth. After Independence in 1947, Delhi became the capital of the newly formed Indian Union and had to face a massive transfer of population following the Partition of India. In the post-Independence period, the population growth of the capital has been remarkably rapid for an urban agglomeration of this size. Population figures rose from 1.4 million in 1951 to 12.8 million in 2001. Migration has played a major role in the demographic evolution of Delhi. Notwithstanding the great diversity of migrants, both in terms of their socio-economic backgrounds and their rural/urban origins, the catchment area of the capital remains dominated by neighbouring states (Dupont, 2000b).

Demographic growth concurred with the spatial expansion of the urban zone. The geographical location of Delhi in the Gangetic plain, and the absence of any significant physical barrier to the progress of urbanization favoured multidirectional spatial expansion (Map 16.2). The widespread growth of the urban agglomeration led to average densities of 163 inhabitants per hectare in 2001 (for an official urban area covering 792 sq. km) with acute variations at a finer scale.

At a city scale, Delhi appears highly fragmented, with abrupt changes in urban morphology, and a mosaic of highly differentiated sections. Physical fractures introduce clear-cut demarcation lines between the urban sectors. The most important one is the Yamuna River with its large bed of agricultural land. The river flows through the metropolis from the north to the south, separating all zones located to the east that are mainly residential neighbourhoods of varied types of settlement, but also include an industrial zone. The Aravelli Hills (or the Delhi Ridge) form another significant natural boundary with its—more or less protected—natural forest, crossing the capital from the south-west to the north.

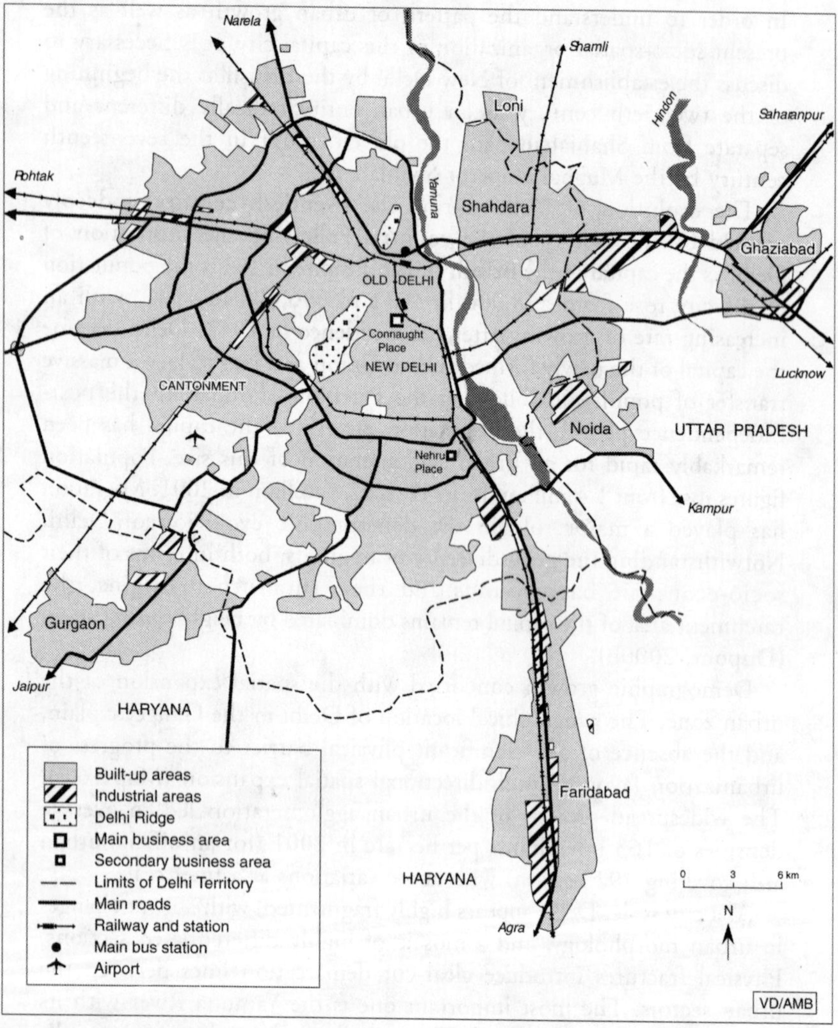


*Source: Eicher City Map of Delhi*, New Delhi: Eicher Goodearth, 1996.

MAP 16.2: SPATIAL ORGANIZATION OF DELHI METROPOLITAN AREA: INFRASTRUCTURE AND FUNCTIONAL SPECIALIZATION (1996).

However, as in the case of Cape Town, historical development and efforts of town planning by the colonial rulers, and later by the independent government, have shaped the urban landscape in a decisive way, and directly contributed to a specific pattern of urban segmentation, even fragmentation.

## The Model of a Fragmented City: From Colonial Thinking to Urban Planning

Although experiencing different histories and development chronologies, Cape Town and Delhi share a common legacy, that of a British colonial settlement. Colonial thinking created new urban models that shaped space along ideological and technocratic lines still functional today (Massiah and Tribillon, 1987). Functionalism, control (of land, populations, migration, ownership, etc.) and technocratic efficiency, prohibition of mixed land use and residential segregation between Europeans and 'natives' were some of its guiding principles (Massiah and Tribillon 1987; Swanson, 1977). In Cape Town and Delhi, these principles introduced intense urban differentiation, opposing a European central space with buffer zones separating it from 'native villages' or indigenous towns. This duality was subsequently consolidated by the importation of international planning ideas, specifically functional specialization of space, strict zoning and separation of places of work and residence, all deeply entrenched trends in the philosophy of twentieth century urban management. They were firmly applied in India and South Africa and contributed to the development of fragmented cities (Maps 16.1 and 16.2).

### *The Colonial Model*

The British model of urbanization in India was based on residential segregation: 'white towns' were separated from native towns; cantonments for army officers and their families were separated from *civil lines*; and distinct housing estates established according to rank in the civil service or the army were built. The planning and building of the new capital of British India, New Delhi, placed under the responsibility of two British architect planners, Edwin Luytens and Herbert Baker, exemplifies this model. The new town was established south of Old Delhi, in a zone where at that time only a few villages were settled. 'The possibility of creating the new city to harmonize visually with the old was never seriously considered. New Delhi was conceived as a purely British settlement juxtaposed to the Indian city' (Evenson, 1989, p. 148). The compact indigenous walled city of Shahjahanabad stood on the one side 'with its intricate web of narrow streets and densely packed buildings' (Evenson, 1981, p. 148). On the other side, separated from the former by a large strip of land cleared and landscaped, lay the new colonial town, the spread garden city with its geometric plan, large roads and vast dimensions. The spatial organization of housing for civil servants in New Delhi directly reflected their position in the hierarchy. Moreover, housing for British employees was separate from that of Indian employees, with the latter located farthest away from the Viceroy's palace. The construction of New Delhi also led to a marked functional division of urban space. Whereas the old city was characterized by a mixed land-use pattern, with a combination of residential use and varied economic activities, the main function assigned to New Delhi was administrative and political, including residential quarters for government employees. It included a central business district, Connaught Place, but no industrial function was envisaged for the new town. The contrast between Old Delhi and New Delhi persisted after Independence, and even today there is differentiation in the urban landscape as well as the socio-spatial organization of the capital.

In Cape Town, Ebenezer Howard's model of the garden city caught the attention of the municipality and its planners (Guillaume, 2001). Although the model was a reference, its progressive social content was generally set aside. What appealed to South African planners in the garden city was:

- a perceived anti-urban feeling and an attempt to bring man and nature together, consistent with a common South African analysis of the social degradation induced by city life;
- an application in the urban realm of the concept of 'community', also central to local social thought;
- a possible solution (even if definitely not present in Howard's project) to the 'urban problems' such as whites' poverty, native presence and population control.

This particular brand of the garden city drew on Howard's model to address colonial preoccupations, in particular, that: autonomous and self-sufficient cities became socially and racially homogeneous residential suburbs in the Cape Town metropolis; localization in a natural environment became isolation through buffer zones where no building was permitted ('the horizontal walls of a defensible city', following Pinnock's analysis, 1989, p. 159); and, 'decent' housing became the world famous 'township matchbox'. Urban fragmentation was again strengthened, and social segmentation inscribed in the urban landscape.

### *Urban Planning in the Second Half of the Twentieth Century*

Urban planning in the second half of the twentieth century followed and even strengthened the same patterns, despite widely varying political contexts in India and South Africa.

In 1948, white South Africans voted the National Party into power and it began to implement its political agenda, apartheid. A global programme to impose and ensure white racist domination over other communities, apartheid has been described as 'a spatial policy, with markedly geographical consequences. Lines were drawn on maps at various scales, and people were evicted and resettled to fit the lines' (Christopher, 1994, p. 6). In large cities such as Cape Town, apartheid systematized earlier policies of segregation:[6] the so-called *locations* were created at the beginning of the twentieth century to house the African population. Forcibly evicted from their homes, Africans bore the brunt of both epidemics and the sanitary syndrome. In Cape Town, after the 1901 outbreak of bubonic plague of which Africans were among the first victims, the location of Ndabeni was created by the municipality, in the hope of saving the rest of the city from the epidemic. With the adoption of the Group Areas Act (GAA) fifty years later,[7] apartheid extended the concept of racially homogeneous residential neighbourhoods to white, Indian and coloured communities. They were to live separately and this social separation was also to be inscribed in the urban space. Using similar planning methods, the apartheid government designed the model of the *township*: a racially homogeneous area, located on the outskirts of the city, devoted to residence only (commercial and productive activities were severely limited if not prohibited outright), poorly equipped, isolated from the rest of the agglomeration by buffer zones, industrial areas and transport infrastructures that constituted physical barriers. The separation of land use was fundamental to planning principles. In consequence, spatial fragmentation was not only practised, but also a guiding line and a proclaimed objective.

India gained Independence in 1947 and Delhi was the place where 'new' concepts of town planning were introduced, and where the first Master Plan was elaborated and implemented after 1962. As the national capital, it was the 'subject of the most comprehensive planning efforts' as 'the visual symbol of a new republic' (Evenson, 1989, p. 184). Dominant ideas in Western planning were directly reflected in decisions regarding the city's urban planning. The Delhi Master Plan was prepared with the assistance of American consultants supported by the Ford Foundation. As in Cape Town, the division of land use in strict mono-functional zones was the basic principle underpinning urban planning. Thus, for K.T. Ravindran (1996, p. 31): 'The result is high commercial concentrations and a fragmented city where people have to commute long distances. [. . .] Zoning has thus been one of the most destructive concepts where the wholeness of the city is concerned.'

The policy of urban and country planning at the regional level was also influenced by the examples of British town planning in the 1950s, in particular the programme of New Towns around London. This was translated into a regional plan prompted by the desire to monitor the capital's growth and to control in-migration into Delhi. It included the promotion of six Ring Towns and later the creation of a new industrial urban centre, Noida.

Today, the Indian capital city is a poly-nuclear metropolis, with several district business centres and commercial complexes, in addition to Connaught Place, the Central Business District inherited from the British colonial period built at the junction of New Delhi and the old city. Administrative functions remain dominant in New Delhi. The southern sector (beyond New Delhi and excluding the south-eastern fringe) accommodates mainly residential areas, but also several flourishing commercial complexes and a major business district (Nehru Place) as well as government offices. On the other hand, the main industrial zones are located in the western and north-western sectors; with an important planned industrial estate in the south-east (Okhla) and another notable industrial zone in the north-east (Shahdara) (Map 16.2). Despite the attempts of the Delhi Development Authority to implement strict zoning, economic activities remain scattered throughout the city, including industrial production that occurs not only in large planned industrial estates, but also in small-scale manufacturing units found in the old urban core as well as in the urbanized villages and in the many unauthorized colonies in the urban periphery.

### Spatial Fragmentation, Social Segmentation

In Cape Town as elsewhere in South Africa, planned spatial fragmentation was accompanied by an ideological restructuring of society: in a classical, if regrettable way, apartheid sought to change society by manipulating the environment, especially space. Spatial fragmentation through careful and thorough planning and brutal implementation was intended to divide society along racial lines. The racist hierarchy of the regime expressed itself in the organization of cities: the higher a racial group in the government's hierarchy, the closer to the centre it could live.[8] The same racial hierarchy factored into every dimension of access to the city, affecting access to urban amenities, education, skilled jobs and landownership, for instance. Consequently, socio-economic status was also dependent on race: blacks (African, Indian and coloured) had limited opportunities, especially in terms of access to jobs. As a result, they experienced high unemployment, in part, because of the explicit policies of job reservation by race and inadequate education opportunities that led to poorly paid, semi-skilled and unskilled jobs. Government-constructed racial differences created massive social division: poverty was far more widespread among blacks than among whites, who not only benefitted from protected and privileged jobs but also profited from state allowances and financial credit. Furthermore, African townships in particular were spatially isolated in marginal under-serviced environments.

The post-apartheid city mirrors this past, still largely characterized by a coincidence between race and class divisions (Maps 16.3 and 16.4). Despite racial desegregation in certain residential neighbourhoods (formerly proclaimed white or newly built areas),[9] the racial map of Cape Town drawn by the Group Areas Act still stands. With few exceptions, former white areas boast a relatively high income, while former African townships suffer enduring poverty. Squatter and informal settlements are inhabited largely by Africans and the socially underprivileged and, like African townships, are located in the urban periphery.

The South African society's highly visible segmentation matches its spatial fragmentation, reflected not only in planning regulations and spatial division, but also in housing. Cape Town's neighbourhoods differ according to housing types, thus the size of the house and plot echoes apartheid racial hierarchy: the 'whiter' the residents, the bigger the house and the plot. Internal arrangement and fittings were also highly

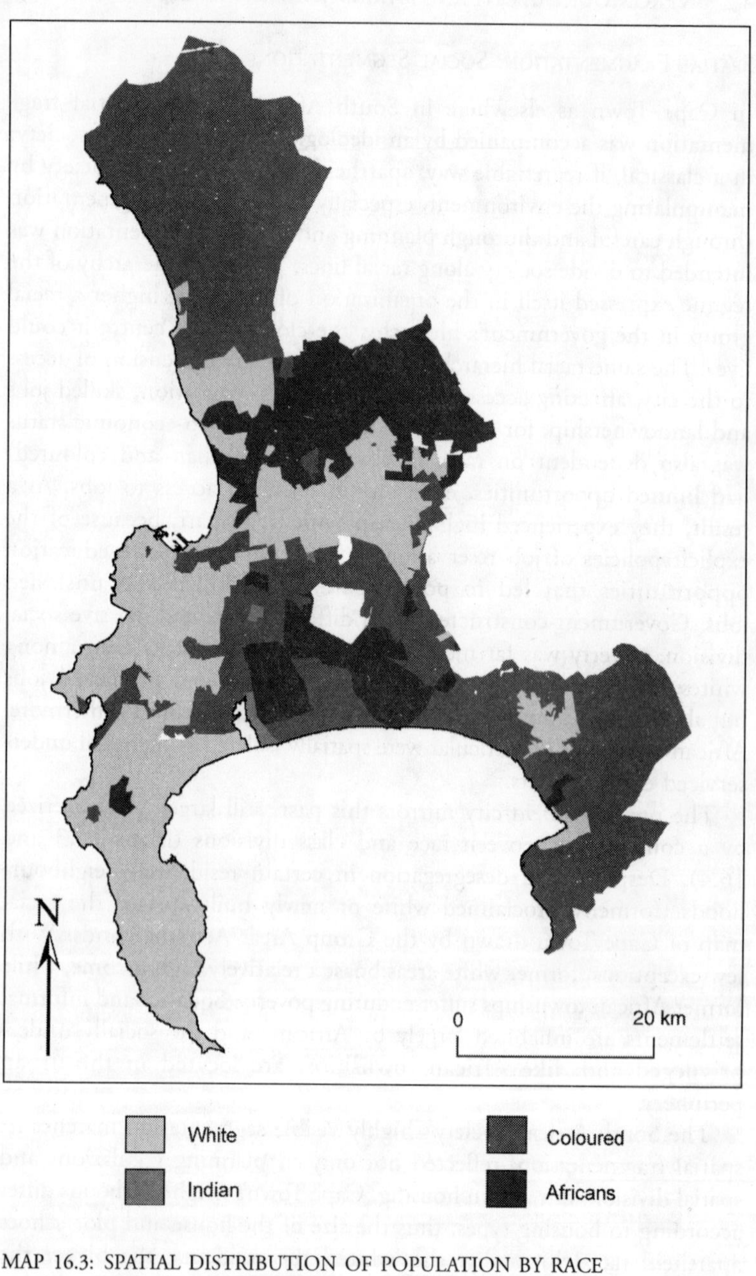


MAP 16.3: SPATIAL DISTRIBUTION OF POPULATION BY RACE IN CAPE TOWN (1996).

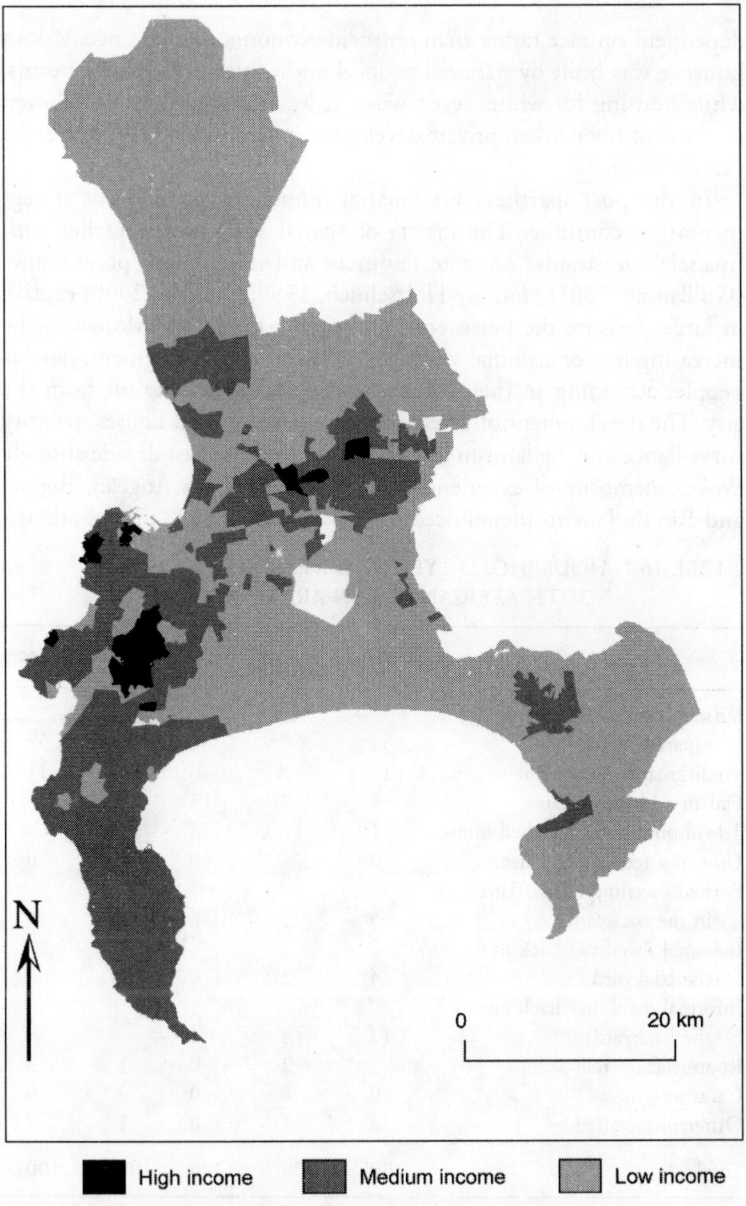


MAP 16.4: SPATIAL DISTRIBUTION OF POPULATION BY INCOME IN CAPE TOWN (1996).

dependent on race rather than on socio-economic status, since African housing was built by national or local authorities under strict norms, while housing for whites, even when it was state-subsidized, followed the laws of the market, private development, and individual preferences (Table 16.1).[10]

In the post-apartheid era, spatial fragmentation and social segmentation continue. The inertia of spatial structures, together with financial constraints on state resources and its building programmes (Guillaume, 2001; Houssay-Holzschuch, 1999; Oldfield, 2000) explain in large measure the persistence of spatial segregation. Moreover, the increasing fear of criminal violence has led to greater fragmentation, as people, according to their means, try to cut themselves off from the city. The development of gated communities, fortified houses, security surveillance and vigilantism in Cape Town over the past decade strongly evokes memories of experiences in cities such as Los Angeles, Bogota and Rio de Janeiro (denounced by Mike Davis, 1990, among others).

TABLE 16.1. HOUSEHOLD TYPE OF DWELLING BY RACE IN SOUTH AFRICAN URBAN AREAS, 1999 (%)

| | African | Coloured | Indian | White | All Races |
|---|---|---|---|---|---|
| Formal dwelling/house on a separate stand | 53 | 67 | 58 | 75 | 57 |
| Traditional dwelling/hut | 14 | 1 | 0 | 0 | 11 |
| Flat in a block of flats | 4 | 9 | 15 | 11 | 6 |
| Townhouse/semi-detached house | 1 | 11 | 18 | 8 | 3 |
| Unit in a retirement village | 0 | – | 0 | 2 | 0 |
| Formal dwelling/house/flat/room in the backyard | 5 | 3 | 6 | 2 | 4 |
| Informal dwelling/shack in the backyard | 4 | 2 | 0 | 0 | 3 |
| Informal dwelling/shack not in the backyard | 12 | 4 | 1 | – | 9 |
| Room/flat on rent | 3 | 2 | 0 | 1 | 3 |
| Caravan/tent | 0 | – | 0 | – | 0 |
| Other/unspecified | 3 | 1 | 0 | 1 | 2 |
| Total | 100 | 100 | 100 | 100 | 100 |

*Notes:* 0: Proportion less than 0.5 per cent or too small to record.
–: Nil or not applicable

*Source*: October Household Survey, 1999.

To a lesser extent, a similar trend can also be observed in the affluent neighbourhoods of Delhi.

In the Indian capital today, the urban landscape is marked not only by the divide between Old and New Delhi, but also by the differentiation of the built environment, affected in large part by state intervention in housing development. The government has implemented extensive housing programmes and land development schemes, such as rehabilitation colonies for refugees, housing estates for government employees,[11] Delhi Development Authority flats, co-operative group housing apartments and resettlement colonies for slum dwellers. Each of these types of housing estate not only presents distinct architectural and urban features, but also tends to house specific socio-economic sections of the urban population, thus contributing to a socially segmented residential pattern (Dupont, 2004).

Furthermore, public housing policies have failed to respond to the demand of large sections of the urban population for housing. Consequently, 'unauthorized colonies' have proliferated in the urban-rural fringe on agricultural land. Poorer groups, approximately 3 million people accounting for almost 25 per cent of the total population of Delhi in 1999, have been relegated to squatter settlements and precarious forms of habitat that have continued to expand in all areas of the capital, despite 'slum clearance' and resettlement programmes. These policies entail the relocation of evicted slum dwellers and squatters in resettlement colonies, or sites providing serviced plots of land located on the urban outskirts (Map 16.5). Pursued most actively during the 'Emergency' (1975-7), resettlement policy led to forced evictions of nearly 700,000 persons. This policy regained momentum in the 1999-2001 period.

Beyond the influence of town planning, housing policies—or their inadequacies—and the forces of the real-estate market, other traditional factors of residential segregation such as caste continue to play a role in shaping the social division of urban space.[12] In Delhi, as in other Indian cities, specific neighbourhoods for former untouchable castes, the Harijan *bastis*, still form part of the urban scene. The residential distribution of scheduled caste populations[13] across Delhi in 1991 revealed the persistence of social ostracism as manifested in residential segregation (Map 16.6). Pockets with high percentages of scheduled castes are, however, not concentrated in the same geographical sector of the urban agglomeration; they are rather scattered, with some located

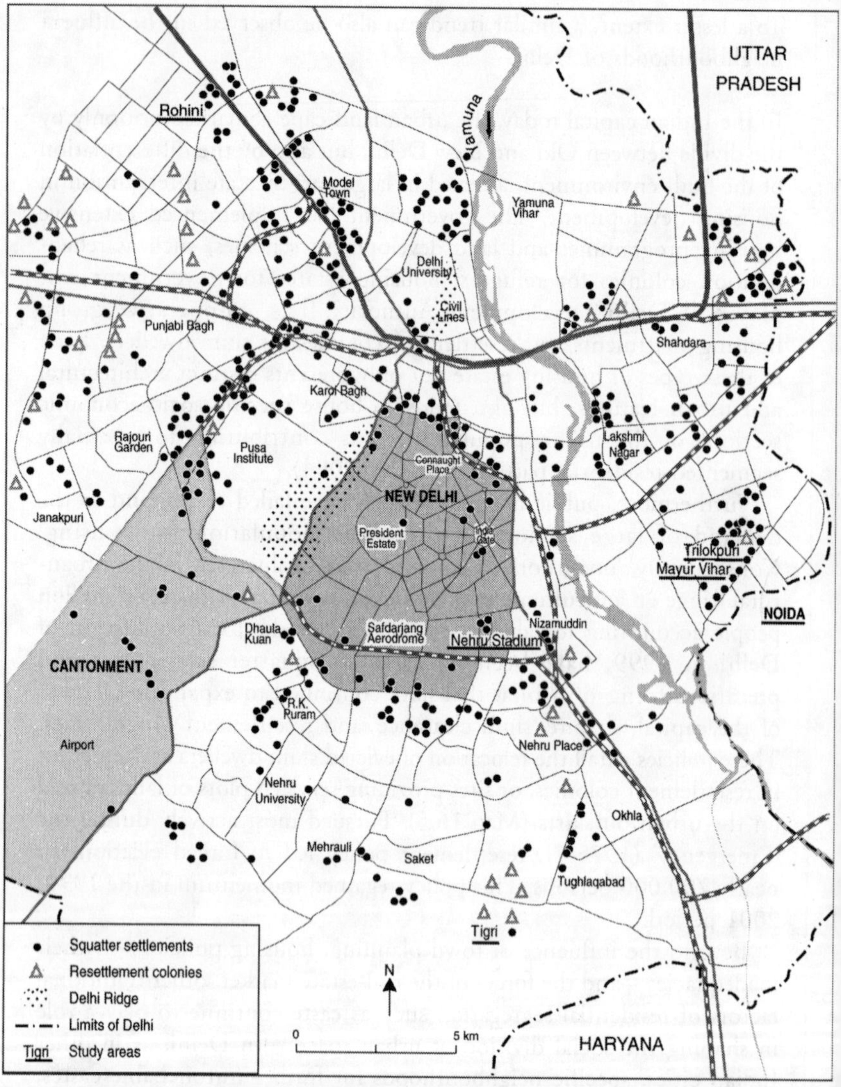


*Sources*: Census of India 1991, District Census Handbook, Delhi, Directorate of Census Operation, Delhi.
Slum & Jhuggi Jhompri Department, Municipal Corporation of Delhi, 1990.
Sabir Ali, *Slums within Slums: a study of resettlement colonies of Delhi*, New Delhi: Council for Social Development, 1990.
Digitised map: UMR ESPACE, Montpellier.

V. Dupont - LCA Bondy - IRD

MAP 16.5: SQUATTER SETTLEMENTS AND RESETTLEMENT COLONIES IN DELHI URBAN AGGLOMERATION (1990).

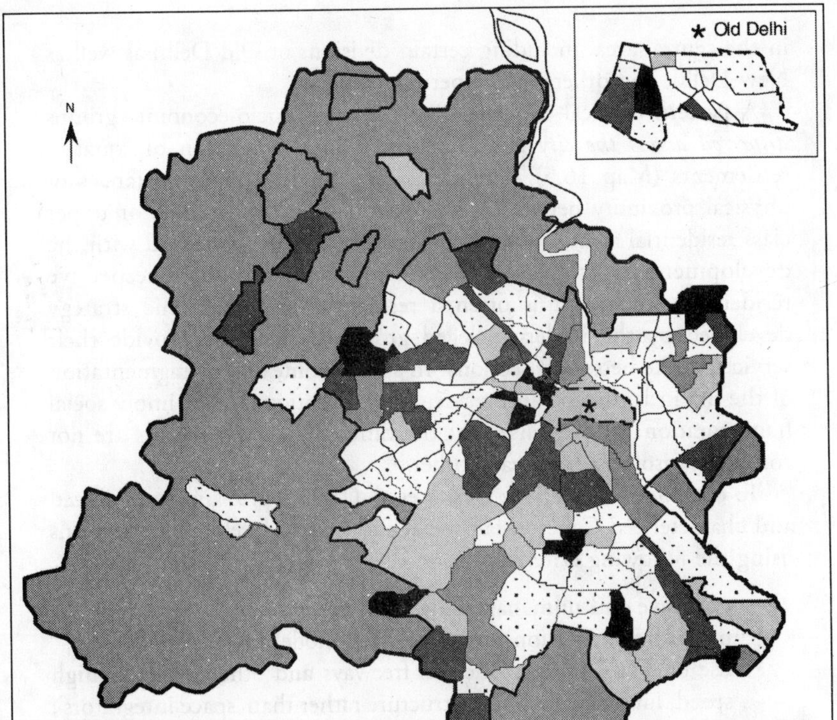


*Source*: *Census of India 1991*, Series 31, Delhi Primary Census Abstract.
Map: Laboratoire de Cartographie Appliquée - IRD (Bondy).

MAP 16.6: RESIDENTIAL DISTRIBUTION OF SCHEDULED CASTE POPULATION IN DELHI URBAN AGGLOMERATION (1991)

in the central area, including certain divisions of Old Delhi as well as New Delhi, and others in the peripheral zones.

A pattern of local concentrations of lower socio-economic groups *dispersed across the city* is also reflected in the location of squatter settlements (Map 16.5). Therefore, one can find many instances of physical proximity between lower class clusters and middle or upper class residential areas. Such patterns are frequently associated with the development of economic relationships between these respective residents.[14] In fact, it is often a residential and economic strategy developed by the underprivileged groups in order to provide their services to the better-off sections. In such a context, the fragmentation of the urban landscape and residential segregation do not imply social fragmentation, in the sense that the different social segments are not completely isolated from each other.

To conclude this section, Dewar et al. (1990, pp. x-xiii) summarized and characterized Capeton-ian social and spatial development patterns using the following criteria:

- explosive and unmanaged low density sprawl;
- urban fragmentation into a 'cellular' model;
- use of 'space bridges' such as freeways and other forms of high speed, limited access, infrastructure rather than 'space integrators';
- separation of land use, urban elements, races and income groups;
- a highly skewed distribution of work, commercial and social facilities and opportunities along the older 'arms' of the city.

The situation in Delhi presents a less alarming or extreme diagnosis of urban fragmentation. Notwithstanding a citywide socio-economic and functional division between the northern and southern halves, the majority of Delhi is relatively heterogeneous in terms of type of settlements and socio-economic groups of residents. However, it would be misleading to conclude that residential segregation in Delhi is moderate: instead, it is at a subtle level. The socio-spatial organization of Delhi could be characterized by a combination of residential and social segregation at the micro-level along with dispersion at the city level. Despite the implementation of separate land use zoning, small-scale economic activities are also located throughout the city.

Physical fragmentation and residential segregation, evident in the two metropolises, do not, therefore, necessarily imply social fragmentation, as observed in the case of Delhi.

## ACCESS TO THE CITY BY UNDERPRIVILEGED SOCIAL GROUPS

The spatial organization of each metropolis, the distribution of jobs and housing types, as well as historical and socio-cultural factors deeply influence the daily life of city dwellers and their mobility. As we focus on access to the city by the underprivileged social groups we address the following questions: To what extent do the poor have the capacity to move in segmented or fragmented metropolises? Do they manage to find their way across the many urban barriers to access different places and thus a vast range of urban opportunities? The very existence and perception of these opportunities is a strong 'pull' factor in rural-urban migration. Physical and symbolic access to those opportunities allows the formation of a common identity as urbanites, and is a condition for collective social development.

For Delhi, our analysis deals with the mobility of the population living in squatter settlements and in resettlement colonies. The findings are based on a statistical survey of 1,249 households conducted in 1995 in five selected zones, including such types of settlements (Map 16.5), and complemented by in-depth interviews and more recent field visits (Dupont and Prakash, 1999; Sidhu, 1995 and 1997). We draw on an analysis of access to Cape Town's opportunities by Africans living in several townships and squatter settlements to provide a comparative perspective. The findings rely on qualitative research conducted in 1995-7 (Houssay-Holzschuch, 1999). We do not dwell here on the question of access to proper housing and basic infrastructure and services for the poor, which was discussed earlier. We focus on access to places of education, work and shopping.

### Contextualizing Mobility: Transportation

Mobility is vital in widely spread and spatially fragmented cities such as Delhi and Cape Town. Access to transport and effective urban mobility of different social groups have the potential to reduce the effects of physical fragmentation or, on the contrary, to aggravate them. Urban transportation and communication networks have the potential power to integrate the city and the potential capacity to favour objective or at least subjective solidarity between urban dwellers in their uses of the city (May, Spector and Veltz, 1998). Transportation means have a considerable impact on urban development; however, their differential access is also a source of social inequalities. Hence, as Kaufmann (2000,

p. 56) pointed out: 'The diversity of ways of living that results produces parallel cities. The fragmented city that ensues is constituted of worlds whose inhabitants rarely meet, due to a collision of speeds and daily life spheres.'

Acute social and economic inequalities in access to urban transportation are commonly observed in metropolises of the South (Diaz Olvera, Plat and Pochet, 1998; Figueroa, Godard and Henry, 1997). Such problems are also common in Delhi and Cape Town. The situation in Cape Town is summarized in Table 16.2.

Public transport in African areas includes buses, trains and group taxis. They are all relatively expensive, forcing people to spend often more than one-third of their wages on transport. Buses and trains are often slow and, as the distances between residences and workplaces are long due to functional specialization and spatial fragmentation, people spend a great part of their day commuting. Group taxis are more efficient, but have long been prone to violence: competition between companies is fierce and conflicts are often resolved by force.

In 1993, walking was a significant means of transport (32 per cent of intra-city trips) in Delhi. Public buses accounted for 62 per cent of trips by vehicle; the rest were distributed equally among cars, scooters or motorcycles, or bicycles and other small carriers (cycle-rickshaws, auto-rickshaws, or horse carts, for instance). The average time spent per intra-city trip was 27 minutes (all purposes combined), 29 minutes for commuting to work, 23 minutes for education, and 28 minutes

TABLE 16.2. MODE OF TRANSPORT OF METROPOLITAN COMMUTERS BY RACE IN 1992

| | Whites | Asians | Coloureds | Africans |
|---|---|---|---|---|
| Public Transport (per cent) | 7 | 33 | 53 | 79 |
| *Bus* | *4* | *22* | *10* | *20* |
| *Taxi* | - | *8* | *8* | *46* |
| *Train* | *3* | *3* | *35* | *13* |
| Car (per cent) | 87 | 57 | 36 | 9 |
| Walking (per cent) | 2 | 4 | 7 | 11 |
| Other (per cent) | 4 | 6 | 4 | 1 |
| Average Monthly Cost (ZAR) | 221 | 134 | 101 | 67 |
| Average Travel Time (mn) | 25 | 36 | 44 | 51 |

*Source*: Vines Mikula Associates, 1994, quoted in Selod and Zenou, 1999.

for other purposes.[15] The case studies of selected neighbourhoods illustrate inequalities in access to various modes of transportation and commuting time.

### Access to Places of Education

Despite a variety of local contexts, in all the five zones studied in Delhi (Map 16.5) (either located in a central area, within the periphery of the urban agglomeration, or in a ring town outside the capital city) a similar pattern of differential access to education was evident.[16] Most (if not all) schoolboys and girls living in squatter settlements attended a school located in the same zone as their residence, and majority of them went on foot. The corresponding frequencies were always higher for children from squatter settlements than those living in other types of settlement. Correlatively, the average time spent in commuting was less. Last, in all the zones, the wider the socio-economic distance as reflected in the type of settlement and housing, the sharper the contrasts between the indicators related to the place of study, the mode of transportation, and the time of commuting.

For example, the Mayur Vihar–Trilokpuri zone houses a large variety of types of settlements and a wide range of socio-economic strata. Among the children living in squatter settlements or resettlement colonies, more than 95 per cent studied in their zone of residence, over 90 per cent walked to school, and on the average they spent 9 to 12 minutes per trip to commute; whereas in the cooperative group housing societies' apartments (housing the better-off sections of this residential zone), only one-third of the students studied in the Mayur Vihar–Trilokpuri zone, only 16 per cent went on foot and on the average they spent 28 minutes per trip.

The distinctive pattern in access to place of education exhibited by school children living in squatter settlements and resettlement colonies reflected two other differentials: differences in the level of education and differences in the type of school attended.

As expected, most of the school children living in squatter settlements attended primary schools (64 per cent to 76 per cent, according to the zone) and not a single student had reached college level. On the other hand, in certain planned housing sectors, among all school children and students, the proportion of those attending higher educational institutions (university or other establishments for higher technical studies) varied from 14 per cent (planned sectors in Noida,

DDA flats in Rohini, for example) to 28 per cent (cooperative group housing societies' apartments in Mayur Vihar). Since there is no university in the zone, those pursuing higher studies had no choice but to travel outside their residential zone to attend a university.

In the case of primary and secondary education, working class children did not attend the same types of establishment as those from better-off families and housing sectors. The former attended government schools, while the latter were enrolled in private schools with a better reputation, and even elitist education establishments located at a distance from the zone of residence. Noida, lying to the east of Delhi is a case in point (Map 16.2). As a new planned town of about 200,000 inhabitants at the time of the survey, it is equipped with many local primary schools and a fair number of secondary schools, including reputed private institutions. Yet, in families living in the planned sectors, 36 per cent of the children attending a secondary school travelled outside Noida to study in Delhi, at the cost of long commuting times (48 minutes on the average per trip), generally travelling by bus. Obviously, such options were completely beyond the financial means of families living in squatter settlements.

The case of Tigri Janta Jeevan Camp, however, revealed that government schools did not necessarily provide better facilities than those the slums dwellers organized for themselves with the help of non-governmental organizations. Tigri J.J. Camp, a very large squatter settlement developed since the 1970s in the southern periphery of Delhi (Map 16.5), comprised approximately 10,000 dwelling units by the mid-1990s, housing nearly 50,000 inhabitants. A number of voluntary non-governmental organizations operating in this slum are very active. A women's association runs a primary school in a newly constructed and well-planned building which includes several classrooms and a courtyard. In 1995, this contrasted with the local government-run primary school that was situated in a park with no formal structure and with children seated on the ground under open tents.[17]

As confirmed by interviews with residents of squatter settlements or resettlement colonies, these case studies illustrate that 'most parents are well aware of the crucial role that school plays in order to climb the social ladder and attain a better status than their own present one' (Milbert, 1997, p. 369). Concern for children's education again came to the fore when Rajiv Gandhi Camp, a squatter settlement centrally located near a new administrative complex and the Nehru Stadium, was demolished in May 2000. The families entitled to resettlement under the scheme[18] were shifted to Narela, a resettlement colony located at a distance of about 30 km from the previous site, in the rural fringe to the north of the Delhi urban agglomeration. Apart from the major issue of access to employment opportunities in the new relocation sites, the lack of adequate school facilities was also a frequent complaint. Hence, the education of some children had been disrupted, as there was no secondary school, and the only primary school was non-functional due to teacher truancy. For some families who had invested in the education of their children in order to improve their socio-economic status, the lack of access to proper educational institutions in the resettlement site jeopardized their strategies for improving their children's future opportunities.

In the South African context under apartheid, schools were segregated. As a consequence of government policy barring them from skilled jobs and the 1953 Bantu Education Act that placed schools firmly under state control, Africans only had access to low quality education in 'African schools', located in African townships. Teachers were poorly trained compared to those in white schools and the pupil-teacher ratio was much higher. Also, curricula were designed to fit job expectations: carpentry for boys and domestic science for girls who were trained as future servants. Besides, the equipment was poor and the school buildings inadequately maintained. This system of 'Bantu education' was systematically opposed and boycotted by the African population during the apartheid years, leading, among other things to a further disinterest of the authorities. On the other side of the racial barrier, affluent private and public schools for whites were in centrally located neighbourhoods with high standards and high fees.

Under the new dispensation, all restrictions on school attendance have been lifted and state-sponsored schools have been reformed. Parents are free to choose a school for their children, the 'only' limitation being their financial resources: the best schools are often very expensive. South Africans parents from all walks of life are deeply convinced of the benefits of education. When asked during the 1996-7 interviews what their wishes for their own future were, their first and main answer was: 'I wish my children to get a good education'. Education is perceived as the best way to eradicate individual and family poverty and thereby reduce inequalities at a more general level. Many families go to great lengths to ensure that their children attend a 'good school': financial sacrifices are made to pay for both the fees and the transport. In Cape Town, African children from townships often travel more than an hour to reach their school in the northern or southern suburbs. Their reception varies from place to place: in Rondebosch, for instance, a wealthy, English-speaking suburb where many students and academics live, negative reactions of the local residents were limited. On the other hand, in Ruyterwacht, a former poor white area which today has coloured and white residents, African children were confronted by barricades erected by the angry residents, reputedly fearing crime and degradation of their environment (Teppo, 2000). In both cases, children's daily commuting is important: coming more often than not from a township, they travel to the city to receive better education. The same process occurs at a lower scale for poorer households: many Khayelitsha families, living in a sprawling township of over 600,000 residents on the outskirts of the city, believe that the nearby schools in the coloured neighbourhood of Mitchell's Plains are better, and that the school year is less disrupted by crime or political conflicts (Fakier, 1998). Fees in these schools are also more affordable than those in the northern and southern suburbs. Therefore, African and coloured children attend schools in Mitchell's Plains: the mobility of the former, even if limited, provides for spaces of social desegregation. Townships schools, however, are not deserted: local children, lacking the will or the means to commute, fill up the classes. In squatter settlements, the situation and access to education follows more or less the same patterns.

### Access to Workplaces: A Delhi Example

Unlike access to places of education, the differential pattern of access to workplaces across various settlement types in Delhi depends on the local context. Although the position of workers living in squatter settlements everywhere has some distinctive features as compared to workers from other neighbouring housing sectors, the differentials do not always operate in the same way.[19] A first distinction has to be made between, on the one hand, the two case studies circumscribed each to a small area (the zones of Nehru Stadium and Tigri) and, on the other hand, the three widely spread zones (Rohini, Mayur Vihar-Trilokpuri and Noida) (Map 16.5).

In large peripheral zones, differential analysis appears more relevant because it include a wider range of socio-economic strata and provides a greater variety of economic activities, and hence employment opportunities. A recurrent differential pattern emerges for workers from squatter settlements (as compared to workers from other neighbouring housing sectors): they tend to work more frequently in the same zone, spend less time commuting, and travel more often on foot or by bicycle. As expected, the contrasts are more marked when compared to residents from planned housing sectors.

The new town of Noida, planned from its inception as an important industrial centre, provides a striking illustration. Almost all the inhabitants of the squatter settlements (98 per cent) work in Noida. The attraction of the employment opportunities offered by the new industrial estate motivated them to migrate. As no arrangements have been made by the town authority to house the majority of industrial workers, they have occupied the vacant land in the gaps and the fringes of the industrial zone where they have constructed precarious housing, while others have rented rooms in the urbanized villages (Dupont, 2001). Not surprisingly, workers living in squatter settlements spend on average only 17 minutes per trip to travel to their workplace, 71 per cent of them go on foot and 19 per cent by bicycle. In the planned sectors, only 51 per cent of the resident workers are employed in Noida, the rest commute daily to Delhi (except for a marginal percentage working elsewhere in the metropolitan area). In contrast, the residents of these sectors spend on average 33 minutes commuting to their workplace, and 80 per cent depend on motorized modes of transport.[20]

In the Badli-Rohini zone, the emergence of certain populated squatter settlements was also linked to the development of an industrial zone. In the case of Rajiv Gandhi Camp near the Nehru Stadium, the origin of this squatter camp was directly linked to the opening of construction sites and the recruitment of migrant workers who settled on their work site.

As illustrated by these examples, the location of squatter settlements in Delhi is often the outcome of strategies aimed at settling in the proximity of sources of livelihood: in industrial zones and near construction sites in particular. These case studies further reveal an important dimension of survival strategies among the urban poor. Since they cannot afford high travel expenses, priority is given to physically accessible employment sources, rather than to housing conditions and security of occupancy. This priority order is exemplified by the case of houseless migrant workers sleeping on pavements or in the night shelters in Old Delhi. In these extreme conditions, under drastic financial constraints, housing is entirely forfeited and transport expenses minimized, in order to maximize available income, as also, in the majority of cases, saving and remittances to the family living in the native village

(Dupont, 2000a). The importance of easy physical access to earning opportunities is crucial for understanding the residential practices of the urban poor (Bharat Sevak Samaj, 1958; Gupta, Kaul and Pandey, 1993; Kundu, 1993; Suri, 1994). The failure of numerous attempts to relocate slum dwellers and squatters in settlement colonies outside city centres is often due to inadequate consideration of this fact.

Today, Trilokpuri, a resettlement colony, is well connected by bus to other parts of the city. However, at the time of their relocation in 1976-7, families found uneven land with only a few hand pumps installed at a distance, a few main roads and very few buses serving the area. Unable to withstand such difficult condition, many of the poorer residents sold their plots and returned to central areas to squat on vacant land in places closer to their sources of livelihood, while others went back to their native villages.

The Delhi Slum Wing and other authorities involved in resettlement programmes have failed to recognize the centrality of economic factors to poverty-stricken families' strategies for survival in cities. At their resettlement site in Narela, for instance, earlier residents of Rajiv Gandhi Camp experience a lack of easy access to transportation (in terms of bus frequency, time and cost of commuting) and hence to their previous workplaces. Those engaged in low paying jobs cannot afford the daily cost of commuting, while local employment opportunities are rare. For example, women who were employed as domestic workers in their old neighbourhood have now been deprived of all prospects to pursue the same activity in the resettlement area. These difficulties are compounded by new rules imposed in resettlement colonies: no small business, shop or workshop is permitted on allotted plots. These restrictions virtually amount to the denial of any survival strategies to people who have been impoverished by eviction from their previous living place, and who have been practically cut-off from their former sources of livelihood. It is not surprising that a team of international human right experts who visited this (and other) relocation site concluded that: 'the Resettlement Programme has been implemented in violation of the Constitution of India, namely the right to life under Article 21', by denying the resettled households their right to livelihood (HIC, 2000).

Even if available data does not allow a strict comparison with Cape Town, some elements may be briefly noted. The first is the high unemployment rate of Africans, compared to other groups. According to the 1999 October Household Survey, unemployment in urban areas in the same year affected almost 41 per cent of Africans, 26 per cent of Coloureds, 20 per cent of Indians and 7 per cent Whites (SAIRR, 2001). At a local level, the situation in African townships may be far worse, despite the vigour and importance of the informal sector in these neighbourhoods. Estimations of unemployment often exceed 60 per cent of the population (Mazur and Quangule, 1995). Mobility is thus dramatically reduced because people do not have the means to commute. Nevertheless, for those residents who have or are looking for a job, commuting to other parts of the city is a necessity (Oldfield, 2000): employment is located in the city centre, in suburbs and industrial areas, while only a few jobs are available in townships. In many households in Cape Town's African townships, women are the breadwinners, working as maids in the more affluent suburbs; in contrast, their unemployed male partners have reduced mobility and access to employment.

### Access to Shopping and Socializing Places: Towards a Post-apartheid Geography of Mobility in Cape Town

During the apartheid era, shopping and socializing places in South Africa were disjointed. Shopping was only done in the city centre or in the White areas, on the way home from work, as commercial development was legally restricted in townships. White commerce benefited from this situation while Black entrepreneurs were forced to operate illegally and informally. Shopping centres in townships were scarce, expensive and generally offered only a limited range of products. In short, laws ensured that shopping created mobility as there was no alternative. For instance, the first supermarket was set up in Khayelitsha township in 1995, a settlement of over 500,000 inhabitants at that time. People shopped in the nearby coloured settlement of Mitchell's Plain. The city centre was also frequently used for shopping (Map 16.7): it drew together commuters' flows, catching a connection between the suburb and the township. All types of transport are available in this centre—trains, buses and collective taxis have their station in the same block, transforming it into a busy hub. The nearby Golden Acre commercial centre was widely used by commuters. The kind of access African people had to shopping places under apartheid is depicted in Map 16.7. Drawn by T, a middle-aged woman from the township of Gugulethu, this mental map illustrates all the major public transport infrastructures present in the centre, on which Africans were largely

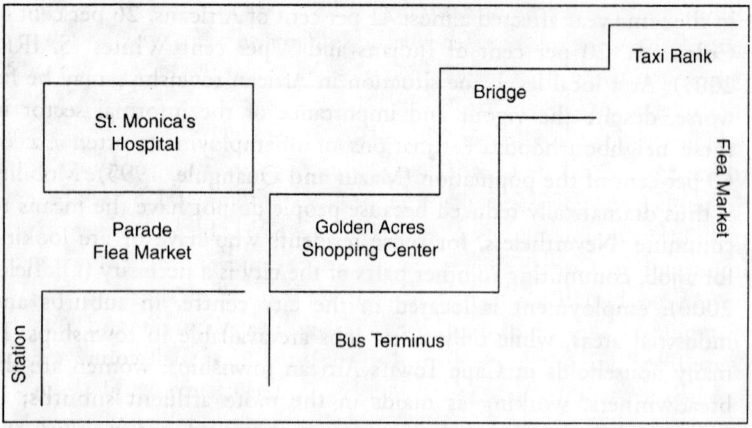


MAP 16.7: A MENTAL MAP OF CAPE TOWN CITY CENTRE, DRAWN IN 1996.

dependent. The space depicted here is a pedestrian's space: from public transport to passageway to commercial centre, one can follow her steps.

In contrast, socializing places in South Africa under apartheid were circumscribed largely to townships (Coplan, 1985): petty apartheid enforced segregation in all public places such as public halls, theatres or movie theatres and clubs. These amenities, often located in the city centre, were seldom accessible to Africans and alternative facilities were scarce in the townships. Also, the local authorities often imposed a public monopoly on the sale and consumption of alcohol, limiting alcohol sales to state-owned township beer halls: a legal multiplicity of bars, restaurants and socializing places was thus impossible. Finally, African areas were constantly subject to police harassment. Therefore, socializing was often difficult or unsafe during the apartheid period: few places could welcome guests legally and many socializing places elsewhere in the city were not open to Africans. Socializing took place instead in private township houses, often transformed into *shebeens*, illegal bars, by their owners. Patrons and owners were at risk of a police raid.

Today, new patterns have emerged as people move freely around the city. Financial constraints continue to influence mobility but people from the township widely use newly accessible facilities. Economic rationality has replaced imposed mobility, such as in the choice of shopping areas. A greater variety of daily products, at more reasonable prices, are available in new township commercial centres. Residents shop in places that are most convenient. For instance, as the Khayelitsha commercial centre is not centrally located, people from the southern half of the settlement prefer Mitchell's Plain centre. Other shopping places such as the city centre or transport hubs like Woodstock continue to attract many people.

The disjunction between shopping and socializing places also seems to have decreased in significance. An exploratory study conducted in September 2001 revealed that the model of shopping and entertainment mall, often branded as a sign of globalization, has become increasingly important in Cape Town. New malls and entertainment complexes have been built on vacant land, bridging some of the gaps of the fragmented city. Older places, such as the Victoria and Albert Waterfront, attracted new patrons during the 1990s: all communities can be seen striding on the quays on a Sunday afternoon. These malls allow varied shopping—for food or daily necessities as well as more exceptional treats. Socializing is also possible as they offer a variety of entertainment in a safe environment (a sought after commodity in the South African context) and at various hours. The main malls are connected by the public transport system.

In short, access to shopping and socializing places have definitely increased for blacks in Cape Town over the last decade as has access to education. The opening of many places legally has triggered an increase in mobility, even for the less privileged. Though spatial fragmentation and residential segregation continue, mobility can be seen as a way to reclaim the city, to restore to Cape Town some of its urbanity.

In Delhi, the question of access to shopping and entertainment places for residents of squatter settlements and resettlement colonies cannot be stated in the same terms, since they have not been subjected to segregation laws or restrictions as severe as under apartheid in Cape Town. Thus, many informal commercial activities, sometimes at a microscale, have developed in these two types of settlements: small shops—often wooden kiosks or even doorstep stalls—provide basic goods and services, and hawkers push their trolleys wherever the streets allow their passage. Provided they manage to obtain their 'ration card' (an administrative procedure that may prove cumbersome for the newly arrived poor migrant families), the recognized residents of any locality also have access to fair-price shops that supply government subsidized staple commodities.

Unlike black South Africans living in townships or squatter camps in Cape Town, in Delhi workers living in squatter settlements are not necessarily disadvantaged in terms of commuting time to reach their workplace, a factor that figures centrally in their livelihood and residential strategies. Yet, the new resettlement programme for slum dwellers has circumscribed residents' spatial and economic opportunities, bringing them close to the conditions that disadvantaged poor black South African families faced in Cape Town in the apartheid era. In particular, resettled Delhi residents have been forcibly shifted far from their places of work and setting up of any trade or business on the plots alloted in the relocation sites has been made illegal.

## CONCLUSION: WHICH MODEL OF CITY ON THE ANVIL?

Cape Town and Delhi are two metropoles whose spatial and social patterns can be described as either fragmented or segmented. We have discussed several common factors that have produced this type of urban configuration:

- the impact of the British colonial urban model;
- powerful town planning that shaped both cities, using similar models of reference, and with comparable effects;
- segmented societies that combine social hierarchy and residential segregation—either as an effect of twentieth century imposed racial segregation, or because of traditional social division based on caste.

This socio-spatial organization has developed in the face of rapid urban growth and the spread of acute social inequality and extensive poverty.

However, Delhi and Cape Town diverge in their present evolutions. While post-apartheid social and housing policies implemented in Cape Town aim to integrate the city and reduce spatial and social fragmentation (in particular through the urbanization of previous buffer zones and the promotion of racially mixed residential areas), the recent trend observed in Delhi is likely, on the contrary, to increase urban fragmentation and foster social fractures. 'Cleaning' the city of its squatter settlements may serve the interests of the better-off sections of the city by improving their visual environment, but this process comes at the cost of thousands of families cut-off from their sources of livelihood as well as their social and economic networks. Furthermore, such 'undesirable' citizens are relegated to the rural fringes of the city, in relocation sites where economic activities are not permitted.

At one time, town planners and policy makers of developing cities, including Cape Town and Delhi, imported Western planning concepts and applied them to local urban contexts without critically assessing them. If Delhi's planners and policy makers had drawn lessons from experiences of other cities of the South, in particular from the disastrous consequences of apartheid planning in South African cities, they would have reformulated their most recent policies in a different way. Comparative urban analysis is not only a heuristic tool for researchers, but also critical for town planners and urban policy makers.

## NOTES

1. All translations from the French are ours.
2. For J. Lévy (1994), urbanity is what differentiates a city from a settlement, specifically the 'putting together a maximum of social objects within a minimal distance' (p. 286).
3. Such findings are not specific to southern contexts such as Delhi and Cape Town. For the French case, see for example, Castells and Godard, 1974; Pinçon, Préteceille and Rendu, 1986.
4. As stated by Godard (1990, p. 9): 'When referring to the concept of strategy, one generally adopts an approach that consists in restoring to the actor his/her share of initiative in the elaboration of his/her own existence'. We subscribe entirely to this approach.
5. The denomination of 'racial' groups in South Africa, especially in post-apartheid South Africa, is an arduous problem as well as a political hot potato. The former apartheid racial classification included
   - 'Whites' (South Africans from European origins), among them:
     - Afrikaners, Afrikaans-speaking descendants of Dutch settlers from the seventeenth century onwards. *Afrikaner* is the Afrikaans word for African and thus includes a political statement, underlining the African identity of this population group.
     - English-speaking South Africans.
     - Other, often more recent, migrants of European origin such as Greeks, Portuguese.
   - 'Indians', South Africans of Indian origin, whose ancestors came as either indentured labourers or free passengers notably at the end of the nineteenth century and at the beginning of the twentieth century (see R. Ebr.-Vally's contribution in this volume);
   - 'Africans' (previously designated as 'Natives' or 'Bantus'), South Africans of African origin;
   - 'Coloureds', an heterogeneous group including people of mixed descent and people not fitting in the above categories.

This classification has been particularly important in the shaping of identities. While condemning the system that designed it, researchers widely use it. Other terms also need to be defined: Indians, Africans and coloureds were collectively designated as 'Non-Europeans', a derogatory term used under apartheid, and, by themselves, as 'blacks'. In this paper, while aware of the political implications of each term, we follow the usual conventions and use the above categories as they are understood in the South African context.

6. Our analysis of the apartheid system is limited to its impact on Cape Town's spatial fragmentation. A fuller analysis and bibliography can be found in numerous publications, see Christopher, 1994; Guillaume, 2001.
7. The 1950 Group Areas Act is one of the legislative pillars of apartheid: it defined racially strict residential zones in the whole country, leading to massive forced removals and the construction of townships in urban areas.
8. A similar principle was applied by the British colonial administration in their planning of New Delhi.
9. See for instance Saff (1998).
10. For further details on housing during apartheid, see Judin and Vladislavic (1998).
11. Since the government employees have been supplied with different categories of housing according to their official status and range of income, this residential model was qualified as 'salaried apartheid' by A. Mitra (1970).
12. For a general discussion, see the contribution by V. Dupont and F. Landy in this volume, and Dupont (2004) for a case study of Delhi.
13. 'Scheduled caste' is the administrative term used to designate the ex-untouchable castes identified for specific public benefits.
14. Such residential patterns can be interpreted as a manifestation of what Schenk (1986, p. 183) has identified as the 'two seemingly contradictory societal forces upon the socio-spatial structure of urban residence : (a) the aim to reside in socially homogeneous areas, and (b) the aim and the need to maintain relations of dependency'.
15. RITES, Household travel survey in Delhi urban area, New Delhi, 1993.
16. The total sample surveyed covered 1,616 students, including 322 living in squatter settlements and 316 in resettlement colonies.
17. However, during our last field visit to this neighbourhood in 1999, this government primary school had been accommodated in a nearby newly constructed building.
18. On the question of 'slum clearance' and 'resettlement policies', see Ramanathan, 2000.
19. The total sample surveyed covered 1,994 workers, including 554 living in squatter settlements and 300 in resettlement colonies.
20. To calculate the average commuting duration per trip, home-based workers were excluded.

## REFERENCES

Bharat Sevak Samaj, *Slums of Old Delhi*, Delhi: Atma Ram & Sons, 1958.

Bickford-Smith, V., E. Van Heyningen and N. Worden, *Cape Town, The Making of a City*, Cape Town: David Philips, 1998.

———, *Cape Town in the Twentieth Century*, Cape Town: David Philips, 1999.

Castells, M., F. Godard, *Monopolville. L'entreprise, l'état, l'urbain*, Paris/La Haye: Mouton, 1974.

Castells, M., *La question urbaine*, 1st edn. 1970, Paris: Maspero, 1981.

Christopher, A.J., *Atlas of Apartheid*, Johannesburg: Witwatersrand University Press, 1994.

Coplan, D.B., *In Township Tonight! South African Black City Music and Theatre*, Johannesburg: Ravan Press, 1985.

Davis, M., *City of Quartz: Excavating the Future in Los Angeles*, London: Verso, 1990.

Détienne, M., *Comparer l'incomparable*, Paris: Ed. du Seuil, 2000.

Dewar, D., V. Watson, A. Bassios and N. Dewar, 'The Structure and Form of Metropolitan Cape Town: its origins, influences and performance', working paper no. 43, Cape Town: Urban Problems Research Unit, University of Cape Town, 1990.

Diaz Olvera, L., D. Plat and P. Pochet, *Villes africaines au quotidien, Mobilités quotidiennes et contraintes sociales à Bamako et Ouagadougou*, Lyon: Laboratoire d'Economie des Transports, 1998.

Dupont, V., 'Mobility Patterns and Economic Strategies of Houseless People in Old Delhi', in *Delhi: Urban Space and Human Destinies*, ed. V. Dupont, E. Tarlo, D. Vidal, Delhi: Manohar-CSH, 2000, pp. 99-124.

———, 'Spatial and Demographic Growth of Delhi and the Main Migration Flows', in *Delhi: Urban Space and Human Destinies*, ed. V. Dupont, E. Tarlo, D. Vidal, Delhi: Manohar-CSH, 2000, pp. 229-39 + 13 maps.

———, 'Noida: nouveau pôle industriel ou ville satellite de Delhi ? Le projet des planificateurs, ses failles et son devenir', *Revue Tiers Monde*, no. 165, January-March 2001, pp. 189-211.

———, 'Socio-spatial Differentiation and Residential Segregation in Delhi: A Question of Scale?', *Geoforum*, vol. 35, no. 2, March 2004, pp. 157-75.

Dupont, V. and J. Prakash, 'Enquête 'Mobilités Spatiales dans l'Aire Métropolitaine de Delhi', in *Biographies d'enquête*, ed. Groupe de réflexion sur l'approche biographique, Paris: INED-PUF/Diffusion, Coll. Méthodes et savoirs, 1999, pp. 279-315.

Evenson, N., *The Indian Metropolis, A View toward the West*, New Haven and London: Yale University Press, 1989.

Fakier, Y., *Grappling with Change*, Cape Town: Idasa, Cape Times, Western Cape Education Department, 1998.

Figueroa, O., X. Godrad and E. Henry, 'Mobilité et politiques de transport dans les villes en développement', INRETS, no. 55, June 1997, pp. 30-1.

Frykenberg, R.E., ed., *Delhi through the Ages: Essays in Urban History, Culture and Society*, New Delhi: Oxford University Press, 1986.

Gervais-Lambony Ph.,'La ségrégation dans la grande ville, un essai de définition', in *Les très grandes villes dans le monde*, ed. M.-A. Gervais-Lambony, Paris: Atlande, 2001, pp. 33-8.

Godard, F., 'Sur le concept de stratégie', in *Stratégies résidentielles*, ed. C. Bonvalet, A.M. Fribourg, Paris: INED-Plan Construction et Architecture, 1990, pp. 9-22.

Grafmeyer, Y., 'Regards sociologiques sur la ségrégation', in *La ségrégation dans la ville*, ed. J. Brun and C. Rhein, Paris: L'Harmattan, 1994, pp. 85-117.

Guillaume, P., *Johannesburg, géographies de l'exclusion*, Paris: IFAS-Karthala, 2001.

Gupta, D.B., S. Kaul and R. Pandey, *Housing and India's Urban Poor*, New Delhi: Har-Anand Publications, 1993.

HIC, 'Visit to Bhalswa and Narela resettlement sites, 6 November 2000', New Delhi: Housing and Land Right Committee, Habitat International Coalition, 2000.

Houssay-Holzschuch, M., *Le Cap, ville sud-africaine: ville blanche, vies noires*, Paris: L'Harmattan, 1999.

Jaglin, S., 'Villes disloquées? Ségrégations et fragmentation urbaine en Afrique australe', *Annales de Géographie*, no. 619, 2001, pp. 243-65.

Judin, H. and I. Vladislavic, eds., *Architecture, Apartheid and After*, Cape Town: David Philips, 1998.

Kaufman, V., *Mobilité quotidienne et dynamiques urbaines. La question du report modal*, Lausanne : Presses Polytechniques et Universitaires Romanes (coll. Sciences, Technique, Société), 2000.

———, 'La mobilité : une notion clef pour revisiter l'urbain', in *Enjeux de la sociologie urbaine*, ed. M. Bassand, V. Kaufmann and D. Joye, Lausanne: Presses polytechniques et universitaires romanes (coll. Sciences, Technique, Société), 2001, pp. 87-102.

Kundu, A., *In the Name of the Urban Poor: Access to Basic Amenities*, New Delhi: Sage, 1993.

Lefevbre, H., *Le droit à la ville*, Paris: Anthropos, 1968.

Lévy, J., *L'espace légitime. Sur la dimension politique de la fonction géographique*, Paris: Presses de la FNSP, 1994.

Lipietz, A., *Le capital et son espace*, Paris: Maspero, 1977.

Massiah, G. and J.-F. Tribillon, *Villes en développement*, Paris: La Découverte, 1987.

May, N., P. Veltz, J, Landrieu and Th. Spector, eds., *La ville éclatée*, Paris: Editions de l'Aube, 1998.

May, N., Th. Spector and P. Veltz, 'Introduction', in *La ville éclatée*, ed. N. May, P. Veltz, J. Landrieu and Th. Spector, Paris: Editions de l'Aube, 1998, pp. 7-19.

Mazur, R.E. and V.N. Quangule, *Household Dynamics and Mobility of Africans in Cape Town: Appropriate Housing Responses*, Cape Town: Western Cape Community-based Housing Trust, 1995.

Milbert, I., 'Quelles politiques pour lutter contre la pauvreté en Inde?', *Historiens et Géographes,* no. 356, February-March 1997 (L'Inde contemporaine), pp. 363-74.

Mitra, A., *Delhi: Capital City,* New Delhi: Thomson Press, 1970.

Navez-Bouchanine, F., 'Des villes entre fragmentation spatiale et fragmentation sociale: une approche critique de la notion de fragmentation', in *Vocabulaire de la ville*, ed. E. Dorier-Apprill, Paris: Editions du Temps, 2001, pp. 109-18.

Oldfield, S., 'State Restructuring and Urban Transformation in South Africa: A Negotiation of Race, Place and Poverty', doctoral dissertation, University of Minnesota, Faculty of the Graduate School, Minnesota, 2000.

Pinçon, M., E. Préteceille and P. Rendu, *Ségrégation urbaine. Classes sociales et équipements collectifs en région parisienne*, Paris: Anthropos, 1986.

Pinnock, D., 'Ideology and Urban Planning: Blue Prints of the Garrison City', in *The Angry Divide, Social and Economic History of the Western Cape*, ed. W. James, M. Simons, Cape Town: David Philips, 1989, pp. 150-68.

Préteceille, E., 'De la ville divisée à la ville éclatée: questions et catégories de la recherche', in *La ville éclatée*, ed. N. May, P. Veltz, J. Landrieu and Th. Spector, Paris: Editions de l'Aube, 1998, pp. 33-58.

Ramanathan, U., 'Illegality, Instability and Redundancy—The Role of Law in the Lives of Slum Dwellers', paper presented at the workshop on 'Space, Territories and Identity: South Africa—India', Cape Town: Department of Environmental and Geographical Science, University of Cape Town, 12-13 October 2000.

Ravindran, K.T., 'Why Planning Failed?', *Seminar*, no. 445, September 1996, pp. 30-5.

Saff, G., *Changing Cape Town: Urban Dynamics, Policy and Planning during the Political Transition in South Africa*, Lanham: University Press of America, 1998.

SAIRR, *South Africa Survey 2000-2001*, Johannesburg: South African Institute of Race Relations, 2001.

Saunders, C., 'Africans in Cape Town in the Nineteenth Century: An Outline', *Studies in the History of Cape Town*, no. 1, 1979, pp. 15-40.

Schenk, H., *Views on Alleppey: socio-historical and socio-spatial perspectives on an industrial port town in Kerala, South India*, Amsterdam: University of Amsterdam, 1986.

Selod, H. and Y. Zenou, 'Education in South African Cities under and after Apartheid', unpublished paper, 1999.

Sidhu, M., 'Residential profile of the studied areas', *Survey on spatial mobilities in the metropolitan area of Delhi*, working paper no. 2, New Delhi: ORSTOM-IEG, 1995.

———, 'In-depth interviews on environmental factors and residential practices', *Survey on spatial mobilities in the metropolitan area of Delhi*, working paper no. 5, vol. II: *Type of Settlement: Resettlement Colony* - Trilokpuri, New Delhi: ORSTOM-CSH, 1997.

Suri, P., *Urban Poor, Their Housing Needs and Government Response*, Delhi: Har-Anand, 1994.

Swanson, M.W., 'The Sanitation Syndrome: Bubonic Plague and Urban Native Policy in the Cape Colony, 1900-1909', *Journal of African History*, vol. XVIII, no. 3, 1977.

Teppo, A., 'Process of Racial/Spatial Desegregation in a Former Poor White Area', paper presented at the workshop on 'Space, Territories and Identity: South Africa-India', Cape Town, Department of Environmental and Geographical Science, University of Cape Town, 12-13 October 2000.

Whittingdale, J. 'The Development and Location of Industries in Greater Cape Town, 1652-1972', Master's dissertation, Department of Geography, University of Cape Town, Cape Town, 1973.

———, 'The Urban Development of Cape Town, 1850-1910', doctoral dissertation, Department of Geography, University of Cape Town, Cape Town, *c.* 1982 (unfinished manuscript).

CHAPTER 17

# Can Institutional Integration Help Reduce Urban Segregation?

## Urban Policies and the Construction of Local Identities: Some Thoughts on the Johannesburg Experience

CLAIRE BÉNIT

South Africa and India have in common partly institutionalized iniquitous social structures: in the form of caste or *jati* in India, and racial and ethnic classification in South Africa—although apartheid racial classifications have been abolished since 1994, they still explain to a great extent social and spatial dynamics in South Africa. In both societies, attention has focused on an almost endless process of constructing national unity, an exercise in which a powerful state is challenged to create and implement policies to transcend regional, social and historical divisions, in many instances creating permanent and dynamic tension between centrifugal and centripetal forces at the national, regional and local levels.

The metropolis is the perfect laboratory for the study of tension between the individual and the group and the local and the national. In the urban context, the spatial expression of all types of social differences are amplified and made more complex by economic growth typical of big cities. Moreover, cities are places for the creation of new identities, where the interplay between multiple identities becomes possible, because of the anonymity provided in an urban context. In addition, there are specific spatial constraints that impact upon the process of settling in the city,[1] such as the economic opportunities on offer. Finally, metropolitan areas are spaces where problems of urban management are raised with the most acuity, generating issues that often transcend the local level if the metropolis has attained sizeable economic and political importance. The metro-polis then becomes the state's international showcase and a political risk for the latter if all economic and political powers are concentrated therein.

Although I have not undertaken a systematic comparison between South African and Indian metropolises (due to limited experience with the Indian case), this paper draws on research from Johannesburg[2] to establish a preliminary analytical grid that could be applied to Indian cities. This reflection seems to me to be a necessary first step to precede a comparative study. My analysis hinges on an apparently simple question central to the post-apartheid context in South Africa: can institutional integration help reduce urban segregation? In other words, what is the role of public policy in the urban sphere—in particular the restructuring of local government with regard to its powers and functions and above all its scale and boundaries—in the (re)construction of local identities?

Between 1994 and 2000, there was an urgent need to 'reconstruct', 'restructure' and 'integrate' cities divided by apartheid along racial and ethnic lines: political and institutional integration of previously segregated social groups was considered essential to this task. The 1994 and 1997 reforms of local government were built on a powerful three-pronged strategy:

1. The setting up of a metropolitan government, uniting the urban area under a single political authority, on a single tax-base in contrast to the apartheid period's institutionally fragmented system with separately constituted racially designated local authorities.
2. The constitution of 'mixed' municipalities that are narrower in their scale, but also merge former black townships with former white municipalities.[3]
3. A political commitment to undertake urban restructuring through large-scale construction of housing and the adoption of a 'compact city' principle, the exact opposite of the apartheid city, which separated groups through distance, segregation and urban sprawl.

These top-down public policies are in no way the only driving force of social and spatial change in the city. In fact, the limited effect of such policies on society is highlighted by the current disenchantment with public policy and with the ongoing institutional reforms that redefine the role of government in relation to civil society, whose participation is being increasingly solicited in the context of economic and political globalization. However, it is worthwhile to consider the role of public policy, especially in the case of post-apartheid Johannesburg, a city characterized with very high expectations that the city government would assume the role of regulator of society and of the urban environment. The role of local government, and of municipal boundaries in particular, has often become a major issue for residents and residents' groups in South African cities. Debates over boundaries have created a public scene where local identities express and even structure themselves and either take over or oppose the local project foisted on them from the 'top'. In such contexts, public involvement in local politics has mobilized people to engage with the state. In the process, local public intervention reveals and also crystallizes existing—or emerging—local identities.

My approach highlights issues of collective local identities generated through political processes. By 'local identity' I mean elements mobilized in a structured way by a group around a specific local stake. This definition, which merges 'local identity' with 'interest group' (at a given time, in a given context), is obviously very restrictive. But it has the advantage of conceptualizing identity in a fluid and dynamic manner that emphasizes how identities evolve over time and in a range of circumstances. In particular, this approach focuses on the strategic dimensions of identities that are necessarily multiple and whose various facets are mobilized in respect to the issues at stake at a given moment and in a given place.

On the basis of several case studies in Johannesburg, I raise two general questions:

1. Do the new local administrative and political boundaries create new territories (space appropriated by a group that proclaims and affirms its identity in relation to the space)? Are these boundaries abstract limits, empty and invisible, or conversely, do they induce the emergence of new local identities, prompting residents living in the space they circumscribe to mobilize as a group?
2. If these boundaries are other than abstract or empty administrative limits, what is their effect on local identities: do they encourage social integration (the formation of a local identity capable of transcending pre-existing local identities)? Conversely, do they define former local racial and ethnic identities and spaces (in the South African context at least) more rigidly? In other words, have new interest groups emerged in reaction to new forms of public intervention (based on redistribution and reconciliation),

or have protest movements surfaced against the integration symbolized by the new local authorities and their urban policies? This question also raises the problem of the efficiency and legitimacy of public intervention in the contemporary urban setting, in relation to its fight against segregation and inequality in urban spaces.

## MUNICIPAL INTEGRATION AND THE FORMATION OF NEW IDENTITIES AT THE MICRO-LOCAL LEVEL—THE RIVERPARK EXAMPLE

Riverpark is one of the five 'integrated housing' schemes launched in Johannesburg in 1995. These housing schemes were intended for low-income families living in substandard housing, in areas considered as improper or even dangerous for urbanization. These housing programmes are located on vacant public land within the established areas of the city: on 'no-man's' lands that had separated the black and white residential areas in the apartheid era. The 'integrated housing' schemes thus seek to encourage racial and social integration by making available subsidized housing (*de facto* benefiting black families) in or near areas where employment and services are concentrated (mainly occupied by white residents).

Out of five integrated housing schemes, only Riverpark took off in 2001. Objections raised by neighbouring residents, who felt that the construction of a group housing estate on their doorstep would create insecurity and lower real estate values, pulled the plug on the other four. The Riverpark project is located between the old Alexandra township and the middle class district of Lombardy East (formerly classed as a 'white' neighbourhood). In 1995, Riverpark became a part of Johannesburg's richest municipality, the Eastern Municipality.

Without going into great detail, I would like to emphasize three important factors to explain the success of this scheme:

1. The objections initially raised by the white inhabitants of Lombardy East were based on the housing construction norms rather than on the scheme itself. The residents' association appealed to the public authorities to increase the subsidy so that better quality housing and services could be provided. From the moment the Eastern Municipality agreed to increase the public subsidy, opposition to the scheme more or less dissipated.

2. The participatory experience of bringing together white residents of Lombardy East with the black future beneficiaries of the scheme, led to the gradual construction of a common identity. This local multiracial identity is clearly evident in a blueprint drafted jointly by the two groups sharing the new neighbourhood. The layout that was drafted by the residents for Riverpark opens on to Lombardy East, indicating the integration of the two groups spatially: numerous access points and spaces for public use are planned. This integration is proposed specifically 'against' a third type of space, the neighbouring Alexandra township, to which access roads are few and indirect. The two groups of private owners[4] share the same perceptions of violence and poverty common in Alexandra and protestd openly against the construction of throughways from Alexandra (only one is planned in the north-east of the estate), setting up joint neighbourhood watches.
3. This new local identity does not take only a spatial or a social form but is also reflected in the complete awareness of being 'the avant garde of the new South Africa'.[5] This valorization of racial integration is sufficiently unusual (except among artist communities or some elite groups) to be worthy of mention.

What can one conclude from this brief analysis? Three elements stand out:

1. *The existence of an integrated municipality* provided the necessary framework for the constitution of a multiracial interest group. It enabled the establishment of local forums where different groups were able to discuss a common future and compare their respective visions.
2. Social integration between private owners—blacks and whites—was made possible by *public intervention at the highest level.* Since the municipality made full use of the normal subsidy for the construction of quality residential housing, which was acceptable to the white residents, the project was allowed to proceed. Thanks to the commitment and tenacity of the municipal council to construct this symbolic housing estate, negotiations between the two groups were able to transcend opposition, misunderstandings and initial differences. Without a stake in the outcome and without financial means, the joint forum would have been an empty shell.
3. Racial integration in this case created a new local identity—to be

homeowners near the Alexandra township. This new multiracial identity created other forms of exclusion, shifting the demarcating line of the definition of the 'other'—which ceased to be a 'black' and became the 'resident from Alexandra' or 'the squatter'.[6]

## METROPOLITAN POLICY AND THE CONSOLIDATION OF THE DIEPSLOOT SLUM: FROM A POLICY OF DESEGREGATION TO A POLICY OF IMAGE-BUILDING

It is important to study the effects of institutional integration on the processes of desegregation and segregation in Johannesburg on a larger scale: for instance, on the northern fringe of the agglomeration. This suburban space essentially houses middle class whites and is dotted with a few small-sized slums situated on private land. In the early 1990s, the apartheid government relocated most of these slum residents to the Diepsloot area, situated in the extreme north of the metropolitan area. The Northern Municipality, democratically elected in 1995, decided not to expand the Diepsloot area. It is believed that such a step would aggravate urban segregation: Diepsloot is situated at some distance from employment centres, amenities and services. Moreover, extending Diepsloot would have been in complete contradiction with the principle of the 'compact city' at the core of the metropolitan master plan. Finally, and more pragmatically, primary urban facilities in Diepsloot are too costly because of the distance from the rest of the city. The infrastructure is just about adequate for the existing households in Diepsloot; to expand this residential zone would have therefore required considerable public investment.

However, much pressure was exerted on the Northern Municipality to alter its decision. First, several associations of white homeowners made efforts to have the few remaining slum pockets in the northern suburban space shifted to Diepsloot. They formed a powerful lobby, often managing to stall the municipality, with the residents resorting to the use of weapons in order to keep a watch on the slums or to block the roads. Second, private developers also expressed an interest in the extension of Diepsloot (they could easily obtain the provincial housing subsidy and construct at a lower cost for greater profit on this cheap, remote, peripheral piece of land). They joined hands with the associations of homeowners in the area to orchestrate the resettlement of the slum residents. Last, the Eastern Municipality collaborated with one of these developers on a Diepsloot extension project. It hoped to resettle its 'own' squatters there—those who had been living, sometimes for as long as ten years and more, in illegal shacks in Alexandra township.

The Northern Municipality successfully resisted these many pressures. However, the situation changed in December 2000. A new reform of local government abolished the municipal level of urban government in favour of a Metropolitan Council that is elected through a direct vote and in which all powers and resources of local government have been concentrated. The Metropolitan Council decided to relocate the Alexandra squatters to Diepsloot in order to showcase what was its principal visible and symbolic project: the redevelopment of Alexandra township.

The former township of Alexandra is located near the Sandton CBD, the greatest area of economic growth at the metropolitan level, where most major national and international enterprises are concentrated. Alexandra is expected to showcase the 'new South Africa' to foreign investors. Its 'redevelopment' is the principal metropolitan project (it has priority over the development of Soweto) and it also enjoys the special subsidies of the national and provincial governments. In this configuration there is no place for the poorly housed of Alexandra: in consequence, thousands of families have been shunted off to be resettled in Diepsloot, which continues to expand into a greater Johannesburg periphery.

What conclusions can be drawn from these two case studies?

1. The South African urban context in the 1990s was *very specific:* the euphoria after the fall of the apartheid regime, large-scale public interventions, and planned institutional integration brought about a sort of state of grace, which facilitated the redefining of local identities, transcending former racial and ethnic boundaries. Such local identities were forged through an idealized property owner—the ideal urbanite if private developers, the public promoters of homeownership, are to be believed. This urban identity was based on the idea of putting down one's roots, but it may also become the instrument of local conservatism. Although NIMBYism is not new in big metropolises, it enjoys greater legitimacy today: the homeowner, responsible for his environment and anxious to enhance the value of his property, is probably the urban citizen most easily mobilized for local participation in the contemporary context.
2. The Riverpark example shows that the *creation of integrated*

*communities through participation in local development can be a success in the context of focused public intervention* via the development of specific projects and the facilitation of finance. Where it is more wobbly, hesitant or absent—as in the Diepsloot case with the multiplicity of actors and the shifting perspectives of public intervention—participation, on the contrary, can bolster the intransigence of existing segregated groups. I stress here the essential importance of public authorities involvement in participatory processes, as only public authorities can regulate and mediate amongst local groups, and promote a long-term project that transcends immediate and narrow interests.[7] Too often, in particular when there is a lack of public funds, participation and 'governance' are conceived as the withdrawal of public authorities as a specific actor, behind what is called 'civil society'.

3. *An integrated form of local government* (combining privileged and underprivileged spaces under a common municipal jurisdiction) *is a necessary condition for urban social integration*: it provides a public political stage where different social groups can express themselves and confront each other. However, this condition is obviously not sufficient. Johannesburg's new Metropolitan Council appeared to be more preoccupied with international investors (and, therefore, with the city's image as a showroom) than with defining the political parameters of an integrated metropolis.[8] Paradoxically, institutional fragmentation (into municipalities themselves 'integrated') provides a better opportunity to fight segregation and favour the 'compact city' than a government at the metropolitan level. However, more than the form of the local government, the dominant political line changed from a commitment to redistribution to one emphasizing economic growth in the 1995 to 2000 period.

## CONCLUSION: THE POSSIBILITY OF COMPARISON BETWEEN INDIAN AND SOUTH AFRICAN CITIES

The case of Johannesburg poses questions that may underpin a comparative Indian-South African urban research project:

1. What are the most pertinent approaches to conceptualize and analyse the relationship between identity, territory and segregation

in Indian cities? In Johannesburg, focus on public policy is essential because the categories of public intervention (and the definition of groups and territories) greatly affect social realities. It is apparently similar in Indian cities where state intervention figures prominently, in particular through the development of various categories of group housing for different target groups. In Indian cities, however, the absence of deliberate spatial segregation, and conversely, the great spatial overlapping of social and ethnic groups and castes (the institutionalization of segregation at the micro-local level), probably renders this notion less relevant in relation to local identity and social integration. Unless the different ways in which castes and religious conflicts express themselves on the political front happen to constitute the reasons for public intervention in cities.

2. This South African study argues that the government has a critical role to play in segregated cities. What is the role of the Indian government in reconfiguring spatial and social inequalities in Indian cities? Have Indian metropolises adopted a multicultural approach and are they characterized by a policy of positive discrimination towards dominated social groups—as is the case, for instance, in a Californian metropolis such as Los Angeles? In the past, apartheid prevented South African towns from taking this path to reconstruction (instead local 'integrated' governments replaced apartheid period 'racial' municipalities); on the other hand, positive discrimination has become increasingly important in South Africa, although not yet as noticeable in the sphere of urban policy. It would seem that urban governments in India continue to remain highly centralized, whether at the level of the federated state or the urban agglomeration. The absence of noticeable segregation at the agglomeration level in India renders an institutional division of territory along ethnic or caste lines less effective. However, like all international metropolizes, Indian cities show a marked tendency towards decentralization and local participation: is there an expression of groups segregated by caste or religion, or the emergence of specific local issues that recompose these identities? It is on this more subtle scale of city governance that the question of the articulation of identity and the constitution of groups and their territories is raised as an interesting point of comparison between the South African and Indian urban contexts.

## NOTES

1. The housing shortage in Johannesburg in the 1970s, for example, often nullified the division of the townships into 'ethnic' localities, which had been envisaged by the architects of urban apartheid. It reached such proportions that the existing townships soon became densely populated, creating an informal sector of rented accommodation (shacks at the far end of plots) which threw the planned ethnic layout out of gear.
2. Based on my doctoral dissertation, see Claire Bénit, 'La fragmentation à Johannesburg. Recompositions du gouvernement local, mobilités de travail et dynamiques résidentielles dans la ville post-apartheid', doctoral dissertation, University of Poitiers, 2001.
3. This second form of institutional integration disappeared in 2000, under the third major reform of local government in South Africa, abolishing the municipal scale to the advantage of the metropolitan scale of governance in the major cities.
4. The future beneficiaries of Riverpark stress the fact that they are 'owners', and not 'squatters', that they have a 'culture' of payment and responsibility, that in sum, they are from the middle class.
5. The citation is taken from the minutes of the Riverpark Committee meetings, 1995-2000.
6. 'Squatter' is the term used in South Africa to designate a specific type of informal resident: a resident living in a shack (on land that has been invaded and is usually not serviced, nor regularized by public authorities).
7. Local authorities are obviously themselves victim of conflict and vested interests: the 'neutrality' of the mediator-authority is more an ideal than a reality. However, the scale (the one immediately above the locality) of their jurisdiction and the exercise of their power enables them to break free from only local interests. Above all, democratic election confers a unique kind of visibility and legitimacy on them whereby a political line can be clearly defined (whether it is or not the product of interactions with civil society). This political (and budgetary) line is imperative for the mobilization of urban citizens and the crystallization of groups and local identities.
8. In this sense, the thinking that originated with the fall of the apartheid regime, in 1994, on the necessity of constructing a 'compact city', especially by bringing areas of residence and employment closer together, did not lead to developments that matched expectations. The South African evolution appears to correspond to that of Indian cities here, despite different political contexts, as pointed out by M. Houssay-Holzschuch and V. Dupont in their work on Delhi and Cape Town in this volume. In these cases, a concern with the image of the town centre led in part to the resettlement of squatters in the far off periphery and to greater economic fragmentation.

CHAPTER 18

# Urban Transition in South Africa: Negotiating Segregation

SOPHIE OLDFIELD

## INTRODUCTION

Post-apartheid urban transition in South Africa has been understood through an analysis of national state restructuring and through the reworking of policies in which the state is the central player (Azadelzah, 1994; Azadelzah and Padayachee, 1996; Nina, 1992; Nzimande, 1997; Wolpe, 1995). In keeping with international trends, researchers and policy makers have also analysed the local state and the decentralization of service responsibilities to the local scale (see Parnell et al., 2002). Together, research on the national and local state has contributed to a better understanding of the uneven role of the state in urban transition. Restructuring takes place, however, in particular cities and towns and rural areas, and within these areas in specific places and communities. In consequence, state-initiated processes and projects are mediated by the socio-economic and physical conditions in communities and by local political structures, all significantly shaped by apartheid period segregation.

Physical and social landscapes at the neighbourhood scale therefore significantly influence the character of urban transition, whether one focuses on racial desegregation and integration, the distribution of physical infrastructure, or on economic and social inequality. Neighbourhoods and communities are, however, complex. They are not uncontested, homogeneous, seamless entities, but often fragmented and in conflict, perhaps racist and authoritarian, or, at other times, unified and democratic in character. In the context of this political, economic and social complexity, communities and neighbourhoods negotiate segregation in varied and uneven ways that critically effect urban transition. An analysis of the varied progressive and regressive processes of transition, therefore, requires an examination of neighbourhoods and communities and the particular ways in which legacies of segregation are negotiated at this scale.

To situate the complexity of community negotiation of urban segregation on a conceptual and empirical level, this paper introduces two communities in the Cape Town area. The first, Green Point, is largely an informal settlement in a former African township. The second, Elsies River, was a former coloured area, built around seventeen different public housing projects of the apartheid period. Despite common poverty and peripheral locations in the city, particular histories of segregation and manifestation of racial identities distinguish these areas from each other physically, socio-politically and inform the ways in which residents of Green Point and Elsies River relate to their neighbours, community and to the rest of the city. Through these case studies, this paper analyses how residents and community organizations negotiate the legacies of racial classification and segregation, place and location in the city, and their experience of urban transition in the post-apartheid period. It explores urban transition and presents three ways to interpret the negotiation of segregation and urban transition at a neighbourhood scale.

## ANALYSING SEGREGATION

South African urbanization has been understood primarily through a racial lens. The history of the Group Areas Act and the state's brutal forced removal of coloured, African and Indian families into peripheral areas of cities and towns across the country has informed research and analysis of the apartheid and post-apartheid city (see Beinart and Dubow, 1995; Christopher, 1991; Hindson, Byerley and Morris, 1994; Mabin, 1991; Mabin, 1995; Maylam, 1995; Parnell and Mabin, 1995; Robinson, 1996). These analyses richly document and explain the historical processes that shaped the present patterns of residential segregation. The apartheid state's strategies for, and opposition by families and communities to the implementation and perpetuation of residential segregation that these studies uncover, are an important part of the stories that underpin an understanding of urban transition in Green Point and Elsies River. Green Point's history in particular builds on the insecurity and illegality of migration between rural homelands and urban townships. In Elsies River, residents' experiences of segregation highlight expropriation of land by the state, dispossession from farmsteads, small holdings and shacks, and installation as tenants in state-provided, racially segregated public housing schemes.

Yet, such histories of segregation are partial, informing representations of urban residential segregation in particular. The impact of segregation remains a complex product of economic, social and political processes built on the foundation of residential separation between races. In this paper, I draw on an exploration of segregation that considers structural legacies evident in the racially skewed urban residential environment, but also the agency that individuals, families and neighbourhoods found to confront these structural constraints in order to create economic livelihoods and make social choices. Whereas residential segregation presents a particular spatial demarcation of the South African city, in the creation of economic and social livelihoods, urban space is used and produced in numerous different ways. Race does persist as a social and spatial marker, but its meanings and residents' identities are more complex. These identities are forged through experience in the city (and elsewhere), through interaction with the state for resources, and through participation in community organizations that conform to neighbourhood boundaries, but are also broader in scale (forged through political parties and religious commitments, for instance). Although a broad-brush pattern of racial segregation continues to demarcate the city, the social and economic landscape has shifted. On the basis of an examination of patterns of residential, economic and social segregation, these changes are studied in the ways that Group Area segregation hierarchies have been fragmented and disrupted in Green Point and Elsies River.

Post-apartheid patterns of economic inequality, for instance, broadly mirror apartheid period racial segregation: people previously classified white tend to be better off than those people formerly labelled as African, and differentiation between neighbourhoods has increased. But, at a finer level, economic polarization has increased within race groups and neighbourhoods, not only since 1994 but during the late apartheid period as well (Crankshaw, 1997; Lohnert et al., 1998; Nattrass and Seekings, 2001). An investigation of such polarization at the micro-level, highlights the mechanisms and spatial strategies that urban residents use to negotiate economic opportunities. Experiences of economic segregation are evident in patterns of access to jobs and the types of places in which informal livelihoods are created. Although structural, the spatial logic of economic processes is not fixed, but generated by whom a person knows, where he or she can buy goods, and the locations from which he or she can sell his materials. Patterns of economic segregation thus both reinforce and disrupt a racial reading of the South African city. An investigation of social segregation, in contrast, presents other interpretations and representations of urban space and agency. Individuals, families and communities build their patterns of socialization around networks connected to culture, religious practice and family traditions. The spatiality of these choices is intimately linked to the diverse urban histories that structure the post-apartheid urban context.

Economic and social networks share a common relational character, constructed around a complex mix of individual and family agency, and the structural and locational constraints that define opportunities in different areas of the city. The spatiality of segregation thus proves complex, multi-layered, and multi-scaled. To explore the ways in which urban histories as well as economic and social processes differentiate the negotiation of urban segregation, I turn to the experience of segregation in Cape Town, in particular in the communities of Green Point and Elsies River, respectively.[1]

## SEGREGATION IN CAPE TOWN

Although the distribution of residences by race in Cape Town does not mirror Group Areas segregation exactly, the city has a racial legacy. Areas formerly classified white occupy a large part of urban land running from the downtown area to the south and the east. A block of formerly coloured neighbourhoods is situated in the geographical centre of the metropolis, with African neighbourhoods located in a diagonal corridor through the middle of this area. Urbanization in Cape Town has been clearly orchestrated by this Group Area configuration. These patterns have been shaped by apartheid segregation and the particular time periods in which different groups of residents moved into the areas that now constitute the Cape Metropolitan Area (CMA). In the section of Cape Town that includes Green Point and Elsies River—the Tygerberg Administration,[2] this temporal context frames urbanization patterns and the spatial development of segregation (Figure 18.1).

A gradual but steady increase in the number of white residents from the 1960s intensified in the 1970s with the development of suburban areas in the City's northern sections. In a similar pattern, but with more fluctuations, the coloured population in the area increased steadily, with each spike on the graph in Figure 18.1 indicating the successive

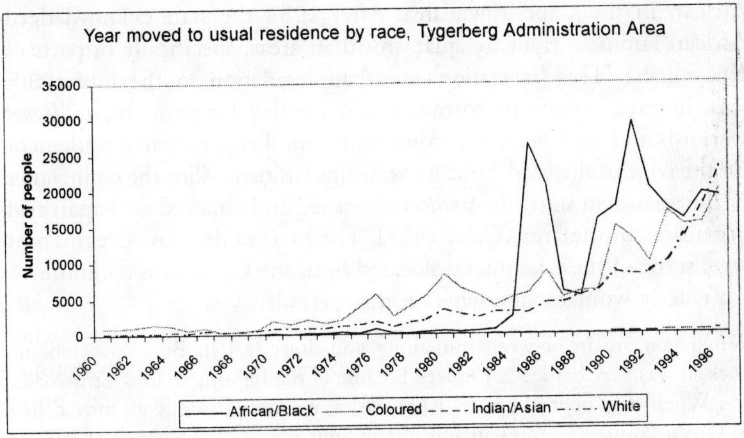


*Source*: Census 1996.

FIGURE 18.1: URBANIZATION BY RACE IN THE TYGERBERG ADMINISTRATION AREA, 1960-96.

building of coloured group areas, initiated with Elsies River in late 1976, continuing with Belhar in 1980-2, and with Delft in 1987 and 1988 at the tail end of the apartheid regime's control.

African population patterns in the Tygerberg area reflect the cessation in 1986 of the enforcement of influx control laws that prohibited African residence in the City. The Khayelitsha township's development in 1984 and 1985 marked the first major move of African residents into Khayelitsha's areas such as Green Point, now under the Tygerberg Administration's jurisdiction. The second peak in 1992 reflects a general relaxation of apartheid laws and an increase in the migration of new residents from the rural areas of the Eastern Cape to the Cape Metropolitan Area. These new residents are found predominantly in this area because its jurisdiction was relatively less densely populated than the older African townships closer to the centre of the metropolitan area.

## Green Point: A Former 'African' Group Area

With just over 2,000 resident families, Green Point stands on the edge of Khayelitsha, the largest and newest township in the Cape Metropolitan Area. The community's history entwines with the legal demarcation of Khayelitsha as a new township for people classified

African in the Cape Town area. After 1984 the state acknowledged African families' 'right to squat' in urban areas, specifically in parts of Khayelitsha. This 'relaxation' in urban regulation in the mid-1980s was, in part, a response to the specific conflict between the *witdoeke*[3] warlords and the Crossroads community, an illegal informal settlement on the edge of the legal African townships (*iKapa*). With the connivance of the apartheid state, the *witdoeke* harassed and attacked anti-apartheid organizers in the area (Cole, 1987). The first residents of Green Point were some of these families dislocated from the Crossroads community. An elderly woman comments on that period:

> When you are in between something you don't feel it. But, now, looking back, it was very hard. . . . I moved because of the fighting in Old Crossroads. . . . When they opened up . . . Khayelitsha, we moved in . . . we moved first to Green Point. . . . You win and lose in your life. (G.M., 4 April 1999)[4]

Allocated land on the edge of Khayelitsha, Green Point was named after the green plastic sheeting donated by the government for shelters.

Some Green Point families moved to the area in the 1990s directly from rural areas or from other parts of the Cape Metropolitan Area. Until the early 1990s, settlement in Green Point was regulated directly by the Lingelethu West Administration, the black local authority in the area. Many of Green Point's present residents are not new migrants from rural areas. They have a longer history in the city. Their residential patterns reflect the areas open or accessible to them when they arrived in Cape Town. In particular, these patterns also build on links with family or work opportunities in Cape Town. For the majority, residential experiences in the Cape Town area were delimited by group area boundaries, with many families located in former African areas. A Green Point pensioner, for example, came to Cape Town in 1958 from the Transkei. She negotiated urban pass laws and the restrictions on her mobility for most of the past forty years, her residential experience reduced in consequence to insecurity, shared living quarters and struggle. She explained how she negotiated the Group area legal web as a woman and a legal urban resident:

> Women were not allowed out without a permit and permits were not issued where I stayed in the Transkei . . . only in Queenstown [a town in the Eastern Cape]. I went [eventually] to Cape Town with a work permit. When I arrived in Cape Town, I stayed with my grandmother who provided a place and then with my mother in Kensington [a racially mixed neighbourhood prior to the enforcement of its group area coloured classification]. Whenever I was out the house I had to carry my pass, a blank piece of paper with my name—

this was the 1st type of pass issued. I was the only one in the household who had it.

Later as a married woman, her residence was technically and legally tied to her husband and his work. Although these laws were applied strictly, she negotiated around their limitations time and time again. She added:

Then I spent 3 years in Nyanga West and from there went to Langa for 3 years in Washington [Street]. We stayed in the township because we were not allowed in the hostel [where my husband was]. If you wanted to visit the hostel you needed a permit and you had to be there at a specific time. If you were there at the wrong time you were arrested. I was working in a butcher in Ndabeni then. [Later] I stayed in Claremont at my work place [as a cleaner] for 15 years, then in Langa for 10 years—in a flat where my husband didn't pay rent because of his work. [I left my husband and] I moved to Khayelitsha in 1990. I first stayed in Mkhaya while my youngest son built a house in Site C. I then moved in with him and stayed with him for 3 years. In 1992 I moved to Green Point. (E.J., 23 March 1999)

Her migration around the city reflects the strictures of changing urban settlement policies and her own agency to negotiate these processes, well-documented trials of negotiating draconian legislation that did not permit a normal life in the city for African families (Lee, 1999; Posel, 1991a) (see Table 18.1).

Although residents have found a place to live in the Green Point area, however inadequate their homes may be, their economic struggles continue. Due to limited financial resources coupled with low levels of schooling, many people depend on informal sector activities to eke out a living in the city. A younger entrepreneur described his various strategies to earn an income:

None of us have a formal job. I started my business with chickens. I added and continued with it when I was working at Bolt [a factory] in Epping. I added cases of beer, two bottles of brandy, and two cartons of cigarettes. I continued but in the long run there was new business in Green Point and the competition was intense. I had to drop the liquor and only continue with the chickens. I had a part time job for four weeks where I saved R400, so I used this money to start selling clothes. But it's a means of survival only, and I'm still suffering. I also learnt about fixing shoes when I saw another person fixing shoes. I copied it from him and now I'm also selling shoes part time. . . . I do want a [formal] job but it's not easy to wake up in the morning to search for work because you need money to buy a [train or taxi] ticket. (N.W., 8 April 1999)

TABLE 18.1: LOCATION AND FORMER RACIAL CLASSIFICATION OF GREEN POINT FAMILIES' RESIDENCES

| Locations: Previous Residences | Group Area Classification |
|---|---|
| Site C: Khayelitsha | *African* |
| Macassar: Khayelitsha | *African* |
| Section 1: Khayelitsha | *African* |
| Harare: Khayelitsha | *African* |
| Site B: Khayelitsha | *African* |
| Old Crossroads | *African* |
| Langa | *African* |
| Gugulethu | *African* |
| Nyanga | *African* |
| Mfuleni | *African* |
| KTC | *African* |
| Cala, Transkei | *African 'Homeland'* |
| Atlantis | *Coloured* |
| Steenberg | *Coloured* |
| Kensington | *Coloured* |
| Belhar | *Coloured* |
| Rylands | *Indian* |
| Claremont | *White* |

Most residents are unemployed (only 24 per cent have paid employment, Census 1996). Those who have found work, tend to have multiple jobs servicing the neighbourhood or selling in other areas of Khayelitsha to make ends meet. Some of the fortunate residents have service jobs at the airport or in Epping, an industrial area 15 km away.

The location of work opportunities for Green Point residents in Capte Town forms a distinctive pattern. They work as cleaners and gardeners in former white and coloured areas predominantly, although many informal sector jobs, especially door-to-door sales and *spaza* (informal shops) activities, are available in areas of Khayelitsha and in the Green Point area itself. Formal sector economic jobs tend to be in industrial areas, which previously served as a buffer between segregated neighbourhoods, or in Mitchell's Plain, a large former-coloured township, where a large shopping centre offers some job opportunities. Since commercial activities were prohibited in African areas until the late 1980s, the lack of formal job opportunities in the Green Point vicinity is not surprising. To date, larger businesses perceive locating in African townships as high risk[5] (see Table 18.2).

In contrast, Green Point residents' social activities fall within the boundaries of former African areas. Their families' choice of church, and mosque in one instance, and the locations of their family and friends whom they visit relatively frequently all fall within areas of the city classified African under the Group Areas laws (see Table 18.3).

After the repeal of Group Areas laws in 1991 (Saff, 1994), African families could move around more freely. By this point, however, access to housing in better-situated or serviced areas had become extremely costly (for instance, areas in proximity to the Green Point community but with formal housing). With work in industrial and former white suburbs and with homes and social lives in townships, economic and social patterns illustrate the complex spatiality of segregation and its persistence despite the repeal of legislation mandating residential segregation.

TABLE 18.2: LOCATION AND FORMER RACIAL CLASSIFICATION OF GREEN POINT RESIDENTS' EMPLOYMENT

| Locations: Employment | Group Area Classification |
|---|---|
| Green Point | *African* |
| Town 2: Khayelitsha | *African* |
| Macassar: Khayelitsha | *African* |
| Gatesville | *Coloured* |
| Site B: Khayelitsha | *African* |
| Parkwood | *Coloured* |
| Mitchell's Plain | *Coloured* |
| Salt River | *Mixed and industrial* |
| Woodstock | *Mixed and industrial* |
| Ndabeni | *Industrial* |
| Epping Industria | *Industrial* |
| Claremont | *White* |
| Pinelands | *White* |
| Gardens | *White* |
| Wynberg | *White* |
| Bellville CBD | *White* |

TABLE 18.3: LOCATION AND FORMER RACIAL CLASSIFICATION OF GREEN POINT RESIDENTS' SOCIAL ACTIVITIES

| Locations: Social Activities | Group Area Classification |
|---|---|
| Green Point | *African* |
| Section F: Khayelitsha | *African* |
| Site B: Khayelitsha | *African* |
| Site C: Khayelitsha | *African* |
| Town 2: Khayelitsha | *African* |
| Macassar: Khayelitsha | *African* |
| Section 1: Khayelitsha | *African* |
| Ikwezi Park: Khayelitsha | *African* |
| Section H: Khayelitsha | *African* |
| Ilita Park: Khayelitsha | *African* |
| Harare: Khayelitsha | *African* |
| Langa | *African* |
| Old Crossroads | *African* |
| Gugulethu | *African* |
| Gatesville | *Coloured* |
| Bishop Lavis | *Coloured* |
| Mannenberg | *Coloured* |

## Elsies River: A Former 'Coloured' Group Area

Images of the post-apartheid city bring to the fore informal settlements such as Green Point. Yet, a large proportion of the population of Cape Town in older 'coloured' communities in particular had a longer history and experience of urbanization that introduces a different type of narrative and another set of challenges to transformation of urban segregation. In Elsies River, the majority of residents are tenants in state-constructed rental housing. Grey blocks of flats four up and four across dominate the landscape of the Elsies River area, shaping the open spaces and wide avenues of the apartheid period. Residents of Elsies River have repeatedly fought with the state over land and housing provision. Unlike many areas in South African cities classified coloured to which residents were relocated under the apartheid system, large numbers of residents of Elsies River had a long history in the area. The majority of residents were not shifted from other areas, but had their roots in Elsies River even before it was proclaimed as a coloured area. This pre-group area connection is important to many families. As one middle-aged man recalled: 'My grandparents came [to Elsies River] because they could afford it, they all owned large tracts of land. People didn't come here to squat, they bought here because they could afford it when they moved from the rural areas' (D.H., 20 July 1999). At that time, Elsies was a rural outpost of the city with scattered farms, small communities of squatters and dirt roads and bush.

The physical and social structure of the community changed immeasurably following the construction of flats as public housing for coloureds in the early 1970s. The history that underlies these patterns builds on repeated land expropriations, congruent with the proclamation and establishment of Elsies River as a coloured area. A resident recalled these bitter memories:

> We used to live behind the old police station, they call it Riverton now. We had to move because the Council took our land. . . . After our land was taken we first stayed on somebody's land in a *pondok* [shack]. But then Council bought this land too—this was in the period when the flats were built. (C.B., 15 July 1999)

The expropriation of land applied to landowners, squatters, renters, i.e. to all the coloured residents of Elsies River regardless of their community status, wealth or social standing. Families failing to 'pass' as coloured were shifted to African townships to the south.

During the building period, residents were moved involuntarily into transit camps, unless they had the money to relocate elsewhere within the confines of the Group Areas laws. From residents' perspective, the process was as follows:

> The Council developed Milton Park as a transit camp for us. Everybody was moved there while the flat building was completed. . . . They said we had to move because our area was *underdeveloped*. They said taking us to the transit camp was part of *developing* us. . . . People were screened there in the transit camp. You had to prove that you could pay and also that you could maintain your place. . . . .If you saw the conditions where we stayed before the transit camp, they were far better, but we had to *improve* ourselves first. (C.B., 15 July 1999)

Schemes of flats and wide, tarred roads physically replaced the open land, squatting areas, and older stone houses and farmsteads. This reconfiguring generated new antagonistic relations between residents and the then Divisional Council. Families not originally based in Elsies River moved to the area in the 1970s and 1980s from other coloured areas such as Athlone and Hanover Park, and from older inner city areas and the centre of Cape Town. The latter areas of the city were proclaimed white and this led to forced removal, to the Elsies River area and to accommodation in state built flats (see Table 18.4).

The implementation of Group Areas under the guise of development imprinted the label 'coloured' on residents. At the same time, the process of removal to flats exacerbated the distinctions between tenants and homeowners in the area. Even within flats, the Council deemed some families as 'economic tenants' able to pay for services, and other families as 'sub-economic tenants' with fewer resources. The former 'economic' group was shifted to flats with hot water geysers. Today, this socio-economic stigma less clearly demarcates flat areas of Elsies River internally as poverty and unemployment are common denominators in all flat areas, but all 'flats' people are aware of the distinctions between themselves and homeowners in the area.

For many residents, the original transition from shacks to flats was a positive one with, for instance, the availability and provision of running water, even hot water for those in the 'economic' group. At the same time, living in flats required all sorts of new monetary obligations such as payments for rental, services and rates. Today, many

TABLE 18.4: LOCATION AND FORMER RACIAL CLASSIFICATION OF ELSIES RIVER FAMILIES' RESIDENCES

| Locations: Previous Residences | Group Area Classification |
|---|---|
| Elsies River | *Coloured* |
| Adriaanse Estate (Elsies River) | *Coloured* |
| Belvenie (Elsies River) | *Coloured* |
| Leonsdale (Elsies River) | *Coloured* |
| Avonwood (Elsies River) | *Coloured* |
| Eureka (Elsies River) | *Coloured* |
| Uitsig | *Coloured* |
| Matroosfontein | *Coloured* |
| Athlone | *Coloured* |
| Atlantis | *Coloured* |
| Ravensmead | *Coloured* |
| Bishop Lavis | *Coloured* |
| Hanover Park | *Coloured* |
| Salt River | *Mixed and industrial* |
| Epping Forest | *White* |
| Vasco | *White* |
| Parow | *White* |
| Observatory | *White* |
| Sea Point | *White* |

residents fear eviction from their flats because of persistent and escalating rates arrears. Arrears stem both from unemployment and poverty, and from boycotts initiated as an anti-apartheid strategy to protest under-servicing and the racist policies and practices of the Divisional Council in the past (J.C., personal communication, August 1999).

Employment rates in many sections of Elsies River are low, in the worst-off areas they parallel rates in Green Point.[6] Elsies River residents' search for work has a particular spatial pattern, evident in where they have found employment. The location of jobs (formal and informal) and shopping activities for residents of Elsies River is concentrated in an area spanning the immediate suburbs to the east and west of and including the Elsies River area. Few exceptions include a particular shopping centre in Mitchell's Plain (the Mitchell's Plain Town Centre) and areas closer to the Cape Town centre where some residents once lived. This east-west concentration reflects, in part, Voortrekker Road, the main arterial road dividing Elsies River from its neighbouring white areas of Parow and Goodwood. Many shops, small electronic businesses and factories are located along this road (see Table 18.5).

In contrast, Elsies River residents attend church and mosque, and visit family and friends in areas other than where they work. Social activities are concentrated almost exclusively in formerly segregated

TABLE 18.5: LOCATION AND FORMER RACIAL CLASSIFICATION OF GREEN POINT RESIDENTS' EMPLOYMENT

| Locations: Employment | Group Area Classification |
|---|---|
| Elsies River | *Coloured* |
| Adriaanse Estate (Elsies River) | *Coloured* |
| Beacon Valley | *Coloured* |
| Belhar | *Coloured* |
| Uitsig | *Coloured* |
| Salt River | *Mixed and industrial* |
| Kalk Bay | *Coloured and White* |
| Ndabeni | *Industrial* |
| Epping Industria | *Industrial* |
| Parow Industria | *Industrial* |
| Parow | *White* |
| Epping Forest | *White* |
| Bellville CBD | *White* |
| Maitland | *White* |
| Seapoint | *White* |

TABLE 18.6: LOCATION AND FORMER RACIAL CLASSIFICATION OF GREEN POINT RESIDENTS' SOCIAL ACTIVITIES

| Locations: Social Activities | Group Area Classification |
|---|---|
| Elsies River | *Coloured* |
| Eureka (Elsies River) | *Coloured* |
| Clarkes Estate (Elsies River) | *Coloured* |
| Belvenie (Elsies River) | *Coloured* |
| Adriaanse Estate (Elsies River) | *Coloured* |
| Salberau (Elsies River) | *Coloured* |
| Avonwood (Elsies River) | *Coloured* |
| Nooitgedacht | *Coloured* |
| Mitchell's Plain | *Coloured* |
| Heideveld | *Coloured* |
| Delft | *Coloured* |
| Eersterivier | *Coloured* |
| Bishop Lavis | *Coloured* |
| Belhar | *Coloured* |
| Ravensmead | *Coloured* |
| Epping Forest | *White* |
| Constantia | *White* |
| Nyanga[7] | *African* |
| Old Crossroads | *African* |

coloured areas. As housing was constructed for coloured families in areas south of Elsies River, many of the residents moved to these areas like Belhar, Ravensmead, Delft (north), and to Mitchell's Plain in particular. Since opportunities for housing in Elsies River itself are limited, moving out of the area was often the only solution to the housing problem. As in Green Point, social patterns and choices reflect old group area boundaries and the urban development of coloured communities, rather than economic choices that are either structurally determined by the location of jobs or by the availability of shopping facilities. In addition, social and economic decisions are also constrained and shaped by transport possibilities and costs, factors that tend to affect residents of flats more than homeowners (see Table 18.6).

## CONCLUSION

Ten years into the post-apartheid period, both Elsies River and Green Point illustrate the persistence of legacies of segregation and the distinct spatial patterns that different forms of segregation assume. The narratives of Green Point and Elsies River introduce the complexities underpinning urban transition. On the level of residential segregation, the physical landscapes of flats and informal settlement persist: Elsies River remains a coloured, low-income suburb with increasing unemployment rates and Green Point, for the majority, endures without basic services and amenities. Both areas share poverty with high unemployment rates and residents' constant search for work in other parts of the Cape Metropolitan Area. But, varying tenures, experiences in the city as well as built and social environments have shaped community structures and agency that allow residents individually and collectively to link to and work in different ways inside and outside of their neighbourhoods. Elsies River and Green Point communities' different experiences in the city have been informed in part by the ways in which inequalities in economic and social opportunities and the urban physical environment were constructed around race in the apartheid period. But these complexities also organize around particular local dynamics that tie individuals and families into broader economic and social networks in the city.

Race thus persists as an important social marker, but racial identities are malleable and disrupted by the particularities of place and the ways in which individuals, families and communities interact with the city, and economic, social and political realities. Racial segregation has left indelible marks on the landscape and built environment, social structures, material conditions, and on the ways in which the state and communities work together. At the same time, however, the post-apartheid city is more complicated and diverse than the delineation of apartheid segregation indicates. Identities do not configure around race alone. Rather, identities are fragmented and multiple, citizens have connections across the city and beyond the city in rural and metropolitan areas in other parts of the country. Citizens organize around their homes and neighbourhoods (the spatial framework of segregation), but also around the church and the mosque and around political affiliation and ideology. The spatiality of these fragmented and multiple urban identities thus perpetuate and rupture the apartheid racial frame.

## NOTES

1. The case studies were based on in-depth interviews with approximately forty resident households and community leaders in each area between 1999 and 2001. The analysis of secondary sources included a range of documents from state institutions and historical archives on each area.

2. From 1996 to 2000 the Cape Metropolitan Area was subdivided into six local municipalities. The 'City of Tygerberg' was one of these structures. With the final restructuring of local government in 2000, these structures were merged into one metropolitan level government. The City of Tygerberg was renamed the 'Tygerberg Administration' in this process.
3. *Witdoeke* means 'white headscarves' and refers to a section of the community collaborating with the police against the movement for the right to live in Crossroads specifically and the City in general.
4. Residents' comments from interviews are labelled with initials to retain anonymity. Full names are used in the case of comments from public officials.
5. Shoprite Checkers, a chain supermarket, moved into a new shopping centre in Khayelitsha in the mid-1990s. It was, however, the first significant retail or commercial venture to take this step (Barnes, 1998).
6. In Adriaanse Estate, one of the worst hit, less than 25 per cent of the residents are employed. Even in the best off areas, an upper limit of 45 per cent of the residents have jobs.
7. The residents with social links to Nyanga and Old Crossroads, African Group Areas, have family in these locations. These residents explained that they 'passed' as 'coloured' to get access to public housing in Elsies River in the period when Group Areas was implemented.

ACKNOWLEDGEMENTS

Funding for this research was generously provided by the Department of Geography, University of Minnesota and the University Research Committee, University of Cape Town.

REFERENCES

Adelzadeh, A., 'From the RDP to GEAR: The Gradual Embracing of Neo-Liberalism in Economic Policy', *Transformation*, 1996, pp. 66-95.

Adelzadeh, A. and V. Padayachee, 'The RDP White Paper: Reconstruction of a Development Vision?', *Transformation*, vol. 25, 1994, pp. 1-18.

Barnes, N., 'Do Retail Centres Enhance Township Economic Development? Lessons from Khayelitsha, Cape Town', Cape Town: Urban Problems Research Unit, 1998.

Beinart, W. and S. Dubow, *Segregation and Apartheid in Twentieth-Century South Africa*, London: Routledge, 1995.

Christopher, A.J., 'Changing Patterns of Group-area Proclamations in South Africa, 1950-1989', *Political Geography Quarterly*, vol. 10, 1991, pp. 240-53.

Cole, J., *Crossroads: The Politics of Reform and Repression. 1976-1986.* Johannesburg: Raven Press, 1987.

Crankshaw, O. *Race, Class and the Changing Division of Labour Under Apartheid,* London: Routledge, 1997.

Hindson, D., M. Byerley and M. Morris, 'From Violence to Reconstruction: The Making, Disintegration and Remaking of an Apartheid City', *Antipode*, vol. 26, 1994, pp. 323-50.

Lee, R., 'African Women, Urban Areas and the Development of the Apartheid State: The Case of Cape Town', unpublished Masters thesis, Department of History, Oxford University, Oxford, 1999.

Lohnert, B., S. Oldfield and S. Parnell, 'Post-apartheid Social Polarizations: The Creation of Sub-urban Identities in Cape Town', *South African Geographical Journal,* vol. 80, no. 2, 1998, pp. 86-92.

Mabin, A., 'The Dynamics of Urbanization Since 1960', in *Apartheid City in Transition*, ed. M. Swilling, R. Humphries and K. Shubane, Cape Town: Oxford University Press, 1991, pp. 33-47.

Maylam, P., 'Explaining the Apartheid City: 20 Years of South African Urban Historiography', *Journal of Southern African Studies*, vol. 21, 1995, pp. 19-38.

Nattrass, N. and J. Seekings, 'Democracy and Distribution in Highly Unequal Economies: The Case of South Africa', *Journal of Modern African Studies*, vol. 39, no. 3, 2001, pp. 471-98.

Nina, D., 'Beyond the Frontier: Civil Society Revisited', *Transformation*, vol. 17, 1992, pp. 61-73.

Nzimande, B., 'Socialism is as Relevant as Ever', *The African Communist*, 1997, pp. 5-14.

Parnell, S. and A. Mabin, 'Rethinking Urban South Africa', *Journal of Southern African Studies*, vol. 21, 1995, pp. 39-61.

Parnell, S. et al., *Democratising Local Government: The South African Experiment*, Cape Town: University of Cape Town Press, 2002.

Posel, D., 'Curbing African Urbanization in the 1950s and 1960s', in *Apartheid City in Transition*, ed. M. Swilling, R. Humphries and K. Shubane, Cape Town: Oxford University Press, 1991, pp. 19-32.

Republic of South Africa, Statistics South Africa, Census (1996).

Robinson, J., *The Power of Apartheid: State, Power and Space in South African Cities*, Oxford: Butterworth Heineman, 1999.

Saff, G., 'The Changing Face of the South African City: From Urban Apartheid to the Deracialization of Space', *International Journal of Urban and Regional Research*, vol. 18, 1994, pp. 377-91.

Wolpe, H., 'The Uneven Transition From Apartheid in South Africa', *Transformation*, 1995, pp. 88-9.

# Contributors

JANE BATTERSBY is a Postdoctoral Research Fellow in the Department of Environmental and Geographical Science, University of Cape Town. Her research interests centre on the intersection of space, place and identity within the post-apartheid context.

SIMON BEKKER is a sociologist who has undertaken research in the fields of collective identities and urban sociology. He is Professor of Sociology at the University of Stellenbosch. He has co-edited *Shifting African Identities*, vol. 2, in the series Identity ? Theory, Politics, History (Pretoria: Human Sciences Research Council, 2001).

CLAIRE BÉNIT is a Senior Lecturer in Geography and Town Planning, University of Aix-Marseille (France). She is currently a Postdoctoral Fellow at the University of the Witwatersrand (Johannesburg). She has been doing research in Johannesburg and Los Angeles; her main research interests are urban fragmentation, local government and community participation.

A.J. CHRISTOPHER is Professor Emeritus of Geography at the Nelson Mandela Metropolitan University in Port Elizabeth, South Africa. He has published extensively in the fields of historical and political geography, more particularly with reference to southern Africa, the impact of British colonialism on the former British Empire and the changing world political map.

SURANJAN DAS is the Pro-Vice-Chancellor for Academic Affairs, University of Calcutta, Director of Netaji Institute for Asian Studies, Kolkata, and member of the University Grants Commission, India. His publications include *Communal Riots in Bengal 1905-1947* (New Delhi: Oxford University Press, 1993), *The Goondas: Towards a Reconstruction of the Calcutta Underworld* (jointly with J.K. Ray) (Calcutta: Firma-KLM, 1996), and *Kashmir and Sindh: Nation-Building, Ethnicity and Regional Politics in South Asia* (Calcutta: K.P. Bagchi, 2001).

VÉRONIQUE DUPONT is a Senior Research Fellow in Economic-Demography from the (French) Institute of Research for Development (IRD, Paris), and presently Director of the Centre de Sciences Humaines in New Delhi. She is also an associated member of the (French) Centre for Indian and South Asian Studies (CEIAS, Paris). She has carried out research on population mobility and the urbanization process in Gujarat and the Delhi region. Her publications include *Delhi: Urban Space and Human Destinies*, edited with Emma Tarlo and Denis Vidal (Delhi: Manohar-CSH, 2000).

REHANA EBR.-VALLY completed her Ph.D. at the Sorbonne in Paris and is in the Anthropology Department at the University of the Witwatersrand. Her current research is on examining rituals and performances, gender and sexuality, as well as relations and politics between settled 'Indians' and recently arrived Indians and Afro-Indian relations in Mayfair, Johannesburg. She has authored *Kala Pani, Colour and Caste in South Africa* (Cape Town: Kwela Books, 2001).

FRANÇOIS-XAVIER FAUVELLE-AYMAR is a researcher in African history at the French National Center for Scientific Research (Institut d'Etudes Africaines, Aix-en-Provence, France). He has written and co-edited several books on the history and historiography of Africa, such as *L'Afrique de Cheikh Anta Diop* (Paris: Karthala, 1996), and *L'invention du Hottentot: Histoire du regard occidental sur les Khoisan* (Paris: Sorbonne, 2002).

PHILIPPE GERVAIS-LAMBONY, Professor of Geography at the University of Paris X, Director of GECKO (research centre of comparative Geography), is a specialist in the urban geography of African cities. He has conducted research in West Africa (Togo) and in Southern Africa (Zimbabwe and South Africa). His main research interest is the relation between territorial organisation and identity construction. His most recent book is *Territoires citadins, 4 villes africaines* (Paris: Belin, 2003).

PHILIPPE GUILLAUME completed a Ph.D. in Geography on Urban Exclusion in post-apartheid Johannesburg (published as *Johannesburg - Géographies de l'exclusion*, Paris: Karthala, 2001). He was the Research Director of the French Institute of South Africa, Johannesburg (2001-3). At present, he is a journalist and test rider for a French motorbike magazine.

MYRIAM HOUSSAY-HOLZSCHUCH is a Senior Lecturer of the Department of Geography, École Normale Supérieure Lettres et Sciences Humaines, Lyon, France. Her research expertise includes social and cultural geography in cities of the South (particularly in South Africa), segregation, public spaces and violence. She currently heads 'A Geography of Public Spaces in Intermediary Countries (China, Mexico, South Africa, South Korea, Turkey)' research project, funded by the French Ministry for Research.

M.A. KALAM is Professor of Anthropology at the University of Madras, Chennai, India. He has been Visiting Professor at the University of Paris X, Nanterre, France; Rockefeller Resident Fellow, Duke University, USA; Human Rights Fellow, Kennedy School of Government, Harvard University, USA; and Commonwealth Academic Staff Fellow at the London School of Economics. He has carried out many sponsored projects and published extensively on tribes, forest management, industrial districts as well as the Indian diaspora.

ATIYA HABEEB KIDWAI is Professor and Co-ordinator UGC Centre for Advanced Studies at the Centre for the Study of Regional Development, Jawaharlal Nehru University, New Delhi, India. She has a professional degree in regional planning from I.I.T. Kharagpur and a Ph.D. from Jawaharlal Nehru University. Her academic interests are varied and she has published on themes in colonial urban history, family history, development and displacement, geography of underdevelopment, port cities and the impacts of liberalization on urban processes.

FRÉDÉRIC LANDY, Associate Professor of Geography at the University of Paris X (GECKO), works on Indian rural issues, food policy and identities. He has co-edited *Globalization and Local Development in India. Examining the Spatial Dimension* (Delhi: Manohar-CSH, 2004) and co-authored *Agriculture and Food in India* (Manohar, forthcoming).

ANNE LEILDÉ is a sociologist who has done extensive qualitative field research in Francophone Africa and South Africa. She is completing a Ph.D. at Stellenbosch University on changing identities in Cape Town.

BRIJ MAHARAJ is a Professor of Geography at the University of KwaZulu-Natal. His primary interest is in urban politics and his research has focused on the transactional relations between the state, municipality and local community over urban geographical organization. His more recent work has focused on the politics of migration in South Africa. He has published in various internationally renowned journals.

HÉLÈNE MAINET-VALLEIX is Associate Professor, Department of Geography, CERAMAC, University of Clermont-Ferrand (France). She works on the social and cultural aspects of urban geography and urban planning. She has authored *Durban, les Indiens, leurs territoires, leur identité* (Paris: IFAS-Karthala, 2002).

SOPHIE OLDFIELD, Senior Lecturer in the Department of Environmental and Geographical Science at the University of Cape Town, was trained as a geographer at Syracuse University and at the University of Minnesota in the United States. She has published on developmental local government, the South African state in transition and on issues of urban and community development.

CHARLES PUTTERGILL is a Sociologist at the University of South Africa. He is completing his Ph.D. at Stellenbosch University on the attitudes of White South Africans to change.

ANNIKA TEPPO received her Ph.D. in Social and Cultural Anthropology at the University of Helsinki in 2004. Her thesis was a historical ethnography of the rehabilitation of poor whites in a suburb of Cape Town. She has also conducted ethnographic fieldwork in Finnish prisons. Currently she is teaching at several Finnish universities and conducting Postdoctoral research at the University of Helsinki Department of Social Policy and Urban Studies.